# Battle-Cruisers

# Battle-Cruisers

## A History 1908–48

Ronald Bassett

**M**

ISBN 0 333 28164 0

First published 1981 by
MACMILLAN LONDON LIMITED
London and Basingstoke

Associated companies in Delhi, Dublin,
Hong Kong, Johannesburg, Lagos, Melbourne,
New York, Singapore and Tokyo

Photoset in Great Britain by
Rowland Phototypesetting Limited
Bury St Edmunds, Suffolk
Printed in Hong Kong

Dedicated
as a token of remembrance to
Admiral of the Fleet Earl Mountbatten of Burma
KG, PC, GCB, OM, GCSI, GCVO, DSO, FRS,
1900–79
an inspiring commander in war and
a statesmanlike leader in peace
who earned the admiration, affection, respect
and supreme confidence
of all who had the privilege
to serve under him

# Contents

## IV    The Ravages of Peace, the Race to Amend

## V    Same Enemy, Different War

## VI    Same War, Different Enemy

## VII    The Cat That Survived but Not to Live

# List of Illustrations

Acknowledgements are due to the Imperial War Museum for all the pictures except 6b and 8.

# List of Maps

# Preface

BATTLE-CRUISERS, the 'Splendid Cats' of two world wars, were a lean and hungry breed of warship that survived for only forty years – probably the shortest lifespan of any type-class in naval history. During those forty years, however, they were involved in the two most widely fought, costly and scientific wars that the world has known and, despite their relatively small number, several of their names have been deeply burned into the annals of sea-warfare.

Without exception they were ships of brave and formidable appearance. HMS *Hood* was arguably the most beautifully balanced warship ever built. Like her sisters, however, she was expected to fulfil a role for which she had not been designed and, like several of her sisters, she died fighting, outmatched, but not in shame.

I saw *Hood* only twice. The first occasion, as a schoolboy, was during Navy Week – it must have been 1936 or 1937 – and I never trod her decks because the queues were so long and I had vowed to be home by nine. I gazed at her from a distance for as long as I dared before sprinting for the railway station.

I next saw her in Scapa Flow in 1941 from the deck of *Norfolk*, distantly, through a grey rain-haze, as we departed that sombre sodden anchorage for the equally inclement Denmark Strait. I forget the date, which does not matter, but I do recall the stately beauty of her as she lay at anchor, a gallant ship that symbolised all the proud strength of our navy. Against a leaden sky her ensign was a white petal splashed with blood, and I did not know then that I would be very near her when she died, at 0600 on 24 May. I did not witness her death, for which I am grateful; I was confined to an action station below decks, alone with a single, older companion who, when the news was passed to us, turned his face from me to hide his tears.

This book describes the lives and times of the sixteen battle-cruisers built for the Royal Navy and the Royal Australian Navy, the men who served in them, their achievements and frustrations, their battles won or lost, and the manner of their going, whether to the roar of high explosive or the clatter of a shipbreaker's yard. I offer no hitherto undisclosed secrets. All that is here has been recorded elsewhere, but perhaps for the first time has been brought together under one cover.

I have written for the layman rather than for the student of naval history, who may claim that my telling is oversimplified, or for the professional sailor, who can screw up an eye and visualise south-west-by-south or sixteen knots and an onion.

I refer to political issues only in so far as they influenced battle-cruiser deployment. Battle-cruiser men considered themselves to be the élite of the Fleet. Well, cruiser men, destroyer men and submariners will dispute that opinion, but there were few operational theatres in which a battle-cruiser did not play some role. The history of the battle-cruiser is very much the history of the Royal Navy between 1908 and 1948. We shall never see their like again – nor, for that matter, shall we see such a navy.

It had been my intention to ask Admiral the Earl Mountbatten of Burma to write a foreword for this book. I had served under his command for two lengthy periods, albeit in a very humble capacity. Once, on Custom House Steps in Malta, seeing me hovering with my camera, he had ordered a distinguished and stately party of British, American, French and Italian admirals to halt, stand in line and stand still, and I swear he winked at me. So I am sure he would have complied with my request. Alas, before I was ready, it was too late.

In addition to the organisations and publications listed in the Select Bibliography, the author is grateful for the personal assistance afforded him by: Lieutenant-Commander N. C. Manley-Cooper, RN (Rtd), late Fleet Air Arm; Commander H. B. C. Gill, DSC, RN (Rtd), the last navigating officer of *Repulse*, and his daughter, Mrs Frederick C. Darwall; Mr H. Murray Taylor, MBE, sometime General Manager and Chief Salvage Officer of Metal Industries (Salvage) Ltd; Mr Maurice Northcott, author; Miss M. W. Thirkettle of the Naval Historical Branch of the Ministry of Defence; Mr M. Willis of the Imperial War Museum; and, not least, eighty-six-year-old Mrs C. M. Pratt, widow of Signalman Pratt, survivor from *Invincible*, 1916.

RONALD BASSETT

Superior numbers in the text refer to the notes at the end of each chapter.

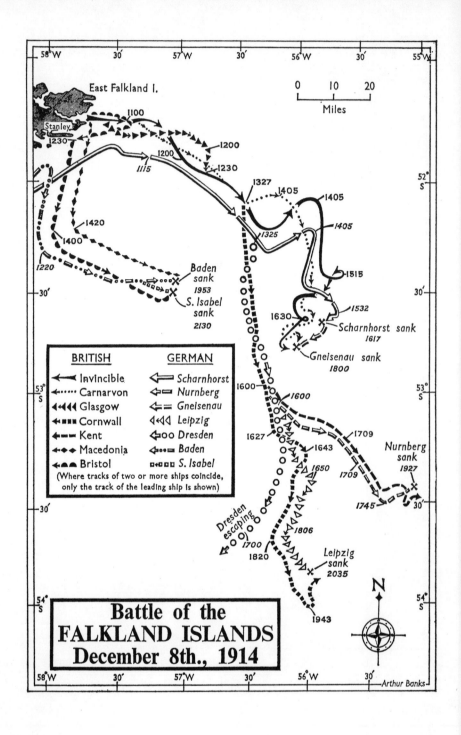

Battle of the
**FALKLAND ISLANDS**
December 8th., 1914

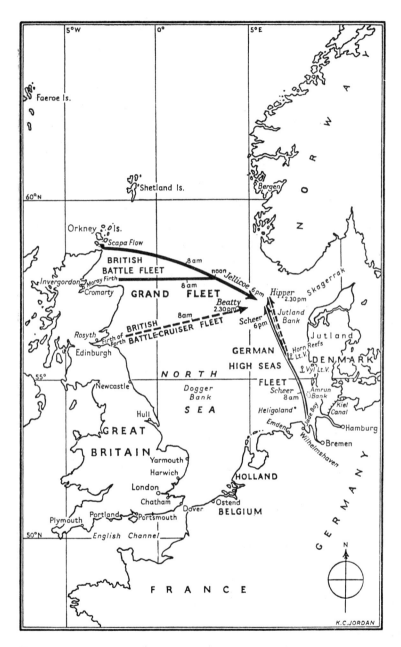

The North Sea, 1914–18, showing the course followed by the British Grand Fleet and the German High Seas Fleet to the Battle of Jutland, 31 May 1916

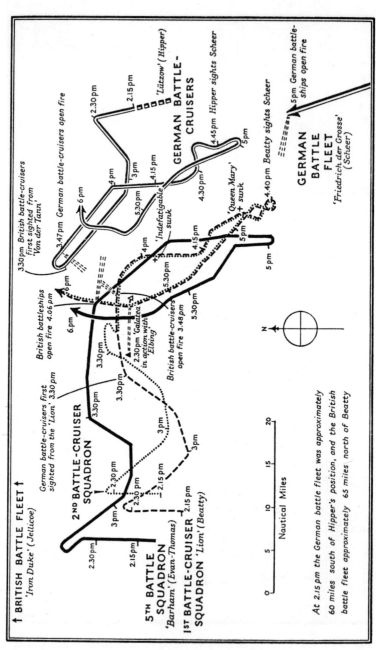

Jutland from 2.15 to 6 p.m. The battle-cruiser action

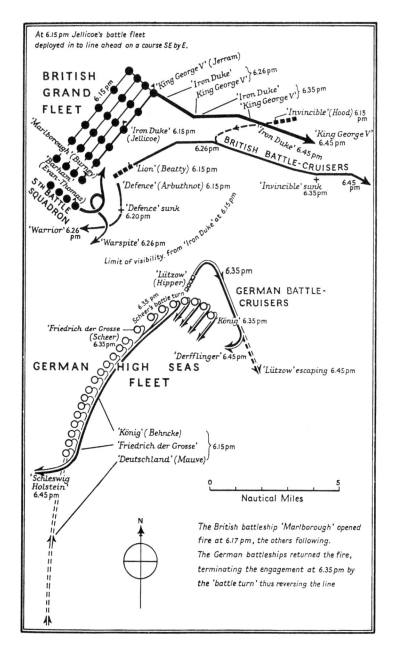

At 6.15 pm Jellicoe's battle fleet deployed in to line ahead on a course SE by E.

BRITISH GRAND FLEET

6.15 pm

'King George V' (Jerram)
'Iron Duke'
'King George V'
6.26 pm

'Iron Duke'
'King George V'
6.35 pm

'Marlborough' (Burney)

'Iron Duke' 6.15 pm (Jellicoe)

6.26 pm

'Invincible' (Hood) 6.15 pm

'Iron Duke' 6.45 pm

'King George V' 6.45 pm

BRITISH BATTLE-CRUISERS

'Barham' (Evan-Thomas)

5TH BATTLE SQUADRON

'Lion' (Beatty) 6.15 pm

'Defence' (Arbuthnot) 6.15 pm

'Invincible' sunk 6.35 pm

6.45 pm

'Warrior' 6.26 pm

'Defence' sunk 6.20 pm

'Warspite' 6.26 pm

Limit of visibility from 'Iron Duke' at 6.15 pm

'Lützow' (Hipper)

6.35 pm

GERMAN BATTLE-CRUISERS

Scheer's battle turn 6.35 pm

'König' 6.35 pm

'Friedrich der Grosse' (Scheer) 6.35 pm

'Derfflinger' 6.45 pm

'Lützow' escaping 6.45 pm

GERMAN HIGH SEAS FLEET

'König' (Behncke)
'Friedrich der Grosse'
'Deutschland' (Mauve)
6.15 pm

'Schleswig Holstein' 6.45 pm

0          5
Nautical Miles

N

The British battleship 'Marlborough' opened
fire at 6.17 pm, the others following.
The German battleships returned the fire,
terminating the engagement at 6.35 pm by
the 'battle turn' thus reversing the line

Jutland from 6.15 to 6.45 p.m. The first clash between the battle-fleets

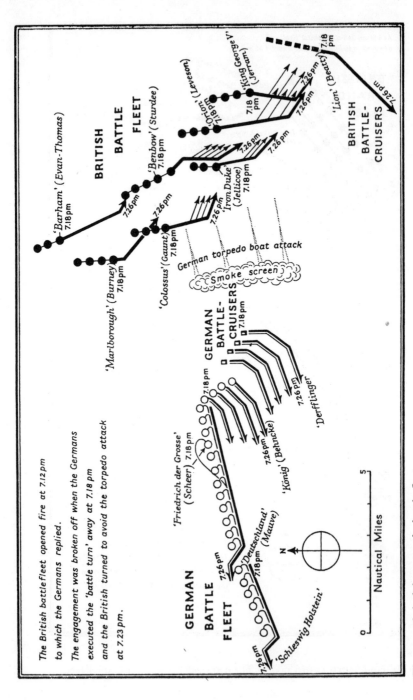

The British battlefleet opened fire at 7.12 pm to which the Germans replied.

The engagement was broken off when the Germans executed the 'battle turn' away at 7.18 pm and the British turned to avoid the torpedo attack at 7.23 pm.

'Barham' (Evan-Thomas) 7.18 pm

7.26 pm

BRITISH BATTLE FLEET

'Benbow' (Sturdee) 7.18 pm

7.26 pm

'Orion' (Leveson) 7.18 pm

'King George V' (Jerram) 7.18 pm

7.26 pm

'Lion' (Beatty) 7.18 pm

7.26 pm

BRITISH BATTLE-CRUISERS

'Marlborough' (Burney) 7.18 pm

'Colossus' (Gaunt) 7.18 pm

7.26 pm

'Iron Duke' (Jellicoe) 7.18 pm

7.26 pm

German torpedo boat attack

Smoke screen

GERMAN BATTLE-CRUISERS 7.18 pm

7.26 pm

'Derfflinger'

'Friedrich der Grosse' (Scheer) 7.18 pm

'König' (Behncke) 7.26 pm

'Deutschland' (Mauve) 7.18 pm

7.26 pm

GERMAN BATTLE FLEET

'Schleswig Holstein'

7.26 pm

N

0        5

Nautical Miles

The second clash between the battle-fleets

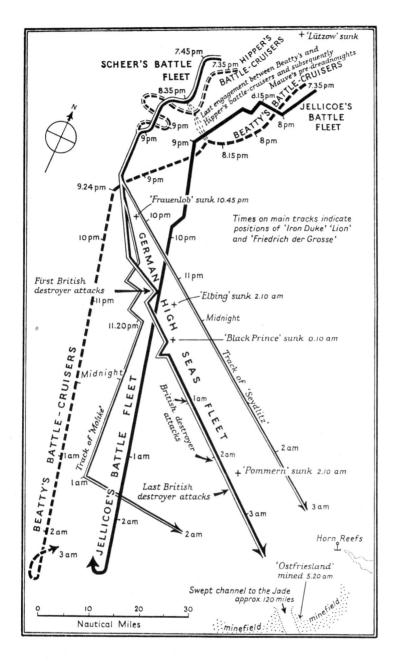

The tracks of the two fleets during the night of 31 May–1 June

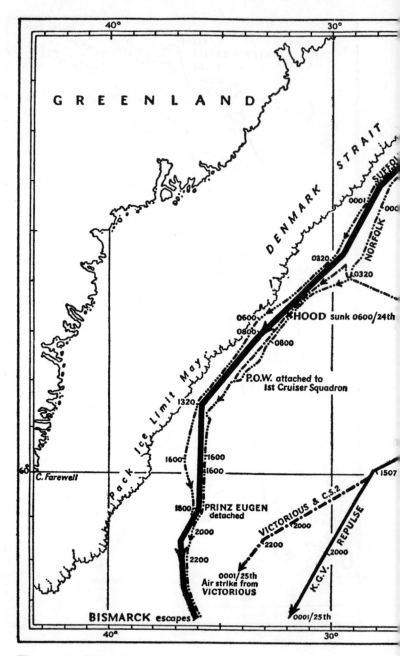

The pursuit of *Bismarck*

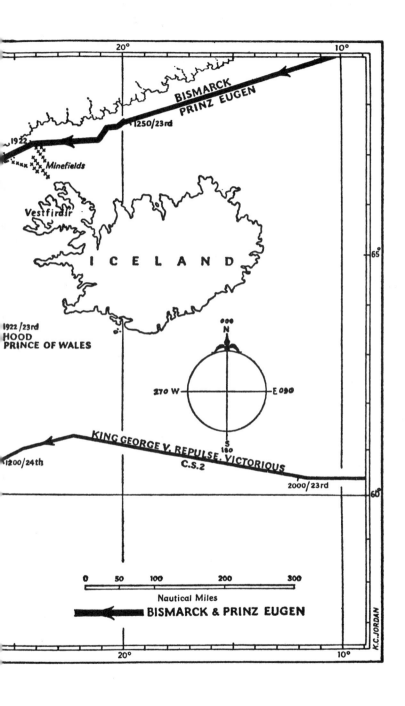

BISMARCK
PRINZ EUGEN

1250/23rd

1922

Minefields

Vestfirðir

I C E L A N D

1922/23rd
HOOD
PRINCE OF WALES

N
000

270 W — — E 090

S
180

KING GEORGE V, REPULSE, VICTORIOUS
C.S.2

1200/24th

2000/23rd

0    50    100         200         300

Nautical Miles

BISMARCK & PRINZ EUGEN

K.C.JORDAN

20°                                    10°

65°

60°

20°                                    10°

# I  To Overhaul Anything That Floats . . .

## Chapter One

*Battleships and armoured cruisers – Admiral Fisher and the years of transition – the first Dreadnought and the evolution of the battle-cruiser – the German challenge*

FOR TWO CENTURIES the major chess-piece of the world's navies had been the ship-of-the-line and later the battleship. Whether sail or steam, the battleship was big by the standards of its time – massively constructed, heavily armed and, because of its weight and unwieldiness, relatively slow. It was, of course, designed almost solely for one purpose: to hit hard and continue hitting while simultaneously absorbing heavy punishment. Only another battleship could challenge a battleship.

The wooden man-o'-war was rarely sunk by gunfire alone. It might be reduced to a mastless waterlogged hulk or be burned to the waterline. Its magazine might blow up or, subsequently, it might run aground or founder in bad weather. Until the introduction of the torpedo, the ironclad, too, was reasonably protected against projectiles. When a heavy warship was destroyed, it was almost always because of an internal explosion – of magazine or boilers – that had been generated by a projectile. The distinction may seem academic, but it is the most important single factor in the story of the battle-cruiser.

The battle-cruiser, however, was a Johnny-come-lately to the theatre-stage of sea-warfare, and it strode it only briefly, if bravely. The public's idol had for long been the battleship.

There has probably never been a sight more impressive, or more ominous to an enemy, than a squadron of battleships in line ahead, no show of strength of which a nation has been more proud, no larger investment of resources to be seen at one time. The British taxpayer always resented every penny spent on his army, but seldom ceased to demand more battleships, which were incalculably more expensive than soldiers. Britain was an island, determined to remain so. The negroes began at Calais, and when there was fog in the Channel it was the Continent that was isolated. Although during the nineteenth century there were periods of economy during which the Navy's size and effectiveness were reduced, instinct and tradition invariably re-established the 'two nations' policy, by which the Navy was maintained at a strength superior to that of any other two navies combined. Until the last decade of the century the fleets of France and Russia were generally regarded as representing the likeliest combined threat.

The demands made upon Britain's navy, however, were much heavier than those imposed upon others'. With a widely flung empire and by far the largest mercantile fleet, it was vital to Britain that the world's sea-lanes should be kept open and safe, and in protecting her own interests Britain inevitably protected those of all who observed international law. Despite criticisms – sometimes based on jealousy, but frequently provoked by high-handedness – the nineteenth-century Royal Navy was a peace-keeping force for which other nations had good reason to be grateful. Policemen, however, are seldom popular.

The ship-of-the-line, or battleship, was unsuited or simply too valuable for many maritime tasks such as reconnaissance and distant patrolling, blockading, commerce-raiding, anti-slavery duties, surveying, or for simply appearing off the coast of some foreign power that threatened to disturb the Queen's peace. For such lesser matters the frigate[1] was employed – smaller, faster, more versatile. The frigate was the father of the cruiser, a maid-of-all-work and the eyes of the Fleet. There have been many other types of warship – sloops, bomb-ketches, corvettes, monitors, destroyers and, later, submarines and aircraft-carriers – but it is with the battleship and the cruiser that we are mainly concerned, because it was from these that the battle-cruiser was born, and survived neither.

Warship development had usually been a process of slow evolution, with the maritime nations watching each other carefully to ensure that none stole a sudden march, but occasionally innovations were introduced that, almost immediately, rendered all existing warships obsolete or completely revolutionised naval tactics. They included the adoption of steam propulsion (although sails were a long time a-dying), the iron and subsequently the steel hull, the breech-loading and turreted gun, submersibles, and finally the Dreadnought, the brainchild of Admiral Sir John Fisher, Royal Navy.

The British have a penchant for playing bowls, dancing all night, or unconcernedly drinking chota pegs while disaster is approaching at frightening speed, and then, when all seems lost or too late, producing like a rabbit from a hat the one man of the century who is capable of saving the situation at the eleventh hour.

'Jacky' Fisher was one of those men, if not among the better-known or the best-loved. Born in 1841, he was thirteen years old when he entered the Navy, a captain at thirty-three, and First Sea Lord in 1904, aged sixty-three, having also, *en route*, held the appointments of Director of Naval Ordnance, Admiral Superintendent for Portsmouth Dockyard, Commander-in-Chief North American and West Indies Station, Commander-in-Chief Mediterranean, and Second Sea Lord.

He was a short man, with the pugnacious vitality so often possessed by men who lack inches, outspoken, ruthless toward those who opposed him and contemptuous of anyone or anything second-rate. By 1904, Fisher had already improved the Navy's gunnery efficiency beyond all recognition, reorganised the Atlantic, Channel and Mediterranean Squadrons, introduced realistic fleet exercises, and modernised the training of officers. In Fisher's opinion, any warship that was not faster and heavier-gunned than its enemy was merely a device for wasting 400 men, and now, as First Sea Lord, he was to insist on the most ambitious building programme undertaken by any navy before or since. To make room for it, he consigned 154 existing warships, including 17 battleships, to the breaker's yard.

One of Fisher's major criticisms of naval design, both British and foreign, related to the number of different gun-sizes within the same ship. The eight 'King Edward VII'-class battleships, for instance – still building when Fisher took office – were to carry 12-inch guns, 9.2-inch guns, 6-inch guns, and 12- and 3-pounders in addition to torpedo-tubes and Maxims. This multiplicity of calibres gave rise to magazine and supply difficulties; and, more seriously, to avoid top-heaviness, many of the secondary guns had to be mounted so low, in sponsons or casemates, that they were useless in a heavy sea or when the ship was at speed. Finally, the improvements, during the previous decade or so, in explosives, fire-control systems and gunnery techniques generally meant that ranges were becoming increasingly longer, and in the next war, Fisher calculated, battles would be fought at ranges of up to 8000 yards.[2] At such a distance smaller guns were inadequate and were thus only superfluous dead-weight. Moreover, the only reliable means of controlling range depended on *salvo-firing*, when a gunnery officer watched for the shell-splashes that fell short, or overshot, and reassessed accordingly. Such calculations were almost impossible when the same ship was firing 12-inch, 9.2-inch and 6-inch guns simultaneously; one splash looked pretty much the same as another.

Fisher had decided several years earlier that the secondary guns of a battleship represented unemployable muscle that could with advantage be added to that of the ship's primary armament. After examining several design-studies he firmly sponsored the building of the first of a new generation of battleships, *Dreadnought*, which mounted ten heavy guns – 12-inch – and virtually nothing else.

The development of the battleship is outside the scope of this book, but a brief glance at *Dreadnought* is necessary because there is no doubt that she strongly influenced the design of the battle-cruisers which were soon to follow her.

It would be wrong to imply that Fisher and the Committee on Designs of 1904 were the first to visualise the all-big-gun warship. Commander William Sims, the United States Navy's gunnery specialist, had already reached the same conclusion; and Vittorio Cuniberti, the distinguished Italian naval constructor, had even described such a ship in the 1903 edition of *Jane's Fighting Ships*. It was plain that a Dreadnought was very soon going to be produced by somebody; the only question was by whom.

The British decision to build a warship that outclassed all others afloat was not as obviously ingenious as it might seem, because it immediately nullified the Royal Navy's longstanding 'two-nations' advantage. Britain had 39 conventional battleships (soon to be known as 'pre-Dreadnoughts') against Germany's 19 – and it was Germany, now, who was emerging as the biggest threat to British naval supremacy. If the proposed Dreadnought negated all Germany's battleships, she did exactly the same to twice the number of British ships, and both nations would be back at the same starting-point.

However, the alternative – that the Imperial German Navy might produce a Dreadnought first – could not be contemplated. HMS *Dreadnought* was laid down in Portsmouth on 2 October 1905 and was completed in the amazingly short time of a year and a day. Of 17,900 tons, she was the first large warship to have turbine engines, giving her better than 22 knots, and mounted ten 12-inch guns of which eight could be fired on either broadside or six ahead and astern. *Dreadnought*, Fisher boasted, could sink the entire German Navy in an afternoon, and the Germans believed him. They immediately began to plan their own all-big-gun ships, and the Anglo-German race for naval supremacy was on.

Sadly, *Dreadnought* was never to be given the chance of proving Fisher's boast. Within the next decade she would herself be superseded by thirty-one improved Dreadnoughts and super-

Dreadnoughts in addition to nine battle-cruisers. Soon after the commencement of hostilities in 1914 she would be relegated to coastal defence duties, her sole moment of glory being the ramming and sinking of the submarine *U29* on 18 March 1916.

There was a growing number of naval theorists who claimed that the next war at sea would not be fought by fleets of massive battleships, or, if such battles were fought, they would be largely irrelevant. A more important role for any navy would be the destruction of an enemy's commerce and lines of communication, the denial of his supplies of food and raw materials, and this was a task for fast well-gunned cruisers, not battleships. In the 1890s the French Navy, in the middle of a fifty-year period of stagnation, had provoked a flurry of consternation in Whitehall by suddenly producing a series of big protected cruisers, mounting 7.6-inch guns and capable of 21 knots, which, if turned loose, could create havoc among British trade-routes.

The Royal Navy's armoured cruisers of the period had been merely relegated second-class battleships, inadequately gunned for the battle-line but too slow for pursue-and-destroy operations. To counter the potential threat of the fast long-ranging commerce-raider, the Admiralty laid down a new breed of armoured cruisers – the 'Duke of Edinburgh', 'Warrior' and 'Minotaur' classes – of 23 knots and 9.3-inch guns. Admiral Fisher, however, wanted better.

Except when circumstances allowed no choice, cruisers were not expected to fight battleships, and no cruiser captain would be criticised for using his superior speed to avoid such an encounter. Indeed, he might expect to be court-martialled if he exposed his ship to such overwhelming odds for no good reason. During set-piece actions between battle-fleets the cruisers sat on the side-lines and watched, perhaps bickered with enemy cruisers, or prowled in the hope of finishing off an enemy that bigger sisters had disabled.

The introduction of the armoured cruiser, which was a larger-than-average cruiser with an armoured belt, heavier-than-average guns and a good turn of speed, had slightly narrowed the gap between cruiser and battleship. It was capable of overhauling and outgunning ordinary cruisers and might, it was hoped, form fast wings to a battle-fleet. However, there was never any possibility of armoured cruisers deliberately exchanging blows with battleships while, alternatively, battleships were too slow to overhaul armoured cruisers. Fisher wanted something that could do both.

He had earlier referred to his super-battleship as HMS *Untouchable*, and, characteristically, had already laid down his qualifications for HMS *Uncatchable*. In addition to being substantially faster than the fastest foreign armoured cruiser, it would have a main armament of 10-inch guns fore and aft (because this was the largest calibre that could be worked entirely manually) and a secondary battery of 7.5-inch quick-firers. The protection of all guns would be such as would resist 8-inch Melinite shells, each with its own fighting-hood and range-finder. There would be no masts or fighting-tops, only a wireless-pole, and only light boats would be carried since none would float after an engagement. Oil fuel was indispensable, and the ships would have telescopic funnels with a very light bridge-structure. There would be no wood anywhere.

Unfortunately the three most relevant features of any warship – hitting power, armoured protection, and speed – were as inter-related as the three angles of a triangle. The dimension of one inevitably influenced the characteristics of the others. If the design requirement was for heavy guns and/or massive protection, then a modest speed had to be accepted. Conversely, if a high speed was insisted upon, over-all weight had to be reduced, which meant that the armour protection usually suffered. Generally, designers sought a compromise that would hopefully satisfy all critics, but from time to time warships had been built in which the compromise was abandoned in order to give one capability greater emphasis. Such a warship was Fisher's *Uncatchable*.

In 1902, Sir Philip Watts, then fifty-six, was appointed Director of Naval Construction. He had begun his working life as an apprentice shipwright in Portsmouth, but outstanding ability had lifted him through the ranks of naval architects in Admiralty employment to the management of Armstrong's Elswick shipyard – the largest in the world – and finally to the Admiralty. Twenty-nine battleships, battle-cruisers, and most of the Navy's cruisers and destroyers would be built during his Directorship between 1902 and 1912, and it was to Watts that the construction of *Uncatchable*, designed from Fisher's outline by Chief Constructor W. H. Gard, was entrusted.

Not surprisingly, Gard had been compelled to ignore several of the more outlandish features of Fisher's projection. What he produced was very much an improved and faster Dreadnought. Or nearly so. In simple terms, Gard put a battleship's guns into a cruiser-weight hull – and that would be the battle-cruiser's damning attribute for the next forty years. The excellent 9.2-inch gun was available, rapid-firing and with a 380 lb projectile capable of pene-trating any cruiser's armour, but the new hybrids were to mount eight 12-inch guns, for which there was only one justification: they could be used against battleships.

The term 'battle-cruiser', of course, had not yet been coined. In early 1906 the keels for a class of three vessels were laid – two on the Clyde and one on Tyneside – and the Admiralty carefully leaked the information that these were for three improved armoured cruisers mounting, as before, 9.2-inch guns. The Germans had no reason to doubt it, and in reply began building their own *Panzer-Kreuzer* – *Blücher* – at Kiel. Armed with eight 210 mm (8.2-inch) guns, she was an excellent armoured cruiser, but even before launching had already been outclassed by her British rivals.

*Invincible, Inflexible* and *Indomitable* were completed in mid-1908. Even their most vociferous critics could not deny that they appeared to be powerful and formidable fighting ships. *Invincible* achieved a mean 26.2 knots on her trials and later bettered 28 knots. Her 12-inch main armament was supplemented by sixteen 4-inch guns, each of which could fire 12 rounds per minute. She carried a peacetime complement of 784 which would be increased to approximately a thousand for war service.

Eyebrows were raised, however, when the figures for armour were examined. Protection was only 6 inches amidships and 4 inches in the bows, with no armoured belt abaft the after turret. No deck was heavier than 2 inches, and areas of the main deck were of only ¾-inch steel. But, stressed the design's supporters, it was never intended that such a ship should slug it out with a battleship on equal terms. She would be able to overhaul and destroy anything afloat *except* a battleship, and could even overtake and keep in touch with a fleeing enemy battle-fleet and engage stragglers at long range. Her speed, Fisher insisted, would be her protection. In any case, the weight-to-speed ratio did not allow for heavier armour, however desirable.

It was an unbalanced design. *Brassey's Naval Annual* commented:

> Vessels of this enormous size and cost are unsuitable for many of the duties of cruisers, but an even stronger objection to the repetition of the type is that an admiral, having 'Invincibles' in his fleet will be certain to put them in the line of battle, where their comparatively light protection will be a disadvantage and their high speed of no value.

In short, because it looked like a battleship, sooner or later a battle-cruiser would be expected to fight like a battleship.

Germany was not slow to take up the Dreadnought challenge, and from 1907 would launch twenty-six battleships and battle-cruisers. Her shipbuilding capacity was smaller than that of Britain, who

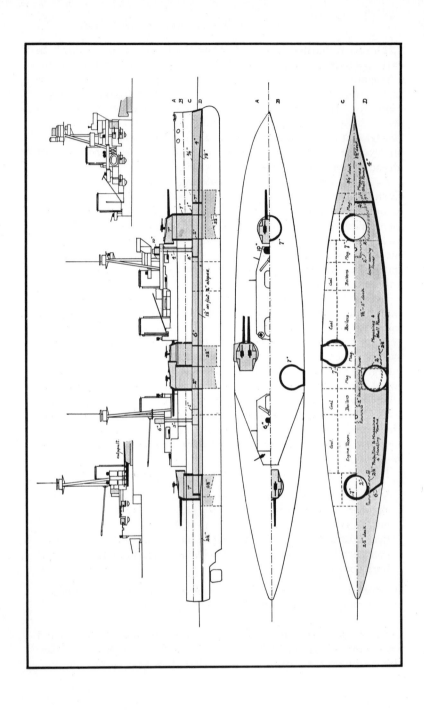

# 'INVINCIBLE'-class BATTLE-CRUISERS

| | Invincible | Inflexible | Indomitable |
|---|---|---|---|
| *Builder* | Elswick | Clydebank | Fairfield |
| *Laid down* | 2 April 1906 | 5 February 1906 | 1 March 1906 |
| *Launched* | 13 April 1907 | 26 June 1907 | 16 March 1907 |
| *Completed* | 20 March 1908 | 20 October 1908 | 25 June 1908 |

*Dimensions*
Length, waterline: 560 feet. Beam 78½ feet. Maximum draught 26.8 feet. Displacement 17,250 tons. Complement (peacetime) 750.

*Armament*
Eight 12-inch guns, 45 calibre; sixteen 4-inch guns, model 1907; three 18-inch torpedo-tubes, submerged.

*Armoured Protection*
6-inch belt amidships reducing to 4-inch at the bows, but no belt abaft the after funnel. Turrets 7-inch above the belt and 2-inch below. Conning tower 10-inch and 6-inch. Main deck 1-inch and ¾-inch, lower deck 2½-, 2- and 1½-inch. Magazine screens 2½-inch.

*Engines*
Parsons' turbines of 41,000 horsepower (the most powerful then afloat) driving four screws. Designed speed 25 knots. Best speeds: *Invincible* 28.6; *Inflexible* 28.4; *Indomitable* 28.7.

*Fuel*
Coal: 1000 tons normal, 3084 tons maximum. Oil: 725 tons. At full speed these ships burned about 500 tons of coal per day and about 125 tons oil.

*Costs*
Part of the 1905–6 Naval Programme, the average cost of each ship was £1,750,000, or about £101.6 per ton. Of this sum, the machinery absorbed £470,000 and the armament £90,000.

built warships for the world, but German yards, of more recent construction, were more sophisticated and German docks were larger. Thus, at battleship level, they were able to build vessels that were beamier than their British counterparts, which allowed for heavier side-armour and meant a steadier gun-platform. Additionally, British ships had to be designed for a world-wide role, to carry large fuel-loads and to accommodate their crews for many months, often years, whether at sea or in harbour. It was not expected that German capital ships would operate beyond the limits of the Baltic and the North Sea, so their bunkers were correspondingly smaller; and, when in harbour, German crews lived in barracks ashore, their shipboard quarters being cramped. All these factors meant wider options with regard to watertight divisions and machinery installations.

Obsessed with keeping pace with British Dreadnought-building, the sudden appearance of the Royal Navy's three battle-cruisers was an annoying distraction for Germany and additionally infuriating because *Blücher* was outclassed even before launching. Germany had no capacity to expend on unproven hybrids but, if the only ships that could overhaul and engage battle-cruisers were other battle-cruisers, then Germany must have them. In October 1908, *Von der Tann* was laid down by Blohm und Voss in Hamburg.

A lesson learned, her details were kept secret, as were those of four Dreadnought-type vessels simultaneously building in German yards, and two years passed before it became known that *Von der Tann* would be bigger in all dimensions than the Invincibles, substantially better-armoured and mounting ten 11-inch and sixteen 5.9-inch guns. Although marginally slower, she was a superior fighting ship in all other respects, but this fact was apparent too late to affect the design of the next generation of British battle-cruisers, the 'Indefatigable' class.

By 1909, Britain had ten new capital ships built or almost built against the Germans' five, and in that year *Indefatigable*, *Australia* and *New Zealand* were laid down amidst a ferment of publicity that credited the new ships with totally spurious qualities. The British public was beginning to develop a battleship-building mania; to the uninitiated the Invincibles had been splendid investments and the new trio could only be better. It was confidently claimed that they would be the first motor-driven warships, that they would be bigger, better-armed and heavier-armoured than the first three battle-cruisers, and capable of 29–30 knots.

They were larger by fifteen hundred tons, and longer and taller by a few feet, but that was all. They had the same armament and, because Fisher did not believe in 'handicapping the racehorses', they had the same inadequate armour. None would match the Invincibles' speed, and, significantly, their average cost was £1,547,500 against the Invincibles' £1,750,000 and *Von der Tann*'s £1,833,000. The economy showed.

*Australia* and *New Zealand* were paid for by the countries after which they were named, the first as a unit of the Royal Australian Navy. At that time the naval service of New Zealand mustered one old gunboat of 805 tons, the small governmental yacht, and two even smaller harbour-vessels. There were no facilities whatsoever for the adoption of a giant battle-cruiser and, wisely, the ship was presented to the Royal Navy with no strings, but doubtless with relief.

Nothing was yet known of *Von der Tann*'s qualities except that she displaced about 19,000 tons. Then, suddenly, in mid-1909, it was learned that Germany had laid down two more battle-cruisers, destined to be *Moltke* and *Goeben*.

This was disconcerting because it meant that the British battle-cruisers – still at this time coyly referred to as 'fast armoured cruisers' – were no longer certain of being capable of overhauling and destroying everything that floated except a battleship or, conversely, of using their speed as protection. The Germans would not repeat their *Blücher* blunder, but would equip their new ships with battleship guns. Intelligent guesswork suggested that *Moltke* and *Goeben* would be bigger than *Von der Tann*, probably as fast as the Invincibles, and would mount either ten or twelve 11-inch guns. (In fact they displaced 23,000 tons, were capable of 27–8 knots, and mounted ten 11-inch guns.) If so, then if both Britain and Germany employed their battle-cruisers as fast wings to their fleets the inevitable would happen, and the Invincibles and Indefatigables could find themselves outmatched.

Such a possibility was anathema to a man of Jackie Fisher's humour. His response was to order bigger, and this time better-armed, British battle-cruisers.

In this direction he was helped by the reintroduction of the 13.5-inch gun, which had last been mounted in the 'Royal Sovereign' class of the early 1890s but abandoned in favour of the 12-inch when smaller and lighter battleships became fashionable. That trend, however, had now been reversed; battleships were becoming bigger and heavier yearly, and if a bigger gun was available, then Fisher wanted it.

As a general rule (although not an invariable one), the larger the

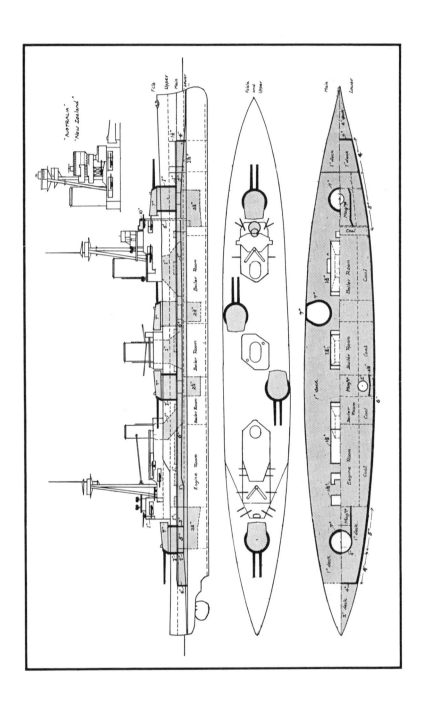

# 'INDEFATIGABLE'-class BATTLE-CRUISERS

|  | Indefatigable | Australia | New Zealand |
|---|---|---|---|
| Builder | Devonport | J. Brown & Co. | Fairfield |
| Laid down | 23 February 1909 | 23 June 1910 | 20 June 1910 |
| Launched | 28 October 1909 | 25 October 1911 | 1 July 1911 |
| Completed | February 1911 | June 1913 | November 1912 |

*Dimensions*
Length, waterline: 578 feet. Beam 80 feet. Maximum draught 27 feet. Displacement 18,500 tons. Complement (peacetime) 800.

*Armament*
Eight 12-inch guns, 50 calibre; sixteen 4-inch guns, model 1907; two 21-inch torpedo-tubes, submerged.

*Armoured Protection*
6-inch belt (11 feet deep) reducing to 4-inch at bows and stern. Turrets and barbettes 7-inch above belt, 4- and 3-inch below. Conning tower 10-inch and 6-inch. Main deck 1-inch, fore and aft 2-inch. Magazine protection 2½-inch.

*Engines*
Parsons' turbines of 44,000 horsepower driving four screws. Designed speed 25 knots. Speeds on trials: *Indefatigable* 26.7; *Australia* 26.9; *New Zealand* 26.3.

*Fuel*
Coal: 1000 tons normal, 3170 tons maximum. Oil: 840 tons.

*Costs*
Part of the 1908 Naval Programme, the average cost of each ship was £1,547,500, or about £82.3 per ton.

gun the longer the range, the heavier the shell the more destructive its impact. However, if a smaller gun has the necessary range and its shells adequate penetrative power, it may compensate for its lack of calibre by being able to load and fire more quickly than a larger opponent. Thus, always given gun-crew proficiency, a ship mounting a large number of modest-calibre guns can saturate an enemy carrying a smaller number of bigger guns *providing it can stay within range.*

The 12-inch gun fulfilled all known battle-requirements, but had been developed to its utmost capacity in range and weight of shell, and to achieve that range its 850 lb projectile required a cordite charge of 307 lb and a muzzle velocity of 3010 feet per second. Barrel erosion was considerable, and accuracy soon began to deteriorate.

The 13.5-inch gun could fire a projectile weighing 1400 lb, for which it required a charge of 297 lb at a muzzle velocity of only 2700 feet per second. So, in addition to its greater hitting effect, barrel wear was considerably reduced, the gun's life was longer and its accuracy more sustained.

For the first time, the 'fast armoured cruisers' were to be bigger and heavier than contemporary Dreadnoughts. The new *Lion* and *Princess Royal* displaced 26,270 tons and *Queen Mary* 27,000 tons. They were the largest and fastest capital ships yet laid down, and the first ships to cost more than £2 million each. This time Fisher wanted no half-measures and, although in retrospect the design still had shortcomings, a number of lessons had been acknowledged.

With 13.5-inch guns, it could again be confidently claimed that these warships could 'destroy anything afloat except battleships'. The latter reservation still applied because, although improved, the protection given to these warships was still very light for 26,000-tonners, but, as before, there could be no alternative if they were to achieve the 27 knots demanded of them. The old weight-to-speed limitation could not be circumvented.

All four twin turrets were installed on the centre line, but the midships 'Q' turret, positioned between the two after funnels, had an arc of fire limited to 120° on each beam. That was probably the design's most serious deficiency. Another annoyance (less important because it could be rectified) was the placing of the tripod foremast immediately *abaft* the forward funnel in order to utilise it as a support for the boat-booms. On trials, as a result, the flames and smoke from *Lion*'s fore funnel at speed rendered her control-top untenable and the ladders within the mast-legs impossible to climb. This defect, however, was subsequently corrected. Crew accommodation was uncomfortable because almost all ratings' messdecks were situated two decks down, forward and aft, below the armoured belt and with no scuttles, while the officers were quartered below the bridge. The quarterdeck was also amidships, which was untraditional and inconvenient in the opinion of both officers and men.

The 'Lion' class was again greeted with extravagant claims with regard to performances. *Lion* was credited with 31.8 knots when in fact, in trials, she had marginally failed to achieve her designed speed. *Princess Royal* was said to have steamed at 34.7 knots when her best-ever speed was actually 28.54. However, they were the best value for money of the battle-cruisers so far. Captain Reginald Hall, commanding *Queen Mary*, had his ship fitted with a bookstall, cinematograph facilities, a chapel, improved bathrooms, *washing machines* for the petty officers, and a number of other refinements that would not be generally adopted until two major wars had come and gone. The extent of his men's appreciation is not recorded, but they would almost certainly have had to suffer the jeers and abuse of other ships' companies.

In January 1910, Admiral (now Lord) Fisher, aged sixty-nine, resigned from his post of First Sea Lord in favour of Sir Arthur Wilson. His ruthlessness and arrogance had made him a number of enemies, and had sometimes miscalculated – although this observation can only be made with hindsight – but there was no doubt that he had dragged a complacent Royal Navy into the twentieth century, enlarged and modernised it, and raised morale and efficiency to their highest levels for a hundred years. His successor, Wilson, was a man of similar character, a hard-working no-nonsense martinet; but the Navy had not yet seen the last of Jackie Fisher.

The Anglo-German naval race was still gathering momentum, with Britain keeping a jump ahead and determined to continue doing so. Perhaps surprisingly, during the last few years before 1914, British yards still had the capacity to lay down battleships for Turkey, Argentina, Chile and Brazil, and cruisers for Russia, Norway, Greece and China. Subsequently the Turks and Chileans never got their battleships, which were appropriated by the Royal Navy, as were the two Norwegian coastal cruisers.[3] In January 1911, however, to the Admiralty's alarm, the Japanese Government ordered a battle-cruiser from Vickers. The alarm was generated by the fact that the specification for the projected *Kongo* outlined a warship that was superior in all respects to *Lion*.

Then, the following month, it was learned that the Germans had laid down their fifth battle-cruiser – *Seydlitz*.

\*

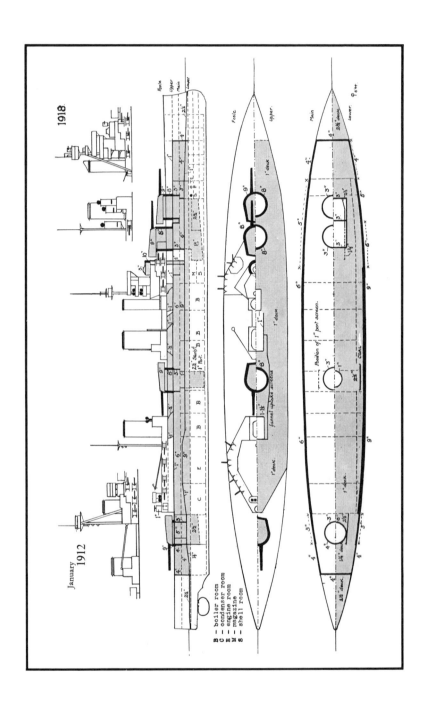

# 'LION'-class BATTLE-CRUISERS

|  | *Lion* | *Princess Royal* | *Queen Mary* |
|---|---|---|---|
| *Builder* | Devonport | Vickers | Fairfield |
| *Laid down* | 29 November 1909 | 2 May 1910 | 6 March 1911 |
| *Launched* | 6 August 1910 | 29 April 1911 | 20 March 1912 |
| *Completed* | May 1912 | November 1912 | September 1913 |

*Dimensions*
Length, waterline: 660 feet. Beam 88.5 feet. Maximum draught 29 feet. Displacement 26,270 tons (*Queen Mary* 89-foot beam and 27,000 tons). Complement (peacetime) 1000.

*Armament*
Eight 13.5-inch guns, 45 calibre; sixteen 4-inch guns, model 1907; two 21-inch torpedo-tubes, submerged.

*Armoured Protection*
Belt of varying 9-, 6-, 5- and 4-inch thickness. Turrets and barbettes 9-inch above belt. Conning tower 10-inch. Signal tower 6-inch. Upper deck 1-inch, lower deck 1¼-inch with 2½-inch fore and aft. Magazine protection 2½-inch.

*Engines*
Parsons' turbines of 70,000 horsepower driving four screws. Designed speed 27 knots. Best speeds: *Lion* 27; *Princess Royal* 28.5; *Queen Mary* 28.

*Fuel*
Coal: 1000 tons normal, 3500 tons maximum. Oil: 1135 tons.

*Cost*
Part of the 1909 and 1910 Naval Programmes, the average cost of each ship was £2,085,000, or about £73.5 per ton. The subsequent cost of moving each foremast was £60,000.

By now, at the conclusion of the 1910 programme, Britain had built, or was in the process of building, eighteen battleships to the Germans' thirteen, in addition to the battle-cruisers already described – the comparative values of which were still vague and their place in the war-plans of their respective navies even more so. Britain still had forty pre-Dreadnought battleships and the Germans had thirty, but these were back-numbers and suitable only for coastal and harbour defence, figuring as small print in the balance of naval power. For Britain the gap between the two fleets was still uncomfortably narrow. In the event of war between the two countries (and it now seemed a racing certainty) it would be logical for the Germans to concentrate and conserve their battle-fleet in fortified anchorages, i.e., a fleet in being, and carefully time their sorties to engage piece-meal elements of the Royal Navy. It was confidently expected that the British would impose a close blockade on the Germans' North Sea bases, but ships could not remain at sea indefinitely – they had to refuel and provision, rest and repair – and it was unlikely that the Royal Navy could maintain much more than fifty per cent of its strength continuously at sea. The initiative would always be with the fleet in being. Fisher, who believed in hitting first and damn the consequences, had suggested to King Edward as early as 1907 that the Navy should not wait for war but should 'Copenhagen the German fleet *à la Nelson*', to which the King retorted: 'Fisher, you must be mad.'

The two navies had exchanged courtesy visits, and their ships' crews had met frequently in Kiel and Portsmouth, Hong Kong, Tsingtao and Singapore, sharing beer, football matches, receptions, tugs-of-war, sailors' yarns and a wary respect for each other. There was an element of fatalism in their exchanges. The officers of a British light cruiser, entertaining those of a German warship of similar type but with one fewer gun, promised their counterparts that, if the two ships ever met in anger, the British cruiser would cover one gun so that the combat would be equal.

There was also a growing uneasy awareness among British experts that the Germans were building very good ships indeed – better in many respects, perhaps, than their own – but it would have been sacrilegious to say so. It was not until a few weeks before the war began, following a speech by Winston Churchill (then First Lord) in which he extolled 'the undoubted superiority of our ships, unit for unit', that Admiral Jellicoe, Commander-in-Chief-elect, warned in confidence that it was 'highly dangerous to consider that our ships as a whole are superior or even equal fighting machines'. But then it was too late.

In assessing the relative merits of two opposing navies, however, the quality of their ships and guns was not the sole yardstick. What mattered as much was the quality of the crews that manned them. It must be remembered that the Royal Navy, except for a few leisurely bombardments and an occasional exchange of shots with some maritime law-breaker, had not fought a fleet action since the days of sail, and had no more *battle* experience than had the Germans and less than the Russians and Japanese or, for that matter, the Americans, whose navy had at least engaged and destroyed Spanish squadrons in Manila and Santiago in 1898. The British, however, did possess a nebulous insouciant confidence, almost arrogance, born of tradition, which Admiral Reinhart Scheer, the German Commander-in-Chief, did not discount when he wrote in 1914:

> The English [sic] fleet had the advantage of looking back on a hundred years of proud tradition which must have given every man a sense of superiority based on the great deeds of the past. This could only be strengthened by the sight of their huge fleet, each unit of which in every class was supposed to represent the last word in the art of marine construction. The feeling was also supported by the British sailor's perfect familiarity with the sea and with conditions of life on board ship.

In truth, there was not much to choose between the admirals of each side. The senior commanders of the Royal Navy, following a lifetime of sterile manœuvres that 'took the form of quadrille-like movements carried out in accordance with geometrical diagrams which entirely ignored all questions of gun and torpedo fire' (Vice-Admiral K. G. B. Dewar), had lost the Nelson touch – that quick initiative with which their predecessors had grasped at half-chances and turned them into victories. Now they merely followed orders, and old dogs were unwilling to learn new tricks. There were not many Fishers among them.

Fortunately there was similar conservatism among the flag officers of the German Navy and a tendency to err on the side of caution, exacerbated by a High Command structure with three bureaux, each responsible for, and jealous of, different aspects of policy: operations, *matériel*, appointments and training. Clear-cut decisions were not easily reached. Furthermore, the Kaiser's Imperial Order of July 1914 would place severe restrictions on the High Seas Fleet's movements; he was unwilling to commit his 'beautiful ships' to the open sea unless they were absolutely certain of success, and such restrictions implied a lack of confidence that was psychologically damaging.

At ship-command level and below, however, the British enjoyed an undoubted advantage. Although the Royal Navy had its share of indifferent officers, most had benefited from Fisher's reforms and had faith in themselves, their ships and their men. It is interesting to glance at the names of those less senior officers of 1914–18 and note those that would emerge as the outstanding sailors of 1939–45 – Tovey, Cunningham, Harwood, Fraser, Burnett, Horton and Noble, and so many others who would exercise again the flair and imagination that their earlier commanders seemed to have lost.

British lower-deck ratings, in general, were also more experienced. They enlisted in the first instance for twelve years, with an optional ten years' re-engagement to follow, and would have spent lengthier periods and much more time in total at sea than the Germans, who were enlisted for three-year terms and might never leave the Baltic. This is not to suggest that German sea-serving personnel were in any way second-rate. Officers were tactically skilful, technically efficient and courageous, while throughout the German Navy there was an almost fanatical devotion to the Fatherland that would not have been apparent on any British messdeck.

Other maritime nations had been watching the Anglo-German rivalry with an amazement not unmixed with annoyance when, as a result, their own warships became increasingly obsolete. Japan, observing her technology to be in arrears, drew up a blueprint for a battle-cruiser that was better than anyone's, and, after Japanese officials had taken £100,000 in bribes from various foreign shipbuilders, the contract was awarded to Vickers Ltd, currently building *Princess Royal*.

Displacing 27,500 tons, carrying eight 14-inch guns and sixteen 6-inch guns, *Kongo*[4] was an embarrassing improvement on the 'Lion'-class battle-cruisers, all still building and of which a fourth version, *Tiger*, was yet to be laid down. There was nothing to be gained, now, in proceeding with this fourth ship, so the Admiralty produced a new design that stole all the best of *Kongo*'s features and began building the completely revised *Tiger* in June 1912, rushing her to completion in eighteen months. She would be commissioned in October 1914 with day-and-night shifts still working on her.

*Tiger* was of 28,430 tons, mounting eight 13.5-inch guns and twelve 6-inch guns, with a designed speed of 29 knots which was easily achieved in her hurried trials before joining the Fleet. It becomes somewhat tedious to repeat that she was a superior fighting unit to her predecessors; it would have been surprising if she were not. This time, however, a battle-cruiser was not, visually, a replica of a battleship, with the same slab-sided funnels and piled-up super-structure. *Tiger*'s lines were finer and more symmetrical without conceding anything in aggression, and she established a new pattern that, at last, gave battle-cruisers identifiable characteristics. A naval writer enthused:

> Speed and beauty were welded into every line of her. The highest ideals of grace and power had taken form at the bidding of the artist's brain of her designer. Wherever she went she satisfied the eye of the sailorman and I have known them to pull miles just that the sweetness of her lines might delight their eyes. She was the last warship built to satisfy the sailor's idea of what a ship should be like, and nobly she fulfilled that ideal. Beside any others she made them look like floating factories. No man who served in her fails to recollect her beauty with pride and thankfulness.

And it was *Tiger* who earned for herself and her sister battle-cruisers the title of 'the Splendid Cats'. She was the last to be built for the Royal Navy to play a significant part in the First World War, and only one of four to survive it for long.

It now seemed that, counting *Australia*, the Royal Navy mustered ten battle-cruisers to the Germans' total of five, which included the outclassed *Blücher*, and that was a handsome enough margin. The Germans, however, had not yet finished. In the yards of Blohm und Voss in Hamburg and of Schichau in Danzig a final two sister battle-cruisers were about to be built: *Derfflinger* and *Lützow*. These were to be armed with 12-inch guns that fired projectiles of 1014 lb – markedly harder-hitting than the British equivalent. They were magnificent ships of 26,180 tons, with armoured protection as good as contemporary battleships and a designed speed of 26.5 knots that was well exceeded in service. It was doubtful if any of the British battle-cruisers, except perhaps *Tiger*, could meet them with con-fidence, and they considerably narrowed the odds between the High Seas Fleet Scouting Group under Vice-Admiral Franz Hipper and the Royal Navy's three battle-cruiser squadrons commanded by Vice-Admiral Sir David Beatty.

Winston Churchill came to the Admiralty as First Lord in October 1911, aged thirty-seven.

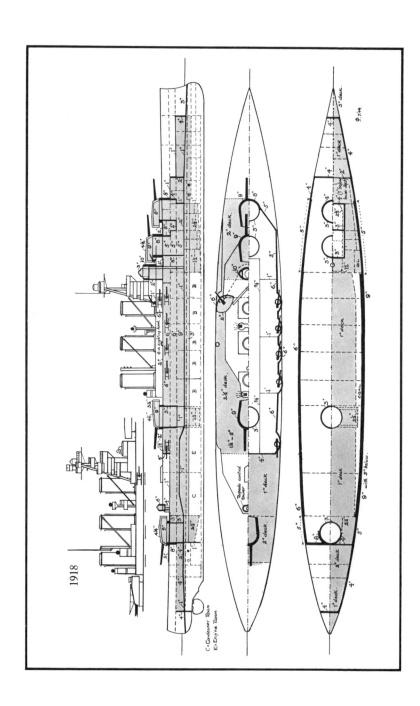

1918

## *TIGER*, BATTLE-CRUISER

*Builder*      Devonport
*Laid down*    20 June 1912
*Launched*     15 December 1913
*Completed*    October 1914

*Dimensions*
Length, waterline: 660 feet. Beam 90.5 feet. Maximum draught 28.5 feet. Displacement 28,430 tons. Complement (peacetime) 1121.

*Armament*
Eight 13.5-inch guns, 45 calibre; twelve 6-inch guns; four 21-inch torpedo-tubes, submerged. Two 3-inch AA guns later added.

*Armoured Protection*
9-inch belt reducing to 4-inch at bows and stern. Turrets and barbettes 9-inch above belt, 6-inch below. Conning tower 10-inch and 3-inch. Forecastle and upper deck 1½-inch, main deck 1-inch, lower deck 3-inch. Magazine protection 2½-inch (improved after Jutland).

*Engines*
Brown-Curtis turbines of 108,000 horsepower driving four screws. Designed speed 29–30 knots. Best speed recorded 29 knots.

*Fuel*
Coal: 3320 tons. Oil: 3480 tons. The ship burned about 1245 tons of fuel daily at 59,500 horsepower.

*Cost*
Part of the 1911–12 Naval Programme, *Tiger* cost £2,593,100. She was the largest and fastest warship to date, and the only British battle-cruiser then or later to mount 6-inch guns. She was also the last coal-burning British capital ship.

## *Notes*

1   The name 'frigate' was reintroduced to describe an ocean escort-vessel developed during the Second World War.

2   Fisher underestimated. At Jutland, only twelve years away, the battle-fleets opened fire at 15,000 yards, and ranges seldom fell below 10,000.

3   The Turkish *Reshadieh* and *Osman I* became *Erin* and *Agincourt* respectively, and the Chilean *Almirante Latorre* became *Canada*. The Norwegian cruisers *Bjoervin* and *Nidaros* were renamed *Gorgon* and *Glatton*.

4   The Japanese themselves built three copies of *Kongo*, named *Hi-Yei*, *Haruna* and *Kirishima*, so successful that Britain wished to lease two of them in 1917. The Japanese declined, explaining that the ships were too dear to Japanese hearts. All four vessels, reconstructed, fought in the Second World War.

# Chapter Two

*Below-decks conditions – messing, provisions and pay – wireless communications – gunnery – coaling and ammunitioning – surgeon probationers*

LIVING-CONDITIONS aboard a battle-cruiser did not differ noticeably from those in battleships of the period or, indeed, in major warships for several decades to come. There were structural variations between classes but, almost invariably, the majority of the ship's company were accommodated on the long main deck (immediately below the upper deck) with the officers' wardroom and cabins aft, the seamen's messes forward, and the Royal Marines' quarters between the two.[1] This arrangement was a legacy from those earlier days when seamen, often forcibly conscripted by press-gangs, had an understandable tendency to mutiny, and it was the marines' responsibility to ensure that they did not.

For off-duty and social activities the quarterdeck – the aftermost area of the upper deck over the stern – belonged exclusively to the officers. Ratings did not trespass here unless on duty or when arraigned as defaulters. On the quarterdeck, too, the captain would indicate by example which half of the deck he preferred for his daily walk, either port or starboard, and all junior officers would stay in the remaining half unless privileged by invitation to share the great man's ten paces in one direction and ten in the other. In harbour the quarterdeck was the ship's entrance foyer, immaculately holystoned and gleamingly polished, with a fine gangway or side-ladder, and continually manned by a frock-coated officer of the watch, a midshipman, quartermaster, bugler and messenger.

Officers' cabins were of necessity cramped, with only the barest of furnishings provided by the Admiralty but usually enhanced by personal effects such as bedcovers, family photographs and potted plants. The wardroom was little more than a communal dining-room which in smaller ships doubled as an off-duty lounge. In larger vessels, however, there was commonly a wardroom anteroom, equipped with easy chairs and a small bar or bar-hatch, supervised by a steward. An officer did not pay cash for his drink but signed a 'chit', or was 'ledgered', and received a monthly invoice accordingly. To those officers who lived only on their meagre service pay, the monthly mess-bill was a constant sword of Damocles.

Sub-lieutenants and midshipmen did not qualify for membership of the wardroom; they were 'subordinate officers' and were confined to the gunroom, which was also not entered by older officers except by invitation. Firmly ruled by the senior sub-lieutenant, midshipmen were subject to a rigid pecking order and, in default, to being chastised by a dirk-scabbard or the toe of a boot. They were, as Captain William Bligh is alleged to have claimed, the lowest form of animal life in the Royal Navy.

A midshipman was paid 1s 9d per day, and his parents were required to allot him £50 a year to cover his uniform and messing expenses, subscriptions to the Sports Fund and occasional rail fares. From what he had left he was compelled to pay 3d a day to the chaplain for his tuition in nautical astronomy. If in harbour and not required for duty, he could go ashore but must return aboard by 2000 hours. If he had the means, a subordinate officer was permitted to take wine at table in his mess to the value of thirty shillings a month, but was forbidden spirits. He slept in a hammock.[2]

The Royal Navy's victualling allowance was the same for both officer and rating – 1s 1d per head per day – but the officer enjoyed a number of extras, the cost of which, like his wines and spirits, was added to his mess-bill. Such extras were provided at the caterer's discretion, so the less affluent officer had to pay for them whether or not he might otherwise have desired them. The wardroom also had its own galley (but not in smaller ships) and the officers had stewards and servants who, in the Home Station, were ratings and marines, Maltese in the Mediterranean and Chinese in the Far East, although this convention might be disrupted if a ship was moved hurriedly from one station to another. Chinese messboys could find themselves in Portsmouth, in inscrutable bewilderment awaiting the next ship to be ordered to Hong Kong.

The ship's seamen occupied the forward one-third of the main deck in 'broadside' messes, which meant that the white-scrubbed wooden tables were aligned at right-angles to the ship's sides as they had always been when men lived and slept over their muzzle-loading guns. The inner ends of the tables could be raised and hooked to the deckhead to facilitate daily deck-scrubbing, and by now most accommodation-decks were covered with 'cortisene', a brown heavy-duty cork lino, pinned at intervals by narrow strips of metal.

Each mess was provided with a mess-locker – a metal dresser to accommodate crockery, utensils, bread, tinned milk and condiments, a chest for tea and sugar, a tea-kettle, several metal pails for the collection of soup, cocoa and rum, and a miscellany of buckets, mops and brushes. In strategic locations were railed-off spaces for the neat stowage of hammocks when not in use.

In the larger ships there would also be segregated messes on the lower deck (next below the main deck). These were likely to include the stokers' messdeck, usually referred to as the Bear Pit, the telegraphists' and signalmen's messes, and those of other ratings who were continually watch-keeping, and the boys' mess.

Boys of the seamen, telegraphist and signals branches enlisted in the Navy between the ages of fifteen years and three months and sixteen years, initially as Boys 2nd Class, to be subjected to a Spartan regimen of training in HMS *Ganges*, Shotley, near Harwich. Educational assessment during this period would classify each as either General Class or Advanced Class. The latter category, the better-educated, would in due course be rated Ordinary Seamen (or Ordinary Telegraphist, Ordinary Signalman) at $17\frac{1}{2}$ years instead of 18, which meant a man's status and pay six months earlier. However, most would still be Boys 1st Class when drafted to a sea-going ship.

The boys' daily routine did not differ significantly from that of their elders, although they were more closely supervised and restricted. They were not encouraged to loiter in the men's messes, and their own mess, usually enclosed, was forbidden to adult ratings except for duty reasons. Boys did not normally keep night watches, but in all other respects assumed realistic, if subordinate, responsibilities in the ship's fighting organisation.

The only seating allowed ratings was the long wooden forms that partnered the mess-tables – or the deck. Conditions below were always congested and noisy, even in the petty officers' messes, which enjoyed a pretence to privacy by being surrounded by half-bulkheads and curtains. There were no personal lockers yet. Men lived out of their kitbags, which meant that all uniform clothing had to be carefully rolled or concertina-folded and tied with string, but they did have a small wooden 'ditty box' in which to secrete their more intimate possessions such as photographs and letters.

A particular nuisance was the sailors' wide-brimmed straw-woven hats, called 'benjies', worn during summer months and in the tropics, whose fragility made them difficult to stow without crushing and, when worn, prone to be torn away by the lightest wind.

Clothes-washing was a primitive business of buckets of water and hard yellow soap, with white duck suits and hammocks scrubbed on the fo'c'sle deck, while drying was a constant problem since no clothing was permitted to be hung above decks and, elsewhere, space was at a premium in even the biggest ships.

Some enterprising ratings organised 'dhobying' services for a few coppers. Others, who had laboured long to buy a small sewing machine, would tailor uniform suits from lengths of serge to a more elegant cut than that prescribed by the Admiralty. Hair-cutting and boot-repairing were two other occupations that could earn a nimble-fingered able seaman a few pence to supplement his pay of £3 a month.

Barefoot sailors had disappeared with the old century; men went shod unless swabbing decks or boats. Anchors were no longer hauled up manually except occasionally for exercise, and the once indispensable carpenter and sailmaker had been usurped by the engine-room artificer. There were now more sophisticated methods of depth-sounding than heaving a lead-line, and there were prismatic range-finders, hydraulics, wireless, and even 'loudspeaking telephones'. Almost all ships, however, even the largest, still relied upon magnetic compasses. In June 1913 the Admiralty had asked the American, Elmer E. Sperry, to supply marine gyro compasses for evaluation, and instruments had been installed in the battleship *St Vincent* and the submarine *E1*. The trials had proved very successful, but by August 1914 few warships had been provided with gyro equipment, an innovation still widely regarded with scepticism.

Battleships and cruisers were being fitted with refrigerators, but destroyers had to take fresh meat aboard every three days, usually by a cutter under oars, loaded to the gunwhales, in the charge of a luckless midshipman. Without the twice-weekly 'blood boat' a small vessel would soon be reduced to corned beef and biscuit.

Under normal circumstances, however, most ships were subject to canteen messing. Each mess elected a caterer, who might be the senior hand but could be anyone with a modest flair for budgeting, and a canny one was an undoubted asset. Hoping to keep within a victualling allowance of 1s 1d per day for every man in his mess – perhaps twenty hands – the caterer would draw raw provisions daily from the stores and butchery, which would be debited in 'the ledger'. The provisions had to be 'made up' by the men. Ships' galleys cooked food but did not prepare it, and there were no automatic peelers or electric mixers. In the messes, potatoes were peeled, meat or fish cut, pastry or stews mixed, and then the end product taken to the galley to be 'given a shock'.

If the caterer did not use the entire monthly allowance, he

achieved 'mess savings', which was a desirable situation so long as he had provided adequately. Alternatively, if he had spent rashly on tinned foods and more expensive meats, the mess would be charged for the excess at the month's end, and the caterer would have to explain why.

Lower-deck ratings had duty-free tobacco and an issue of half a gill of Jamaica rum each midday if they were twenty years old, but paydays were long separated and their pay was niggardly. Married men with families were particularly straitened; they were called 'bundlemen' because they frequently went ashore with spare food bundled in their blue kerchiefs. They lived on coppers and denied themselves the simplest of luxuries.

There was a wide social gap between officers and men, and, although they were not as estranged as were the officers and ranks of the Army, they shared only brief moments of forced *bonhomie*, at Christmas, and during concert parties, regattas, and such other recreational activities that did not require too much physical contact. Officers might play cricket against ratings but would never spar with them; their shore-going leisure interests were poles apart, and ratings preferred it so. They were less than comfortable when involved in what were clearly 'officer' occasions – as had been tragically demonstrated in 1912 when Petty Officer Evans participated in Scott's final dash for the Pole, for his physical rather than for his intellectual attributes. Unable to fraternise with his four officer companions, nor they with him, he was a man isolated, unwilling even to report the ghastly frostbite that contributed to his death.

If the social gap remained wide, however, the educational disparity between wardroom and lower deck had narrowed considerably during the previous few decades, allowing ratings to assume responsibilities that would have totally defeated their fathers. Stokers could be taught the fundamentals of triple expansion engines and steam turbines, while electrical circuitry, torpedoes and gunnery hydraulics demanded increasingly high technical abilities. Finally there was wireless telegraphy, which promised to change the entire conduct of sea-warfare. It was significant that, while the mercantile marine decided that wireless operators had to be officers, in the Royal Navy they were ratings, initially selected from among better-schooled seamen and signalmen, and subsequently specifically recruited.

The days had long passed when the only means of communication between the Admiralty and a distant fleet was a fast frigate, and in

1914 the Navy had 435 ships equipped with wireless and about 30 shore wireless stations. Transmission-ranges varied widely, depending on the quality of the equipment and atmospheric conditions, but for the first time orders and intelligence could be passed to and from units at sea in hours rather than weeks or even months. Wireless was still unpredictable, but when it succeeded it did so brilliantly.

The areas around the British Isles were covered by transmitting stations at Cullercoats, Caistor, North Foreland, Niton, Land's End and Crookhaven, but overseas the network was much more thinly stretched. It was still necessary for almost all signals to travel at least part of their route by undersea cable, and, if intended for a ship operating outside the range of a local wireless station, to be addressed to the British consul or *chargé d'affaires* at the ship's next expected port of call. Despite the use of codes and ciphers there was a security risk with both wireless and cable; the first because it was open to interception and the second because it would almost certainly have to pass through non-British hands at some stage.

The Germans had far fewer overseas locations in which to establish wireless stations, but they had taken full advantage of those they did have, particularly in the Pacific. They were well aware that such stations would be captured or destroyed within weeks of a war starting, and had made elaborate arrangements accordingly. It was not wholly by chance that a number of German merchant ships, with excellent wireless apparatus, found themselves interned in American and other neutral ports, while German personnel supervised a number of Telefunken stations throughout Central and South America. The Germans also compensated for the anticipated loss of their overseas colonies by building transmitters which were technically superior to, and of much higher power than, those of the British. The Nauern station, near Berlin, had a range of 6200 miles and was commonly heard at 10,000. This allowed communication with Windhoek in South-West Africa, thence with Togoland and Dar-es-Salaam. The Austrian station at Pola reached Spain, Constantinople, and thus the Balkan theatre, while Eilwese, in Hanover, communicated with Tuckerton, New Jersey.

The British, however, had early realised the importance of intercepting enemy signals traffic, not only as a source of intelligence but also as a means of plotting the position of an enemy ship or force. A chain of listening stations on the east coast recorded all German transmissions, and by a process of simple triangulation could quickly pinpoint the vessels responsible. In addition, the Germans were creatures of habit, and U-boats leaving or approaching their bases would infallibly pass close to the North Hinder, a rusting old light-vessel belonging to the Dutch Government, to check their navigation and report accordingly. The light-vessel became the axial point of a British chart, called the Spider's Web, which by the end of the war was becoming a death-trap for submarines. Any unusual increase in wireless activity in the vicinity of Wilhelmshaven, or Heligoland, or Cuxhaven could mean that the German High Seas Fleet, or a portion of it, was preparing for sea.

Finally, the Germans were unaware that their naval codes had been salvaged by the Russians from the cruiser *Magdeburg*, wrecked in the Gulf of Finland, and sent to London. There, in the Admiralty's Room 40 OB, a team of cipher experts under Sir Alfred Ewing was able to anticipate a number of German movements, although not always to the Royal Navy's advantage. The Admiralty also had its share of obtuseness and resistance to innovation.

In both naval and merchant ships the location of wireless equipment was very much an afterthought. The wireless office was usually situated abaft the bridge, vulnerable to weather damage and even more to shell-fire. Aerials were fragile, though juries could be rigged quickly, albeit hazardously; but a single shell-splinter could irreparably destroy a ship's wireless facility, which might have been fully protected if positioned below decks.

The wireless office was almost invariably a small compartment smelling of overheated rubber insulation. Above the operator's bench a teak cabinet with massive tuning-dials housed the transmitter from which emerged two highly polished copper conductors each terminated by a small shining ball separated from its twin by about four inches. By the manipulation of a clumsy Post Office Morse key the gap was bridged by an electrical discharge, alarming to the uninitiated but used by the operator when lighting a cigarette. This was the 'spark', the father of a hoarse-toned Morse transmission that frequently jammed the reception of all other ships in the vicinity while remaining obstinately unheard by the station for which it was intended. The receiver was a complexity of glass valves, wires and condensers, often mounted, without covering, on a bulkhead, flanked by shelves for books, dirty cocoa-cups, paper spills, tobacco, signal-pads. There might be a small safe, perforated so that it would sink if thrown overboard – although nobody had invented one that would float – in which were kept the ship's codes and confidential publications. Most of the remaining bulkhead space would be occupied by lists of call-signs, frequencies and transmitter calibrations, emergency code-groups, broadcasting schedules and the watchkeeping-table.

In 1914 the range of wireless transmitters in smaller warships was only about twenty-five miles, but this performance was soon improved. A number of imaginative, although usually unsuccessful, experiments were made toward increasing aerial capacity, such as lifting them by box-kites, or using jets of water. Even in the largest ships an output of two kilowatts would be considered highly satisfactory, and the British had nothing to compare with the Germans' twenty-kilowatt equipment in Cologne and Nauern.

Wireless communication with aircraft developed gradually, but throughout the war would remain a hit-or-miss activity with a preponderance of misses. Radar was twenty-five years away; the limit of visibility was still the horizon.

In the final analysis, however, all warships were floating gun-platforms. It mattered less how an enemy ship could be intercepted than how it could be hit quickly, accurately and repeatedly. In short, it was the ship that scored 'the fastest with the mostest' that would emerge successful.

Until the turn of the century, or just after, the standard of gunnery in all navies was poor, partly because of inefficient instruments but equally as the result of 'go-as-you-please' procedures that included independent firing, salvoes, broadsides, controlled firing, rapid and slow firing, and group volleys. There was no standard pattern, and gun-crews merely did their best with the orders given. If their officers were satisfied, then there was no reason why seamen gunners should feel particularly concerned.

Some officers were not satisfied. Captain Percy Scott, commanding the second-class cruiser *Scylla* in the Mediterranean, introduced a new procedure of his own devising that involved rapid handling and loading of ammunition, a chart for recording hits and misses, and extemporised telescopic sights which his men were trained to maintain on target when the ship rolled. In her target shoot of 1899 *Scylla*'s six 4.7-inch guns made 56 hits with 70 rounds fired – 80 per cent – which was so superior to the Fleet's 20–40 per cent average as to be condemned as a fluke.

The following year Scott used the same drill in his new ship, the heavy cruiser *Terrible*, which, in her first test, scored 77 per cent hits to rounds fired against the Fleet's average of 28 per cent. Then, in 1901, *Terrible* achieved 80 per cent with her 6-inch guns, with ten men hitting with every round they fired and one petty officer establishing a record with eight hits with eight rounds in one minute.

Scott's *Terrible* was suddenly big news. Other commanders were stung into following suit, and by 1902 a number of ships were performing as efficiently. There was, however, a wide disparity between the best shooting and the worst. Among ships mounting 13.5-inch guns, for instance, *Hood* scored 88.35 but *Empress of India* only 13.25, and with 12-inch guns *Ocean* achieved 70.13 against *Formidable*'s paltry 4.12.

Not just a wind of change, however, but a blizzard was about to blow through the corridors of the Admiralty. In October 1904, Admiral Sir John Fisher became First Sea Lord. Four months later Scott was promoted to flag rank and appointed Inspector of Target Practice, while Sir John Jellicoe became Director of Naval Ordnance. Realistic battle practice was introduced, requiring ships to fire at long-range towed targets while simultaneously altering course. That year, 1905, the Navy's *average* proficiency exceeded 50 per cent for the first time, and by 1907 had reached 79 per cent, the best, so far as was known, in the world.

The 'Queen Elizabeth'-class battleships, laid down in 1913, would be the first to be totally oil-fired. All other major war-vessels burned a combination of coal and oil.

Both fuels were devoured in staggering amounts, and hundreds of colliers were continually engaged in replenishing the stocks of coaling stations around the world or waited in harbours to bunker ships as they arrived. A battleship or battle-cruiser carried up to 3500 tons of Welsh steam-coal and 1000 tons of oil, and, except in an emergency, did not allow fuel-levels to fall below 25 per cent. At high speed, coal could be consumed at the rate of 500 tons a day and oil at 125, but at the more economical speeds of ten or twelve knots a ship would have a maximum range of about 8000 miles.

Inevitably, coaling was a dirty and unpopular business, and everyone aboard not otherwise essentially engaged, including midshipmen, would be involved. Ventilators and scuttles were closed and vulnerable paintwork draped with canvas. Progress depended largely on the size of the collier's hatches and the efficiency of her winches, but a ship's company could hope to transfer 150 tons per hour. In the gloom of the collier's hold men shovelled the coal into two-hundredweight sacks which were hoisted in whips of ten and deposited on the upper deck of the receiving vessel, then wheeled on hand-trolleys to open chutes that fed the bunkers. Below, stokers stowed and trimmed, blackened, sweating and choking, aware that the whole procedure must be repeated in a couple of weeks. The coal-dust fouled everything and seeped everywhere, carpeting the decks, clogging machinery, and speckling linen and papers in the most inaccessible cabins. On completion, several more hours would be devoted to hosing and scrubbing, with the bathrooms crowded with naked filthy men and the drains running black.

Ammunitioning was another, though less frequent, operation that was required to be completed as quickly as possible. Explosives were embarked either from an ammunition jetty or from lighters alongside, with a red warning-flag hoisted and all smoking forbidden throughout the ship. A battleship carried a hundred projectiles and twice that number of cordite charges for each gun of her main armament. A 12-inch projectile weighed 850 lb, a 13.5-inch projectile 1400 lb, and full cordite charges about 300 lb. All were stowed in the magazines and shell-rooms below each turret, and the magazine-crews, who were normally cooks, writers, storemen and marine bandsmen, were expected to accommodate a rate of fire of two rounds per gun per minute. If there were a threat of fire, the magazine with its crew was flooded by the Officer of Quarters above.

The only other commodity of importance to be periodically embarked was food. The quality of provisions provided by the Admiralty was generally good, if somewhat unimaginative, and 1*s* 1*d* per head per day was more generous than might be thought today. In what form food appeared on the plate depended on the ingenuity of the mess caterer, earlier described, and the integrity of the cooks, who could make or mar any culinary adventure.

To feed her officers and men for two weeks, a battleship or battle-cruiser would take aboard 60 tons of potatoes, 30 tons of fresh beef, half a ton of kidneys, 180 sides of bacon, 2400 lb of margarine, 15 hundredweight of salt cod, 10 hundredweight each of kippers, haddock and bloaters, half a ton of onions, 6 hundredweight of salt, macaroni, lard, tinned herrings in tomato sauce (known to the lower deck as 'herrings-in'), 720 dozen eggs, prunes, tapioca, slab cake, tinned apples, tinned peaches, brawn, cheese, tinned peas, 36 cooked hams, 24 dozen bottles of sauce and 12 dozen bottles of curry powder.

Both fresh and dry provisions were issued at routine times daily. There were usually no restrictions on bread and potatoes; each mess might draw what it wished, providing there was no waste. Other commodities, such as tea, sugar, evaporated milk and margarine, would be issued in quantities based on the number in each mess, while meats, fish, tinned goods and similar preserves would be a matter for the caterer's discretion and debited accordingly. Larger ships baked their own bread and supplied it to smaller ships which could not.

Probably the least popular man in any ship was the Master-at-

Arms, in sailing days responsible for instructing men in the use of pike and cutlass but later given police duties and nicknamed 'Jaunty', from the French *gendarme*. He had been assisted by several Royal Marine corporals, referred to as 'crushers' and detested by naval ratings who regarded all marines as merely soldiers – a distinctly inferior species. Indeed, any seaman who was clumsy or inadequate was derisively dubbed a 'soldier'. Just prior to the First World War, however, the marine provost corporals were replaced by regulating petty officers who, if still named 'crushers', were more attuned to the naval rating's way of life and less resented. At the conclusion of the Second World War the Regulating Branch would be further reinforced by the introduction of Leading Patrolmen.

With the Navy's sudden and massive increase in personnel during late 1914, the Admiralty found it impossible to recruit an adequate number of qualified doctors to meet wartime requirements, and an appeal was made to medical students in the final stages of training to volunteer to serve as surgeon-probationers for the duration of hostilities. More than a thousand were taken into the service, to be drafted to every class of warship from battleships to destroyers and sloops. It is very probable that most of these young men considered that their careers were to be interrupted for only a few months. In the event, however, they served for four years, often in action, in confined and difficult circumstances, frequently with no senior to consult, and aided only by a book of clinical notes – but so many with ability and gallantry.

For a hundred years the Royal Navy had not fought a major battle, but had policed the world's sea-lanes, hunted down Chinese pirates and Arab slave-traders, wagged warning fingers at upstart dictators and brought succour to the victims of earthquakes and typhoons. Ships like *Beagle* and *Challenger* had charted oceans and coastlines, recorded depths and marine phenomena for the benefit of all; the Admiralty's Hydrographic Department was the envy of the world. If the Royal Navy had been the biggest, its muscle had been applied to the furtherance of safe navigation, communications and the establishment of maritime law. There had been jealousies and resentments, but the British had little for which to apologise. Every other navy in the world copied British procedures and customs, dressed their sailors in the square blue collar and ribboned cap of the British tar, and patterned their officers' behaviour on that which had been developed at Dartmouth and Osborne.

The century of comparative calm, however, was now ending and a challenge was being offered by the Imperial German Navy which, it was known, was powerfully equipped, well trained, determined, and enjoying the advantage of being able to choose the timing and direction of its forays, intent, in the words of Grand Admiral Alfred von Tirpitz, on waging 'guerrilla warfare against the English [sic] until we have achieved such a weakening of their fleet that we can safely send out our own'.

## Notes

1   *Dreadnought* had reversed the traditional arrangement by having her officers berthed forward and her men aft, because of the otherwise long distance from the admiral's stern cabin to the bridge. Her ratings believed it was because the officers could not tolerate the vibrations from her 23,000-horsepower engines, while ratings were expected to put up with anything. In fact the men had far the better of the exchange. The 'Lion'-class battle-cruisers also had an unconventional accommodation arrangement (see p. 15).

2   Officers-to-be entered *Britannia*, the Royal Naval College at Dartmouth, as thirteen-year-old cadets. After three and a half years they were drafted to sea as midshipmen, still regarded as under training, until they qualified as sub-lieutenants. This procedure was modified in the 1970s, when the age for admission to Dartmouth was raised to 16½. The cadet now goes to sea at twenty, assuming qualification, as a sub-lieutenant. The rank of midshipman has been abolished.

# II 1914: The Cats Show Their Claws

## Chapter Three

*Mobilisation and war – the chase of* Goeben *– the RNVR – Heligoland Bight*

IN AUGUST 1914, Europe went to war with cheering crowds, songs and flowers. The victorious soldiers of Germany, promised the Kaiser, would be home before the leaves had fallen. The British agreed that it would all be over by Christmas and flocked in their scores of thousands to enlist.

During the summer of that year the reserve squadrons of the Royal Navy had been manned for manœuvres in view of the darkening international situation, and had 800 warships afloat, grossing almost three million tons. On 26 July, a week before Britain's declaration of war, Admiral Prince Louis of Battenberg, the First Sea Lord since 1913, ordered that the reserve ships and their crews should not be dispersed. It was a decision taken in the absence of the First Lord, Winston Churchill, with whom Prince Louis enjoyed an amicable relationship, and there is little doubt that Churchill approved of the action – at least in retrospect, since he accepted the major share of the credit for it. Within three months, during which time the public's anti-German feelings were expressed in smashing the windows of anyone with a vaguely German-sounding name, Prince Louis was the subject of a scurrilous newspaper campaign and asked by the Cabinet to resign.

On 30 October 1914, at Churchill's insistence, Admiral of the Fleet Lord Fisher, now in his seventy-fourth year, was recalled from retirement to assume once again the office of First Sea Lord.

Not all of the Navy's 800 ships were ready for war. Some of them, like the cruisers of the 'Edgar' and 'Royal Arthur' classes, were almost a quarter of a century old and had been gathering rust and barnacles for years, used only for the gunnery and boat-handling training of disinterested reservists. Still, they would be good for something, and, unlike the Army, the Navy had an embarrassing superfluity of personnel. The men had to be put somewhere, and the old ships were hauled from their moorings. They were stripped of excess woodwork and horsehair furnishings, and entire crews were set to chipping away the paint of two decades, as thick as the armour beneath it. Simultaneously, dozens of passenger-liners were appropriated by the Admiralty for conversion into armed merchant cruisers. Armies of dockyard workers swarmed over these stately vessels of Cunard and White Star, tearing out expensive panelling and draperies, smothering everything in thick black paint, and hoisting inboard guns, ammunition and splinter-mats. It would soon prove to be a needless exercise, because within weeks the German mercantile fleet – the only justification for the British auxiliaries – had been sunk or captured, or had achieved sanctuary in home or neutral ports.

When it was realised that three Cunard liners – *Aquitania*, *Lusitania* and *Mauretania* – alone devoured 30,000 tons of coal every week, which was exactly what the entire Grand Fleet needed, they were hastily released from naval service.

The battle-cruisers had spent the immediate pre-war years in much the same way as most of the Navy had spent those Indian-summer years – exercising, cruising and showing the flag at home and abroad. In 1908, *Indomitable* had taken His Royal Highness George, Prince of Wales to Quebec, allowing him to work as a stoker during the voyage, and in the same year *Inflexible* had attended the Hudson–Fulton celebrations in New York. In March 1911 she had collided with the battleship *Bellerophon* off Portland, damaging her bows. *Invincible*, too, in March 1913, had collided with the submarine *C34* in Stokes Bay, off Portsmouth, but there had been no casualties and little damage.

*Indefatigable* had gone to the Mediterranean, while *Australia*, on completion, had sailed for Australian waters. *New Zealand* had undertaken a world cruise, returning to the Home Station for a visit to Russian Baltic ports in December 1913.

*Lion*, *Princess Royal* and *Queen Mary* had been commissioned too recently to have enjoyed any foreign adventures and, indeed, prolonged industrial disputes had delayed *Queen Mary*'s completion until September 1913. *Tiger* was still in John Brown's yard on Clyde-bank and would join the Grand Fleet at Scapa Flow on 6 November 1914 after less than a month's shake-down, too late for the war's opening shots.

A second vessel of the *Tiger* type, intended to be *Leopard*, was proposed under the 1912 Navy Estimates. Construction was postponed until 1914, but in that year was cancelled.

\*

If the German Navy had expected a close blockade on their bases, presumably with British warships patrolling just outside gunshot range in the old Nelson style, they were to be disappointed. Almost three years earlier Prince Louis of Battenberg (then Second Sea Lord) and Sir Francis Bridgeman (then First Sea Lord) had decided on a new strategy of *distant* blockade. With scouting submarines, wireless interception, and with battle-cruisers capable of 28 knots, cruisers of 30 knots, destroyers of 36 knots, and east-coast harbours only two hundred miles away, it was no longer necessary to have storm-battered squadrons at sea for weeks while the enemy sat warm and chuckling, awaiting a few hours of fog in which to slip the net or, worse, the moment when he could pounce on a weak British off-shore force and then quickly regain sanctuary.

It had not occurred to the Germans that their fleet in being might be balanced by an even larger fleet in being with its heavy units based on Scapa Flow, Cromarty and Rosyth, and light cruisers and destroyer flotillas operating from Dover, Harwich and Lowestoft. The theme was perhaps negative, but at least it did not play into German hands, and it might even tempt their ships to venture farther than was wise into the North Sea, which would suit the British well.

Since early 1913, however, in anticipation of an Anglo-German war, Winston Churchill had cherished plans for capturing a base or bases on the coast of Holland, Denmark, Norway or Sweden, in disregard of the fact that these countries would be neutral and that neither the British Army nor the Royal Navy had any experience of amphibious operations. His proposal involved the seizure of the Dutch island of Borkum and the German island of Sylt, possibly Heligoland and even an advance up the Elbe. The War Staff firmly rejected the plan as strategically and tactically futile.

Fisher's return to the Admiralty only added fuel to Churchill's swashbuckling calculations, for the old Admiral was also obsessed with a scheme for landing a British or Russian army on the Baltic coast of Germany, eighty miles from Berlin, and he would nurse this obsession until the end of the war. To equip the project Fisher would progressively place contracts for 612 vessels – concealing his motives from a disapproving Treasury – which would include battle-cruisers, monitors, light cruisers and destroyers.

In due course Churchill and Fisher would turn their attention to the Gallipoli peninsula (Fisher albeit with reluctance) – an operation to which the Navy's contribution would be less than impressive, and both men would be sacked as a result.

But we are ahead of ourselves.

*

On the eve of war, *Indefatigable, Inflexible* and *Indomitable* constituted the nucleus of the Mediterranean Fleet, commanded by Admiral Sir Berkeley Milne, supported by four armoured cruisers (*Defence, Black Prince, Duke of Edinburgh* and *Warrior*), four light cruisers (*Gloucester, Weymouth, Chatham* and *Dublin*), sixteen coal-burning destroyers, sixteen obsolete torpedo-boats and six small submarines.

Milne was an officer totally lacking in initiative; his second-in-command, Rear-Admiral Thomas Troubridge, by his own boast, had never disobeyed an order nor questioned one; and this unfortunate combination would be responsible for the first body-blow to British naval prestige.

The only German warships in the Mediterranean (on 2 August 1914) were the battle-cruiser *Goeben* and the light cruiser *Breslau*. There was a powerful French force of sixteen battleships (although only one was of Dreadnought quality), six cruisers and fourteen destroyers.

Everyone knew, without a shadow of doubt, that war was only hours away and that Britain and France would be allied against Germany. Milne had been told by signal, initiated by Winston Churchill, that his (Milne's) *first responsibility* was to protect the French transference of troops from north Africa to metropolitan France – *but*, Churchill added, Milne must also 'if possible bring to action individual German ships, particularly *Goeben*'.

The secondary instruction would have confused a commander brighter than Milne. The obvious thing to do was to eliminate *Goeben* and *Breslau* (which Fisher would have unhesitatingly ordered, but Fisher was not yet back in office), after which there would have been no threat to the French, but, to baffle Milne further, Churchill warned that the British 'should not at this stage be brought to action against superior forces, except in combination with the French . . .'.

'At this stage' neither France nor Britain was at war with Germany, but on 3 August the French were. *Goeben* and *Breslau*, hoisting Russian ensigns, bombarded the Algerian embarkation-ports of Philipville and Bône, inflicting negligible damage, then ran for Messina to take on coal. That same day the Admiralty had announced that the entire Navy was 'on a war footing', which was, however, not quite the same thing as being at war. When, at 0930 on the morning of 4 August, *Indomitable* and *Indefatigable* met *Goeben* and *Breslau* – steaming eastward – there still remained 13½ hours before Britain's ultimatum to Germany would expire. The two British battle-cruisers reported the encounter by wireless to Admiral Milne in Malta, refrained from saluting the German pair, and then turned to follow them.

From Malta, Milne told the Admiralty: '*Indomitable* and *Indefatigable* shadowing *Goeben* and *Breslau* 37.44N 7.56E.' Churchill responded: 'Very good. Hold her. War imminent.' It is difficult in retrospect to understand what the phrase 'Hold her' was meant to imply. War may have been imminent but it was not yet fact and, indeed, there still remained time for the German Government to agree with British demands, however unlikely this might be. *Goeben* and *Breslau* were about their lawful business, for the moment. If this typically Churchillian vagary meant 'Hold her in sight', which was the only sensible interpretation, then that was what *Indefatigable* and *Indomitable* tried to do.

Aboard *Goeben*, however, Admiral Wilhelm Souchon had no intention of tamely waiting for 11 p.m. to legalise his destruction. He piled on steam, eastward, passing close to the northern coast of Sicily and heading for the narrow Straits of Messina. The senior British captain, Francis Kennedy, did the same and, for the first time, German and British battle-cruisers were comparing performances. Hour followed hour under a hot August sun, through morning and into afternoon, with the officers on each bridge watching their clocks and the two German ships gradually widening the gap that separated them from *Indefatigable* and *Indomitable*. By evening only the light cruiser *Dublin* remained in touch until dusk and mist closed around *Goeben* and *Breslau*. In the stokehold of the German battle-cruiser four men had collapsed and died, but Souchon had reached the neutral Italian port of Messina, sanctuary and coal.

Milne, and consequently Kennedy, had been forbidden to enter neutral waters, which meant the entire length of the Straits of Messina, although such a proscription would not have bothered a Nelson or a Fisher. Earlier, in London, Battenberg had been pleading that it was still possible to destroy the German warships before dark (and this was the man who was to be hounded from office because of his alleged German sympathies), but Churchill, denied by the Cabinet, could make no move except to approve the signal to be despatched at 11 p.m. GMT to all British ships throughout the world: 'Commence hostilities against Germany.'

In Messina, *Goeben* and *Breslau* were coaling. Waiting for them to emerge, Admiral Milne leisurely redeployed his own forces.

Assuming that Souchon did not mean to remain in Messina to be interned, he had the choice of three lines of escape. He could steam westward, in the direction of Sardinia, Gibraltar and sixteen French battleships; he could turn eastward toward the coasts of neutral Greece, Turkey and the cul-de-sac of the eastern Mediterranean; or, finally, he could *begin* steaming eastward but then turn northward around the toe of Italy into the Adriatic, to join the Austrian fleet in Pola or Trieste.

It did not occur to Milne that the Germans might run for the Dardanelles, which would be against all the rules. He ordered Rear-Admiral Troubridge to patrol the mouth of the Adriatic with his four armoured cruisers, and himself held the three battle-cruisers (*Indomitable* and *Indefatigable* now joined by *Inflexible*) south of Sicily 'on a defensive line from Bizerta to Sardinia'. When Souchon sailed from Messina at 1700 hours on 6 August he found, to his surprise, only the light cruiser *Gloucester* waiting for him at the eastward entrance to the Straits.

Milne had miscalculated, but it was not an entirely unreasonable miscalculation, and the situation could still be rescued if he moved quickly. Captain Howard Kelly, commanding *Gloucester* – the only officer to emerge from the operation with any credit – followed grimly in the wake of the enemy and wirelessed his course to Milne. A little later Souchon edged north-eastward to give the impression that he was, indeed, turning into the Adriatic, and *Gloucester* reported this, too, to both Milne and Troubridge. Everything seemed to be happening as the British had expected, and Troubridge moved southward to intercept.

Kelly clung to *Goeben* and *Breslau* throughout the night of the sixth, keeping his distance from the enemy's heavy guns and waiting for Troubridge's heavy cruisers to appear ahead or Milne's battle-cruisers to overtake him from astern, but neither happened. Milne was steaming slowly from the direction of Malta, still convinced that Souchon was bound for the Adriatic, while Troubridge, at 0400 on the morning of the seventh, decided not to continue his attempt to intercept *Goeben* and *Breslau* because his force was inferior to that of the enemy, and the Admiralty had earlier expressly ordered that British ships 'should not at this stage be brought to action against superior forces . . .'. Since Troubridge's squadron mounted twenty-two 9.5-inch guns against *Goeben*'s ten 11-inch, plus fourteen 7.5-inch and twenty 6-inch guns against the enemy's total of twelve 6-inch and twelve 4.1-inch guns, with the additional advantage of being four ships against two, his reasoning was highly questionable, and to allow that he was only obeying orders is to be generous in the extreme. Winston Churchill would later suggest that his order re-ferred only to the *Austrian* fleet, but this claim was as inept as Troubridge's.

Idling until 1000 hours, Troubridge took his squadron into the Greek port of Zante to await further developments – hopefully the arrival of Milne's battle-cruisers. Milne, however, was three hundred miles to the westward, steaming tranquilly at 12 knots.

Howard Kelly, in *Gloucester*, was still pounding after *Goeben* and *Breslau*, but at 0530 Milne ordered him to 'gradually drop astern to avoid capture'. Kelly ignored the order and, observing *Breslau* falling back, presumably to turn him away, decided to engage. Both *Breslau* and *Goeben* returned his fire, and Kelly, outgunned, and aware of the importance of his shadowing role, broke off the action but remained in contact. Nothing would be gained by getting *Gloucester* sunk or disabled, but Kelly was wishing that someone else cared.

For a further three hours *Gloucester*, alone, clung to the enemy, until Milne ordered categorically that Kelly should not continue beyond Cape Matapan. At 1630, aware of the futility of it, Kelly gave up the chase, and *Goeben* and *Breslau* disappeared gratefully among the islands of the southern Aegean.

At 1400 hours on the following day, 8 August, Milne was informed by London that Austria, now, was at war with Britain. The signal was a pre-arranged coded group which an Admiralty clerk had released in error and would be cancelled in due course, but it was sufficient to persuade Milne that the pursuit of *Goeben* was of secondary importance to the possible emergence of the Austrian fleet. Indeed, if Souchon intended to reinforce the Austrians (Milne was still convinced of this), then there was even more reason for shutting the door to the Adriatic. He ordered Troubridge's squadron and *Gloucester* to rejoin him in a position where he 'could not be cut off from Malta by the possible emergence of the Austrian fleet'. Milne was quite happy to have *Goeben* and *Breslau* bottled up in the neutral Aegean 'to the north'.

It had not remotely occurred to him, nor to the Admiralty, that Souchon would take his ships to Constantinople and turn them over to the Turkish Navy. It simply wasn't cricket.

Turkey was sitting on the international fence, watching both sides but with sympathies becoming progressively pro-German. On 3 August the British Foreign Secretary, Sir Edward Grey, had incensed the Turks by casually informing them by telegram that their two battleships, *Reshadieh* and *Osman I*, building in Britain at a cost of £7½ million, were being requisitioned by the Royal Navy.[1] The money had been raised by public subscription throughout Turkey, and Grey added that the financial loss was a matter of 'sincere regret' to His Majesty's Government, and would be given 'due consideration'. The Turks were not appeased, and on that very day signed a secret treaty of alliance with Germany.

*Goeben*'s arrival in Turkish waters was not unannounced. For hours German diplomats in Constantinople had been pleading that Souchon be allowed to take his ships through the Dardanelles into the Black Sea; but the Turks were anxious to maintain a façade of neutrality, and to agree to the German request would undoubtedly seriously damage Turkey's delicate relationship with Russia. The appearance of the two warships before the fortress of Chanak, however, meant that a decision had to be taken. The German ambassador refused to allow the vessels to be interned and demilitarised, the Turks had no way of compelling them, and presumably the British fleet would soon be arriving to insist that they were. (In fact Milne and his battle-cruisers were still sauntering around the southerly waters of the Aegean, 'in case the German ships came out'.)

Then someone in Constantinople offered an inspired solution. Why shouldn't the Germans 'sell' the two warships to the Turkish Government? It was perfectly legal. And hadn't the British seized two battleships that were rightfully Turkish?

Both Germans and Turks were delighted. *Goeben* and *Breslau*, renamed *Jawus Sultan Selim* and *Midilli*, hoisted the Turkish ensign, and their crews, wearing Turkish tarbushes, were inspected by the Sultan. Souchon was appointed Commander-in-Chief of the Turkish Navy, and millions of Turks became jubilantly pro-German.

'It does not much matter,' shrugged the Prime Minister, Asquith, in London. 'We shall insist on the *Goeben*'s crew being replaced by Turks who will not be able to navigate her.'

The Admiralty, too, was unruffled, announcing on 11 August that 'with the dismantling and internment of these ships the safety of trade will have been almost entirely secured'.

A few weeks later Souchon and his German crews, without Turkish approval, took the two warships into the Black Sea to shell Odessa, Sevastopol and Feodosia, and sink a Russian gunboat. Russia declared war on Turkey – to Germany's satisfaction – and Britain and France followed suit. It was a sequence of events that would draw half a million troops from the Allied armies in France and subsequently drag Bulgaria, Greece, Italy and Romania into the world conflict. Gallipoli would be suffered and the campaigns of the Middle East fought, while Russia, deprived of her Black Sea lifeline, would be choked to death.

The Splendid Cats had not been allowed to show their claws, and the Navy was enraged. Rear-Admiral Beatty, with a proprietary interest in battle-cruisers, fumed: 'To think that it is for the Navy to provide the first and only instance of failure. God, it makes me sick!' Fisher, still simmering in retirement, considered Milne to be an 'utterly useless commander', a 'backstairs cad' and a 'serpent of the lowest type'. Milne was recalled from the Mediterranean on 18 August, anticipating his next appointment as Commander-in-Chief Nore, only to find himself retired, which was a generous fate, but the Admiralty dared not be accusative. Milne's conduct and dispositions had been 'subjected to the careful examination of the Board of Admiralty with the result that their Lordships have approved of the measures taken in all respects'. In the language of a later generation, a whitewash.

With the Navy's contemptuous eyes on him, Troubridge demanded a court of enquiry which subsequently ordered a court-martial on the charge that he 'did forbear to chase HIGM's ship *Goeben*, being an enemy then flying'.

Troubridge was exonerated; any other verdict would have pointed another doubting finger at the Admiralty's indecisive handling of the operation. There would, however, be no further sea-commands for Troubridge. In 1915 he led the Naval Mission to Serbia, which gave artillery support to the Serbs against the Austrians, and received the Order of Kara George from King Peter.

Captain Howard Kelly, of *Gloucester*, was awarded the Companionship of the Bath.

In home waters both navies were making aggressive noises like two boxers in their respective corners before the first exchange of blows. There had been a confused and indecisive flurry of shots between German light cruisers and a British destroyer force which an Admiralty communiqué described as 'a certain liveliness' but, in general, the British were more concerned with the transportation of the British Expeditionary Force to France (which the enemy hardly knew had happened until they collided with the BEF at Mons) and with combing out some of the earlier, probably inevitable, anomalies, muddles in ship dispositions, blockade and patrol priorities rather than with seeking an early confrontation. It was inappropriate, for instance, to employ the battle-cruiser *Invincible* for halting and searching neutral ships in the waters south of Ireland, even if the neutrals were impressed, and equally incongruous for slow obsolete cruisers like *Aboukir*, *Hogue* and *Cressy*, manned by reservists, to patrol unescorted only a few miles off the Hook of Holland. *Invincible* was withdrawn from Queenstown to join *New Zealand* in the Humber, where both would shortly be reinforced by *Inflexible*, ordered home from the Mediterranean. Three other battle-cruisers, under Sir David Beatty, were based at Cromarty. *Aboukir*, *Hogue* and *Cressy*, the 'Live Bait Squadron', were left where they were.

By late August, however, the Royal Navy was ready to demonstrate who was master in the North Sea and, besides, a success of some kind was badly needed to offset the long series of reverses in France, the gravity of which even the most vigorous propaganda failed to hide. It was planned that two flotillas of destroyers led by two light cruisers should stage a dawn attack on the German naval patrols off Heligoland Bight. At this early hour the Germans' level of vigilance would be at its lowest, and the surprise assault could have them reeling. If, when they had gathered their wits, they pursued the retiring British to seaward, there would be six submarines waiting for them and, better still, the battle-cruisers *Invincible* and *New Zealand* out of the Humber.

It was realised, however – almost too late – that the date of this adventure coincided with that of the transportation of 3000 marines and naval ratings across the Channel to bolster the threatened defences of Antwerp. It was thought that the German High Seas Fleet, in the Jade river, might make a move to intercept. In addition to the deployment outlined in the original plan for the Heligoland operation, therefore, the Admiralty ordered *Lion*, *Queen Mary* and *Princess Royal*, accompanied by six light cruisers, to provide additional cover for both the Heligoland enterprise and the possible emergence of the High Seas Fleet.

The Royal Naval Volunteer Reserve, imposed by Parliament on an uninterested Admiralty in 1903 and since almost ignored, still mustered 5000 officers and men in 1914. Few of them were drafted to sea-going ships; the majority were formed into brigades with their counterparts, the Royal Marine Volunteers, and sent to reinforce the Army, initially in Belgium. From one viewpoint this was a convenient means of disposing of the unwanted amateur sailors, but must also be seen as a commendable attempt on the part of Winston Churchill to stem the German advance – rather spoiled by his offer to resign his Admiralty appointment and 'take command of the forces in the field', which was received by the Cabinet 'with roars of incredulous laughter'. However, this bid to stabilise the Belgian theatre and hold the key bases of Ostend and Zeebrugge might have been more successful if some of the eleven Territorial divisions idling in England, for which Kitchener had only contempt, had also been sent across the Channel at this time.

The day, 28 August, began with confusion. Commodore Sir Reginald Tyrwhitt, commanding the assault force in the newly commissioned light cruiser *Arethusa*, together with the older *Fearless*, was not informed of the latest change in plans – that there were going to be a lot more warships around than he had expected, and that not all the ships he met would be hostile. Commodore Roger Keyes, in the destroyer *Lurcher*, commanding the submarines, was also left in ignorance. Finally, none of the supporting battle-cruisers knew where the British submarines were to be deployed. Tyrwhitt, at 0330 on the morning of the operation, would sight six light cruisers and be within seconds of engaging them before realising that they were British, and Keyes would be similarly baffled, much later, when he sighted the same vessels and reported them as enemy.

There was worse. *Arethusa* had been in commission for only fifteen days and was in no condition to lead any such raid into enemy waters. Her engines were giving her only 25 knots instead of their designed 30. Only the previous day it remained apparent that each time her semi-automatic 4-inch guns fired they almost invariably jammed. Such was the enthusiasm for the operation, however, that it was decided not to attempt to remedy the guns' defects *in case they would not be ready for the next morning*. It was better, presumably, to take part with guns that persistently jammed than not to take part at all.

That the operation did not become a death-trap was even more incredible because before midnight on the twenty-seventh incautious British wireless exchanges had warned the Germans that a force was approaching Heligoland, and it would have been perfectly possible to have had heavy units from the Jade at sea and ready, but nobody seemed to have guessed the scale of the raid. In the event, all the heavy ships of the High Seas Fleet were locked behind the tidal bar at the river's mouth, unable to emerge before about midday.

Shortly before 0700, however, *Arethusa* sighted enemy destroyers through the dawn mist at about four miles and the British flotillas gave joyful chase. They were soon lost to sight in the haze, but Tyrwhitt, following the sound of gunfire to give support, stumbled into one of the German patrolling cruisers, *Stettin*, which unbelievably had been at anchor and had not yet raised steam for full speed. *Arethusa* altered course to engage.

Almost immediately, inevitably, her guns began to jam. Both ships were running southward, on parallel courses, when a second German cruiser, *Frauenlob*, raced into range from the direction of Heligoland.

*Arethusa* was now in trouble. With only one gun functioning, she was hit thirty-five times in ten minutes, suffering 27 casualties including 11 dead. With her forward engine-room awash with three feet of water, speed was reduced to ten knots. There was a cordite fire aft, her wireless was destroyed and her signal halyards shot away. Then her single gun put a shell below *Frauenlob*'s bridge, inflicting 37 casualties, and with *Fearless*, commanded by Captain W. F. Blunt, closing fast both German ships turned away, *Frauenlob* to take no further part in the general action.

Elsewhere the destroyers of the assault force were scampering recklessly around in the mist, firing at anything that moved and achieving more than their indiscipline deserved. The enemy destroyer *V1* and two torpedo-boats, *D8* and *T33*, were severely punished but all managed to crawl for the safety of Heligoland. Then out of the mist burst the big destroyer *V187*, the German commodore's ship. She whirled away southward, with the British snapping at her heels. Within minutes, however, she suddenly put her helm over and doubled back to meet her pursuers. She had sighted, ahead, the cruisers *Nottingham* and *Lowestoft*, two units of the 1st Light Cruiser Squadron which, with Beatty's battle-cruisers, had been belatedly assigned to supporting the raid. There was no hope for *V187* now. She fought, but, pounced upon by eight destroyers, was torn to shreds and sank, burning, with her ensign flying. The British picked up the survivors, retained a few 'just as a sample', and gave the others biscuits, water, a compass, and pointed the way home to Heligoland. It was still a gentleman's war.

By mid-afternoon there seemed to be nobody else around to shoot at, and *Arethusa* was in a poor state of seaworthiness, so Tyrwhitt decided to terminate the inshore operation and retire seaward.

By now, however, the Germans were recovering from the shock of an enemy force running wild within sight of the red cliffs of Heligoland. The heavy ships of the High Seas Fleet were still frustratingly imprisoned in the Jade estuary, but all available cruisers were ordered to pursue and engage the retiring British ships. *Mainz* was under way by 0900, *Strassburg* by 0930, followed in quick succession by *Köln*, *Ariadne*, *Stralsund*, *Kolberg*, *Hela* and *Danzig*. Encouraged, *Stettin* – which had earlier fled from the action – turned back for another run at the enemy.

Commodore William Goodenough, aboard *Southampton* leading the 1st Light Cruiser Squadron, believing that any further involvement of his ships would only further confuse matters and that, anyway, his presence was no longer required, had also withdrawn from the Heligoland area and was twenty miles to the north-west. *Nottingham* and *Lowestoft*, however, were being shadowed by Commodore Keyes in the destroyer *Lurcher*. Keyes, unaware that there were any four-funnelled cruisers on *his* side, reported to *Invincible* by wireless that he was in touch with the enemy. Goodenough, intercepting this signal, decided to take *Southampton* and *Falmouth* to *Lurcher*'s assistance, whereupon Keyes reported the approach of *two more* enemy cruisers which he intended leading toward *Invincible*'s position. Finally, *Southampton* sighted a submarine periscope and turned to ram at high speed. The submarine was the British *E6*, which avoided destruction by crash-diving.

While these off-stage drolleries were being played out, *Arethusa* was limping westward accompanied by *Fearless* and her destroyers. Their situation was perilous. By 1100 they had covered barely fifteen miles, and at noon the tide in the Jade would be sufficiently high to release fast powerful ships like *Von der Tann*, *Seydlitz* and *Moltke*, any one of which could annihilate the little British armada.

The first enemy ship to appear from the south-west was the cruiser *Strassburg*, which fired a few ineffectual salvoes at long range before turning away into the mist. Minutes later, *Köln* was sighted. She also fired, then followed in the direction of her sister.

It seemed to Tyrwhitt that the two reluctant Germans might very well be outriders of a heavy squadron unleashed from the Jade, a possibility strengthened by intercepted wireless signals which suggested that Keyes in *Lurcher* was also in contact with *four* enemy cruisers. While it had been hoped that German ships would indeed be lured into the sights of the waiting British submarines and perhaps the battle-cruisers, there was no means of communicating with the submarines, the battle-cruisers were forty miles away, and *Arethusa* was a cripple.

Tyrwhitt's apprehension was not relieved when yet another cruiser materialised to northward and opened fire on the crawling *Arethusa*, this time with uncomfortable accuracy. Several salvoes had erupted within thirty feet of the ship when the escorting British destroyers flung themselves in the direction of this new enemy, threatening a torpedo attack. She was, in fact, *Strassburg* again, but in the thick visibility she appeared to be a larger vessel. However, as uncertain as were the British of enemy strength, *Strassburg* again turned away.

To Vice-Admiral Beatty in *Lion*, far to seaward, the excited exchange of wireless enemy-reports was causing increasing concern. He ordered Goodenough to detach two of his cruisers to *Arethusa*'s assistance, and then, a little later, ordered the remaining four to follow. Commodore Goodenough, having now convinced *Lurcher* that both were fighting the same war, pounded off to the south-east. He was more than an hour's fast steaming from *Arethusa*.

Beatty then received a polite signal from *Arethusa*: 'Respectfully request that I be supported. Am hard pressed.'

It was time, Beatty decided, to take the battle-cruisers inshore to clear up the entire confused situation. To risk his five battle-cruisers in the thickening eastward mist, among both British and German submarines, minefields and, not least, the German High Seas Fleet, was something not to be casually undertaken, but *Arethusa*, *Fearless*, their destroyers, and perhaps even Goodenough's cruisers, might need Beatty's big guns if they were to escape being overwhelmed. *Lion*, *Queen Mary*, *Princess Royal*, *Invincible* and *New Zealand* turned in line toward Heligoland and began working up to full speed, their crews at action stations and all guns ready.

*Mainz* had left the Ems river at 1000 hours, using all of her 25 knots to intercept the British force by 1130, and she did not flinch from the destroyers when they raced into attack; she hit back angrily. Nor were the destroyers less determined. In the running fight that followed for twenty minutes, *Laurel* received a shell in her engine-room that killed three men, a second that scythed down the forward gun's crew, and a third that ignited ready-use lyddite ammunition, disabled the after gun and wrecked a funnel. Commander Frank Rose, hit in his left leg, balanced on his right. Then he was hit in his right leg and, not surprisingly, fell down, but continued in command until he lost consciousness. The bridge of *Liberty*, following, was squarely hit by a shell that also brought down her mast, killing her captain and a signalman, while *Laertes* received four shells in one salvo that killed two, wounded six, and damaged her boilers sufficiently to bring her to a halt.

Miraculously, however, all three destroyers would later be brought home by their crews to fight again. They would also be told by the Admiralty that their consumption of torpedoes had been unnecessarily lavish and that supplies of these expensive items were not inexhaustible.

Meanwhile *Mainz*, fighting superbly, found herself in exactly the same predicament as had *V187*, earlier. She ran straight into the arms of Goodenough's cruisers.

Her captain, Paschen, turned her desperately, but the vengeful destroyers were waiting; they were not going to allow her to escape now. On fire forward and aft, with her port engine disabled, her rudder jammed and most of her guns silenced, there was nowhere for her to run. A torpedo smashed into her, amidships. The British cruisers were hitting her with every salvo, tearing down her funnels, then her mainmast. In ten minutes *Mainz* was a chaos of torn metal, flame and corpses. She struck her flag at 1250, and her crew began to abandon her. The British lowered boats immediately, and *Lurcher*, having just come up, went alongside the stricken German to take off survivors more quickly – among them Lieutenant Wolf von Tirpitz, son of the Grand Admiral. Shortly after 1300 *Mainz* rolled over and sank as *Lurcher* backed clear with only seconds to spare, the Germans on her deck giving three cheers for His Majesty the Emperor. Even as *Mainz* disappeared beneath a sea floating with burning cordite and scattered debris, orders were being given to heavy units of the High Seas Fleet, already with steam raised, to clear the Jade bar, and *Von der Tann*, *Seydlitz* and *Moltke* were capable of reaching the battle-area in two hours. To the units engaged, however, of both sides, the situation was just as confused as it had ever been. The cruisers *Köln* and *Ariadne*, believing that their own battle-cruisers were already at sea, were racing through the mist to join company. *Strassburg* was still being hounded by destroyers, while *Stralsund* and *Stettin* steamed aimlessly, firing occasionally at distant shapes but achieving little.

The entrance of Beatty's five big ships into this chaotic arena was like that of a file of sedate policemen into a playground of brawling schoolboys – and as immediately effective. A salvo from *Lion* and *Princess Royal* stopped *Köln* in her tracks, to wallow helplessly with ruined engines. Then *Ariadne* sighted *Lion* and, totally ignorant of the presence of British battle-cruisers in the area, signalled her by searchlight. The reply was a thunder of gunfire that wrecked one of *Ariadne*'s boiler-rooms, ignited a coal-bunker, and set her upper-works ablaze. Listing heavily, and with shells still smashing into her, the cruiser reeled away into the fog, to founder.

Beatty led his squadron in a wide circle, signalling the order for retirement to all warships, and then the battle-cruisers turned their guns back to *Köln*, which had managed to get under way again. They steamed past her slowly and, since her flag was still flying, shot her to pieces at a mere 3500 yards range as calmly as if at target practice. Only one survivor from *Köln* would be picked up, by his own countrymen, two days later. Among her dead was Rear-Admiral Leberecht Maass, commanding Heligoland's destroyers and torpedo-boats.

In the first exchange of any significance the German Navy had lost three cruisers and a destroyer, with three smaller ships badly damaged. Casualties amounted to 712 dead and 149 wounded, with 381 men taken prisoner. British losses totalled 35 killed and 40 wounded and, although *Arethusa* and *Laurel* were towed home, no ships were sunk.

It was a heartening success at the right time, but superficial planning and poor communication might have proved disastrous if the Germans had not been equally badly organised and, with their best ships protectively locked away in the Jade, outnumbered and outgunned. The Germans, Winston Churchill would later confess, 'knew nothing of our defective staff work and of the risks we had run'.

Only the battle-cruisers, their crews could claim, had added a little dignity to a day of unruly and futile skirmishing.

## Note

1    The two ships' final completion and trials had been deliberately delayed on Churchill's orders. Five hundred Turkish seamen aboard a transport on Tyneside, waiting to crew the new ships, threatened to take them by force, but the Admiralty warned that such a move would be met by military action.

# Chapter Four

*Coronel – Sturdee, von Spee and the Falklands battle*

THE BRITISH PUBLIC was elated. The Bulldog had growled; the Heligoland exploit had been worthy of Drake and Nelson, and the Kaiser's fleet had not dared to emerge from its fortified anchorages to face the Sons of the Sea ('all British born'). 'An operation of some consequence,' the Admiralty agreed modestly, and Winston Churchill informed Admiral von Tirpitz, through the International Red Cross, that his son, Wolf, taken off *Mainz*, was safe. Newspapers printed the usual 'eyewitness accounts' of enemy warships shelling British sailors as they rescued German survivors, and of German officers shooting their own men who had abandoned ship without orders, but coyly refrained from identifying the eyewitnesses; it was all part of a campaign to convert the cricket mentality of the British into one of blood-boiling hate for the Huns, who bayoneted babies and old ladies.

However, despite the confusion, of which the public was unaware, the Heligoland operation was seen to confirm British naval superiority, and Grand Admiral von Tirpitz, ever the pessimist, conceded that 'August 28th [was] a day fateful both in its after effects and incidental results for the work of our Navy'. What he meant was that the Kaiser, as a result, clamped down even harder on the initiative of his admirals. In essence, only submarines and minelayers would now venture into open waters without his express permission. Only he, the All Highest, would decide if and when his beautiful ships would fight the British.

Unknowingly the Kaiser, having closed the door on massive fleet actions – in which his High Seas Fleet, by schoolboy arithmetic, must suffer destruction – had opened another door, that of insidious submarine-warfare. This was the *only* weapon by which the British, so overwhelmingly superior in surface strength, might be brought down by hacking at their ankles. The Kaiser had not envisaged such a strategy, the German naval hierarchy was opposed to it, and the British were too arrogant to believe it.

There was a new name to enliven the conversation of armchair strategists. It was that of Sir David Beatty, a man with a square chin, his cap at a rakish angle and, in defiance of regulations, six buttons on his jacket instead of eight. Success had marked every step of his career, not wholly unattributable to the acquisition of an extremely wealthy, American-born wife whose lavish entertainment of ministers and senior officers, frequently on a yacht in which she was able to follow the Fleet's cruises, did much to influence his prospects of promotion. He was a captain at twenty-nine and achieved flag rank at the incredibly early age of thirty-eight. Despite the resentment of less fortunate colleagues, however, Beatty was an able and intrepid commander, and there were few others better qualified to lead a battle-cruiser force. He had a reputation for rebelling against restraint, and was popular among lower-ranking officers, the lower deck – and now the public, anxious to pin hopes on anyone who could win battles, and with such panache.

For the moment, unfortunately, there were no more opportunities for Beatty to demonstrate the lethal efficacy of battle-cruisers. On 14 September the armed merchant cruiser *Carmania*, on passage to join Rear-Admiral Sir Christopher Cradock's 5th Cruiser Squadron in South American waters, fought and sank the armed German liner *Cap Trafalgar*, but this was modest fare. Then, only eight days later, the old 'Live Bait Squadron' of *Aboukir*, *Cressy* and *Hogue* (the last had towed *Arethusa* home from the Heligoland action) were all torpedoed and sunk by a single submarine with the loss of 1459 lives, off the coast of Holland – a disaster that effectively cancelled out the casualties suffered by the Germans off Heligoland. On 27 October the 23,000-ton Dreadnought *Audacious* struck a mine during gunnery exercises off northern Ireland and sank after an internal explosion, but the news of her loss would not be admitted until the end of the war.

Finally, on 1 November, the old armoured cruisers *Good Hope* and *Monmouth*, and the armed merchantman *Otranto* – three of the four ships of Cradock's 5th Cruiser Squadron – were annihilated at Coronel by the German East Asiatic Squadron commanded by Rear-Admiral Maximilian von Spee.

The German squadron comprised the armoured cruisers *Scharnhorst* and *Gneisenau* and the light cruisers *Dresden*, *Leipzig* and *Nürnberg*, the most powerful concentration of enemy warships outside European waters. None was more than eight years old, all were manned by seasoned well-drilled crews excellently led.

Cradock, too, was a fine seaman of the old school who 'fought hard and played hard and did not suffer fools gladly'. There is little doubt that his determination to seek action at any cost, however commendable, clouded his judgement, but he and his squadron should never have been placed by the Admiralty in the position they were – where they might meet von Spee. Cradock had two old armoured cruisers, *Good Hope* and *Monmouth*, both built before the turn of the century and manned by reservists recruited from among Scottish fishermen and coastguards, the lightly armed merchantman *Otranto*, which limited the squadron's speed to sixteen knots, and the light cruiser *Glasgow*, the only ship in company to match the quality of any of the Germans.

To some extent Cradock's predicament derived from the problem always faced by the Royal Navy before and since, of stretching its resources, often thinly, to cover all contingencies, while the enemy was free to conserve and then concentrate his own forces at times and locations of his own choosing. However, the Admiralty was well aware that von Spee was loose in the Pacific, and it could be assumed that he would try to inflict as much damage as possible on Allied shipping and shore installations before either interning his squadron or attempting to run for Germany. There had been ample time to reinforce Cradock, whose area of responsibility was impossibly vast – from Halifax, Nova Scotia, down to the southern tip of South America and the west coast of the sub-continent up to Panama. While the British commander can be criticised for several errors of judgement, including that of discarding the fifth ship of his force, the ancient battleship *Canopus*, because of her decrepit engines, responsibility for the Coronel disaster must also be shared by three others: the First Sea Lord, Battenberg, the Chief of the Naval Staff, Vice-Admiral Sir Doveton Sturdee, and finally the First Lord, Winston Churchill.

The Germans were an effective force only so long as their ammunition lasted. Coal, water and provisions could be obtained fairly easily, but once his ammunition was expended von Spee was finished. He would not lightly seek an encounter with British warships, even Cradock's, for this reason, and also because battle damage could prove impossible to repair; he had no dockyard facilities and could spend only hours in a neutral port. There was never any doubt, however, that if Cradock came within reach he would fight.

And off the Chilean coast Cradock fought. His last wireless

message was: 'I am going to attack the enemy now.' He then hoisted the flag signal, 'Follow in the Admiral's wake', and turned toward the enemy and annihilation. As the sun set, when *Good Hope, Monmouth* and *Otranto* had been destroyed with the total loss of their crews, the little *Glasgow* – the only British ship to hit an enemy with her 4-inch shells – escaped into the darkness.

Only two days earlier, in London, Prince Louis of Battenberg had written to Winston Churchill: 'I have lately been driven to the painful conclusion that at this juncture my birth and parentage have the effect of impairing in some respects my usefulness. . . .'

Within hours Admiral Fisher, aged seventy-four, was reappointed First Sea Lord. His first action, at five in the morning, was to sack Sir Doveton Sturdee, the Chief of Naval Staff. His second was to signal Cradock: '*Defence* has been ordered to join your flag with all despatch.'

*Defence* was a six-year-old armoured cruiser of 14,600 tons, but neither she nor the signal would reach Cradock. As Churchill later commented: 'We were already talking to a void.'

There was yet another bitter pill for the Royal Navy to swallow. At dawn on 3 November, even before the Admiralty had received the telegram from the British Consul-Agent in Valparaiso telling of the defeat at Coronel, the German battle-cruisers *Von der Tann, Seydlitz* and *Moltke*, accompanied by the armoured cruisers *Blücher, Yorck* and *Roon*, appeared off Yarmouth and shelled the town and an old fishery patrol-vessel, *Halcyon*, for thirty minutes and then returned to Wilhelmshaven as easily as they had come. The British submarine *D5*, attempting to intercept, struck a mine and was lost with almost all hands, and the only consolations were that the bombardment did negligible damage while *Yorck* also struck a mine and sank off the Jade.

'You, Sturdee, were responsible for this bloody mess,' Fisher snarled. 'Now *you* can go and clean it up. And don't come back until your orders have been carried out to the letter – until von Spee and his squadron have been wiped off the face of the earth!'

It was still 4 November. Admiral Sir John Jellicoe had already been ordered to detach *Invincible* and *Inflexible* from the Fleet at Cromarty immediately. They were to proceed to Devonport to prepare urgently for foreign service and, although their orders were secret, there could be only one objective. Rear-Admiral Sir Archibald Moore, flying his flag in *Invincible*, was considered too junior for the task and would transfer to *New Zealand*. The new appointment of Commander-in-Chief South Atlantic and South Pacific would go to Sturdee.

Fisher detested Sturdee and had already made it plain to Churchill that he would not work with the Chief of Staff. Churchill, having himself earlier threatened to resign if Fisher were not appointed First Sea Lord, had no choice but to consent to Sturdee's removal from the Admiralty, but it was convenient to imply that Sturdee was to correct the mischief that had resulted from his own negligence. The appointment was Churchill's.[1]

Fisher's order to Jellicoe was followed by another. The battle-cruiser *Princess Royal* was also to be released to proceed forthwith to cover the possibility of von Spee emerging from the Panama Canal; all loopholes were to be closed. Jellicoe, having lost *Audacious* only a week earlier, protested that this further weakening of the Grand Fleet could have serious consequences, while Beatty also complained that his battle-cruiser force was being dangerously depleted. Fisher scrawled 'Rot!' across Beatty's letter. *Invincible* and *Inflexible* departed Cromarty so hurriedly that numbers of their crews were left ashore, and would have to undertake the long journey to Devonport by train.

The two ships reached the Channel base before dawn on Sunday, 8 November and were immediately passed into dry dock for scraping and painting and the correction of defects, whilst simultaneously embarking coal, three months' supplies of stores for themselves and other ships on the South American station, and ammunition for *Glasgow*. Churchill personally sent a ciphered signal to Commander-in-Chief Devonport:

> *Inflexible* and *Invincible* are to sail on Wednesday 11th. They are needed for war service and dockyard arrangements must be made to conform. If necessary dockyard men should be sent away in the ships to return as opportunity may offer. You are held responsible for the speedy despatch of these ships in a thoroughly efficient condition. Acknowledge.

Compliance with such orders seemed contrary to reason. When built, *Invincible* had been fitted with experimental electrical instead of hydraulic turret machinery, which had not proved entirely satisfactory, and when the war started she was in the process of having a hydraulic system installed. Despite having fought at Heligoland, engineers of Vickers Ltd were still aboard monitoring the conversion and also equipping the ship for director firing. Furthermore, in the opinion of the Dockyard Superintendent, it was impossible to brick up the fire-boxes of two battle-cruisers in forty-eight hours. On Tuesday, 10 November, braver than he was wise, he took a train to London to remonstrate with the First Sea Lord.

Meanwhile, Sturdee had hoisted his flag in *Invincible*. The officers and men of both ships, reinforced by working parties from the nearby barracks, were labouring around the clock, hoisting coal, crates and ammunition – 'begrimed, haggard and weary, staggering around like flies' – while dockyard workmen and technicians crawled everywhere, frantically aware that, if they did not finish, they would find themselves voyaging to South America and a battle with von Spee. Never had dockyard civilians worked so hard and selflessly; in the mid-forenoon of Tuesday, 10 November – a day early – the ships were ready for sea.

Sturdee nodded. 'Very well. We sail at 1600.'

There was a final dilemma. Plymouth Sound and the Channel were thick with fog which, at this season, might persist for days. The ships' magnetic compasses, following the riveting and welding of the hurried refit, could no longer be considered reliable, and there was no time for recalibration. Somebody remembered Elmer Sperry, who had hopefully opened an office at 57 Victoria Street, London. He was located, bundled into a train at Paddington with one of his Yankee devices, and a few hours later the gyroscopic compass was being fitted in *Invincible*. Sperry would be still demonstrating his instrument as the two battle-cruisers nosed through the fog into the Channel. He was taken off by launch, damp but happily convinced that the Royal Navy would now seriously adopt his invention. It did, and the American established the Sperry Gyroscope Company Ltd on 26 January 1915. By the end of the war 1022 Mark II Sperry gyro compasses would be in service and Sperry would receive a commendation from the Lords Commissioners of the Admiralty.

As the mooring-ropes had been tossed from bollards, gangplanks removed, and a Royal Marine band brayed on *Invincible*'s quarter-deck, eight midshipmen flung their baggage and themselves aboard, having raced forty miles in taxi-cabs to fulfil their first drafting orders. In London the Dockyard Superintendent's persistence had earned him an interview with Fisher. The First Sea Lord listened to the man's grievances, then drew out his watch. The two battle-cruisers, he told his subordinate, were already in the Channel, steering west, and if the Devonport workmen had not finished their tasks they would remain on board until they had, to be dropped off when convenient. It would be a matter of complete indifference to Fisher if they were dropped over the side.

Opinions of Vice-Admiral Sir Frederick Charles Doveton Sturdee, both at the time and later, vary widely. Fisher regarded him as 'a pedantic ass' and would later accuse him of criminal ineptitude; he was not alone in his view. Churchill, however – at least prior to Coronel – described Sturdee as 'an officer of keen intelligence and great practical ability, a man who could handle and fight his ship and his squadron with the utmost skill and resolution'.

The true picture obviously lies somewhere between these extremes. Sturdee was fifty-five when he hoisted his flag in *Invincible*. During the forty-three years he had already served he had shown competence rather than brilliance, perseverance rather than intrepidity; he lacked the dash of a Beatty or the pugnacity of a Cradock, but although he had not distinguished himself in the role of Chief of Staff – a post for which he was probably intellectually unsuited – his sea-going qualifications could not be disputed. There was absolutely no reason why Sturdee, with the force he was about to command, should not quickly overwhelm von Spee, always assuming he could corner the German in the vast area to be searched.

Inexplicably after the feverish haste of departure, however, Sturdee did not steam at the 25 knots of which his two ships were capable. He reduced to a leisurely 10 knots, halted occasionally to challenge merchant ships, coaled in the Cape Verde Islands on 19 November, carried out battle practice (during which he contrived to wrap a target-towing wire around *Invincible*'s screws) and reached the coast of Brazil on the twenty-sixth.

It was here, off the Abrolhos Rocks, that Sturdee was joined by Rear-Admiral Archibald Stoddart and a miscellany of old and not-so-old warships hastily garnered by the Admiralty from adjoining stations. When Sturdee had ordered away several to secondary duties he was left, in addition to his two battle-cruisers, with the patched-up *Glasgow* and her sister *Bristol*, the armoured cruisers *Kent* and *Cornwall* (identical to the old *Monmouth*, sunk at Coronel), the marginally younger armoured cruiser *Carnarvon*, and two armed merchantmen, *Macedonia* and *Orama*, which would be assigned to escorting the colliers that would follow the ill-assortment of warships.

'Your main and most important task', the Admiralty's orders had emphasised, 'is to search for the German armoured cruisers *Scharnhorst* and *Gneisenau* and bring them to action. All other considerations are to be subordinate to this end.' To Sturdee, apparently, this did not convey any sense of urgency. He confessed that he was 'completely in the dark' with regard to the German squadron's whereabouts, although the Admiralty's situation-reports suggested that it was still on the Chilean coast. Captain John Luce, commanding *Glasgow*, was disgruntled with Sturdee's decision to remain at the

Abrolhos Rocks for three days. The crew of his little cruiser had fought von Spee once, unhappily, and, like schoolboys worsted in a brawl but now reinforced by bigger accomplices, they were eager for another fight. Luce remonstrated. The British were still 2500 miles from the Falklands, which was where von Spee was probably making for, and for the past two weeks the two battle-cruisers' wireless operators had been chattering carelessly, so that by now every shore station in South America and West Africa knew of their presence. That meant that von Spee would know, and he was no fool.

Sturdee shrugged, only mildly concerned. 'Very well, Luce. If you believe that's important, we'll sail tomorrow.'

Aboard the ships the crews were in tropical ducks – ill-fitting white canvas that soiled easily and, despite repeated scrubbing, tended to become progressively greyer. The battle-cruiser men had celebrated crossing the Equator a few days before, and Sturdee had addressed *Invincible*'s company. Few on the lower decks of any of his ships had heard of him before, and they reserved judgement. The warm weather was a delight after the November bleakness of Cromarty and the North Sea, and they had taken aboard pineapples, oranges and bananas at St Vincente. The older men assumed nonchalance; they had done this all before. *Invincible* had sniffed cordite smoke at Heligoland and *Inflexible* had lately returned from the Mediterranean. The recently joined – the midshipmen, the seaman boys and ordinary seamen – tried to appear nonchalant also, hoaxed into asking the engine-room for a bucketful of revs or the bosun's store for green oil for the starboard lamps. Lime juice was issued daily. The sky was golden, the sea a wonderful blue flashing silver that dazzled the eyes. There were dolphins and flying fish, great white seabirds on gliding wings, and at night the stars were like diamonds strewn across black velvet. For nine of those nights the British squadron ploughed southward, the five cruisers in a line abreast that covered a front of fifty miles. It began to get colder.

The men returned to blue serge. Even so, the weather was clear and sunny, the sea calm and visibility superb. This time Sturdee ordered that the battle-cruisers should maintain wireless silence, and the precaution was sobering. There was a tingling awareness that every hour brought them nearer to von Spee's squadron which, the Admiralty was saying, seemed still to be off the Chilean coast. 'Use Falkland Islands as main base for colliers. After coaling proceed to Chilean coast, avoiding letting your large ships be seen in Magellan Straits. Search the Straits inlets and channels taking colliers with you as necessary.' The task facing the British was daunting; the Pacific coast of Chile was fringed by scores of islands like broken and scattered jigsaw pieces. Von Spee had the choice of a number of routes around the toe of South America and, if he avoided Sturdee, the Falklands station would be at his mercy, then the important trade-routes of the South Atlantic, the African coast, or the Indian Ocean. A tiger would be loose.

At 1030 on Monday, 7 December the British squadron arrived at Stanley in the Falklands. Von Spee, at least, had not reached here yet.

There was already a warship in Stanley's inner harbour. She was the old battleship *Canopus*, member of a class of 1896 designed specifically for the China Station. Even when new she had been an 'economy' battleship, of only 12,950 tons, mounting four 12-inch guns in two turrets. The geriatric *Canopus* should have gone to the breaker's yard years before; she had been reprieved by the war, and only then to be consigned to an area in which, it was thought, she would spend most of her time at anchor. She had not enjoyed a refit since 1907. Her speed was restricted to 12 knots. In a desperate emergency she could manage 14 knots, when her engines almost invariably broke down. (She was also forbidden to use full helm at any speed above 15 knots because of the danger of capsizing, but the proscription was somewhat presumptuous.) Because of her deplorable condition, Rear-Admiral Cradock had abandoned her when he sought battle with von Spee at Coronel. Whether or not her antique guns, despite their calibre, would have influenced the engagement is a question that naval historians have debated for sixty-five years. The Admiralty had provided Cradock with four 12-inch guns which, in the event, he did not use. That, at least, was the Admiralty's excuse for shrugging disclaiming shoulders.

Having escaped conflict with von Spee, *Canopus* was still afloat; more accurately, she was aground, her commander, Captain Heathcote Grant, having received the typically Churchillian order to

remain in Stanley Harbour. Moor the ship so that your guns command the entrance. Extemporize mines outside the entrance. Be prepared for bombardment from outside the harbour: send down your topmasts. Stimulate the Governor to organize all local forces and make determined defence. Arrange observation stations on shore to enable you to direct fire on ships outside. Land guns or use torpedoes to sink a blocking ship before she reaches the narrows. No objection to you grounding ship to obtain a good berth. . . .

Grant had complied. *Canopus* sat with her bottom firmly in the harbour mud and her turrets turned to seaward, her topmasts lowered and her funnels and upperworks daubed with green and brown paint to blend with the shoreline. Her ten 12-pounder guns, each weighing more than half a ton, had been unshipped and set up as shore batteries, while a line of mines, improvised from oil-drums filled with explosive, was laid across the harbour entrance ready to be electronically detonated. The Captain of Marines drilled a defence force of three hundred farmers, fishermen and the two local undertakers, and the wives and children had been herded inland.

Once von Spee's ships had got the range of *Canopus*, however, her situation would have been suicidal. There had been some excitement, therefore, when the two elderly ladies posted as look-outs on their farmhouse roof telephoned the old battleship to report smoke on the northerly horizon. Minutes later they were counting the ships as they appeared – two, six . . . seven warships and a merchant cruiser. It was not von Spee, thank God, but Sturdee.

The squadron's colliers, following with *Orama*, were not expected to arrive until the eleventh, but there were three already in Stanley Harbour,[2] and Sturdee wished to resume passage for the Chilean coast within forty-eight hours. Leaving the AMC *Macedonia* to patrol outside, the seven warships were ordered into the anchorage. *Glasgow* and *Carnarvon* would begin coaling immediately, the others at 0400 on the following morning, the eighth. Meanwhile, officers might proceed ashore. *Bristol*'s captain requested permission to draw his fires to effect engine repairs, and *Cornwall* also had machinery defects. The fortunate shore-going parties in their No. 6 white drills and pipe-clayed shoes hastened to depart their ships before coal-dust smothered everything, and the gun-crews of *Canopus* were told that the Admiral would watch them fire a practice salvo next morning.

All commanding officers were summoned to attend a conference in *Invincible*. There were weeks of arduous steaming ahead; von Spee could be anywhere – off Chile or making for Panama, or already past Cape Horn and heading for West Africa.

Nobody suspected that von Spee was only a few hours away, heading for the Falkland Islands.

Von Spee and his men had been enthusiastically fêted by German nationals in neutral Valparaiso, but the Admiral had responded sourly. When a civilian raised a glass to toast damnation to the British Navy, von Spee shook his head. 'I drink', he said icily, 'to the memory of a gallant and honourable foe'; and to a woman who offered him flowers he suggested that she saved them for his funeral. Time, he knew, was running out; he clung to no illusions. The Japanese had taken Tsingtao, which meant there was no longer a sanctuary for him across the Pacific, and his remaining options were being reduced daily. He could not remain indefinitely off the Chilean coast, and to allow his squadron to be interned would be despicable. Nor dare he contemplate passing through the Panama Canal; for certain the British would be waiting for him to attempt just that. Berlin, however, had strongly implied (by cable through the German consulate in Valparaiso) that von Spee should 'break through with all ships and return to Germany', which only proved that there were as many armchairs in the Admiralstab as there were in Whitehall.

'I am quite homeless,' von Spee confided privately. 'I cannot reach Germany; we possess no other secure harbour. I must plough the seas of the world, doing as much mischief as I can, until my ammunition is exhausted or until a superior enemy succeeds in catching me.' There was, of course, only one possible escape-route – via Cape Horn and into the South Atlantic.

This route was perhaps not just possible but even probable. Cape Horn offered not a single channel and a single exit, like the Panama Canal, but several channels and several exits into the Atlantic – and, once beyond, von Spee was relatively free. However, he needed to move very quickly. There was no doubt that the incensed British would be racing warships to intercept him, and it was vitally necessary for the German squadron to pass through the Cape Horn danger-point before the British reached it.

Von Spee did not move quickly. He cruised leisurely southward, as Sturdee was doing, simultaneously, on the opposite coast, and anchored in St Quintin Bay for four precious days to coal and to distribute 300 Iron Crosses Second Class on behalf of the Kaiser. Every ship was now fully bunkered and there were three colliers in company. Furthermore, he halted a British vessel, *Drummuir*, and transferred from her yet another 3000 tons of coal. It can hardly be claimed that his modest speed was necessary to conserve fuel; once in the Atlantic there would be German colliers waiting to break out of their internment in Argentinian, Uruguayan or Brazilian ports to assist the squadron homeward. The German Government could apologise afterwards.

It was on 6 December that von Spee revealed his plans, which, at the same time, emphasised his pessimism with regard to fighting his ships through to Germany. The East Asiatic Squadron was going to *attack and capture the Falkland Islands base*, destroy its wireless station and any enemy patrol-vessels in the harbour, hoist the German flag and make a prisoner of the Governor, William Allerdyce. A German governor would be appointed, and a message sent throughout Argentina and Brazil asking for volunteers to garrison the ex-British colony. There were no British warships of consequence at Stanley, von Spee asserted,[3] and the operation would be a massive blow in retaliation for the enemy's capture of German possessions in the Pacific, Africa and China. If the Falklands could not be garrisoned and held, then everything of military value would be destroyed and the squadron, carrying the Governor, would resume passage for Germany as originally envisaged.

It was almost a death wish; von Spee's captains were aghast. The squadron had done well, but it was already living on borrowed time. Ammunition stocks were down to about fifty per cent, and they would need every round to get them through the Royal Navy's closely knit blockade. Of what use were the Falkland Islands to Germany, anyway, other than for a few days of propaganda jeering that would be abruptly silenced by two or three British battle-cruisers and a few companies of marines? No, the captains reasoned, much more would be gained if the East Asiatic Squadron could tiptoe back to Wilhelmshaven. Luck could be pushed too far, and the Falklands should be avoided like the plague.

Von Spee had been ill-served with intelligence by his own Admiralty; neither had he sought any. He had also loitered un-necessarily in a potentially dangerous locality, but there was still time for him to run for the South Atlantic where he could savagely maul enemy shipping and entertain a hope of regaining Germany. His captains were right. The Falkland Islands were simply not worth it, nor the pleasure of seeing a German ensign flying briefly over a remote British dependency. Von Spee, however, was deter-mined, and his desire for an easily achieved and equally short-lived success was unworthy and uncharacteristic of a man who had hitherto outwitted the British.

The squadron would be approaching Port Stanley on the morning of 8 December. *Gneisenau* and *Nürnberg* would be detached and the first would send armed cutters ashore, carrying an ultimatum to the Governor. The other ships would follow fifteen miles behind.

It was doubly unfortunate that, early in the morning of the seventh, von Spee received confirmation by wireless from a German agent that Port Stanley was empty of warships. This was true, except for the camouflaged *Canopus*. Sturdee and his battle-cruisers did not arrive until 1030.

*

On the morning of Tuesday, 8 December, in Port Stanley, *Invincible* and *Inflexible* began coaling at 0400. The other ships of the squadron were in various states of unpreparedness; *Glasgow* and *Carnarvon* had finished coaling, but both *Cornwall* and *Bristol* had engines opened for repair. Only *Kent* had steam, and was preparing to relieve *Macedonia*, patrolling off-shore.

For most of the year the Falklands experienced mist and intermittent rain, damp cold and overcast skies. It was Scapa Flow all over again, the men complained, and no better ashore – the same treeless terrain, the same muddy sheep and screeching seabirds, no women, and no pubs that could be called pubs. If the Germans wanted the Falklands, they could bleedin' have 'em.

This morning, however, despite being cold, the weather was fine and sunny, with visibility clear for twenty miles – but not from the flag-decks of the battle-cruisers, around which coal-dust swirled like smoke.

By 0730 most of the officers had finished breakfast; a few lingered below with their second or third cup of coffee, deferring the moment they must go on deck. Admiral Sturdee was in his cabin, shaving.

At 0745 the look-out on Sapper Hill, 450 feet higher than the anchorage, telephoned *Canopus*, sitting in the mud of the inner harbour: 'A four-funnelled and a two-funnelled man-of-war in sight south-east steering northwards.' He did not know it yet, but he was looking at *Gneisenau* and *Nürnberg*, steaming ahead of von Spee's squadron.

Captain Grant of *Canopus* did not know it, either, but he could make an educated guess. He had no telephone connection with the flagship, nor could he reach *Invincible* by Morse lamp or semaphore. *Canopus* hoisted the flag signal 'Enemy in sight'.

Only the alert *Glasgow* saw the signal. The two battle-cruisers, a mile away in the outer harbour, were only vaguely visible through a floating haze of coal-dust. For several minutes *Glasgow* tried unsuccessfully to attract the attention of *Invincible*, first by Morse lamp and then by 24-inch searchlight. At 0756, in desperation, she fired a 3-pounder.

Sturdee had finished dressing. Informed of the sighting, he, like Grant, had no doubt with regard to the approaching vessels' identity. If they were warships they must be German. 'He [von Spee]', he claimed later, 'came at a very convenient hour.' He ordered *Kent* to slip and proceed to sea (she did so, commendably, by 0845), for *Invincible* and *Inflexible* to stop coaling and for all other ships to raise steam for full speed and to report when ready for 12 knots. This could take two hours. Then, imperturbably, Sturdee

ordered hands to breakfast and to change into clean underclothes.[4]
Then he sat down to porridge, kippers and tea. By this time the two
distant ships had been reinforced by five more, of which two would
later be identified as the supply-ships *Baden* and *Santa Isabel*. The
leading pair were now only eight miles from Port Stanley.

At sea-level, the unsuspecting *Gneisenau* and *Nürnberg* did not sight
the masts of the Falklands wireless station until 0830; the harbour
was hidden by a long out-thrust tongue of land which the Germans
would not round for another hour. They could, however, see a
merchant ship hastening shoreward. Had they been able to identify
her they might have questioned why the P. & O. liner *Macedonia* was
running into Stanley Harbour instead of steaming somewhere between Southampton and the Mediterranean, her usual occupation.
There also seemed to be a great deal of smoke over the harbour area,
which suggested to Maerker, *Gneisenau*'s captain, that the British
had observed the German cruisers' approach and were burning their
coal-stocks. It was of little consequence. *Gneisenau* and *Nürnberg*
ranged their guns on the wireless station, closing, and when the
disappeared *Macedonia* was suddenly replaced by a 'Monmouth'-
class cruiser (it was *Kent*) emerging from behind the headland there
was surprise but no consternation. Maerker increased speed to cut
her off; she was a bonus victim.

At 0900, however, *Gneisenau*'s gunnery commander, Johann
Busche, reported that there were other ships in Stanley Harbour and
he could swear that, through the smoke, he could see *two pairs of
tripod masts*.

Tripod masts were a characteristic of only two classes of warship:
battleships and battle-cruisers of the Dreadnought type. Captain
Maerker was confident that no such enemy warships were nearer
than the Mediterranean, and he told Busche so, acidly. Busche, high
in the control-top, was adamant. There were not only tripod masts
in Stanley Harbour, he insisted, there were heavy-cruiser masts also.
The smoke was not coming from burning heaps of coal; it was
coming from the funnels of large warships – a lot of them – and
some of those funnels were already moving seaward, very ominously.

Well, Maerker shrugged, the old *Canopus* was around here somewhere, but she offered little threat to the East Asiatic Squadron. He
ordered battle ensigns to be hoisted. Range 13,500 yards.

Far distant, to westward of the smoke-hazed Stanley Harbour,
there erupted a tiny yellow puffball that as quickly dispersed. It was
interesting, and the Germans turned their binoculars. Within

seconds there appeared a second yellow mushroom, just as brief. At this time *Gneisenau*'s wireless operator was transmitting to von Spee's flagship, *Scharnhorst*: 'Probably three enemy "County"-class cruisers and one light cruiser in Port Stanley and possibly *Canopus*. . . .'

Maerker was right, at least, about *Canopus*.[5] The two old guns of her fore turret, forged in 1890, had flung their 12-inch shells almost six miles. Firing blind (*Canopus* could not see her target from the inner harbour) the first two missiles burst in the sea only a thousand yards short of *Gneisenau*. The second salvo, from the after turret, went even closer. One of the shells ricocheted off the water and sheared through the base of the cruiser's after funnel.

For Sturdee, despite his impassivity, the next hour was perilous. The battle-cruisers, his trump card, were land-locked, only partially coaled and totally unready for action; firing from the anchorage would present serious problems. If von Spee chose to attack on a bearing unfavourable to the British, his 8.2-inch guns and their highly proficient crews could impose savage punishment. Sturdee was a sitting duck. It was also a crucial test for the battle-cruiser as a class; this hunt-and-destroy operation was precisely the role for which it had, allegedly, been designed. The Heligoland action had proved very little, and if two Invincibles were to be battered to impotence by the enemy cruisers they had been assigned to destroy, then the battle-cruiser's future was bleak – and it would be the most humiliating reverse in the Royal Navy's history. The entire world would laugh, not just at the battle-cruisers but also at Jackie Fisher, whose pets they were.

And at the Admiralty in London, where the time was 1330 GMT, Winston Churchill shuddered when Rear-Admiral Sir Henry Oliver (who had succeeded Sturdee as Chief of Staff) brought to him a telegram from the Governor of the Falkland Islands which stated that 'Admiral Spee arrived at daylight this morning with all his ships and is now in action with Admiral Sturdee's whole fleet, *which was coaling*'.

'We had so many unpleasant surprises', Churchill confessed, 'that these last words sent a shiver up my spine. Had we in fact been taken by surprise and, in spite of our superiority, mauled, unready at anchor?' The telegram merely confirmed Fisher's view that Sturdee was a 'damn fool'.

Von Spee, however, had already decided that he would tempt fate no longer. He would not bring his ships within range of a battle-ship's 12-inch guns, even if they were old. He would run for safety. The German squadron could outsteam both battleships and

'County'-class cruisers, and had nothing to fear from British light cruisers. He altered course to south-eastward, increasing speed and at 0937 signalling Maerker: 'Do not accept action. Rejoin the flag at full speed.'

Maerker complied. In the engine-rooms of *Gneisenau* and *Nürnberg* the valves were opened wide, the ships shuddered and, astern, their wakes frothed as they turned away from the Falklands shoreline. It was a pity, their gun-crews reflected, because *Kent* was almost within range.

It is, of course, not difficult for any historian, many years later and with the benefit of both sides' records, to criticise the action of a naval or military commander who *at the time* possessed only limited, often suspect, information – and, furthermore, had only minutes or even seconds in which to make a crucial decision. There is no doubt that von Spee's decision was the wrong one, but he reached it quickly on the basis of the intelligence available to him. He could not know that he had thrown away his only hope of survival. Had he pressed home his attack against Port Stanley he would have enjoyed a better than even chance of at least temporarily disabling his tethered enemy, of delaying the larger ships' pursuit sufficiently for him to get well clear. Discredited, the role of the battle-cruiser would have been the subject of reassessment and the class might well have been relegated to less exposed duties. With the promise of the fast battleships, then building, it is possible that all further work on battle-cruisers would have been stopped. Certainly none would have been retained to serve in the Second World War. History, however, is full of 'ifs'.

Maerker sighted his flagship at 1030 and within a further half-hour all five German warships were in line ahead in the sequence *Gneisenau, Nürnberg, Scharnhorst, Dresden, Leipzig*, steering south-east and working up to 22 knots. There was no alarm in the squadron. Indeed, even those who had earlier opposed the Falklands adventure were saying that, since they had come so close, they might as well have given the station and settlement a few salvoes. There was nothing to fear from the British, who must be twenty-five, perhaps thirty, miles astern and with no hope of a big-gunned ship closing that gap. Tortoises didn't catch hares.

The day was beautifully clear, which was a nuisance because, far behind, fine on the squadron's port quarter, there followed the little *Glasgow*, of no consequence except that she was capable of shadowing them at least during daylight, and the day was still young. No, astern of *Glasgow* there was more smoke, increasing in volume – and as the minutes passed it was becoming sickeningly apparent that the smoke was vomiting from the funnels of two big ships, bigger than *Scharnhorst* and *Gneisenau*, and moving with intimidating speed. Glasses were turned from every German bridge. In God's name, what were *these*?

Three funnels irregularly spaced. Tripod masts.

Battle-cruisers; 12-inch guns and five knots faster than the German squadron.

Tortoises didn't catch hares, but greyhounds did.

In baffling contrast to the leisurely procedure of previous weeks, Sturdee's ships had cleared the harbour of Port Stanley quicker than any seamanship manual would have conceded possible. Hard on the heels of *Kent* followed the little terrier *Glasgow*, spoiling for a fight. *Carnarvon* and *Invincible*, with Sturdee still at breakfast, pounded past the lighthouse at 1000 hours followed by the cheers of the crew of old *Canopus*, who had manned their rigging. They had waited in this forsaken anchorage a long time for this moment. *Inflexible* and *Cornwall* (whose engine-room artificers were still reassembling one engine) were only minutes behind, and even *Bristol*, with both engines opened and her boilers cold, would be under way by 1100. In the open sea, with most of his squadron gathered, Sturdee hoisted the signal which for two centuries had never failed to arouse the fighting fury of British seamen, volunteers or pressed men.

General Chase.

Now, at last, the picture was painted exactly as Fisher had visualised it – his hunter-killer Invincibles thundering through the sea and overhauling, mile by mile, a fleeing enemy cruiser squadron, the conclusion inevitable. There remained only one thin thread of hope for von Spee – that some of his ships might hold their distance sufficiently long for either night or fog to offer sanctuary. No, night was too far away. Fog was more likely; these southern seas were notorious for crawling fog, sleet and squall clouds. Why, God, was today so different, the skies so blue and filled with sunshine, so crystal clear?

The two battle-cruisers were steaming at 26 knots, a speed that was not only rapidly closing the twenty-mile gap separating them from the enemy but also equally rapidly taking them ahead of *Cornwall*, *Carnarvon* and *Kent*, none of which had made better than 18 knots for years. Sturdee reduced speed to 22 knots, then 19 knots, allowing his older ships to come up. It was not a popular order below decks. Both officers and men had been watching the enemy cruiser force, ahead, growing slowly larger in their gunsights. They remembered the action of Coronel, following which not a single British seaman had been picked up by von Spee; there was a killing hate in them, but now they could see the enemy drawing away again. Sturdee was unconcerned. There would be time, he signalled to all ships, for crews to take a meal before the action began. It was 1132, with twelve hours of daylight remaining.

Below, the messdecks were in a state of disarray. Tables were still littered with unwashed breakfast-plates, scattered with crumbs and puddled with tea. The refuse-buckets had not been emptied, nor potatoes or bread drawn from the issue-room. Unwanted clothing lay where it had been flung when the hands had been summoned to quarters – not, as in a later war, provided with steel helmets, respirators, anti-flash gear and life-belts, but simply as they stood, usually in overalls. Some unfortunates were still grimed by coal-dust; the bathrooms were locked and all water switched to fire hydrants. Damage-control parties had run out old holed hoses across all decks, to sprinkle water when action began, partly to reduce the hazard of fire but also because there was a theory that wet steel was more resistant to shell-impact than dry. When the men, sent away from their stations, reached their messes, they were in no mood for soup, boiled beef, potatoes and suet pudding. They hacked wedges from the mess-lockers' stale loaves, spread them with margarine, stuffed them into mouths violent with obscenities, and returned to their guns. Even the meekest sailor breathed murderous fire, cursing Sturdee for being a stupid bastard of an old woman.

Forty minutes later Sturdee, coming up from his lunch, decided that the two battle-cruisers would never come to grips with the enemy if they continued to wait for the slower ships. He ordered both to work up to 26 knots again and, at 1247, when the range had narrowed to 16,500 yards, *Invincible* hoisted Flag 5.[6]

The enemy were fine on the starboard bow, more than nine miles away, the maximum range for 12-inch guns – and those of the two battle-cruisers had not been calibrated above 12,000 yards; no warship had ever engaged beyond this distance nor had anyone envisaged doing so. The first salvoes fell short, and continued falling short for twenty frustrating minutes as Sturdee remorselessly crept nearer. His most effective battle-range would be something between 8000 and 10,000 yards, but if he came down to this he would be putting his own ships within reach of von Spee's 8.2-inch guns – and they were not to be despised. Any naval commander who throws away the advantage of superior gunnery-ranging merely to place his ship closer to the enemy is not being gallant, only irresponsible. Between them, *Invincible* and *Inflexible* had 1600 12-inch shells and an entire afternoon and evening in which to fire them. Sturdee knew it, and so did von Spee. The British gunnery was poor, but the law of averages insisted that, sooner or later, the big guns would hit. Von Spee elected to hedge his bets. To his light cruisers, *Nürnberg*, *Dresden* and *Leipzig*, he signalled: 'Leave the line. Take independent avoiding action.' Sturdee, von Spee calculated, must now either split his own force or allow three German cruisers to escape, and if the two battle-cruisers continued in pursuit of *Scharnhorst* and *Gneisenau*, as was likely, then it was also probable that the smaller German warships, scattering, could outpace the older British cruisers that laboured astern.

Von Spee, however, underestimated both Sturdee and the engine-room crews of *Kent* and *Cornwall*. Sturdee had anticipated this situation. 'The main duty of the battle-cruisers is to deal with the armoured cruisers,' he had instructed his captains ten days earlier. 'The British armoured cruisers and light cruisers should not seek action with the enemy's armoured cruisers in the early stages but, *in the event of the enemy's light cruisers separating or trying to escape, make it their business to deal with them.* . . .'

So, as the three German light cruisers turned out of their line to southward, *Kent*, *Cornwall* and *Glasgow* turned also, as if tied by string; no orders were needed. *Invincible* and *Inflexible* pounded after von Spee.

The British battle-cruisers were hampered by their own dense funnel-smoke, which was being blown ahead of them by a wind from almost directly astern, so they could seldom tell whether or not they were hitting. Inevitably, however, the 12-inch guns were finding their mark. Both *Scharnhorst* and *Gneisenau* were being found, the big shells tearing into the German ships' casemate decks, the lyddite high explosive drenching wreckage and corpses with yellow dye. Then, unwarily, Sturdee came too close, and von Spee hit back. Nobody had thought the Germans capable of engaging at 15,500 yards, but their expertly served 8.2-inch salvoes straddled *Invincible* repeatedly. To add insult to injury, at 12,500 yards they opened fire with their 5.9-inch secondary armament, to which the British 4-inch guns could make no reply. *Invincible* received a shell from *Gneisenau* which, descending at a steep angle, sheared through the upper deck and, without exploding, *went out through the ship's side.* Hastily, Sturdee widened the range.

In due course Sturdee would be strongly criticised in naval circles, even by his own men, predictably and vociferously by Jackie Fisher, and, by inference, by the silence of Winston Churchill, for his alleged timidity in destroying von Spee's heavy ships; each of the battle-cruisers expended some six hundred 12-inch shells in doing so. Sturdee, however – to use a modern vulgarism – did not intend to give a sucker an even break. He was not in the heroics business. It is not easy to explain to a widow or a bereaved mother that a loved one is dead because the Admiral wanted to cut a dash. Nor was Sturdee responsible for his ships' poor shooting, largely the result of blinding smoke[7] (to which von Spee was not a victim), the speed vibration and flung spray that bedevilled less-than-perfect gunnery optics. Several years would elapse before ballistics experts conceded that, at ranges of nine or ten miles, the chances of hitting a moving enemy were about five per cent.

Both pairs of ships jockeyed for advantage, von Spee attempting to close the range while simultaneously edging toward the rain clouds on the south-westerly horizon, Sturdee determined that his enemy should do neither, having the speed to dictate terms. By 1510 *Scharnhorst* was on fire with several guns disabled and many dead, seriously holed and listing. *Gneisenau* was similarly afire, with one boiler-room flooded and abandoned and a second becoming un-tenable. Von Spee and Maerker exchanged encouraging signals but, as *Scharnhorst* slowed ominously, von Spee flashed to his subordinate, who had opposed the Falklands operation from the beginning, 'You were right after all,' and, a little later, 'Try to escape if your engines are still adequate.'

*Scharnhorst* died first, a reeling shambles of twisted steel, gutted by fire and shrouded in smoke and escaping steam, yet with her re-maining guns still firing with remarkable discipline. *Inflexible* closed for the kill, pounding the waterlogged hulk until it rolled to port. *Scharnhorst*'s fore turret was only six feet above water when it fired its last defiant shot.

This time the British did not pause to pick up survivors – perhaps they remembered Coronel as they raced on to overhaul *Gneisenau* – and von Spee and his entire ship's company perished. It was no longer a gentleman's war.

*Gneisenau*'s speed had been reduced to 16 knots, so that the elderly *Carnarvon* came up to add her 7.5-inch broadsides to those of *Invincible* and *Inflexible*. Incredibly, the German cruiser survived for almost two further hours – a credit to her Bremen builders, who had given her armour superior to that of the pursuing British battle-cruisers. The inevitable, however, was only being delayed. By 1730 *Gneisenau* was stopped, utterly wrecked and only just afloat.

Although her last gun was still spitting, Sturdee hoisted Flag 6 at 1750 and ordered boats to be lowered. Fortunately, *Gneisenau* settled slowly, allowing a good percentage of her men to jump clear, and when *Carnarvon*'s contribution appeared to be somewhat reluctant Sturdee angrily signalled: 'Lower all your boats at once!' *Invincible* recovered 108 survivors, *Inflexible* 62 and *Carnarvon* 20, but many succumbed to the near-freezing temperature of sea and wind or, more horribly, to the vicious attacks of predatory albatrosses, which the British tried to beat off with their oars. Admiral von Spee's youngest son, Heinrich, serving aboard *Gneisenau*, was not among the rescued.

The battle-cruisers were not unbruised. *Invincible* had been hit twenty-two times, but damage was largely superficial. The starboard leg of her foremast tripod had been shot through and a bunker had been flooded, the wardroom, canteen and several seamen's messes wrecked. One 8.2-inch shell had penetrated as far as the Admiral's pantry, failing to explode and coming to rest on a shelf of Sturdee's marmalade. There were no casualties. *Inflexible* was hit three times, only losing the head of her main derrick, but had one seaman killed and two wounded.

There were still two other battles being fought beyond the southerly horizon. Brave old *Kent* had laboured after *Nürnberg*, opening fire at 1700 and gradually closing to a mere 3000 yards, at which range both ships were hitting freely. *Kent*'s guns were heavier, however, and her gunnery excellent; she had her sister *Monmouth* to avenge. At 1845 *Nürnberg*, pulverised, stopped and sinking, hauled down her ensign. *Kent* had been struck thirty-eight times – with four killed and twelve wounded – and all her boats were holed, but she patched them hastily. The task consumed twenty vital minutes, as a result of which only seven survivors were plucked alive from the icy water. Von Spee's elder son, Otto, serving in *Nürnberg*, was not one of them.

Still further southward *Cornwall* was hammering after *Leipzig*, and *Glasgow* after *Dresden*. John Luce, commanding *Glasgow*, was soon aware that he was overhauling *Dresden* only very slowly, and there was a distinct possibility that he could not come within effective range before dark. Further, he was not convinced that the old *Cornwall* was capable of catching *Leipzig*. Luce decided to settle for one certain kill rather than risk losing both. He abandoned his pursuit of *Dresden* and turned to engage *Leipzig* until *Cornwall* came up. Between them, the two British ships overwhelmed *Leipzig*, but German casualties might have been far fewer if the German commander, Haun – strolling his bridge with a cigar between his lips – had not ignored repeated British signals requesting his surrender so that lives could be saved. He allowed his ship's company to be reduced to seven officers and eleven men before someone else fired a green rocket to indicate compliance.

*Cornwall*, however, working her engines to near-destruction, had arrived on the scene with ample time to deal with *Leipzig* alone, and John Luce had allowed *Dresden* to slip away into the mist and hazed rain to the south-west; *Glasgow* would never catch her now. With hindsight, it was Luce's one tactical error, excusable in the circumstances but expensive. *Dresden*, although content merely to play hide-and-seek off the Chilean coast, would have five British cruisers searching for her for three months until, on 14 March 1915, she would be cornered off the island of Mas a Fuera, four hundred miles west of Valparaiso – in sweet justice by *Glasgow* and *Kent*. Hit by two salvoes, she would hoist a white flag and then scuttle.

Meanwhile, von Spee's two remaining colliers had been sunk, somewhat unnecessarily, by *Bristol* and *Macedonia*. Sturdee did not intend to use his two big ships in a prolonged search for one light cruiser, and on 11 December he took them back to Port Stanley to resume coaling. The local defence force fired off its guns, Governor William Allerdyce invited all officers to Government House, and the ratings of *Invincible* hauled the battered leg of their tripod mast to the top of Sapper Hill, where they mounted it as a memorial to 8 December 1914, on which day they had sent four German cruisers and 2300 sailors to the bottom of the Southern Ocean, and avenged Coronel.

Sturdee received telegrams of congratulations from the King, Winston Churchill on behalf of the Admiralty (but not personally), Jellicoe and Beatty, the French and Russian navies, and from many of his senior colleagues. From Fisher, who regarded Sturdee's conduct as inept and the victory fortuitous, there was only belittling acrimony. The First Sea Lord considered the escape of *Dresden* to be unforgivable, and would have kept Sturdee in the South Atlantic aboard an old cruiser until the fugitive was apprehended, but even Fisher could not defy overwhelming public opinion; in 1914 victories were too few to be cheapened by petty dispute. Sturdee was appointed to the command of the 4th Battle Squadron of the Grand Fleet, hoisting his flag in *Benbow*, awarded a baronetcy, granted £10,000 by Parliament and, after Fisher's death, promoted to the rank of Admiral of the Fleet.

In January 1916, more than a year later, an empty, weather-beaten dinghy was lifted from the sea by German fishermen off the coast of Schleswig. The little boat had travelled 7000 miles to reach its home, for on its salt-bleached bows was faintly painted the name *Nürnberg.*

Before leaving the story of the Falklands action it would be unjust to ignore the performance of the cruisers in company; on balance they earned rather greater credit than their bigger and faster sisters. From the table below it can be seen that, on paper, only *Glasgow* was capable of overhauling any of the German ships, and she was the lightest-gunned. True, the differences in speeds amounted to only a knot or so, but, in addition to a ten-mile start, a knot meant more than a mile every hour.

|  | *Age* | *Designed speed* | *Best recorded speed* |
| --- | --- | --- | --- |
| *Kent* | 14 years | 23 knots | 24.1 knots |
| *Cornwall* | 13 | 23 | 24 |
| *Glasgow* | 5 | 25 | 26.7 |
| *Dresden* | 7 | 24.5 | 25.1 |
| *Nürnberg* | 8 | 23.5 | 25.7 |
| *Leipzig* | 9 | 23 | 23.7 |

There can, however, be few more vicious goads to extreme effort than lust for vengeance on one hand and a fight for survival on the other. In the three ships fleeing and the three pursuing, stokers and engine-room artificers pushed boilers and pistons far beyond the limits of safety. *Kent,* the oldest of all the ships involved, was running light with her bunkers very low. She burned wood – ladders, hatch-covers, mess-stools, capstan-bars, the chaplain's lectern, chicken-coops – with the desperate stokers thrusting everything into the fires as it was flung down to them. The ship's pressure-gauges climbed deep into red danger; *Kent*'s maximum designed horsepower was exceeded by 5000, and she steamed 2 knots faster that day than she had ever steamed in her life. Her funnels glowed orange, then white, and she vibrated so violently that her gun-sights were blurred and useless, but, yard by yard, she clawed after *Nürnberg.* Soon after 1700 the exhausted men in the stokehold heard the sudden rumble of guns above them, and they knew *Kent* was within range; they had won their battle. Every hair was burned from their legs and would never grow again.

## Notes

1   Churchill alone insisted (*The World Crisis*) that 'I cannot accept for the Admiralty any share of the responsibility for what followed' (i.e., Coronel), but was angrily criticised by naval circles. His further attempts at justification in the *Morning Post* were also rejected in an editorial that retorted that by 'attacking the memory of an heroic martyr to his duty (and his orders)' Churchill had put the blame 'upon the principal victims of his own error of judgement'.

2   On examination, the cargo of one collier was found to have deteriorated so much as to be useless, so only two colliers were available for immediate fuel replenishment.

3   Incredibly, although the arrival of Sturdee's battle-cruisers in the South Atlantic was the subject of common gossip in the clubs and bars of Rio de Janeiro, Montevideo and (after von Spee's departure) Valparaiso nobody seems to have made a sustained effort to warn von Spee, partly because of the German commander's desire for wireless security and his avoidance of shore locations which might report him, but apparently also because everyone ashore seemed to believe that *someone else* was passing him such vital information. In the event, nobody did.

4   In days of sail it was held that Frenchmen fought best when starving, Dutchmen when drunk (thus 'Dutch courage') and Englishmen with a full belly. British captains, given time, always fed their crews before action and ordered clean clothing to minimise the infection of wounds. These two traditions were adhered to in both world wars and, during prolonged periods of action – sometimes of several days – strenuous efforts were made under very difficult conditions to keep men fed, albeit with only corned beef, bread and soup.

5   Neither *Canopus* nor any other pre-Dreadnought warship had tripod masts. All had pole masts, usually reinforced by booms for boat-hoisting but which could not be confused with tripods by an experienced officer. At ten miles, through smoke, there would be little to differentiate between the masts of an old battleship and those of an armoured cruiser.

6   The full meaning of Flag 5 was 'Open Fire; May be obeyed as soon as seen'. The rider was added because some ships might not be in a position to range on the enemy immediately, or fire without hazard to others in company. Flag 6 ordered 'Cease Fire; *Must* be obeyed as soon as seen'.

7   *Indomitable*'s fore funnel had been heightened in 1910 and *Inflexible*'s in 1911, but *Invincible*'s was not raised until February 1915, at Gibraltar, when she was returning from the Falklands.

# Chapter Five

*The east-coast bombardments – Dogger Bank – the Dardanelles*

IN AUGUST 1914 the British warship-building programme was interrupted in order to concentrate materials and labour on those ships that could be completed and got to sea within six months, the expected duration of the war. This marked the introduction of the Emergency War Programme, which was to be progressively extended because the war did not end in six months.

Turkey had declared war on 1 November and, two days later, *Indefatigable* and *Indomitable*, still smarting over the escape of *Goeben* and *Breslau*, were joined by the French pre-Dreadnoughts *Suffren* and *Vérité* in a long-range bombardment of Turkish fortifications at the entrance to the Dardanelles. Seventy-six 12-inch shells were lobbed at Sedd-el-Bahr and Kum Kale, both – according to long-range observation – being reduced to rubble. The only consequence was that the alarmed Turks immediately began to strengthen their shore defences and minefields, on which the Gallipoli operation would founder six months later.

By the beginning of 1915 the Germans' western-offensive plan had failed – but only just. They had been halted at the Marne, but they occupied most of Belgium and a huge area of France, had severely mauled the Russians and, although on the Western Front they had passed to the defensive, they held a well-prepared and almost impregnable line against which the French and British would hurl themselves repeatedly, at ghastly cost, for the next four years.

Alone among the Allies, however, the British had the consolation of holding one card which, they were confident, could not be trumped. It was the Royal Navy. Whatever might happen on the Continent or elsewhere, the war could not reach Britain. 'I do not say that [they] cannot come,' Earl St Vincent had once said of another enemy invasion threat, 'I only say that they cannot come by sea.' And so, agreed the nation, say all of us.

It was disconcerting, therefore, when on 16 December 1914 the German battle-cruisers *Seydlitz, Moltke, Von der Tann* and *Derfflinger*, the heavy cruiser *Blücher*, light cruisers and two flotillas of destroyers appeared off the east coast for the second time to bombard West Hartlepool, Scarborough and Whitby.

The raid was inspired largely by a desire for revenge (von Spee's squadron had been destroyed by Sturdee during the previous week), but was also intended to undermine civilian morale while simultaneously imposing duress on British naval defences. In the first objective it failed completely, as the *Blitzkrieg* would so fail in a later war. The British public's faith in the Navy, whether justified or not, was too firmly rooted to be shaken by such hit-and-run attacks on almost helpless targets. They were only puzzling, and the fact that the 120 people killed and some 700 wounded were almost entirely civilian provided excellent propaganda to be turned against the German 'baby-killers'. Public morale, indeed, was stiffened.

At this time *Invincible* and *Inflexible* were in the South Atlantic, *Indefatigable* was still in the Mediterranean (soon to be relieved by *Inflexible*), while *Indomitable*, having returned from Malta, was refitting. *Australia* was in the Pacific. *Tiger*, completed only in October, had joined the Grand Fleet in Scapa Flow on 6 November and was still working up. It was from Cromarty that Beatty, in *Lion*, leading *Princess Royal, Queen Mary* and *New Zealand*, roared southward to intercept the enemy raiding force under Admiral Hipper. He almost did, but the patchwork of minefields off the east coast, heavy seas, fog, and yet more signalling confusion combined to thwart him. Outflanking light units of both sides exchanged shots, but once again the Germans slipped safely away. It was British naval pride that was stung, not public opinion, which was still conditioned to the view that the Navy never failed.

At the Admiralty, Jackie Fisher was still nursing his 'Baltic Project', the details of which were obscure but undeniably involved the forcing of the Kattegat narrows and a landing on the Pomeranian coast. He exploited the success of the two Invincibles at the Falklands (for which he had so vehemently castigated Sturdee) and the melting-pot of the Emergency War Programme to achieve Cabinet permission to build two more improved and very fast battle-cruisers, of 'a special type for a special purpose'. They would be laid down on 25 January 1915 and subsequently named *Renown* and *Repulse*. Of these two ships there is much more to tell, but before they were completed for service Fisher would be dethroned and there would be a great deal of rethinking about battle-cruisers.

*

Encouraged by their success on two earlier occasions, on 24 January the German battle-cruiser 1st Scouting Group, supported by four cruisers and nineteen destroyers, made a third sortie across the North Sea, intending a sweep of the Dogger Bank area to destroy the British fishing fleet, its escorts and any other light forces that might be in the vicinity. This time, however, the German naval command overplayed its hand, choosing a moment when *Von der Tann* was in dockyard hands and so reducing the primary attack force to *Seydlitz*, *Derfflinger* and *Moltke* accompanied by *Blücher* – a splendid heavy cruiser but no match for battle-cruisers, and capable of only a nominal 25 knots. *Blücher* was a liability.

And this time, superbly, the Admiralty's intelligence service was on its toes. Intercepted enemy wireless traffic and *Magdeburg*'s captured code-books revealed that something big was afoot, and the increasingly efficient system of radio direction-finding filled in the blanks. As Hipper's battle-cruisers slipped their moorings in the Jade estuary during the dark of night, so did Beatty's reception committee, this time starting from Rosyth.

It was slightly unfortunate that the non-participation of *Van der Tann* was balanced by the absence of *Queen Mary*, probably Beatty's most efficient ship, which had been sent to Portsmouth for dockyard attention. She had been replaced by *Tiger*, similarly gunned but a poor substitute, in commission for only weeks and not yet a competent fighting machine. Moreover, for reasons never explained, *Tiger*'s crew included an unusually high percentage of serious defaulters, recovered deserters and several less-than-adequate officers. During the entire war the performance of this magnificent warship would always be disappointing.

*Lion*, *Tiger*, *Princess Royal*, *New Zealand* and *Indomitable* steamed through a night in which sea and sky were swept clear of mist by a north-easterly wind. There was only a moderate white-flecked swell and, when dawn rose, visibility would be excellent. Strict wireless silence was maintained. Unsuspecting but wary, Hipper's squadron was closing on an almost reciprocal course – 'a beast of prey', rejoiced Winston Churchill, 'moving stealthily forward hour by hour into the trap'.

At 0715, in half-light north of the Dogger Bank, the British light cruiser *Aurora*, leading the 35 destroyers of the Harwich Flotilla, sighted her German counterpart *Kolberg*, a member of Hipper's screen which totalled 4 cruisers and 19 destroyers. The advantage was *Kolberg*'s, aware that any ship she encountered must be an enemy, while *Aurora* could not be so immediately certain. The German cruiser opened fire first, hitting *Aurora* three times, fortunately inflicting only superficial damage, before the British ship could reply, but a shell struck *Kolberg*'s fore-bridge, killing two men. She turned away to eastward, signalling Hipper by wireless that the raid had been compromised.

Hipper had been steaming north-westward on the northerly fringe of the Dogger Bank. Now he swung his squadron around and headed for home, although *Kolberg* had warned him only of enemy light forces, the destruction of which was the purpose of the German operation. In the event, through sudden apprehension rather than tactical ability, Hipper avoided total destruction, for Beatty's five battle-cruisers were only 28,000 yards behind him and working up to 28 knots. The Admiralty had predicted the interception position with pinpoint accuracy.

It was the German Navy's misfortune that almost all its major actions were to be fought whilst withdrawing, or, as propagandists more cruelly preferred, when running away, provoking the jeer that German warships had their heaviest armament aft, which of course was juvenile nonsense. The fact was that, after Coronel (in addition to the Kaiser's Imperial Order of July 1914, which forbade units of the High Seas Fleet to venture beyond the Horns Reef unless success was absolutely assured), German surface forces were invariably out-gunned. Hipper's four heavy ships mounted eight 12-inch guns, twenty 11-inch and twelve 8.2-inch against Beatty's twenty-four 13.5 inch and sixteen 12-inch guns. The disparity was not quite as wide as it appeared because of *Tiger*'s inept gunnery, but Hipper could not know this, and had every reason to run for safety. He ordered his escorting cruisers to race ahead and his heavy squadron to make 25 knots, which was *Blücher*'s best speed.[1]

It took Beatty's three leading ships (*Lion, Tiger* and *Princess Royal*) eighty-two minutes to close to 22,000 yards of the trailing German ship, the unfortunate *Blücher*, but at the same time *New Zealand* and *Indomitable* had fallen astern of their faster sisters and were not in contention. At 0852 *Lion*'s ranging salvo fell short. Ten minutes later, at 20,000 yards, she hit *Blücher*, and by 0915 all three British ships were finding the same target. *Lion* was able to turn her guns on *Moltke*.

Both squadrons, at high speed, were in line ahead with the British on the starboard quarter of their quarries. Hipper ordered his four ships into echelon so that a maximum number of his guns would bear, and, for the same reason, the three British battle-cruisers turned slightly to starboard. *New Zealand* and *Indomitable* were still out of range, and the 1st Cruiser Squadron of *Southampton, Birmingham,*

*Nottingham* and *Lowestoft*, clinging with difficulty to the race, were unable to intervene.

In the War Room of the Admiralty, Winston Churchill and his three senior strategists, Admirals Fisher, Wilson and Oliver, had been watching the situation for several hours. Consensus of opinion had it that the Germans were only attempting another hit-and-run adventure, but there was always the possibility of more ambitious developments. To insure against the possibility of Hipper slipping past Beatty, the pre-Dreadnoughts of the 3rd Battle Squadron,[2] accompanied by four light cruisers, had already been ordered out of the Forth and were deployed some forty miles north-west of the Dogger Bank. More significantly, to meet the unlikely event of the High Seas Fleet following Hipper's battle-cruisers into the North Sea, the Grand Fleet had slipped from Scapa Flow during the previous evening, and twenty-two super-Dreadnoughts were steaming slowly southward, cleared for action.

The German Admiralstab did not learn until the early forenoon of the twenty-fourth that Hipper and his battle-cruisers had been intercepted 180 miles from Wilhelmshaven, without support. All available ships of the High Seas Fleet were ordered to raise steam, but everyone knew it was too late. Hipper was on his own.

Hit repeatedly by 13.5-inch salvoes, *Blücher* was suffering severe damage. A shell had penetrated a boiler-room, her after superstructure and two turrets had been destroyed, and more than two hundred dead and wounded littered her decks. Her speed began to slacken and, progressively, she was falling even farther astern of the German battle-cruisers.

*Lion*, however, closest to the enemy and the most exposed, was also being punished; it was German practice to concentrate fire, whenever practicable, on the head of the enemy line. At 0928 Beatty's flagship suffered a hit that penetrated her bunkers, and at 0935, informed that *New Zealand* was coming within reach of the stricken *Blücher*, the British commander ordered his now four ships to turn their fire on 'opposite numbers' *from left to right*.

This had been the standard British battle procedure for almost two centuries, although there were gunnery experts who considered that the German method of chopping down one opponent at a time by concentrated fire was more effective. Ideally, *Lion* should now engage *Seydlitz*, *Tiger* fire at *Moltke*, *Princess Royal* at *Derfflinger*, and *New Zealand* – coming up from astern – should finish off *Blücher*.

The order, however, was not interpreted in this manner by

Captain Henry Pelly, commanding *Tiger*. He assumed that *Indomitable* had also joined the British battle-line from astern, in which case the sequence of fleet numbers would indicate that *Tiger* should fire at *Seydlitz*.

In one respect this miscalculation was not too serious. It meant that both *Lion* and *Tiger* were concentrating their broadsides on the enemy flagship, *Seydlitz* – it was a leaf from the German gunnery manual. It also meant, unfortunately, that *Moltke*, the second battle-cruiser in line, was left completely undisturbed to fire salvo after salvo at *Lion*.

Again, this development was not necessarily disastrous if *Tiger's* eight 13.5-inch guns had made any useful contribution. The ship, although the only one in company equipped with a director fire-control, had never fired at a moving target, and the doubtful quality of many of her company has already been referred to. More damaging, however, was the inadequacy of her gunnery officer, whom Lord Fisher later described as 'villainously bad', who persistently reported *Lion's* shell-splashes as being those of his own ship. During the relevant period of the action *Tiger* was overshooting by 3000 yards, and there is no evidence that she achieved a single hit on the enemy.

In return for being the admiral's chosen ship and by implication the best in the squadron, it was also the flagship's doubtful privilege to occupy always the position of greatest hazard, in the van. *Seydlitz* had her two after turrets demolished by *Lion's* first salvo and escaped total destruction by seconds. An explosion in one barbette ignited cordite in the loading-chamber, flared down the turret-trunk to the ammunition-handling chamber, and then penetrated an open door to the chamber of the second turret. Six tons of cordite propellant erupted, wrecking the entire stern and killing 159 men instantly. The magazines, and thus the ship, were saved by a petty officer who opened the flooding-valves, turning their red-hot wheels with his bare hands.

*Lion*, now the target of *Seydlitz*, *Moltke* and *Derfflinger*, was hit twelve times. At 1000 hours her forward turret was disabled, and minutes later her after fire-control position and the secondary armament circuitry were put out of action. Then, at 1018, a massive concussion forward suggested that the ship had been torpedoed, but two shells from *Derfflinger* had struck simultaneously, one penetrating below the waterline to flood the forward port bunkers and the other bursting in the torpedo flat, with the result that, very quickly, all adjoining compartments were also flooded up to the main deck. Beatty was forced to zig-zag.

Despite this, the British situation was promising. *Blücher*, being hammered by *New Zealand*, was ablaze and listing, defiant still but obviously a doomed ship and abandoned by Hipper, who was maintaining 25 knots toward the south-east. *Derfflinger*, hit by *Princess Royal*, was also on fire, and the German squadron was still more than a hundred miles from the sanctuary of Heligoland with five or six hours of daylight remaining. Only *Moltke* was still unscathed. *Lion*, although hurt, was still holding her best speed and none of her following squadron had been damaged.

At 1035, however, Beatty's *Lion* was struck again, and at 1041 yet another shell started a fire in 'A' turret magazine, which was extinguished by flooding, but the flagship's speed was now reduced to 20 knots. She was beginning to be overtaken by *Tiger* when, at 1100, an enemy salvo tore through her waterline armour, damaging feed-tank and boiler-room sufficiently to disable the port engine. *Lion* slowed to 15 knots, listing 10° to port with power and lighting failed. She turned out of the line, and *Tiger*, *Princess Royal* and *New Zealand* swept past her.

There now followed the most controversial period of the Dogger Bank action. Assuming that *Lion* was incapable of playing any further part in the chase, authority now passed to Beatty's second-in-command, Rear-Admiral Sir Archibald Moore, flying his flag in *New Zealand* (unless or until Beatty transferred to another ship, which was obviously no easy procedure under the circumstances). It was unfortunate that *Lion*'s disablement had occurred just as she had hoisted a change-of-course signal, provoked by a submarine-sighting report. In fact there were no submarines in the vicinity, and the deviation would have not long delayed resumption of the action. Even so, the new heading did swing the British squadron temporarily away from Hipper and rather more toward the crippled *Blücher*.

*Lion*, without electrical power, was unable to use Morse by wireless or lamp, with which orders could have been expressed precisely; flag-hoists allowed only a limited selection of standard phrases that did not always meet the requirements of a given situation and, when Beatty wanted to urge Moore to continue his pursuit of Hipper, the best that the Fleet signal-book could offer was 'Attack the rear of the enemy'. Moreover, this signal was flying from *Lion*'s yardarm in company with the earlier hoist, 'Course NE', suggesting to Moore that the enemy to be attacked was to the north-east – where *Blücher* still struggled.

*Lion* had only two halyards remaining, and a frustrated Beatty, watching his squadron turn away from Hipper's battle-cruisers only to blaze away at the waterlogged *Blücher*, could only hoist 'Keep nearer to the enemy' – again, the most appropriate phrase that the signal-book offered. In any case, Moore was out of sight. Beatty transferred to the destroyer *Attack* and raced to reassume control of the situation, only to meet *Princess Royal*, who was *coming back*, ordered by Moore to investigate the flagship's predicament. Beatty boarded her at 1220, but by this time it was beginning to dawn on Moore that, while the three British battle-cruisers, with the cruiser *Aurora* and three destroyers, were yapping around the tortured *Blücher*, Hipper's half-beaten squadron was twelve miles away and disappearing south-eastward at 25 knots. It would take the British two hours to come within range again, but then Hipper would be getting dangerously near to Heligoland and the High Seas Fleet. Beatty, in command again and breathing fire, ordered all ships to resume the chase. Minutes later, however, realising that the game had been lost, he turned his battle-cruisers for home.

The dying *Blücher* was still snarling at the ships gathered around her, now joined at last by *Indomitable*. The German cruiser put a shell into the destroyer *Meteor*, who had ventured too close, killing four, but then received two torpedoes from *Arethusa*. Shortly after noon *Blücher* began to roll over to port, and *Arethusa*, closing again, lowered her boats. Having been hit by a total of seven torpedoes and more than seventy heavy shells, *Blücher* died well. She had 792 killed, while 234, including many wounded, were picked up by the British.

For several hours the fast-moving battle had been followed from above by the German naval Zeppelin *LZ5*, commanded by Kapitan-leutnant Klaus Hirsch. While on routine patrol, he had intercepted Hipper's first action-report, had hurried to the scene, but was compelled to watch helplessly as *Blücher* was battered to destruction. Hirsch also saw Hipper's three battle-cruisers escaping at high speed south-eastward, and then, fired at by the British cruisers, he sought safety above cloud-level and made wireless contact with Hipper. In so doing, Hirsch did not observe that the damaged *Lion* had dropped out of the chase and, when asked by Hipper how many British battle-cruisers were still in action, he replied that there were four. Elatedly, Hipper jumped to the conclusion that he had sunk one of his pursuers, and wirelessed this claim ahead to Wilhelms-haven.

That evening Admiral Hugo von Pohl, the Chief of the German Naval Staff, reported to the Kaiser that, although *Blücher* had been lost, Hipper had sunk an enemy battle-cruiser, probably the flagship *Lion*. The Kaiser was delighted, immediately announcing that he would personally decorate all the officers and men involved. When, hours later, the sobering truth was learned, the Kaiser's delight turned to anger; he demanded that heads should roll, and they did. Admiral Friedrich von Ingenohl, Commander-in-Chief of the High Seas Fleet, and his Chief of Staff, Rear-Admiral Eckermann, were both dismissed, the first for failing to support Hipper and the second for planning the Dogger Bank raid in the first instance. Hipper escaped similar punishment only because of the intervention of senior colleagues who argued that he was more sinned against than sinning.

There was another minor embarrassment for the Germans. As the boats of *Arethusa* and several destroyers were engaged in picking up *Blücher*'s survivors, a German seaplane had appeared from nowhere and dropped a number of small bombs. No record exists of any damage being caused, but British newspapers pounced gleefully on the incident, even claiming that 'one bomb fell among the drowning men and blew four of them to pieces'. The Germans, already smarting from accusations of mass atrocities, murder, rape and 'frightfulness' in Belgium, were forced to condemn the attack by 'an interloping seaplane out of Borkum' flown by an inexperienced pilot who, it was claimed, was trying to bomb the destroyers, not their rescuing-boats.

With only *Blücher* sunk, Beatty had returned to *Lion*, bitterly disappointed that Hipper had slipped through his fingers yet again and so cheaply. His flagship had fired 243 rounds and had received twelve hits, although her casualties numbered only twelve wounded. She had some 3000 tons of water in her, mostly forward, and was six feet down by the bows. *Tiger*, hit six times, had ten killed and eleven wounded, among whom was the foreman of a party of dockyard electricians, still working aboard, who had surrendered to hysterical panic and run amok. One shell had penetrated 'B' turret, killing two, a second had exploded in the signals-distribution centre, killing eight, while the petrol-tank of a motor-launch had erupted into flames sufficiently spectacular to convince the fleeing Germans that she was disabled. In fact she suffered little more than blistered paint.

    *Lion*, taken in tow by *Indomitable*, regained Rosyth at dawn on 26 January. Her injuries were too extensive for the facilities of the newly commissioned dockyard, and she should have been taken to Devonport, but to Jackie Fisher this would have been tantamount to an admission that one of his Splendid Cats had been maimed by a few 12-inch shells. *Lion*, he ordered, would go to Armstrong's yard on the Tyne – and she did, remaining there for four months, cradled in coffer dams. Tons of concrete had earlier been poured into her leaking compartments by the Salvage Corps, and this had to be progressively and painstakingly broken up by small charges of dynamite before repairs could begin.

Beatty's detailed despatch to the Admiralty was completely rewritten before being released to the press and was supplemented by the fiction that 'the presence of the enemy's submarines necessitated the action being broken off'. If this were true, an American naval correspondent wrote, then Beatty ought to be shot. And Beatty, shown the article, nodded, 'I quite agree with him.'

However, he had little for which to apologise, and the blame for allowing Hipper's battle-cruisers to escape was directed at Moore, whom Fisher described as 'despicable' and 'utterly incomprehensible'. Moore was subsequently relegated to the command of a cruiser squadron off the Canaries, where he would be unlikely to be required to make any important decisions. He claimed, with some justification, that he had only obeyed what he interpreted to be his orders, but Fisher retorted that 'in war the first principle is to disobey orders; any fool can obey orders'.

When emotions had cooled, however, a closer analysis of the Dogger Bank action provided the Admiralty with a number of comforting statistics. This was the first time that British battle-cruisers had been matched against their counterparts and, since *New Zealand* and *Indomitable* had played no part in the exchange, and *Tiger*, although in company, had contributed nothing,[3] it was true to say that *Lion* and *Princess Royal* had engaged and held their own against *Seydlitz*, *Derfflinger* and *Moltke*, sinking *Blücher*, with the Germans suffering a thousand dead in addition to more than two hundred as prisoners. 'This combat between the finest ships of both navies', Churchill could boast to the House, 'is of immense significance and value in the light it throws upon the rival systems of design and armament. Although the German shell is a most formidable instrument of destruction, the bursting, smashing power of the heavier British projectile is decidedly greater, and – this is the great thing – our shooting is at least as good as theirs!'

Our shooting, of course, was not. Beatty had achieved a moral and material victory which, but for Moore's lack of initiative, and *Tiger*'s disregard for the golden rule that 'no ship should be left unfired upon' – Captain Pelly, accused Fisher, was a 'poltroon' – might have been an annihilation of Hipper's entire squadron. The British success, such as it was, could be attributable to superior range and weight of projectile, not to efficient gun-laying.

Both British and Germans had learned several lessons. The Royal Navy added a number of more relevant phrases to the Fleet signal-book, revised the orders regarding the concentration of fire on an enemy battle-line, and installed auxiliary wireless offices in ships so that, should the main W/T apparatus be destroyed, there existed stand-by equipment. Gunnery practice was intensified. There was a growing awareness of the vulnerability of battle-cruiser armour to plunging shot, particularly that of the turret roofs, but no remedies were undertaken. It was the Germans, as the result of the *Seydlitz* near-disaster, who more clearly realised the potential danger of an explosive flash in a turret descending the trunk to the cordite-handling room. They immediately began to modify the system of interlocking flash-proof doors in the magazine-hoists of their capital ships and, to counter the British advantage in gunnery range and calibre, install improved Zeiss stereoscopic rangefinders which would prove more accurate than the Barr & Stroud coincident type fitted in British ships.

The circumstances leading up to the Gallipoli landings in the spring of 1915 and the campaign that followed have been thoroughly explored elsewhere. Only the first phase of the operation, the naval bombardment of the Dardanelles shore defences, has any relevance to this book: only one battle-cruiser was briefly involved.

The plan to force a passage through the Dardanelles straits had been enthusiastically endorsed by Winston Churchill, who envisaged a 'methodical piecemeal reduction of the [Turkish] forts as the Germans did at Antwerp', ignoring the fact (if he was ever cognisant of it or, if he was, whether it would have made any difference) that the performance of naval guns was significantly different from that of the high-trajectory howitzers used against the fortifications in Belgium. It also seems incredible, in retrospect, that initially the Navy alone should have been expected to 'bombard and take the Gallipoli peninsula, with Constantinople as its objective', and difficult to understand, assuming that the warships involved, with only two battalions of marines, had the capability to *take* anything, how the Navy would subsequently proceed without massive military support.

Fisher blew hot and cold, first supporting the proposal and then, realising that the resources he had been accumulating for his nebulous 'Baltic Project' were to be siphoned off into the Dardanelles scheme, opposing it. In the end he surrendered to Churchill's insistent eloquence and, to his credit, made every effort to provide the operation with the facilities necessary for success.

Following the Falklands action, *Inflexible* had refitted at Gibraltar and on 24 January 1915 relieved *Indefatigable* in the Mediterranean, hoisting the flag of Admiral Sackville Carden. It was Carden, an irresolute commander and an unfortunate choice, who would be given the responsibility for destroying the Dardanelles defences a month later.

The bombardment fleet consisted of eighteen heavy ships. Most of these were old pre-Dreadnoughts (including four French) which could no longer claim a place in a battle line but whose big guns were quite adequate for a leisurely off-shore bombardment. Four, however, were vessels of better quality. They were *Queen Elizabeth*,[4] *Inflexible*, *Lord Nelson* and *Agamemnon*. The last two, although indeed pre-Dreadnoughts, were the youngest of that generation, completed as late as 1908, and were formidable if rather slow battleships. Carden's plan was to deal with the enemy's batteries in three stages: first those at the mouth of the Straits, then the intermediate positions on both sides of the seaway, and finally the inner forts that guarded the Narrows – the entrance to the Sea of Marmara. Minesweeping trawlers, escorted by destroyers, would sweep ahead of the fleet before each stage, and parties of seamen and marines would be landed to demolish what remained of the Turkish fortifications when the warships had ceased firing.

The bombardment of the outer forts began at 0950 on 19 March at long range, reducing to 6000 yards and, by the late afternoon, to 5000 yards. The results were not encouraging; it was clear that the older ships must be at anchor to fire with the accuracy necessary to hit individual targets and that merely hitting the forts was not enough; direct hits must be registered on the enemy's guns in order to disable them.

Bad weather delayed further action until the twenty-fifth, when all four emplacements at the mouth of the Straits were silenced. Demolition parties met no opposition when landed, but it was not until 2 March that the entire outer defence system had been destroyed and Carden could proceed to stage 2.

The preceding minesweeping operation was to be carried out by trawlers manned by non-naval personnel who, although accepting that their role involved some risk, protested that they 'had not joined up to be shot at' – and the Turkish defenders, stiffened by German officers, who in turn were grateful for the lack of urgency in Carden's programme, were beginning to hit back. The minesweeping trawler-crews were reluctant to enter far into the Dardanelles until the shore batteries were silenced, while the bombarding ships could not approach to within range until their path had been swept clear of mines.

Carden, never an optimist, was already aware that the entire operation was going sour and that the Straits would not be forced unless one shore or the other was occupied. Even when the trawlers were manned by naval volunteers, sweeping progressed very slowly. The Admiralty was getting impatient and, although Churchill informed Jellicoe that 'our affairs in the Dardanelles are prospering although we have not yet cracked the nut', two days later he telegraphed Carden, 'The results to be gained are . . . great enough to justify loss of ships and men if success cannot be obtained without. We shall support you in well-conceived action for forcing a decision, even if regrettable losses are entailed.' He followed this with: 'The operation should now be pressed forward methodically and resolutely at night and day. The unavoidable losses must be accepted.'

For two weeks Carden's big ships had been reduced to ineffective long-range shelling. Now, despite his lack of confidence, he determined to attack with his entire force on 17 March. Minesweeping efforts were intensified, resulting in four trawlers being sunk and their supporting cruiser *Amethyst* suffering severe damage with 25 killed and 45 wounded. Then, on the fifteenth, Carden broke down and asked to be relieved of his command. He was replaced by Vice-Admiral J. M. de Robeck.

Whatever de Robeck's views on the feasibility of his task might have been, he had little choice but to follow his predecessor's plan of attack – albeit a day later. At 1045 on Thursday, 18 March sixteen Allied capital ships, in three lines abreast, weighed anchor and advanced into the Dardanelles. It was a brilliantly sunny morning with the sky cloudless and the sea richly blue and calm. It was also to be one of the blackest days in the history of the Royal Navy.

The first line consisted of *Queen Elizabeth*, *Agamemnon*, *Lord Nelson* and *Inflexible*, the second of the old French battleships *Gaulois*, *Charlemagne*, *Bouvet* and *Suffren*, and the third of *Albion*, *Irresistible*, *Vengeance* and *Ocean*. The remaining four, *Majestic*, *Prince George*, *Swiftsure* and *Triumph*, steamed on the flanks.

At first all went well. Despite the determined fire of enemy batteries the Allied ships pushed steadily on until the leading line 'A' was within 14,000 yards of the inner fortifications. At 1130 the bombardment began, and observers were soon reporting hits on the forts defending the Narrows. Great clouds of smoke and dust, pitted with flame, hung over the target, and a magazine erupted with a thunderous roar that echoed and re-echoed among the hills. It was the enemy's smaller guns, now within range, that were responding accurately and effectively. It was often difficult to determine from which shore the shells were coming, Turkish mobile howitzer batteries changed positions repeatedly, and counter-fire was also drawn to smoke-emitting dummy guns. *Agamemnon*'s upperworks were hit twelve times in twenty-five minutes and *Inflexible* had her tripod damaged, her bridge wrecked and set ablaze and her fore control-top disabled with three men killed and six wounded. However, by noon de Robeck was sufficiently encouraged to bring the second line of French pre-Dreadnoughts forward to join the attack, whereupon *Gaulois* was severely damaged, having to be withdrawn and beached, and *Inflexible* was holed again.

*Bouvet*, hit repeatedly by 14-inch shells, ran over a mine. Her magazine exploded and she capsized and sank within two minutes, taking 700 men with her – and now the day that had begun so promisingly was turning into a nightmare. At 1400 de Robeck had ordered the remaining French warships to retire and his third line of British pre-Dreadnoughts to come into action. *Inflexible*, having withdrawn out of range to get her wounded below, returned to her place to resume firing, but was immediately hit again and then, at 1611, struck a mine and began to list. Four minutes later the pre-Dreadnought *Irresistible*, having had both her primary turrets disabled, was also mined and drifted out of control as destroyers raced to take off her crew. She was abandoned, and would sink unseen during the coming night.

De Robeck was baffled. He did not know (nor would it be known until after the war) that his ships had been manœuvring all day in a minefield laid ten days earlier. Evening was approaching and, with two of his big ships sunk, a third beached and another seriously crippled, he decided to postpone further action until the following day – but the nightmare was not yet finished. *Ocean*, continuing to blaze away at the shore defences, was suddenly rocked by a violent explosion – another mine – and, with her steering-control ruptured, circled helplessly. Again, destroyers took off her crew, but the hulk was abandoned to sink, like *Irresistible*, under the cloak of darkness. By dawn nothing would be seen of the two veteran battleships.

The battle-cruiser *Inflexible*, now with a total of 29 killed, with her hull at the level of her torpedo-flat torn open, with 2000 tons of water in her, down by the bows and in danger of sinking, managed to steam out of the Straits at slow speed to reach the island of Tenedos and anchor in shallow water. Here she was temporarily patched, and reached Malta only with extreme difficulty. She was repaired at Gibraltar and subsequently rejoined the Grand Fleet in home waters on 19 June.

There was never any possibility of de Robeck resuming the attack on the following day. In addition to the losses already mentioned,

*Charlemagne* had a stokehold flooded, *Agamemnon* a 12-inch gun disabled, and *Albion*'s fore turret was out of action. The total death-toll of about 800 – predominantly French – might be considered modest. Even had the ships succeeded in forcing a passage through the Dardanelles they could not have remained long in the Marmara, nor could their supply-vessels have followed. Far from compelling Constantinople to surrender, de Robeck would have found the Germans and Turks well prepared to receive him, and might well have experienced as much difficulty in withdrawing as he had in entering.

De Robeck abandoned the entire operation on 23 March, although the First Lord, Churchill, continued to urge him to renew the assault – this despite the fact that the War Council had already decided to mount a full-scale military operation in five weeks' time. Churchill would later claim that it was this period of delay which was responsible for the even more tragic failure of the subsequent Gallipoli campaign, but the assertion was hardly compatible with his earlier assurances to the War Council that the Navy alone could bring the Turks to their knees.

Fisher, having resigned himself to the failure of the naval operation, was becoming progressively less tolerant of the First Lord's volatility, his criticisms and constant meddling in professional matters. He was finally incensed when Churchill, on 15 May, proposed sending still more ships to the Dardanelles. Fisher tendered his resignation to the Prime Minister, and Asquith accepted it.

Churchill's own position was now the focus of severe criticism, and it was plain that he would have to leave the Admiralty. The Prime Minister offered Churchill the Colonial Office, which he refused, but he finally accepted the office of Chancellor of the Duchy of Lancaster, without a seat in the Cabinet. He resigned this post, too, in late 1915, asking Asquith to appoint him Governor and Commander-in-Chief in British East Africa. Refused, he went to France, following training, to command the 6th Royal Scots Fusiliers, and so passes out of our story for the next twenty-four years.

By the end of 1915, Beatty had all ten battle-cruisers under his immediate command, based on Rosyth; all, including *Australia*, had returned to home waters during the year. Neither Beatty nor Jellicoe cared for the Forth as an anchorage. Its approaches, they claimed, could be easily mined and were accessible to submarines,[5] while there were no facilities for full-calibre gunnery practice, for which the battle-cruisers would have to be sent north to Scapa Flow. Rosyth, however, was more convenient for launching counter-attacks against the Germans' hit-and-run activities and, if the Admirals did not like Rosyth, their ships' companies were well satisfied. They hated the bleak and deprived environment of Scapa Flow; in Rosyth the delights of Edinburgh were only an hour away.

With Beatty flying his flag in *Lion*, the other nine battle-cruisers of the force were now organised into three squadrons. The 1st (under Rear-Admiral O. de B. Brock) consisted of *Princess Royal*, *Queen Mary* and *Tiger*, the 2nd (Rear-Admiral W. C. Pakenham) of *New Zealand*, *Indefatigable* and *Australia*, and the 3rd (Rear-Admiral the Hon. H. L. A. Hood) of *Invincible*, *Inflexible* and *Indomitable*. The twenty-nine battleships of Jellicoe's Grand Fleet were shared between Scapa Flow and Cromarty.

There were, during early 1916, several occasions on which the British and German heavy units came very near to clashing, and on 22 April the battle-cruiser force, racing to intercept a reported enemy sortie – which, in the event, did not materialise – ran into dense fog, and *Australia* and *New Zealand* collided. *Australia*, the more seriously damaged, was in dockyard hands until 5 June, and thus did not participate in the biggest and most controversial action in naval history – Jutland, during 31 May and 1 June. She would be the only battle-cruiser never to fire a shot in battle.[6]

## Notes

1    *Blücher*'s best recorded speed was 26.4 knots in 1909, running light. During the Dogger Bank action she did not exceed 23 knots before being overhauled.

2    The 3rd Battle Squadron consisted of *Hibernia*, *Africa*, *Zealandia*, *Dominion*, *Britannia* and *Hindustan*. They each mounted four 12-inch and four 9.2-inch guns, but were only 18-knotters, so their ability to maintain contact with Hipper for very long is doubtful.

3    When *Lion* had turned out of line, *Tiger* became the leading ship and then the target for the three enemy battle-cruisers. It can be argued, there-fore, that she contributed by taking punishment which might otherwise have been directed at *Princess Royal*.

4    The new and fast battleship *Queen Elizabeth*, in commission for only weeks, had been designated flagship of the East Mediterranean Squadron, a device for consigning her to safe waters for the purpose of calibrating her eight 15-inch guns, the most powerful afloat. It was decided that she might as well calibrate them with the Turkish forts as her target.

5 Scapa Flow was not secure. As early as November 1914, *U18* had penetrated into Hoxa Sound but was seen by a patrol-boat and rammed. *UB116* did the same in October 1918, but detonated a series of mines. Finally, on 13 October 1939, *U47* slipped through the Flow's defences to torpedo *Royal Oak*.

6 *Australia* did, however, sink the German freighter *Eleonore Woermann* on 6 January 1915, off the Falklands, when on passage from the Pacific to join the Grand Fleet.

# Chapter Six

*Action stations and the sailor – new battle-cruiser construction – the scene set for a major confrontation*

IT IS AN ODD FACT that soldiers have always written of their experiences more readily than sailors. Our library shelves are filled with military literature but offer only a comparatively few seafaring memoirs, usually taken from collected letters (and among the most lucidly interesting are those written by the lower-deck sailors of Howe and Nelson).

The First World War produced an unprecedented number of soldier poets and writers, some idealistically euphoric, others bitterly cynical; millions of words were written, during and after the war, about Ypres, the Somme, Gallipoli and Mesopotamia, telling of bravery and sacrifice, the mud and stench, privation and death. Rightly so, for it was a soldier's war.

We must search more diligently for an insight into the sailor's environment. He seemed content to leave history in the hands of the official recorder, who painted with a broad unemotional brush and with small regard for the minutiae of messdeck life and the day-to-day problems of the common bluejacket. Those authors who do tell us something of the war at sea, such as Captain Taprell Dorling ('Taffrail') and Paymaster-Commander L. da C. Ricci ('Bartimeus'), wrote from an officer's viewpoint and an almost total ignorance of the lower deck; their attitude toward naval ratings was paternally condescending, like that of a country gentleman toward his forelock-tugging tenants.

The naval rating, however, enjoyed one important psychological advantage over his counterpart in the trenches. Officers, even the most senior, shared the same dangerous situations as their men. There were no generals sending scores of thousands of men into an attack without themselves having ventured nearer than ten miles from the battle-area, no orders by telephone from staff officers in some far-distant château. The ship's captain stood on an open bridge, and so did the admiral, his flagship was the first and most exposed in the line, and a few inches of gold braid were no protection against shrapnel and high explosive.

In both wars sea-actions fell into two different patterns. The first was that which developed with little or no warning, such as a submarine or aircraft attack (although the latter was rare during the First World War), and the other was the battle which everyone had been anticipating for hours. With the first – the immediate – an action-alarm bell hammered or a bugle sounded 'General Quarters' and, within seconds, hatches and watertight doors were crashing shut and ladders and passageways teemed with men scurrying for their action stations, upward to gun-positions, flagdeck and bridge, downward to engine-room, transmitting station or magazines. Throats might choke, but there was little time for real fear. It was during the long period of anticipation that preceded other actions that,[1] whilst men had time to bath, change clothing, eat, possibly snatch uneasy sleep, even write letters which might or might not leave the ship, they also had time to speculate.

Unlike the soldier before battle, who might be comforted by the thought that he had a number of avenues of survival which included flight and surrender, the sailor had nowhere to run, nowhere to hide; no part of his ship was safer than any other. He resigned himself, not necessarily with equanimity, and his captain's measured voice, assuring him that 'we expect to intercept the enemy at 0330. I have every confidence that our ship will give a good account of herself', did not provoke any sudden determination to be heroic. The sailor was better informed of developments than the man in the trenches (who often did not know where he was, far less where he was going, or why) but he was also uncomfortably aware how devastatingly swiftly a ship could sink, be utterly destroyed in one colossal explosion. Any officer or rating whose battle station was two or three decks below could entertain little hope of escape. If he had avoided death by blast, ragged steel or scalding steam, he was still separated from the upper deck by several ladders, clamped watertight doors, crazily tilted decks perhaps choked with smoke, in darkness or already flooding. After all this, if he prevailed, there was still the other enemy, the sea, floating with lung-clogging oil, burning cordite and the upturned clay-coloured faces of the dead. There was not much to choose between the Arctic, in which a man died in three minutes, or the Atlantic and North Sea, where the cold penetrated agonisingly, more slowly, until muscles atrophied and respiration failed. And ships in company, he knew, did not pause to pick up survivors during a battle situation.

Men might think of these things as each hour brought their ship nearer to its rendezvous with the enemy and, as the hour approached, some would begin to drift in the direction of their stations even before being ordered to 'First State of Readiness'. Sailors of the earlier war had little survival or protective equipment, but those of 1939–45 were provided with steel helmets, respirators, flash-resistant coverings for face, hands and arms, and an inflatable life-belt to which was clipped a small battery-fed and waterproof red lamp. In both wars most men were employed in those duties for which they had been specifically trained – e.g., wireless operators went to the main wireless office or to one or more auxiliary, or standby, wireless locations; gunlayers manned gun positions, torpedomen their torpedo-tubes, and signalmen went to the flag-deck or a signals distribution office. There were others, however – cooks and stewards, writers, Royal Marine bandsmen, storemen – whose normal pursuits were irrelevant to a combat organisation, who provided those services which were *only* required during action. These included the handling of ammunition in the magazine, the control of shell damage and fire, and the collection of wounded.

Damage-control parties were positioned in several strategic locations throughout the ship, provided with hydrants and hoses, axes and crowbars, timber, wooden plugs and belts of 'fearnought' – a blanket-like, fire-resistant material. In the later war there would also be foam extinguishers, acetylene cutters, portable fire-pumps and breathing apparatus.

A ship's sick-bay was inadequate for the demands of battle, and an operating-theatre and casualty receiving stations would be established in roomier accommodation – perhaps the wardroom, the chapel or the office flat. During action movement between one part of the ship to another, in addition to being strongly discouraged, was also extremely difficult. All doors in watertight bulkheads and the massive hatch-covers between decks were firmly clamped shut and *must not be opened*, so that anyone wishing to pass from one compartment to the next could be faced with an arduous and frustrating negotiation with numerous blanked-off passageways and ladders, maze-like in complexity, before reaching his goal.

In practice, of course, once the ship was in action none left his station except for a specifically approved reason. During lulls in a prolonged intermittent engagement, such as the pursuit of *Bismarck* in May 1941, which extended over four days, one man might be sent away from each position to collect food or beverages from the galley for his fellows. At the captain's discretion it might even be possible briefly to stand down one watch at a time for ablutionary purposes and to snatch a breath of fresh air on deck. Protracted uninterrupted duty in a confined, often overheated location below decks (or, for that matter, in an icily cold position above) was exhausting and progressively prejudicial to mental alertness.

It was unlikely that more than a comparatively small number of a ship's company would see the enemy they were fighting, and even those on bridge, flag-deck, lookout and gun position might only fleetingly glimpse a smudge of smoke, a vague distant shape on the horizon or, at night, the enemy's gun-flashes. Most men were confined, blind to all that was happening above them, hearing only the rumble of their own guns above the noise of their immediate environment – the clatter of shell-hoists and hydraulic rams, the throb of turbines, the teeter of Morse or the *peenk-peenk* of an Asdic echo. It was under such circumstances that imagination could run riot, and a thoughtful commander would endeavour to keep his imprisoned crewmen informed of a situation which, below, could often sound more threatening than it was.

In 1915 a newspaperman, referring to the Dogger Bank action, could write: 'One of the crew [of *Lion*] afterwards remarked that the noise of the German shells was like the rattle of peas on a corrugated-iron roof. The distance was too great for the German gunfire to take effect.'

This was pure fabrication; none of *Lion*'s crew could have said it. Twelve-inch shells do not rattle like peas; they smash into a ship, tear through heavy armour and explode with a shattering concussion in the confined spaces beyond, wreck gun-positions, machinery and circuitry, scythe down men and turn below-deck compartments into reeking death-traps. Nor is a shell's effect lessened by distance. The longer the range, the more steep is the angle of descent, and it was a warship's thin horizontal armour – the decks and turret-roofs – which was so easily penetrated. The newspaperman, writing his war despatches in the King Lud, was unaware that the shells which 'rattled like peas' on *Lion* had put her into dock for four months.

In both 1914 and 1939 the regular Royal Navy went to war with a confidence amounting almost to arrogance, born of centuries of maritime supremacy, which compensated for the fact that on many occasions British ships and weapons were inferior to those of the enemy. Further, this confidence was absorbed by the thousands of wartime volunteers and conscripts, conditioned since infancy to believe in the unchallengeable qualities of their service. There was never an engagement, despite the odds, during which a British crew speculated that *it might not win*. Conversely, German surface operations often lacked incisiveness because of a subliminal feeling of inferiority (exacerbated by a discipline that allowed commanders at sea very little freedom of action) or an awareness that the British strength in depth was such that its surface was only being scratched by the most heroic German effort.

Occasions arose, however, when the German Navy found it necessary to undertake some sort of demonstration to justify its existence, and one such occasion arose in the spring of 1916. For four months the French and German armies had been locked in savage battle at Verdun. The losses on both sides were horrendous, while it was suspected that the British were preparing for a massive offensive on the Somme. During the preceding winter, too, the German people had begun to learn the realities of war under blockade; there were increasing shortages of food, clothing and fuel. Twice the leaves had fallen but the Kaiser's soldiers had not come home, and already half a million never would. Many could not understand why, if the English were being strangled to death by the U-boat offensive, the fine great battleships and battle-cruisers of the High Seas Fleet seldom left the security of Wilhelmshaven, Cuxhaven, Heligoland and Kiel, and scores of thousands of sailors lived idly, strolled the streets and slept nightly in dry bunks.

In London, Churchill had been succeeded as First Lord by Arthur Balfour and Fisher by Admiral Sir Henry Jackson; while, across the North Sea, Admiral Reinhard Scheer was now Commander-in-Chief of the High Seas Fleet with Hipper still commanding the fleet's battle-cruiser force.

Scheer had a problem. He knew exactly where the British ships were based and that Beatty's battle-cruisers would come pounding out of Rosyth at the slightest provocation. What he would like his own battle-cruisers to do was either ambush the cruisers and destroyers of the Harwich Force and destroy them before they could be supported, and/or (either as a development of such an action or as a separate operation) lure Beatty's ships toward Heligoland and the guns of the High Seas Fleet. What he wanted to avoid at all costs was to allow the High Seas Fleet to be caught in the open by Jellicoe's superior battle squadrons – but these were far away in Cromarty and Scapa Flow. Beatty, he assessed correctly, would come roaring after the bait – Hipper's battle-cruisers – and, given a little luck, could be cut off and overwhelmed long before Jellicoe could reach the scene.

Jellicoe, in turn, could read Scheer's thoughts as clearly as if they had been written out for him. Furthermore, with his wireless listening stations and possession of German code-books, he could be warned of Scheer's intentions (or could make an educated guess)

even before the High Seas Fleet had raised its anchors. Elements of
the Harwich Force had deliberately trailed their coats in the hope of
enticing the enemy's battle-cruisers to attempt the opening phase of
their plan but, for a number of reasons including the German
tendency to bolt for home at the first threat of action, had failed.

Despite the cards he held, Jellicoe knew that Scheer was no fool
and always had the advantage of a 'fleet in being', of choosing the
most favourable time and circumstances. Jellicoe would also have
agreed with Scheer that Beatty was inclined to be headstrong, and
that a situation could easily arise when he would decide that his
Splendid Cats could 'finish the job' without any help from anyone
else. Jellicoe had already warned Beatty that 'they know that if they
can get you in chase, the odds are that you will be a 100 miles away
from me, and they can under such conditions draw you well down to
the Heligoland Bight without my being in effective support. . . . The
Germans might well get the High Seas Fleet so placed as to cut in
behind you. . . .'

British and Germans were engaged in a tactical quadrille in which
the merest stumble could be disastrous.

Both navies had been substantially reinforced since the beginning of
the war, the British in particular by the five 'Queen Elizabeth'
battleships, the German by three 'Königs' and another battle-
cruiser, *Lützow*, a sister to *Derfflinger*. By mid-1916, therefore, Beatty
held the advantage, at least on paper, of ten to five, although one of
his number, *Australia*, was out of service.

The dockyards of each country were still building. *Renown* and
*Repulse* had been launched, due for completion toward the end of
that year, and the Director of Naval Construction, now E. Tennyson
d'Eyncourt, had been instructed to prepare designs for a class of *four*
super battle-cruisers – *Hood, Howe, Anson* and *Rodney* – to be laid
down in late 1916. While all this building was progressing under the
somewhat confused circumstances of the Emergency War Programme, few people were aware that, as a legacy of Fisher's 'Baltic
Project', three extraordinary warships had reached an advanced
stage of construction in the yards of Vickers and Harland & Wolff.
Fisher had coyly referred to them as 'large light cruisers' in order to
obtain Treasury sanction but, since two would mount 15-inch guns
and the third, amazingly, 18-inch guns, such a classification was
facetious. They were battle-cruisers, albeit eccentric, and would be
named *Courageous, Glorious* and *Furious*.

## *Note*

1   Jellicoe's battleships steamed for twenty hours in order to intercept the German fleet at Jutland in 1916, but this was a modest prelude compared with those of other actions, such as the Normandy landings in 1944 or several of the battles of the Pacific during the Second World War.

# III Who Blundered?
# The Beginning of Doubt

## Chapter Seven

*Jutland, the opening phase and the battle-cruisers' meeting – the loss of* Indefatigable *and* Queen Mary

JUTLAND has been analysed more thoroughly than any other battle in maritime history, debated by strategists, refought by tacticians, disputed by its participants. Both sides claimed a victory and both were justified from their respective viewpoints. It was a clash of two massive battle-fleets; neither side was expecting it, and the first day was followed by a night of confusion, the whole battle being punctuated by a series of missed opportunities. Millions of words have been written about Jutland and there is little more to add, but it was an engagement where, as the Admiralty afterwards admitted, 'the British ships on which the brunt of the fighting fell were the Battle-cruiser Fleet . . .'.

It all began on the morning of 30 May 1916, when the Admiralty was informed that an intercepted coded signal, originated by the German Admiralstab, had ordered the High Seas Fleet to slip and assemble in the outer Jade by 1900 hours of that day. The Admiralty alerted Jellicoe and Beatty, while supporting units in the Humber and at Harwich were ordered to raise steam.

During the afternoon another coded signal was logged. It read simply, '31 Gg 2490', which the Admiralty's Room 40 OB was unable to interpret. However, following upon the earlier instruction, and in view of its brevity, it almost certainly ordered the execution of orders previously issued.

Jellicoe was directed to take the Grand Fleet to sea.

The cryptic '31 Gg 2490' in fact indicated that the secret order No. 2490 was to be put into effect on 31 May. Hipper's High Seas Scouting Force[1] was to carry out a 'reconnaissance in force' off the Danish coast in the full knowledge that the British would quickly learn of it and despatch Beatty's force to intercept. Only fifty miles to southward, however, Scheer's more than twenty battleships would be hovering, waiting to annihilate Beatty's battle-cruisers. The plan was a modified version of another, more complex, which, since it was abandoned, is of interest only to the theorist. Scheer wished to avoid, at all costs, a confrontation with Jellicoe's battle-squadrons; he would be content to devour Beatty and then run for cover. Unfortunately he was unaware that both Beatty and Jellicoe would be at sea and steaming to meet him four or five hours before his own fleet had left harbour.

Similarly, Jellicoe was later advised by the Admiralty that, if any enemy ships had left the Jade, they did not include Scheer's flagship *Friedrich der Grosse* (and therefore probably not the High Seas Fleet) because her wireless call-sign, DK, was still being transmitted from Wilhelmshaven. Any wireless operator, if asked, could have supplied the information that DK was merely the German Commander-in-Chief's harbour call-sign which, on departure, was transferred to the shore station.

Off Rosyth, on the evening of 30 May, Beatty had hoisted the flag signal 'Raise steam for 22 knots and report when ready to proceed', and at 2130 *Lion* slipped her moorings and led her sisters out of the darkening Forth into the North Sea. This, however, was not the force that Beatty had expected, or perhaps wished, to command. Three of his battle-cruisers, *Invincible*, *Indomitable* and *Inflexible*, were absent from his line. Ten days earlier they had gone north to Scapa Flow for full-calibre gunnery practice and had been temporarily substituted by the 5th Battle Squadron consisting of the new battleships *Barham*, *Valiant*, *Warspite* and *Malaya* under Rear-Admiral Hugh Evan-Thomas, detached from the Grand Fleet. The exchange would have been reversed within a further few days, but now, for Beatty, the battleships constituted a mixed blessing. They each mounted eight 15-inch guns and were massively armoured, but they were also three knots slower than the slowest of the battle-cruisers, which must adjust their speed accordingly and so throw away the one virtue to have justified their construction. Inadvertently, battle-cruisers were being required to share a battle-line with battleships, as *Brassey* had predicted eight years before.

Also in company, moving up from astern to assume their screening stations, were fourteen light cruisers, eight destroyers and, by no means least, *Engadine* – a seaplane-carrier converted from a cross-Channel steamer and carrying a pair of two-seater Short 827 seaplanes. It was necessary for these wood-and-wire machines to be hoisted out by crane, if the sea was sufficiently calm, and to be hoisted aboard again, but the ungainly little steamer was the first 'aircraft-carrier' to be involved in a major fleet action, the forerunner of a class of warship, yet undreamed of, which would reduce to obsolescence the proud giants in whose wake *Engadine* trailed apologetically.

There is little doubt that Beatty would have preferred to have had a full muster of battle-cruisers under his hand; he understood battle-cruisers and they understood him. The battleships, despite their potency, were incompatible with battle-cruiser tactics. Still, there could have been few men in those battle-cruisers as they moved slowly in line ahead under the Forth bridge – *Lion, Princess Royal, Queen Mary, Tiger, New Zealand* and *Indefatigable* – who really thought that this sortie would achieve anything more than those earlier. Hopefully by this time tomorrow they would be anchored again in mid-river with the off-duty watch ashore.

A hundred miles to the north the three errant ships of the 3rd Battle-Cruiser Squadron were leading the larger part of the Grand Fleet out of Scapa Flow. Their crews were heartily sick of the bleak Orkneys anchorage, congested with moored capital ships and with the inhospitable island of Flotta accessible only by cutter or picket boat across a mile of choppy grey water. There were football pitches and a nine-hole golf course ashore, but all too frequently sheeted with water or lashed by rain and unfit for play, a few small piers and a clutter of undistinguished buildings that included a YMCA hut. There were no trees, no civilian houses, and only the most primitive of roads, no shops, no bars, no women, only unremitting mud with a scattering of gulls and a few sheep. The battle-cruiser men were glad to have Scapa Flow behind them; when this latest excursion was concluded – and it was certain to be abortive – they would surely be returned to Rosyth and the pubs and willing lassies of Edinburgh.

Rear-Admiral the Hon. H. L. A. Hood, CB, MVO, DSO, stood with feet apart on the dark open bridge of *Invincible*. Of medium height, stolid, he had the ruddy untroubled face of an English farmer rather than that of one of the Navy's most capable younger admirals. He was the last of a distinguished line of fighting seamen, but his own rapid promotion had been thoroughly earned and few would have disputed it. A popular commander of Osborne Naval College between 1910 and 1913, then Naval Secretary to the First Lord, Winston Churchill, he had also flown his admiral's flag over Dover, regarded as the key to the Channel. That flag now flew at the head of the 3rd Battle-Cruiser Squadron, and there was every probability that, in due course, he would succeed Beatty in command of the Battle-Cruiser Fleet as a further step toward even higher responsibility.

Hood was in a frustrating position. His squadron's rightful place was with Beatty, who had been ordered to make for a specified position eastward of the Long Forties, reaching it by 1400 on the thirty-first. If he had not sighted the enemy, he would turn to rendezvous with the Grand Fleet, which should by then be about seventy miles to the northward, and the combined force would extend their reconnaissance toward the Horns Reef, off the west coast of Jutland. Initially, therefore, there was no need for haste on Jellicoe's part, particularly in view of the Admiralty's advice suggesting that Scheer was not at sea anyway. The Grand Fleet steamed through the night at 16 knots. The battleships' maximum station-keeping speed, in any case, was only 20 knots, and Hood must keep pace unless or until Jellicoe released him – while with every hour Beatty was drawing farther away.

Scheer was steaming his twenty-two battleships northward, parallel to the Danish coast. Sixty miles ahead of him Hipper's battle-cruisers represented the bait which Scheer was hoping would lure Beatty to annihilation. If Jellicoe's Grand Fleet subsequently put to sea, Scheer was confident, it would be far too distant to threaten intervention; Jellicoe would only be wasting thousands of tons of fuel. As late as 1400 hours on the afternoon of 31 May, however, the German Commander-in-Chief did not know if Beatty was out. Far more important, he had no idea that Jellicoe was *already half-way across the North Sea*.

It has often been overlooked that at this time Beatty's battle-cruisers were regarded as not merely an advanced squadron of the Grand Fleet but as an independent force responsible for intercepting the Germans' raids on the east coast. Jellicoe's battleships were deployed only as insurance against the possibility of Hipper slipping past Beatty, which, as we shall see, almost happened. Jellicoe was described as the only man on either side who could lose the war in a single afternoon, but he would more likely be aware that neither could he win it. A crushing defeat of the German High Seas Fleet would not unravel the deadlock on the Western Front, and, on balance, Jellicoe would as soon keep the enemy ships penned up in their harbours. Although, as he had told his admirals a few weeks earlier, 'the total destruction of the High Seas Fleet gives a greater sense of security, it is not, in my opinion, wise to risk unduly the heavy ships of the Grand Fleet in an attempt to hasten the end of the High Seas Fleet, particularly if the risks come not from the High Seas Fleet itself but from such attributes as mines and submarines'. He shared the older school's intense dislike for undersea warfare and was far from alone in his somewhat exaggerated fear of the torpedo and mine, although, to be fair, the British had suffered overwhelmingly greater losses by these two weapons than in surface actions. Jellicoe's tendency always to analyse a problem, to weigh the probable losses in ships and men against the potential gain, has often been interpreted as over-caution. Haig called him 'an old woman' but, then, Jellicoe would never have a Somme on his conscience – if Haig had a conscience.

David Beatty possessed one Nelsonic virtue that Jellicoe did not – 'the great gift of insubordination' – but, if he was inclined to be headstrong, he was not irresponsible, and was as aware as his superior of the long-term importance of the Navy's advantage in numbers. He might, and did, commit tactical errors, but never a strategic one; he had the panache to achieve more with an ill-judged manoeuvre than someone else would with a copybook one. Beatty's belief in his ships' battleworthiness was over-sanguine, but until Jutland the battle-cruisers had done all that Fisher had claimed they would. Even so, Beatty well knew his place in the mosaic of sea-warfare. He would hurl his squadrons at Hipper's but would never trade blows with Scheer unless he was sure of holding on, and surviving, until support arrived.

At noon Jellicoe, steaming his battleships in six divisions in line abreast, reduced to 14 knots to avoid approaching too soon the position in which he was to rendezvous with Beatty. Hood's squadron was twenty miles ahead of the Grand Fleet, steering south-east.

The day was sunny, the sea calm, with a mild south-easterly breeze. Seventy miles to the south Beatty's six battle-cruisers, with Evan-Thomas's battleships about five miles astern, reached the turn-around point at 1400 hours. From *Lion*'s bridge the sea was empty to the horizon except for the far-screening cruisers, and at 1415 Beatty ordered his ships to alter course to northward in order to close with the Grand Fleet. He was unaware, at this moment, that just beyond the curve of the easterly horizon Hipper's battle-cruisers, cruisers and destroyers – also ignorant – were steering an almost identical course.

It was an innocent Danish steamer, *N. J. Fjord*, positioned precisely between the two forces, which unwittingly flashed the powder-keg and probably saved Hipper (who, like Beatty, was steering directly toward the Grand Fleet) from certain destruction. Two destroyers from the German squadron's *western* wing were detached to investigate the neutral ship while, almost simultaneously, the light cruiser *Galatea* peeled away from Beatty's *eastern* screen to do exactly the same thing. Minutes later the Danish steamer was no longer of importance to anyone except its crew, who doubtless were wishing they were anywhere else but where they were.

Suddenly, after sixteen hours of routine steaming, which had been suffered so often before, everything was happening. *Galatea*, now sighting the German cruiser *Elbing*, flashed the confidential challenge signal, and *Elbing*, realising what it was, passed this to Hipper, in *Lützow*, with her enemy report. The German flagship chose to interpret the odd signal as a report of 24–6 battleships, and Hipper, aghast, immediately swung his squadron round towards the south-south-west to avoid action. Within minutes, however, reassured by another signal to the effect that *Elbing* was in contact with only four enemy cruisers (probably *Galatea*, *Phaeton*, *Inconstant* and *Cordelia*²), he came back to west-north-west for the kill.

*Galatea*, too, had been hammering out her enemy report to *Lion* – 'Two cruisers probably hostile bearing east-south-east. Course unknown.' Beatty received it, and so did Jellicoe, seventy miles to the north, but neither was excited; this sort of alarm had been raised before. Still, Beatty hoisted a signal that ordered a turn in succession to the south-south-east, telling Captain Chatfield,³ *Lion*'s commander, to put the helm over before the following ships acknowledged.

This was an irregular procedure, but neither unprecedented nor unreasonable under the circumstances and, indeed, all the battle-cruisers followed *Lion*'s turn without hesitation. Someone, however – probably *Lion*'s signals officer – had not realised that *Tiger*, responsible for relaying the Admiral's flag signals to the battleships five miles astern, was now unable to do so because of the earlier evolution. Evan-Thomas, leading the battleships in *Barham*, and unaccustomed to Beatty's mercurial propensity, continued filing his squadron on its original course for seven minutes before *Lion*'s searchlight ordered him to the new bearing. By that time the battleships were not just five but ten miles astern, with Beatty increasing speed and widening the discrepancy even further.

Eight minutes later, at 1440, *Galatea* signalled that she had sighted substantial smoke on a bearing east-north-east, following this with an amplifying report that 'Smoke seems to be seven vessels besides destroyers and cruisers. They have turned north.' The British battle-cruisers were working up to full speed, and at 1447 Beatty ordered *Engadine* to fly off a seaplane. It took Flight-Lieutenant F. S. Rutland and his observer, Paymaster G. S. Trewer, some twenty minutes to get their aircraft launched, into the air and flying at sixty miles per hour toward the gun-flashes to the north. This was an error, if understandable, for they saw only the enemy cruisers, to which Rutland closed to within a mile and a half, at a mere thousand feet. Trewer leaned over the side of the flimsy machine, counting and identifying the ships, and then, as his pilot circled, tapped out his report to *Engadine*. Rutland unfortunately expended some of his limited flying-time admiring, from aloft, the battleships of his own force, and was then compelled to return to the carrier with an engine defect, to be hauled inboard. *Engadine* had received the wireless report but was unable to make contact with *Lion*, so the first aircraft to be involved in a naval action did not achieve story-book success.

This was a pity, because early intelligence might have persuaded Beatty, who still did not know that he was about to meet Hipper, to give his four trailing battleships an opportunity to move closer. Steaming at 25 knots, the ships following *Lion*, in sequence *Princess Royal*, *Queen Mary*, *Tiger*, *New Zealand* and *Indefatigable*, hoisted additional battle-ensigns, and Beatty flew the flags Baker Johnnie One – 'Assume complete readiness for action' – but this was only a gloating formality. His squadron was fully ready, and on *New Zealand*'s compass-platform Captain J. F. E. Green pulled on a *piu-piu*, a Maori feathered war-coat.

It was Hipper, with a slight visibility advantage, and expecting to be about to scoop up a squadron of British light cruisers, who sighted Beatty's ships at 1520; the earliest British sighting was logged at 1533. Since the opponents were still some fourteen miles apart, however, this discrepancy was of no immediate relevance. Beatty, observing that Hipper was steering toward the north (and Jellicoe), swung around to eastward to get behind the enemy and his home base, whereupon Hipper wheeled toward the south-east, from where, he knew, Scheer's battle-fleet was approaching. The net result was that the two battle-cruiser forces were now on converging courses with the range closing.

Beatty, with four of his six ships mounting 13.5-inch guns, could have opened fire at 23,000 yards, although this was unlikely to have been profitable. He had *intended* to fire at 16,000 yards. In the event, partly because of unusual visibility conditions, partly because the short-based British range-finders tended to overestimate distance, but also because, at the crucial moment, Beatty had left the compass-platform to dictate a signal to Jellicoe, the range had closed to 15,500 yards before Captain Chatfield ordered Flag Five to be hoisted. The Germans opened fire seconds before the British.

It is interesting, at this point, to look at the situation as it *appeared* to each of the opposing commanders.

Hipper thought that, as planned, the German operation had succeeded in luring the British battle-cruiser force into the open, and now he could lead Beatty into the jaws of his following battle-fleet. Scheer was about fifty miles away but had now increased speed to 16 knots[4] and could expect to join the action well before dusk. Hipper was momentarily dismayed to be told that Beatty was being followed, at a distance, by a squadron of 'Queen Elizabeth'-class battleships. He reported to Scheer, mistakenly, that all five of the class were in company when in fact *Queen Elizabeth* was in dock, refitting. However, on consideration, the unexpected presence of the British battleships could prove to be a windfall. As powerful as they were, they could not survive against the entire High Seas Fleet. Hipper had only to draw them in the right direction, but first he had to keep Beatty at bay.

Like Hipper, of course, Beatty did not remotely imagine that there were soon to be far more enemy ships to contend with than those in the immediate vicinity. For him today was a second Dogger Bank, from which action Hipper had escaped with the loss of only one heavy cruiser. Hipper was running now, but Beatty had no intention of letting him off the hook this time. The British commander had not forgotten the battleships trying hard to keep pace, but for the present he had no employment for them; his Splendid Cats could 'finish the job'. Evan-Thomas in fact had worked his four ships up to a commendable 24 knots and, by taking the shorter line each time the battle-cruisers altered course ahead, would gradually come to within 19,000 yards of the enemy, and so, at 1606, be able to open fire at extreme range.

But much would happen before 1606.

In each battle-cruiser turret the officer of quarters gripped his bracing-rail, dividing his attention between the narrow slit in his observation-hood and the brass-rimmed repeaters that relayed gun-laying data from the transmitting station below the ship's waterline. The steel cavern of the gun-house was hot, reeking of cordite smoke, deafening with the clatter of shell-hoists and the stinging hiss of hydraulic rams. The two great gun-breeches, closed and loaded, were sunk into the wells that allowed their barrels to elevate twenty degrees above horizontal. To serve each monstrous pair, in magazine and shell-room, to hoist charges and projectiles, load and ram, train and lay, eighty men on several deck-levels hauled and thrust, sweated and blasphemed, but in the gun-house were only nine – the seated breech-operators and loaders, sight-setters, trainers and layers. As the huge breeches closed and locked, red 'gun-ready' lamps would flicker in the transmitting station below and in the director tower above and abaft the bridge. A bell tinkled – *ding-ding!* – and then there was an awful concussion that shocked the senses. The whole turret lurched, with each gun, of seventy-five tons, heaving backward in recoil, then to be subdued and slide slowly forward again. Immediately, the breeches crashed open, releasing a blast of burned cordite gas that filled the chamber, stinging eyes and throats. Fresh shells and charges were already in the loading-cages, and the range-pointers jerked.

Below each turret, below barbette and upper deck, main deck and lower, in the caves of the cordite-handling rooms and magazines where steel bulkheads streamed with condensation, laboured the troglodytes who fed the ever-hungry guns. The magazine, they had been told, was the safest place in the ship – unless of course it blew up, when nobody would be likely to complain afterwards. But cordite, ruled the experts, never exploded unless confined within a gun-breech; gelatinised smokeless powder only burned slowly, however fierce the heat. Tests had proved it.

The cylindrical cordite charges for a 13.5-inch gun, each weighing 297 pounds, were encapsulated in pure silk which, after firing, left less glowing residue in the barrel than any other known material, easily extinguished by the thrust of the wet mop referred to as a 'woolly-headed bastard'. The charges were stowed, in the cordite-room, in metal bins from which they were transferred to the hoist-trays in the turret-trunk, joining company with the 1400 lb projectiles similarly taken from the magazine immediately below. Shells and charges were then hoisted by cage to the working-chamber under the gun-house, where they were rolled off into waiting containers, hydraulically rammed into a second cage, and raised through the deck of the gun-house to the open breech.

Under drill conditions well-trained magazine personnel could feed their heavy guns at the rate of two rounds per minute per gun, but such a rapid firing-cycle would not be sustained in action, even if it were desirable. During drill, errors through haste carried no serious penalties; in battle they could be disastrous. After the first flush of nervous excitement, men tended to function more deliberately, perhaps mildly surprised that, with each passing minute, the situation was not as devastating as they had expected. Moreover, after each salvo, gunnery officers needed a few seconds in which to assess the fall of shot and correct ranges – again, a little more deliberately than during a drill.

Despite all this, however, any unwanted delay in the arrival of ammunition at the gun-breeches, for whatever reason – and there were many technical reasons – was seriously disruptive. To counter such a delay each gun-house accommodated a number of stand-by (or 'ready-use') charges and projectiles which, as events would tragically prove, were a lethal hazard.

Eager to get to grips, Beatty had led his ships in line ahead almost directly at the starboard beam of the enemy column, in effect allowing his own 'T' to be crossed, with the result that Hipper's squadron, in addition to seeing the British ships sharply profiled against the lighter western sky, was able to open fire with a full broadside of guns, while only the forward guns of Beatty's ships could bear. The latter were soon to alter course to duplicate the Germans', but Hipper's guns had found their range with painful accuracy, and at 1551 *Lion* was hit twice by *Lützow* before *New Zealand* and *Indefatigable* had even opened fire. Almost immediately *Princess Royal* and *Tiger* were damaged, and a further five minutes elapsed before the efficient *Queen Mary* disabled one of *Seydlitz*'s turrets and then scored a hit on *Derfflinger*. By 1600, however, the German squadron's guns had found their targets thirteen times, the British only four. Both admirals were aware that the range – now only 12,000 yards – was sufficiently narrow for secondary armament to be brought into play, and this was just too close for capital ships. Each, as if by mutual agreement, turned two points away from the other, and the distance between the smoke-wreathed battle-lines opened again to 21,000 yards, or about twelve miles.

Even as this was happening, *Lion*'s 'Q' turret, amidships, was hit by a shell that tore off the roof armour, lifted a sheet of flame as high as her funnels, killed or mortally wounded every man within, and ignited the ready-use cordite in the working-chamber below. Major Francis Harvey, Royal Marines, officer of quarters, ordered all magazine doors to be closed just as he died. This undoubtedly saved the magazine and, indeed, the ship. The magazine crewmen – the cooks and stewards – also died to a man, and some would be found later, charred beyond recognition, with their hands still on the clamped door-clips.

The smoke over *Lion* had not cleared when two projectiles from *Von der Tann* fell on the fo'c'sle and forward turret of *Indefatigable*, the last in line, flaring explosively almost simultaneously. From *New Zealand*, the next ahead, it seemed that she had survived, for nothing further happened for thirty seconds. Then, suddenly, *Indefatigable* disintegrated in a series of violent eruptions, starting from forward, which enveloped the battle-cruiser in dense smoke. When the smoke had dispersed, *Indefatigable* had disappeared.

From her thousand crew only two survivors, later in the day, would be picked up from among the splintered wreckage which, for the next few weeks, was to be washed up on the beaches of Denmark. The destruction of *Indefatigable* was a sobering shock, scarcely believable. During the preceding twenty-two months of war other British heavy ships had been lost, but all except *Audacious* had been slow pre-Dreadnoughts and all had succumbed to mines or torpedoes. A British ship of the line had not been sunk in a surface action since the Anglo-Dutch wars of the seventeenth century.

For a few minutes, with the range widened, the guns of both sides were silent, the ships' crews getting the wounded down and extinguishing fires, repairing damage and jettisoning debris. There was jubilation in the German battle-cruisers, tinged with apprehension, for one sinking did not mean a battle won, but at least the odds were levelled; they were now five against five. Among the British there was perplexity and guilt. In material terms the loss of *Indefatigable* was not crippling, but it should not have happened. Later, many would reflect that Beatty had been wrong so heedlessly to close the enemy when five battleships with 15-inch guns were trailing astern of him, ignored.

And it was those 15-inch guns that now began to emphasise such an opinion. For twenty minutes Evan-Thomas's 5th Battle Squadron had been labouring in pursuit, and at 1606, from more than ten miles away, *Barham* opened fire on the rear of the German line; minutes later her sisters followed suit. This was speculative shooting indeed, for at such a distance the battleships' gunlayers could see no more than the white smear of the enemy's stern-wash and the tumble of his smoke, but almost immediately *Von der Tann* was holed below the waterline, flooding with 600 tons of water, and another of *Seydlitz*'s turrets was disabled.

It is impossible to guess Beatty's thoughts at this moment. The battleships' gunlaying, even allowing for their wider-based range-finders, was markedly superior to that of his own squadron; they had enjoyed the benefit of realistic gunnery exercising in the vicinity of Scapa Flow, and Beatty might have mused that the only three of his own battle-cruisers that had been allowed the same facilities were now with Jellicoe's Grand Fleet. It could be expected that Hipper, despite having drawn blood, was not going to loiter around to be hammered by Evan-Thomas, but would make even greater efforts to escape to the south-south-east, while Beatty, having lost a ship *perhaps* because of his impetuosity, would be equally determined to hit back. Although *Lion*'s midships turret was wrecked and her wireless destroyed so that all signals to Jellicoe had first to be passed by light to *Princess Royal*, Beatty turned his battle-cruisers four points toward the enemy, to resume the action.

Hipper, unexpectedly, did not continue racing for the south-south-east, but altered to the southward to narrow the range even as Beatty was trying to do. Beatty, of course, was unaware that his opponent was not so much running away as running to meet Scheer's High Seas Fleet, which, if both groups of ships, closing head-on, held their courses, was only thirty minutes away. To achieve this rendezvous, Hipper's battle-cruisers must risk heavy punishment from the British ships, and this they did, firing with every gun that could bear.

It is only just that a mention should be made of the secondary but equally vicious battle being fought between the smaller ships accompanying each battle force. Between 1555 and 1609, ordered by Beatty to attack with torpedoes, twelve destroyers (a mixed bag drawn from all three escorting flotillas) steamed pell-mell, at 34 knots, to loosen their torpedoes at 9000 yards. Almost immediately they were embroiled with fifteen enemy destroyers, led by the light cruiser *Regensburg*, similarly launched by Hipper to relieve the pressure on his battle-cruisers. There followed a confused mêlée among a welter of shell-splashes, smoke and blazing guns, impossible to describe logically, but which ended with the German destroyers making off for the comparative safety of their own battle line and leaving two of their number, *V27* and *V29*, waterlogged and sinking. The German destroyers fired eighteen torpedoes, all of which were evaded by Beatty and Evan-Thomas; the British craft fired twenty. One, from *Petard* (which had also torpedoed *V27* and then finished her off with 4-inch shells), struck *Seydlitz*, tearing a hole thirteen feet by thirty-nine under her armoured belt. Creditably, the German battle-cruiser maintained her place and speed in the line.

The British *Nestor* and *Nomad* also lay stopped, two miles from each other, wallowing helplessly as the battle moved away from them. *Nestor*'s commander, the Hon. Barry Bingham, had already declined a tow from *Petard*. 'I was obliged to refuse, for I could not see my way to involving a second destroyer in a danger which only applied to one, for at the time we were still under fire and able to steam slowly. . . .'

Both British and German battle-cruisers had disappeared beyond a smoke-hazed horizon, and only the sullen rumble of their guns could be heard across a sea that was completely empty except for the two injured destroyers. Their respite, however, was to be only brief, for from the south, at first distant but growing larger every minute, there came into sight a long line of silver-grey battleships, squadron following squadron, light cruisers, torpedo boats, more light cruisers. . . .

It was the German High Seas Fleet.

Aboard *Nomad*, Lieutenant-Commander Paul Whitfield was jettisoning his weighted confidential books when his ship came under fire from four enemy battleships which closed to a mere five hundred yards. Her forward magazine exploded and Whitfield, wounded, ordered his men over the side. He was the last to leave, and *Nomad* sank in ninety seconds. Seventy-two men, including wounded, were picked up to become prisoners of war.

The men of *Nestor* watched their sister ship's destruction helplessly and then waited for their own. With the confidential books and maps disposed of, the wounded lowered into the motor-boat and the Carley floats hoisted out, the enemy had not yet begun firing. The First Lieutenant, Maurice Bethell, suggested that the cables might be got ready on the fo'c'sle, *just in case they got a tow*, but there was to be no reprieve. The enemy ships had turned their guns and, hit savagely and repeatedly, *Nestor* began to roll to starboard and settle by the stern. Still, defiantly, she got away her last torpedo before Bingham ordered his men into the boats; there was nothing left to fight with and the end was only seconds away.

Seeing the whaler and motor-boat standing by, Bingham glanced at his First Lieutenant. 'Now, Bethell – where shall we go?'

Bethell chuckled. 'To heaven, I trust, sir.' He turned his attention to a wounded signalman only to be torn down by splinters from a bursting shell, and was not seen again.

*Nestor* sank, stern first, with her ensign flying. Bingham and seventy-nine others, despite the whaler foundering and the motor-boat almost swamped, were hauled aboard the German destroyer *S16* twenty minutes later.

Hipper's 'run to the south' during the late afternoon of 31 May 1916 has to be acknowledged as one of the most heroic feats of fighting seamanship in the history of sea-warfare. He could not shake off the British battle-cruisers, even had he wanted to, because of their slightly better speed, and his necessary turn southward kept him within range of Evan-Thomas's force, which was only marginally slower and was able to turn on the inner, tighter line, and thus keep within reach. Understandably, it was Beatty who was the more anxious to resume the exchange. At 16,000 yards *Lion* hit the German flagship *Lützow*, but *Queen Mary*, third in line, was firing superbly, twice putting shells into *Derfflinger* and straddling her repeatedly. Between 16,000 and 14,500 yards the most effective of the British battle-cruisers was trading salvoes with both *Derfflinger* and *Seydlitz* – and these were odds that she could not sustain for long. At 1624 three enemy projectiles of a salvo of four struck her, flashing dull red forward and amidships. Again, like *Indefatigable* earlier, it seemed that she was not seriously hurt, for she ploughed on majestically, still firing. Then she shuddered and, as an officer in *Tiger* observed, 'the ship seemed to open out like a puffball or one of those toadstool things when one squeezes it . . . the whole ship seemed to collapse inwards . . .'. A shattering explosion tore *Queen Mary* apart, flung the massive turret-roofs hundreds of feet skyward, and then the wrecked 27,000-ton battle-cruiser was completely hidden in a dense pall of brown cordite smoke.

*Tiger*, next astern, swerved through the smoke at 24 knots as debris from her hidden stricken sister rained on her decks. Only *New Zealand*, last in line and hauling out to starboard to pass within fifty feet of *Queen Mary*, saw during a few moments of thinning smoke the stern in the air with screws still churning and, on deck, men swarming from hatchways and turrets. Seconds later, as the smoke closed again like a curtain, the men of *New Zealand* heard a final rumbling explosion, but the nightmare had fallen astern, and there were other things to think about.

A total of 1266 men went to their deaths with *Queen Mary*. Six survivors were picked up by the destroyer *Laurel* and, later, two more by German destroyers. Another, Petty Officer E. Francis, had miraculously escaped from *Queen Mary*'s 'X' turret, aft, had taken to the sea, but was less than fifty yards from his sinking ship when she finally exploded, yet incredibly found himself still alive when that holocaust had subsided. Clinging to wreckage, he was picked up by the destroyer *Petard*, choking, vomiting and half-blinded by fuel oil. He was taken to the destroyer's wardroom but, hours later, again in action, *Petard* would be badly hit and her stern wrecked, with nine killed (including the surgeon-probationer attending Francis) and six wounded. By another miracle, Francis lived to tell of it.

Whatever criticisms have been levelled at Beatty, lack of courage was never one of them. *Lion* herself had been hit repeatedly, already suffering 95 killed and 49 wounded, and the unexpected loss of both *Indefatigable* and *Queen Mary* might have unnerved a lesser man. Now, from *Lion*'s flag-deck, an excited signalman shouted that *Princess Royal*, too, had blown up. She had not, but was merely momentarily enveloped in heavy smoke – now, however, anything could happen. Beatty's immediate comment to his flag captain, Chatfield, that 'there seems to be something wrong with our bloody ships today', may have been a flippancy to mask his disappointment, but there was nothing flippant about his next order, to turn yet nearer to the enemy to engage more closely. It required a cold determination which matched Hipper's, and Beatty must have experienced relief to see, astern, *Princess Royal, Tiger* and *New Zealand* still in line and firing steadily. Moreover, at 1628 the German battle-cruisers *turned away*.

This was not, as was claimed, solely because Hipper was 'no longer able to stand up to the greater weight of British shellfire' but as much because of the British destroyers' torpedo attack, referred to earlier, which was launched at this time, and also because Scheer's High Seas Fleet was now only minutes away; Hipper could afford to pull Beatty and Evan-Thomas around to a more easterly course so that Scheer, approaching from the south-east, could achieve a positional overlap and thus have the British trapped between his own fleet and Hipper's squadron.

At 1638 Beatty received an electrifying enemy-report from the light cruiser *Southampton*, two miles ahead. The report – 'Have sighted enemy battle fleet bearing south-east course north' – was immediately relayed to Jellicoe by *Princess Royal*, whose communications officer added, somewhat unnecessarily, 'probably hostile'.

Jellicoe altered course to south-east, increased speed to 20 knots, and signalled the Admiralty: 'Fleet action imminent.'

Typically, Beatty held his course until he could see for himself the head of the German battle-fleet – *König, Grosser Kurfürst, Kronprinz Wilhelm, Markgraf, Kaiser, Kaiserin* and *Prinz Regent Luitpold* – and the following miles of smoke-wreathed fighting-tops climbing ominously over the horizon. He signalled an immediate course-alteration of sixteen points, a complete U-turn, which would bring his ships heading back toward Jellicoe. He was no longer the hunter but the hunted; he had been trapped because the Admiralty had said that Scheer was still in Wilhelmshaven.

Still, Beatty had one gilt-edged ace up his sleeve – assuming he was allowed the opportunity to play it, because Jellicoe's Grand Fleet was still fifty miles away.

*Notes*

1   Hipper now had five battle-cruisers – *Lützow* (his flagship), *Derfflinger*, *Moltke*, *Seydlitz* and *Von der Tann* – the four light cruisers *Frankfurt*, *Wiesbaden*, *Pillau* and *Elbing*, and thirty destroyers led by the cruiser *Regensburg*.

2   The 3800-ton *Cordelia* was commanded by Captain T. P. H. Beamish, who had commanded *Invincible* at the Falklands as Sturdee's flag captain, and had suffered this demotion as the result of Fisher's disapproval.

3   Later Admiral of the Fleet Lord Chatfield, First Sea Lord 1932–5, and Minister for Co-ordination of Defence at the beginning of the Second World War.

4   Scheer's maximum station-keeping speed was only sixteen knots because, rather against his better judgement, he had allowed six pre-Dreadnoughts to accompany his fleet, which had to adjust its speed to that of the older ships.

# Chapter Eight

*Jutland, the second phase and the loss of* Invincible – *the fleets collide – missed opportunities and the German withdrawal*

EARLIER that afternoon Rear-Admiral Hood's 3rd Battle-Cruiser Squadron – *Invincible, Indomitable* and *Inflexible*, accompanied by the light cruisers *Chester* and *Canterbury*, and the destroyers *Shark, Acasta, Ophelia* and *Christopher* – had intercepted the first alarm-report transmitted by *Galatea*, and at 1513 increased speed to twenty-two knots. The squadron, it will be remembered, was twenty miles ahead of the Grand Fleet, steering south-east with a reserve of speed that it was unable to utilise. (Although the oldest of the battle-cruisers on both sides, the three Invincibles were probably still marginally the fastest.) At 1600 hours, receiving no orders from Jellicoe or further intelligence from Beatty, Hood increased speed again, on his own initiative, to twenty-four knots, turning to the south-south-east. Five minutes later, however, he received wirelessed sanction from Jellicoe to proceed immediately to support Beatty.

This was the instruction which Hood had been impatient for since departing Scapa Flow. Now he signalled maximum speed and ordered his crews to action stations, pushed *Canterbury* five miles ahead, *Chester* the same distance on his battle-cruisers' starboard beam, and deployed the four destroyers in a line-abreast anti-submarine screen.

Shortly after 1700 hours a low-flying sea-mist began to reduce visibility to seven or eight miles, in some directions as little as three. Hood was starved of information (as was Jellicoe), but he intuitively maintained his south-south-easterly course to get between Hipper's battle-cruisers – still the only enemy force reported – and the bolt-hole of the Skagerrak. Hood, in fact, had already reached to the *eastward* of Hipper when his outriding cruiser *Chester* found herself on a collision course with four enemy cruisers at a distance of only 6000 yards. These were *Frankfurt, Wiesbaden, Pillau* and *Elbing*, leading thirty destroyers, only four miles north-east of Hipper's *Lützow*.

*Chester* swung around to starboard, firing as she flung herself back toward the 3rd Battle-Cruiser Squadron, zig-zagging. Overwhelmingly outgunned, however, she was hit seventeen times; in minutes thirty-five of her crew were dead, with forty-two wounded, and most of her guns disabled.

The British battle-cruisers sighted *Chester* reeling out of the haze, a floating shambles, ablaze with cordite fires, but drawing her pursuers on to the guns of the bigger ships. From *Invincible*'s director-control Commander Hubert Dannreuther, the gunnery officer, reported: 'Four cruisers, Wiesbaden class. Five-point-nines, ranging eleven thousand. Speed twenty-four knots, sir.'

Aboard *Chester* was Boy 1st Class John Travers Cornwell, just sixteen and sometime pupil of Walton Road School, London. Severely wounded when an exploding shell killed all others of the forward gun-crew of which he was the junior member, he continued to work the gun alone and managed to get away a final projectile – which allegedly struck *Wiesbaden* – before dying. Without detracting from young Cornwell's courageous behaviour, it is fair to suggest that there were very many acts of heroism that day which would pass unnoticed, but Cornwell's tender years marked him out for special attention; England needed youthful heroes. He would be awarded a posthumous Victoria Cross, received by his widowed mother from His Majesty the King at Buckingham Palace, and John Travers Cornwell would become firmly established as the beau idéal for thousands of the Navy's boy sailors during the years to come.

Whether or not *Wiesbaden* was hit by John Travers Cornwell, however, was largely academic. The four German cruisers, suddenly seeing the three big warships toward which they had been led by *Chester*, whirled frantically. How could there be a British battle squadron in *this* direction? Too late. *Wiesbaden* was torn to smoking wreckage and both *Pillau* and *Frankfurt* severely damaged. All four cruisers would almost certainly have been annihilated if Hood had not been compelled to alter course in the face of a torpedo attack by thirty-one destroyers led by the cruiser *Regensburg*.

For a second time the insolent aggressiveness of the British destroyers was to prove too much for their German counterparts. *Shark*, *Acasta*, *Ophelia* and *Christopher*, each of less than a thousand tons, armed with puny 4-inch guns and a pair of torpedo-tubes but as eager as unleashed puppies, hurled themselves at the enemy flotillas, which managed to fire only twelve torpedoes in the direction of Hood's squadron before turning away. None struck, and only

*Indomitable* reported seeing any as the battle-cruisers altered course to the north-westward, from where Hood could hear the rumble of heavy guns.

At 1820, off *Invincible*'s port bow, Beatty's ships, led by *Lion*, suddenly loomed out of the mist, steaming in the *opposite direction* and firing at a yet unidentifiable enemy to the southward. And Hood's men, puzzled, counted their approaching sisters and counted again. *Lion* led only three other ships; *Queen Mary* and *Indefatigable* were missing.

It was about now that a horrible truth began to dawn on Admiral Scheer. For almost two hours the entire High Seas Fleet had been in hot pursuit of a numerically inferior enemy – Beatty's and Evan-Thomas's squadrons – and it should have appeared odd to both Scheer and Hipper that Beatty was leading them to the north-north-west, and then north-*east*, instead of running for home, which could only be westerly. The faster British battle-cruisers had drawn out of effective range, although the 15-inch guns of Evan-Thomas's four battleships had been punishing the Germans' leading ships each time they ventured too close. It must have been apparent to Scheer that Beatty was capable of getting clear away, yet he seemed to suspect no threat in the British commander's insistence on pulling around to easterly at 1735. The immediate result of this manœuvre was to put Beatty's battle-cruisers again within range of Hipper's, yet still Scheer recognised nothing more sinister than a tactical indiscretion on the part of the enemy, to be exploited. He did not know that the British Grand Fleet was only fifteen miles from him, that the two fleets were closing at a combined speed of forty miles per hour, and that Beatty was steering his own ships across Hipper's bows to mask Jellicoe's approach until the last moment.

Only at 1800, when Scheer was informed that three enemy *battleships* (Hood's battle-cruisers) had mysteriously appeared to his *easterly* did he begin to have misgivings. Hipper, not yet having sighted Hood's squadron, ordered *Regensburg*'s flotillas to attack in the hopeful assumption that the Invincibles were only three more battleships to be isolated and destroyed but, now wary, swung his own five battle-cruisers around to take station ahead of the German 3rd Battle Squadron, the van of the High Seas Fleet.

The inexpert reader attempting to follow these evolutions will have found them confusing – and, indeed, professional sailors would debate them hotly for years. However, at about 1815 on the evening of 31 May the situation was, simply, as follows:

1. The German High Seas Fleet's twenty-two battleships, pre-

ceded by Hipper's five battle-cruisers – all in line ahead – were steaming roughly north-eastward.

2. The British Grand Fleet's twenty-four battleships (shortly to be joined by Evan-Thomas's four) were closing fast, just over the horizon to the north-west, i.e., on the Germans' port bow. The British were deployed in six columns of fours, the columns aligned abreast, on a course roughly south-east.

3. The German Commander-in-Chief, Scheer, was completely unaware of the Grand Fleet's proximity, while the British Commander-in-Chief, Jellicoe, knew that the enemy was somewhere ahead but, because of inadequate intelligence from Beatty, did not know exactly where. He could make an educated guess, but was about to sight Scheer's fleet twenty minutes earlier than he had anticipated, and so have that much less time in which to redispose his fleet.

4. Beatty's four surviving battle-cruisers (*Lion, Princess Royal, Tiger* and *New Zealand*), battered but still game, were the only ships on either side to know what was happening, and it would have been helpful if Beatty had kept Jellicoe more informed. Beatty had been steaming ahead of, and on roughly the same course as, his German pursuers, leading them across the projected path of the Grand Fleet. Now, with the outriding ships of both British forces in visual contact, Beatty turned to starboard across the face of the High Seas Fleet's advance, led by Hipper's battle-cruisers, so that he (Beatty) was now in effect leading the Grand Fleet, albeit at a distance, to cross Scheer's 'T'.

5. There was, of course, a 'joker' in the pack. It was Hood's three battle-cruisers, *Invincible, Indomitable* and *Inflexible*, which had first steamed too far to the eastward but, turning, had roughly handled the four cruisers of the German 2nd Scouting Group and then – much more important – shrugged off a torpedo attack by three destroyer flotillas, inadvertently pulling those thirty warships away from the fleet positions from which they might have launched a damaging assault on Jellicoe's battleships. Nobody knew where Hood's battle-cruisers were, perhaps not even Hood himself, until, at 1820, *Invincible* shook free of the crawling mist to see Beatty's four ships on her port bow, enveloped in smoke and with guns pounding, but thrusting through the slate-coloured sea on an almost reciprocal course.

There was no time to question why only three ships followed astern of *Lion*. Flags climbed to *Invincible*'s yardarm, then fell. Hood wheeled about, *inside* Beatty's line, leading *Indomitable* and *Inflexible* into a U-turn to bring them abeam of Beatty's squadron, and finally forging ahead to station the three Invincibles neatly in the leading position. The manœuvre took three minutes – an exhibition of precision seamanship that would have earned approval on a calm day off Portland Bill at twelve knots. However, at twice that speed, with guns crashing, the sea torn by explosions and shrouded in smoke, it was a feat that might have provoked even Admiral Scheer's admiration.

Then, suddenly, Admiral Scheer had other problems. The far horizon, through gaps in the swirling haze, was twinkling with the flashes of guns – the big guns of the twenty-eight battleships of Jellicoe's Grand Fleet. For the British the day had come at last; for the Germans, *der Tag*.

The battle had now entered into its most crucial and bitter phase. The Germans were stunned. 'We had no intimation', confessed Commander Erich Raeder[1] aboard *Lützow*, 'that the British Grand Fleet was also on the scene.' Nothing, it seemed, could now prevent the trial of strength for which the British had waited so long. 'Remember tradition of Glorious First of June and avenge Belgium!' enthusiastically signalled Vice-Admiral Sir Cecil Burney in *Marlborough*, the first battleship to open fire – and Sub-Lieutenant His Royal Highness Prince Albert, later to be King George VI, ran to his action station in the forward turret of *Collingwood*.

However, unlike Nelson, Howe or Jervis, who were able to see all their own warships and the enemy's at the same time, Jellicoe's field of battle extended over some three hundred square miles, while the extent of visibility was only about five in any direction. He had brought more than a hundred ships into an area already being criss-crossed by Scheer's and Beatty's squadrons, and although he had repeatedly asked Beatty, by wireless, for the enemy's bearing, course and speed he had received only the vaguest references which, in any case, were probably invalid before they could be studied. By lamp and semaphore the battleships were asking each other, 'Where *is* the enemy?', 'What can you see?' It would take Jellicoe an appreciable time to redeploy his battle-fleet to exploit his massive advantage in gunpower. As delighted as Beatty's battle-cruiser men were to learn of the Grand Fleet's arrival, they must continue, un-aided by even the four battleships of Evan-Thomas (who had prematurely decided to transfer his allegiance to the Grand Fleet) to hold the German High Seas Fleet at bay.

The addition of Hood's three Invincibles to Beatty's line had an immediate effect. The range had closed to 9000 yards and, despite the unpredictable mist, they were firing rapidly and accurately at Hipper's ships, hitting repeatedly. *Lützow*, the flagship, was little more than a floating wreck, listing heavily and with her bows down, while *Derfflinger* had suffered 180 casualties, hit by twenty 12-inch shells which, her gunnery commander, George von Hase, observed, 'pierced our ship with terrific force and exploded with a tremendous roar which shook every seam and rivet'. *Seydlitz* was half awash, and all of *Von der Tann*'s main armament was disabled, although her captain, Zenker, maintained her in line to absorb some of the enemy's fire which might otherwise be directed against his companions. Only *Moltke* remained relatively unscathed but, although hideously damaged, the German ships were stoutly built and well served by their damage-control organisations. Moreover, astern of Hipper's squadron followed the seven modern battleships of the 3rd Battle Squadron, led by *König* – and battle-cruisers were not intended to fight battleships on equal terms.

*Invincible* had been hit several times; one shell had penetrated forward and another had torn through the flimsy two-inch plating below the after funnel. Several boats had been smashed, but fires were under control and nowhere was fighting efficiency impaired. In return she had scored hits on both *Lützow* and *Derfflinger* – and then, even more satisfying, on the 28,000-ton *König*. Hood, fighting his squadron from *Invincible*'s open bridge with the battle-cruiser's captain, Arthur Cay, was delighted. He telephoned his gunnery commander in the director-control, Hubert Dannreuther. 'Your firing's very good, Dannreuther,' he shouted above the shuddering noise. 'Keep at it as fast as you can. Every shot's telling.'

These were probably the last words that Hood spoke. The ubiquitous shroud of mist and crawling cordite smoke that had clung so persistently to the racing warships was suddenly wrenched aside and, simultaneously, the sun – only ninety minutes from setting – burst brilliantly from the westerly clouds. *Invincible*, at the head of the British line, was exposed, starkly silhouetted against a clear sky and only 8000 yards from the enemy. *Derfflinger*, at last steering out of station to avoid further punishment, fired her final salvo at a range from which it was almost impossible to miss, while the guns of *König*, following, pounced on the same target. It will never be known which of the two was responsible for *Invincible*'s destruction. A heavy shell tore through the roof-armour of the British battle-cruiser's 'Q' turret, amidships, and exploded in the gun-house. There was a secondary explosion as ready-use cordite in the chamber erupted, and officers and men died instantly. The searing flash ignited the cordite in the gun-loading cages, roared down the turret-trunk in which the protective doors were open, and burst ferociously into the cordite-handling room. 'Q' turret, trunk and magazine disintegrated. 'P' turret, adjacent, followed suit seconds later.

'A great crimson rose of flame,' said a horrified spectator in *Indomitable*, 'a hundred feet high and perhaps two hundred broad . . . climbed leisurely, contemptuously, with an awful majestic dignity to a good four hundred feet, at its top an immense baulk of ship's plating and many lesser bits. Then the deep red faded and there remained only a black pall below, merging into the general pall that the many ships' smoke at full speed was creating. . . .'

With all boilers ruptured and the entire midships gouged out of her, *Invincible*'s back broke between her second and third funnels. She sank in a welter of flame, steam and spitting cordite, as 'a gentle shower, like the first snowfall, of ashes fell or rather came drifting down' on the ships swerving past their dying sister.

Of 560 feet in length, and sinking in only 30 fathoms of water, the two halves of *Invincible* were still visible an hour later, when the battleship *Hercules* steamed across the debris-scattered position. Aboard *Hercules*, the naval observer for the Czar of Russia, Commodore G. Schoultz, writing furiously, noted that 'at 7.30 p.m. I am told from the fore-top that we are passing floating wreckage of a large ship. Looking over the port-side I see through my glasses two objects like sailing boats. They are very close together, and are apparently the stern and bow of a ship whose middle part is below the surface. English or German? The fore-top cannot answer, and we sweep past. . . .'

There were only six survivors from *Invincible*'s total crew of 1026. One of them was Commander Dannreuther, the gunnery officer, who claimed that he had 'simply stepped from the falling fore-top into the water', and another was the torpedo officer, Lieutenant Sandford. All clung to a raft among floating oil, filth and unidentifiable wreckage, but rose to their knees to cheer as the other ships of Beatty's squadron sped by, still firing at the enemy. Following vessels took them to be Germans, including the destroyer *Badger*, which hauled them aboard thirty minutes later – with an armed guard waiting.

Until about this time the action had been almost exclusively between the two opposing battle-cruiser forces, but was now developing into a full fleet engagement in which the battle-cruisers' role would become a subsidiary one – although not irrelevant. Both Beatty's and Hipper's squadrons were relegated to heavy-cruiser duties, their independent status ended. Beatty had lost three ships, but the six surviving were in good fighting condition; while Hipper's squadron, although its five were still afloat, could hardly be reckoned a viable fighting group. Minutes after the sinking of *Invincible* the entire High Seas Fleet was ordered by Scheer to reverse its course away from the British – not in succession (which would have been a prolonged and vulnerable manœuvre) but with all ships turning about simultaneously, so that by 1845 the long German line was retiring to the westward with Hipper's badly mauled battle-cruisers covering the rear. *Lützow* was so severely damaged as to be almost useless, and the destroyer *G39* was called alongside to transfer the Vice-Admiral to *Seydlitz*; but this vessel, too, was found to be totally unfit for flagship duty. *Derfflinger* was ordered temporarily to assume command until Hipper could board *Moltke* – it took him almost two hours – and hoist his flag again.

Jellicoe had already been poorly served by Beatty with regard to intelligence, and would now continue to be neglected by his cruisers, whose most important task was to act as his 'eyes'. None of the many ships that watched Scheer's turn-away (not even *Iron Duke*'s own gunnery control) reported it to the Commander-in-Chief, and some thirty minutes elapsed before Jellicoe decided to turn the Grand Fleet – now in line ahead – to south-west-by-south and so more nearly follow the enemy's westerly course. Meanwhile Beatty, in *Lion*, having resumed leadership of the battle-cruiser force, had reduced speed to 18 knots to enable the main fleet to overhaul, and then, at 1853, apparently attempted a wide S turn for the same reason, but instead turned *Lion* in a complete circle. At a later date Beatty would claim that he had initially ordered a 90° turn to starboard which, because of a gyro compass failure, became one of 180° which he then corrected by ordering a 180° turn to port. This explanation, however, does not stand up to scrutiny, since the 'overshoot' of 90° to starboard would have been corrected by only a 90° return to port. In fact, *Lion* steered a complete 360° turn. Beatty, after his first order (90° to starboard?), left the bridge to examine his ship's damage, and it is highly probable that nobody remaining on the bridge had the initiative to halt the evolution. *Lion* continued blithely to turn full circle.

Jellicoe would confess that 'at this stage it was not clear whether the enemy battle fleet was ahead of our battle fleet or on the starboard beam' but, in the event, it hardly mattered because, a few minutes later, Scheer *again* reversed course and, from fifteen miles, steered directly for Jellicoe's line, led by an attack force of twenty-one destroyers and, of course, Hipper's ravaged battle-cruisers.

The German Commander-in-Chief's reasons for this bizarre manœuvre are still not entirely clear; even Scheer's own explanations, later, were less than convincing. He had been leading the High Seas Fleet westward, into the North Sea, sunset was only an hour away, and neither he nor Jellicoe would relish a night action. Scheer would undoubtedly have been concerned that he was drawing farther away from his bases and, if the British cut off his line of retreat during the night, then the High Seas Fleet would be in a perilous situation next day. However, he had also been misled with regard to the British battle-fleet's position and deployment; he still believed that Hood's ships were battleships. Probably Scheer was juggling with several possibilities in the Micawberish hope that one of them would turn out well. The Germans' sudden *volte-face* would certainly surprise the British, and the initiative would change hands. Scheer might well cross the 'T' of the Grand Fleet's rear, give help to *Wiesbaden* (wrecked and waterlogged but still just afloat) and finally, if the German fleet broke through, be that much nearer to Heligoland with a clear path eastward.

None of these things happened because *Southampton*, one of the few British cruisers to achieve any distinction that day, reported the enemy's approach at 1904 and, anyway, Scheer had misjudged the position and course of the Grand Fleet, which was steaming across *his* 'T' when the battered *Lützow*, leading Hipper's battle-cruisers and the German 3rd Battle Squadron, emerged from the westerly mist, 9000 yards to starboard.

The British could hardly believe their eyes – nor, aboard *Friedrich der Grosse*, could Admiral Scheer. 'The entire arc stretching from north to east was a sea of fire,' he declared. 'The flash from the muzzles of the guns was distinctly seen through the mist and smoke on the horizon, though the ships themselves were not distinguishable.' He had steered his fleet into a semi-circle of enemy guns and was about to be punished for it. *Lützow*, pounded by both *Colossus* and *Collingwood* at only 8400 yards, at last reeled out of station, afire, now having been hit by twenty-four heavy projectiles. Astern of the tortured German battle-cruisers the battleships were also being repeatedly found – *König* ten times and *Grosser Kurfürst* eight. 'We were in a regular death trap,' observed von Hase in *Derfflinger*. 'There was only one way of escape from this unfavourable tactical situation; to turn the line about and withdraw on the opposite course.'

This time, however, a withdrawal was not going to be a simple matter of reversing course; the enemy was too close and would have to be distracted. At 1912 Scheer signalled '9R' – 'Panzerkreuzer ran an den feind' ('Battle-cruisers close the enemy and ram').

With *Lützow*[2] in a sinking condition and clawing away to the south-west, *Derfflinger* led *Seydlitz*, *Moltke* and *Von der Tann* in what could only be a suicidal attack, and within two minutes had two turrets blown to pieces, her control system disabled, and was ablaze fore and aft with 150 more dead. It was highly unlikely that the four ships would have survived long enough to ram, but fortunately, at 1915, Scheer also ordered his destroyer flotillas to attack with torpedoes while simultaneously making smoke. Only seventeen of an original fifty-one were in a position to comply, but these overhauled the battle-cruisers and flung themselves into the shell-torn cauldron ahead, turned to present their tubes – at extreme range, 8000 yards – and loosed thirty-one torpedoes.

All missed – a poor reward for such heroism – and, indeed, only ten carried as far as the British line. However, although several of the German destroyers were hit by heavy projectiles, only *S35* broke her back and sank with her own men and those she had previously rescued from *V29*. Nor did the German battle-fleet, replying desperately to the overwhelming British fire, achieve any greater success. During the entire exchange only *Colossus*, commanded by Captain A. D. P. R. Pound,[3] was hit with minor damage to her fore superstructure. Earlier, at 1855, *Marlborough* had struck, or had been struck by, a torpedo which reduced her to 17 knots, possibly fired by the stricken *Wiesbaden* but equally likely to have been any of a number of distance-run nomads floating that day.

It was now, however, that Jellicoe made the decision which would be debated in every naval college for decades. Like most senior officers on both sides he overestimated the effectiveness of torpedoes – the *bête noire* of the conservative sailor – and the smoke-obscured sortie by the enemy's destroyers suggested that the Grand Fleet was about to be subjected to massed torpedo attacks. It was not this presumption (which was a reasonable one) that would be later questioned, but his reaction to it.

It was never disputed that the best counter-measure in the event of a torpedo attack was to present a ship's narrowest profile, i.e., bows or stern, and to 'comb the tracks' of the missiles, which were usually visible. There was some advantage in turning *toward* approaching torpedoes; damage sustained to the bows was likely to be less crippling than the destruction of screws and rudder. On the other hand, in turning and steering *away*, a ship had more time to manœuvre evasively and might also outrun the torpedoes' limited range.

Jellicoe chose the more cautious alternative. He turned his battle-ships two points, then another two points – 45° – *away* from the enemy.

Assuming that Scheer was holding to his last-reported course (and nobody thought it necessary to inform Jellicoe otherwise), the British Commander-in-Chief's avoiding action would have lost the Grand Fleet only two or three thousand yards, but, with Scheer turning away during the confusion, the distance between the two fleets was widening at the rate of twenty-five miles per hour. The Germans began to breathe again. Out of range, they wheeled to south-westward, and that was the last seen of them by Jellicoe's battleships. The light was failing, sunset was only thirty minutes away, and in an hour it would be completely dark.

Only Beatty's six surviving Splendid Cats had not turned away. They were still exchanging salvoes with the enemy, and at 1945 Beatty wirelessed Scheer's bearing and course to Jellicoe. Minutes later he pleaded: 'Submit van of battleships follow battle-cruisers. We can then cut off whole of enemy battle fleet.' It was still just possible, but now the nearest British battleships, the 2nd Battle Squadron, would need two hours to come up with the scene of action, so Beatty held to his guns alone. At 2017 he closed to 10,000 yards of his old foes, Hipper's battle-cruisers. Before they could seek sanctuary on the disengaged side of the High Seas Fleet, *Derfflinger*'s last turret was demolished and all *Seydlitz*'s fore-bridge personnel were killed. *Moltke*, hitherto relatively undamaged, had shipped 1000 tons of water.

Beatty now turned his attention to the German 2nd Battle Squadron of six elderly battleships led by Rear-Admiral Mauve in *Deutschland*, who had begged Scheer to be allowed to accompany the fleet to sea on the previous evening. The 11-inch guns of the slow 13,200-tonners were no match for even the reduced firepower of the battle-cruisers, and *Hessen, Pommern*[4] and *Schleswig-Holstein* were all hit as Mauve broke away for the westward.

With darkness now fallen, firing ceased; it was no longer possible to recognise enemy from friend.

And darkness marked the end of the battle between the big ships of the two fleets. During the night there would continue to be fierce and confused encounters between opposing light cruisers and destroyers, resulting in a number of casualties, but neither commander-in-chief was sure of his position in relation to the other. Jellicoe, whose ships were not trained for night fighting, did not wish to provoke a night action unnecessarily, but had every reason to believe that, since the Grand Fleet was astride the enemy's line of retreat, there would be ample opportunity at daylight to locate Scheer again and, this time, annihilate him. Scheer had only one desperate desire – to reach the sanctuary of the Jade estuary.

He succeeded, miraculously. Both fleets were steering a southerly course with the British nearer to the German coastline – which Jellicoe correctly suspected to be the situation – but neither was aware that Scheer, nursing his damaged ships, was making only sixteen knots and falling progressively astern, which meant that at 2130 the High Seas Fleet collided with the light cruiser and de-stroyer screen covering Jellicoe's rear, and broke through it only three miles astern of *Barnham*, *Valiant* and *Malaya*. The captains of these ships could see the action being fought but refrained from doing anything because *someone else was probably seeing and reporting it and, anyway, they must wait for orders from their divisional commander*. The log of *Bellerophon* noted that 'there was quite a lot of firing going on to the north-east and a cruiser seemed to be on fire pretty badly. [Later] there was further firing from astern and . . . intermittent firing on the port quarter. *Otherwise the night passed without incident*.' The Grand Fleet continued to steam determinedly southward, and now there was nothing between Scheer and the Horns Reef light-ship.

The last shot of the battle was fired at 0330 by the light cruiser *Champion*, who sighted four enemy destroyers which subsequently fled into the dawn mist. It was a pity that *Champion* did not pursue, for these vessels – *G37*, *G38*, *G40* and *V45* – were carrying 1250 officers and men taken off *Lützow*, which had been finally despatched by a German torpedo shortly before.

By now, however, Scheer's battle-fleet was thankfully anchoring in the Jade estuary, and during the next few hours scores of smaller ships would be limping into Cuxhaven, Heligoland and Bremer-haven. The entire High Seas Fleet had steamed safely over three British submarines lying on the bottom, off-shore, which knew noth-ing of the Jutland battle until they regained their Yarmouth base eight days later.

If, even so, during early forenoon, an orbiting satellite could have surveyed the grey wind-whipped expanses of the North Sea, it would have seen hundreds of warships still scattered from the Orkneys across the Great Fisher Bank, from Wight to the Skagerrak – long files of battleships, battle-cruisers, armoured cruisers, squadrons of light cruisers and flotillas of destroyers. All flew the White Ensign, none the black-crossed flag of the Imperial German Navy. A few, usually solitary, holed and listing, struggled westward into the teeth of a rising wind and sea already beginning to disperse the great slicks of oil that floated with splintered boats, Carley floats, sodden hammocks and broken mess-stools, but most of all the tumbled dozens of seamen's corpses, clustering together in final comradeship.

Below decks in the broken ships of both sides the surgeons' battles were continuing to be fought, more so in those British vessels that still had to claw their way painfully homeward, often with decks wrecked and smoke-filled, with no electrical power, the only lighting being from candles and torches. Typical of so many was the scene in the crippled *Warrior*, who would fight gamely to bring her crew to a home port before the sea claimed her at 0800.

A bathroom forward of the sick bay was selected as an operating-theatre. As soon as it was ready the surgeons set to work. . . . All through the long hours they toiled, knowing little or nothing of what passed upon the seas about them, of the position of their ship, of the chances of personal safety. The injuries received were of the most terrible kind. Several bodies were rent in pieces; many limbs were torn from bodies; some men were stripped naked. Among the operations performed by the light of the guttering candles, upon a sinking ship in a gale of wind, were amputations, ligaturing of bleeding vessels, the removal of shell splinters. . . .

There were many burials at sea on that first day of June – ninety-five alone from the quarterdeck of *Lion*, including the chaplain and a surgeon-probationer who had unaccountably been handling ammunition in 'Q' turret magazine. Yet most of the British fleet remained at sea. The few compelled to seek the havens of Rosyth, Aberdeen, the Tyne and Humber transferred their blanket-wrapped wounded by cargo-hoists to tugs and lighters alongside and then to ambulances waiting on the jetties.

On Tyneside dockyard workers shouted abuse at the exhausted sailors; the German press was already announcing a crushing defeat for the Royal Navy. England's invincibility on the seas was broken, crowed German headlines. The High Seas Fleet had torn the venerable Trafalgar legend to shreds. Although, as early as 2145 on Thursday, 1 June, Jellicoe was able to tell the Admiralty that his battle-fleet was 'again ready for action and at four hours' notice', it was not for another two days that Whitehall declared that 'the German fleet, aided by low visibility, avoided prolonged action with our main forces, and soon after these appeared on the scene the enemy returned to port, though not before receiving severe damage from our battleships . . .'.

But it was too late and too constrained. For the first time in several hundred years, it seemed to many, the Navy's image of infallibility was in doubt.

If the action were to be judged by a score-sheet of ships sunk and men killed, then Scheer was justified in claiming a victory. The

British had lost three battle-cruisers, three armoured cruisers and eight destroyers against the Germans' one old battleship, one battle-cruiser, four light cruisers and five destroyers; 6097 British were killed, 2551 German; the numbers wounded were almost identical – 510 and 507 respectively.

Cold figures, however, did not tell the whole story, which would not be apparent until the end of the war. They did not explain that, although three of Beatty's battle-cruisers had been sunk, the remaining six were still an efficient fighting squadron, while Hipper, having lost *Lützow*, had only one ship, *Moltke*, which was better than a floating wreck. *Seydlitz*, listing eight degrees and drawing forty-three feet of water (twice her normal draught) crawled into the Jade, stern first, after twice running aground, and would not be seaworthy again until mid-September. *Derfflinger*, almost as badly damaged, would be under repair until late October, and it was necessary to put *König, Grosser Kurfurst* and *Markgraf* immediately into dry dock to save them. On paper the High Seas Fleet's score was flattering, but the German warships would never again put to sea with the intention of provoking an action with the British. 'Our fleet's losses are very severe,' confessed a senior German officer. 'On June 1st it was clear to any thinking person that this battle must, and would be, the last.' It was. A New York newspaper had the final word: 'The German Fleet has assaulted its jailor, but it is still in jail.'

In Britain, disappointment with regard to Jellicoe's failure to pursue more determinedly Scheer's ships was widespread, and understandably so, but when emotions on both sides had cooled Rear-Admiral Werner Stichling, German Navy, was able to say:

> The British superior fleet could have, perhaps, the next day inflicted heavy damage on the German fleet but not without damage to itself, [but] nothing would have changed, even in the improbable eventuality of the annihilation of the German fleet. The fleet was for all practical purposes paralysed in its harbours and could never again mount a decisive assault. The British Admiralty had no need to take any risk. One could go so far as to say that a crushing defeat of the High Seas Fleet would have had a completely unanticipated effect . . . the total German ship-building capacity and the total personnel of the navy would have been put to work on the U-boat fleet. . . .

Jutland had been an acid test for Fisher's 'speed instead of armour' obsession and, *prima facie*, the British battle-cruisers had failed. Equivocally, however, the apparent ease with which three of

Beatty's ships had been destroyed was less the result of flimsy armour than the sensitivity of British cordite when exposed to flash and the careless handling of that cordite in magazine-areas. It had always been said that cordite, a gelatinised smokeless powder, would not *explode* unless tightly confined – i.e., within a gun-breech – but would only *burn*, comparatively slowly. Secondly, while German propellant charges were not removed from their protective brass containers until they arrived at the gun-breech, in British ships the silk-encased charges were taken from their bins at magazine-level before being transferred to the hoist-trays in the turret-trunk. Furthermore, in their enthusiasm to maintain a rapid loading-rate, magazine-parties were tempted to 'pile up' exposed charges in the handling room, ready for hoisting, and similarly to ignore a number of other anti-fire measures. It is significant that, among the British battle-cruisers, only four turrets were penetrated by shells but three ships blew up. Among the German ships nine turrets were penetrated (with eight being burned out) but no ships were blown up.

There were other, less relevant, contributory factors. Undoubtedly the gunnery of Beatty's 1st and 2nd Squadrons (excepting *Queen Mary*) was less accurate than that of Hipper's ships during the initial phase of the battle, but this was the penalty for insufficient practice. Hood's three Invincibles performed markedly better, and the shooting of Evan-Thomas's battleships was extremely good. In the final analysis there was little difference between the number of *hits per gun* achieved by both fleets (about 0.4 per gun, 11-inch and above) and, taking into account the larger number of British guns participating (344 to 244) and the generally heavier calibre of British armament, it is plain that the German warships had to absorb heavier punishment than their enemies. They survived because of their heavier armour-to-tonnage ratio, more subdivisioning below decks, and an excellent damage-control discipline which involved counter-flooding, drainage and pumping to keep vessels on an even keel despite the intake of thousands of tons of water.

Perhaps, however, the major reason for the miscarriage of British hopes was the failure of so many commanders to provide the flagship with information on the enemy's changes of course and disposition, without which Jellicoe could only guess at Scheer's intentions. Commodore William Goodenough, in *Southampton*, was almost alone in trying to keep Jellicoe informed, and even he neglected to report the German fleet's crucial reversal of course at 1835. Throughout the entire action the cruisers neglected their most important role, and this time the vagaries of wireless communication could not be blamed. Intoxicated by the vastness of the occasion, everyone seemed to be assuming that someone else was advising the Commander-in-Chief. Nobody did.

The post-Jutland disenchantment with the battle-cruiser was not ameliorated by the knowledge that the hulls of four more ships of this type had already been launched, a fifth was about to be, and yet a further four were to be laid down before the end of 1916. The price demanded for high speed was too great, it was claimed. Was it logical to persevere with these flimsily protected ships when the new, massively armoured and oil-fired 'Queen Elizabeth' battleships – virtually unsinkable – were capable of twenty-four knots anyway?

It would, however, be many years before the Navy saw the last of the Fisher legacy.

## *Notes*

1    Later Grand Admiral Raeder, Commander-in-Chief of Hitler's navy until 1943. Sentenced to life imprisonment at Nuremberg but released in 1955.

2    *Lützow*, with 8300 tons of water in her, and on the point of foundering, was finally torpedoed by the destroyer *G38* during the early hours of the following morning after her surviving crew had been taken off.

3    Later Admiral of the Fleet Sir Dudley Pound, First Sea Lord during the Second World War until October 1943.

4    *Pommern* would be torpedoed by British destroyers during the early hours of the following morning, to explode with the loss of her entire 830 crew.

# Chapter Nine

*The Rhadamanthus project and the unwanted hybrids – flying trials – actions off Norway and Heligoland – the birth of the super battle-cruiser*

As part of the 1914–15 warship-building programme it had been intended that the five 'R'-class battleships laid down during the previous year (*Revenge, Royal Oak, Royal Sovereign, Ramillies* and *Resolution*) should be supplemented by three more, slightly improved in several particulars and provisionally named *Resistance, Repulse* and *Renown*. In December 1914, however, Jackie Fisher, convinced by the performance of the battle-cruisers at Heligoland Bight and the Falklands that these were the warships of the future, ordered that the contracts for two of the projected battleships should be cancelled and substituted by others for two battle-cruisers. The new ships, it was specified, would mount four 15-inch guns in two turrets, twenty 4-inch guns, and be capable of 32 knots. Within twenty-four hours Fisher added a third 15-inch turret (a total of six guns) which, in fact, consumed all the 15-inch guns available. A six-gun ship was incompatible with the standard procedure for eight-gun salvo-firing, but this was a complication that the First Sea Lord could shrug aside. Nobody argued with Jackie Fisher.

To baffle the landsmen of the Cabinet, the new design project carried the title 'Rhadamanthus: Ocean-Going Battle-Cruiser', but before completion, and too late for dispute, would become simply 'Very Fast Battle-Cruiser', and there is little doubt that Fisher added '– for Baltic Project'.

With the drawings approved, incredibly, within ten days, the keels of both ships were laid down on Clydebank on 25 January 1915 (Fisher's birthday), and the building-time of just over a year and a half for ships of 28,000 tons was an outstanding dockyard achievement. The original intention to install an entirely new system of turbine propulsion was abandoned, and the machinery designed for *Tiger* was repeated, but with an additional three boilers (making a total of forty-two). There were a number of other constructional short cuts, including the omission of wooden planking on the weather-decks, which were merely provided with metal foot-strips to improve grip, and torpedo-net defences were dispensed with.

Speed and gunnery trials were carried out off Arran during August and September 1916. The results have not survived, but subsequently both ships were good for 32 knots. At speeds above 25 knots vibration was severe, with the quarterdeck awash at full speed, and it was necessary to raise the height of the forward funnel in both ships by ten feet to lift fumes away from the bridge, but they were otherwise good sea-boats and steady gun-platforms. However, *Renown*'s gunnery trials strained her hull considerably, and in later years both ships' frequent need for dockyard attention would earn them the nicknames 'Refit' and 'Repair'.

Completed, *Renown* and *Repulse* incorporated a number of novel features. They were, of course, the longest (794 feet over all) and the fastest capital ships afloat,[1] and were the first to have torpedo-protection bulges built *within* the hull proper instead of outside, which meant a more finely tempered, leaner line. The superstructure was uniquely economical in layout, and searchlight platforms were splayed from the funnels. Finally, for the first time, the secondary 4-inch guns were mounted in triples, and since, hitherto, these guns had not yet been even mounted in pairs the innovation was many years ahead of its time. It was a brave experiment which, in theory, allowed for a spectacular concentration of fire – thirteen guns abeam, eight ahead, or twelve astern. In practice, unfortunately, the triple mounting was a disappointment. Probably because of rushed development, the design was clumsy, with separate instead of co-ordinated mechanisms requiring a crew of thirty-two men to serve each three-gun installation. The desired rate of fire was never achieved, and it is tragic that *Repulse* would be defending herself unsuccessfully with these same manually worked and less-than-adequate guns against swarming Japanese bombers and torpedo aircraft twenty-five years later.

*Renown* and *Repulse* joined the Grand Fleet for working up in September 1916, and met critical eyes as they steamed into Scapa Flow. Their armour had been based on the scale provided for *Indefatigable*, and everyone knew what had happened to her. Along the entire length of each new battle-cruiser were two uninterrupted rows of scuttles, which meant hulls almost devoid of protection; above a 6-inch belt that extended only 26 inches below the waterline, the sides were of merely 1½-inch plating. These two ships, well gunned, fast, and outstandingly handsome, were 'tin cans'.

It was an assessment not ignored by Jellicoe. In October he recommended heavier deck protection for the crowns of the magazines and over the engine-rooms. This reinforcement to both ships was carried out at Rosyth – adding 500 tons to their tonnage calculated at design stage – before they were allocated to Beatty's Battle-Cruiser Force. Nothing, however, could be done about that paltry side-armour.

Before the end of 1916, Jellicoe had been appointed First Sea Lord, handing over command of the Grand Fleet to Beatty. The battle-cruiser force, reduced to two squadrons, was now led by Vice-Admiral William Pakenham, and the arrival of the two Renowns, even if there was a problem with regard to their employment, brought his complement up to nine.

| 1st B.C.S. | 2nd B.C.S. |
|---|---|
| *Lion* | *Australia* |
| *Tiger* | *New Zealand* |
| *Princess Royal* | *Inflexible* |
| *Renown* | *Indomitable* |
| *Repulse* | |

If the new battle-cruisers had been eyed askance, however, there was a greater shock in store for the Grand Fleet – or, more accurately, three shocks. They were named *Courageous, Glorious* and *Furious*.

Jackie Fisher had referred to them as 'large light cruisers', a contradiction in terms calculated to deceive the Treasury, which had already approved the construction of light cruisers but would almost certainly oppose any suggestion of battle-cruisers. When built, *Courageous, Glorious* and *Furious* would defy any sensible classification, and the Navy dubbed them 'Outrageous', 'Curious' and 'Spurious'. However, they were later officially listed as battle-cruisers, and must so be described.

All three, of course, were figments of Fisher's dream of an amphibious operation in the Baltic. 'The *Furious* and all her breed', he claimed, 'were not built for salvoes. They were built for Berlin, and that's why they drew so little water and were built so fragile.' Indeed, their specification called for a draught of 22 feet – five feet less than any ship of comparable size – to facilitate inshore operations, while their massive guns 'were built to make it impossible for the Germans to prevent the Russians from landing on the Pomeranian coast'. In hulls larger than any battleship's but ready to crumple under the impact of only modest-calibre projectiles, *Courageous* and *Glorious*

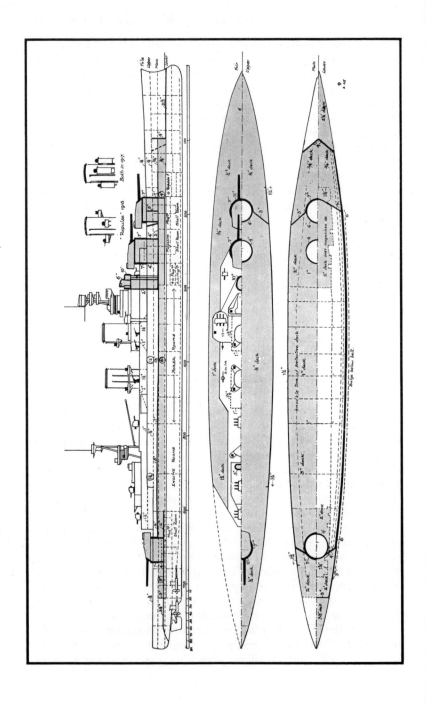

## 'RENOWN'-class BATTLE-CRUISERS

|  | *Renown* | *Repulse* |
|---|---|---|
| *Builder* | Fairfield | J. Brown & Co. |
| *Laid down* | 25 January 1915 | 25 January 1915 |
| *Launched* | 4 March 1916 | 8 January 1916 |
| *Completed* | 20 September 1916 | 18 August 1916 |

*Dimensions*
Length, waterline: 750 feet. Beam 90 feet. Maximum draught 27.5 feet. Displacement: *Renown* 27,947 tons; *Repulse* 27,333 tons. Complement (peacetime) 967.

*Armament*
Six 15-inch guns; seventeen 4-inch guns; two 3-inch AA guns; two 21-inch torpedo-tubes, submerged.

*Armoured Protection*
Belt of 6-, 4-, 3- and 1½-inch thickness. Turrets 11-inch, barbettes 7-inch above belt. Conning tower 10-inch. Forecastle 1½-inch, upper deck ½-inch, main deck 3- reducing to 1-inch.

*Engines*
Brown-Curtis turbines of 120,000 horsepower driving four screws. Designed speed 31.5 knots. No record of best speeds exists, but *Renown* achieved a mean 32.68 knots on trials and both were good for 32 knots in service.

*Fuel*
Oil: 4243 tons. Consumption at full speed was about 1400 tons a day.

*General*
Built in a record time for their size, *Renown* and *Repulse* were, on completion, the fastest capital ships afloat. They were the first warships to mount their 4-inch guns in triples, and the first to have' bulges enclosed within the hull structure proper.

would mount four 15-inch guns and *Furious* (initially) two 18-inch guns, the heaviest afloat in the world. Speeds would not be less than 32 knots.

If intended for shore bombardment, such large guns would have been more profitably mounted in monitors; the Dardanelles operation had demonstrated how severely large floating targets could be punished by shore batteries. However, a Baltic offensive had not been talked about since Fisher departed from the Admiralty – and had been allowed little credence before. It would have demanded far greater resources than the French or British could possibly provide, while Russia was already near to breaking-point. Designed for a project that would never materialise, it was difficult to imagine a role in which the three new ships could be usefully employed.

Nor was their irrelevance mitigated by their appearance. A single large funnel precisely amidships, partnered by a lightweight super-structure and mainmast, presented a profile that had none of the aggression of *Tiger* or the majesty of *Renown* and *Repulse*, in return for which a sailor can forgive many sins. The secondary armament of *Courageous* and *Glorious* – eighteen 4-inch guns – were disposed in the triple mountings which were to prove unsuccessful, but this is a retrospective criticism. *Furious*, completed later than her sisters, mounted ten single 5.5-inch guns. Her two eighteen-inch guns[2] (reduced to one before she was commissioned) each weighed 150 tons and fired a projectile of 3600 lb, but the rate of fire was so slow and the range-finding of two-gun salvoes so difficult that the chances of ever hitting at long range must have been almost non-existent. In 1918 two spare 18-inch guns were fitted in the monitors *Lord Clive* and *General Wolfe*, but the war ended before any real assessment could be made of their effectiveness.

*Courageous* and *Glorious* were commissioned in October 1916, but were not regarded as *completed* until January 1917, when both were temporarily assigned to the 3rd Light Cruiser Squadron, with *Glorious* flying the flag of Vice-Admiral Trevylyan Napier. *Furious*, however, even before leaving her Tyneside dock, was undergoing sweeping modification, and would soon become completely un-recognisable as a warship type-class. She was about to become the world's first true aircraft-carrier.

Jutland had demonstrated the need for ships fast enough to keep up with the battle-fleet and able to fly off and recover aircraft more efficiently than by the hoist-out, hoist-on procedure employed by vessels like *Engadine*. A lengthy take-off deck was indicated, and to apply such an innovation to *Furious* it was necessary to dispense with her forward 18-inch turret. The flight-platform, laid between superstructure and bows, was 160 feet long, with a hangar accommodating ten aircraft below it. The after 18-inch turret was left *in situ*.

The ugly hybrid carried out her trials during June, July and August 1917. Taking off presented few problems, and the first successful landing was made by Squadron Leader E. H. Dunning in a Sopwith Pup on 3 August. With *Furious* steaming into the wind, Dunning approached from astern, jockeyed around the superstructure, and sat the aircraft down on the flight-platform as he switched off the ignition. There was no arrester gear yet, so waiting deck personnel grappled with the plane while it was still several feet off the planks and dragged it to a halt. Such a haphazard procedure could hardly be considered satisfactory, so Dunning instructed that, for his second attempt, his machine should not be handled until it had touched down. This time, however, a tyre burst as he landed. The light plane spun in the wind and, before it could be halted, plunged over the side as *Furious* ploughed on. Dunning was drowned.

It was at this stage of semi-development that *Furious*, never a credible battle-cruiser nor yet a successful aircraft-carrier, joined *Courageous* and *Glorious* in the North Sea, the odd trio constituting the 1st Cruiser Squadron. On only one occasion were they to be aggressively deployed in company – on 17 October, when they were ordered with other units to intercept enemy raiders that had attacked a convoy of Scandinavian ships off the coast of Norway. The interception attempt was initiated too late to achieve anything; the convoy lost nine merchant ships and two escorting destroyers, and *Furious*, whose participation (with one 18-inch gun mounted aft) was of doubtful relevance, was immediately returned to her builders for further modification. This entailed the removal of her remaining big gun and the substitution of an after flight-deck of 300 feet, a second hangar and lifts fore and aft. Now she was an aircraft-carrier pure and simple, to be subjected to further reconstruction between the wars and serve with distinction during the Second World War. She would survive, to be broken up in Dalmuir and Troon in 1948.

The problems of getting a flying machine into the air from the deck of a conventional warship had been studied by the Royal Naval Air Service since 1912, and experiments with light cruisers had been sufficiently promising to justify attention being given to larger vessels, but Jellicoe had been unwilling to equip capital ships with aircraft because of the undesirability of battleships turning out of line in order to launch into the wind. However, by 1917 aircraft were becoming more reliable and the Grand Fleet Aircraft Committee

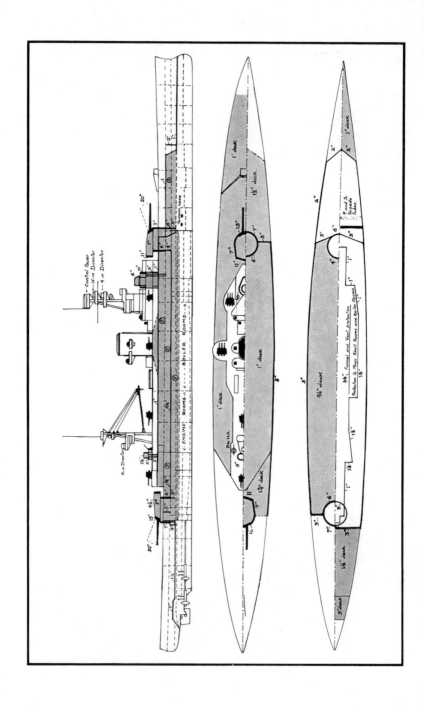

# 'COURAGEOUS'-class LIGHT BATTLE-CRUISERS

|  | *Courageous* | *Glorious* |
|---|---|---|
| *Builder* | Armstrong-Whitworth | Harland & Wolff |
| *Laid down* | May 1915 | May 1915 |
| *Launched* | 5 February 1916 | 20 April 1916 |
| *Completed* | January 1917 | January 1917 |

*Dimensions*
Length, waterline: 735 feet. Beam 81 feet. Maximum draught 23.4 feet. Displacement 22,690 tons. Complement 840.

*Armament*
Four 15-inch guns; eighteen 4-inch guns; two 3-inch HA guns; sixteen 21-inch torpedo-tubes.

*Armoured Protection*
3-inch belt reducing to 2-inch. Turrets, 13-inch faces, 11-inch rears, 7- and 4½-inch sides. Conning tower 10-inch. Upper decks 1-inch, others up to 1¾ inches with 3 inches over steering.

*Engines*
Parsons' all-geared turbines of 90,000 horsepower driving four screws. Designed speed 31–2 knots, exceeded by both ships on service.

*Fuel*
Oil: 3160 tons.

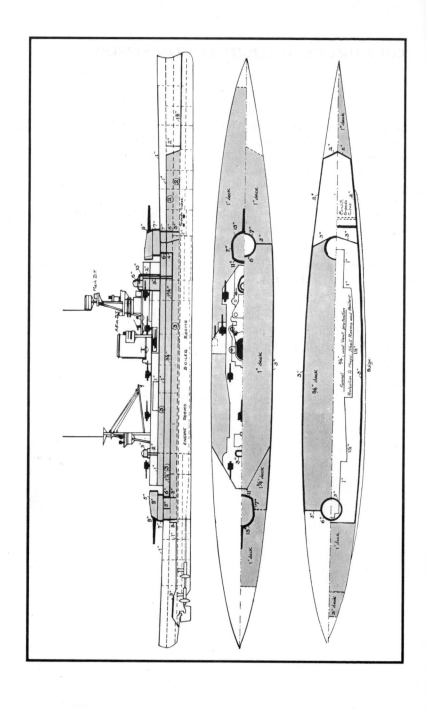

## *FURIOUS*, LIGHT BATTLE-CRUISER

*Builder*          Armstrong-Whitworth
*Laid down*     June 1915
*Launched*      15 August 1916
*Completed*    July 1917

*Dimensions*
Length, waterline: 750 feet. Beam 88 feet. Maximum draught 20
feet. Displacement 22,890 tons. Complement 880.

*Armament*
Two 18-inch guns (as laid down, one as commissioned); ten 5.5-inch
guns; five 3-inch HA guns; eighteen 21-inch torpedo-tubes.

*Armoured Protection*
Sides 2–3-inch armour over 1-inch plating. Turrets, 13-inch faces,
11-inch rears, 7- and 4½-inch sides. Conning tower 10-inch. Upper
decks 1-inch, others up to 1¾ inches with 3 inches over steering.

*Engines*
Brown-Curtis all-geared turbines of 94,000 horsepower driving four
screws. Designed speed 31½ knots.

*Fuel*
Oil: 3160 tons.

had developed a flying-off platform which, mounted on the roof of a gun turret, could be trained as required and a machine launched without the ship leaving her station.

*Repulse* was the first capital ship to be fitted with the new platform, and on 1 October 1917 – only a few weeks after Dunning had plunged to his death from the deck of *Furious* – Squadron Leader Rutland (earlier of *Engadine*) lifted off an identical single-seater Sopwith Pup from the roof of *Repulse*'s forward 'B' turret, which was turned 45° off the bow. On 8 October he repeated the experiment from a similar platform over the after 'Y' turret, which was trained 30° before the beam and the aircraft flown off the *rear* of the turret.

In a wood-and-wire machine, with an engine of 130 horsepower, and in complete ignorance of the consequences when the chocks were snatched from the undercarriage – except that the last pilot was dead – this was a feat that demanded as much courage as would be necessary to take an aircraft through the sound barrier many years later. Rutland proved the practicability of launching from capital ships, and both *Repulse* and *Renown* were provided with permanent fore and aft turret platforms which would be retained until replaced by midships catapults during the 1930s.

Aboard *Lion*, Beatty's flagship and then Pakenham's, was a seventeen-year-old midshipman, recently graduated from Dartmouth, named by courtesy Lord Louis Mountbatten. He was the second son of Prince Louis of Battenberg, now the 1st Marquess of Milford Haven. The young Louis was soon to transfer to *Queen Elizabeth*, again Beatty's flagship, but would meet with battle-cruisers again, and thirty-eight years later would not only assume the post that his father had been compelled to relinquish – First Sea Lord – but would also be appointed Chief of the Defence Staff, chairman of the Chiefs of Staff Committee, the last Viceroy and the first Governor-General of India.

The last significant sea-action of the war, like the very first, was a confused exchange and, similarly, involved the Splendid Cats, now under Pakenham, who, however, did not enjoy quite the same cavalier freedom of activity as had Beatty earlier. Beatty, now Commander-in-Chief, kept Pakenham on a tight rein and had made it clear that the battle-cruisers were an integral part of the Grand Fleet, not an independent force. Otherwise Beatty had suggested no sweeping changes in the Navy's role. He accepted Jellicoe's philosophy that massive fleet-actions in the North Sea were unlikely to solve anything and so should not be deliberately provoked. Time was on the side of the Allies. Six American battleships and several destroyer flotillas had already joined the Grand Fleet and, although the Navy was beginning to suffer a bad press as a result of its lack of initiative, it was plain that a High Seas Fleet confined to and impotent in its harbours was a cheaper alternative to another Jutland.

In any case, notwithstanding Beatty's superiority of 43 capital ships to Scheer's 24, the Grand Fleet was embarrassed by a shortage of destroyers, increasing numbers of which were being detached to anti-submarine and convoy escort duties. It was the unrestricted U-boat offensive that now represented the greater threat, and it was not one that the British were well equipped to counter. However, by late 1917 the Navy's strategy was clear-cut – to defeat the U-boats by denying their passage into the Atlantic, protect convoyed merchant ships against those that succeeded, and allow the enemy's big ships and their crews' morale to deteriorate at their anchorages in Kiel and Wilhelmshaven. It was a play-safe, play-for-time strategy that would earn the Navy no applause from Fleet Street but, with merchant shipping losses so serious that the nation's food and oil reserves were reduced to six weeks' supply, heroics could wait. The French and British armies on the Western Front were bracing themselves to meet the offensive that must surely be launched in the spring of 1918; German reinforcements, pouring into the line following the collapse of the Russians, considerably outweighed the trickle of Americans on the Allied side.

British minelaying operations in the vicinity of enemy submarine bases had been intensified. The conversion of ships for minelaying purposes was a relatively simple procedure although, for obvious reasons, vessels with a good turn of speed were necessary for working in areas patrolled by enemy light cruisers and destroyers. Even *Courageous* served briefly as a minelayer with her quarterdeck, fitted with four sets of trolley-rails, being known as 'Clapham Junction'.

In response, the Germans stepped up their sweeping operations, and with minefields being laid increasingly to seaward, particularly off the Heligoland Bight, their minesweepers were being drawn as much as 150 miles from the Jade, with the inevitable result that they and their destroyer escorts were attacked. The Germans added cruisers to their escorts, and the British similarly strengthened their attack forces. Scheer ordered battleships to be deployed in support of his cruisers, and that was the final straw for Beatty.

At dawn on 17 November a sizeable British surface force was steaming toward the Heligoland Bight, looking for trouble, smarting under press criticism and anxious to rectify the Jutland imbalance.

It was led by *Courageous* (Vice-Admiral Napier), *Glorious*, eight light cruisers of the new 'Caledon' class and ten destroyers. Speculatively in support were the five battle-cruisers of the 1st BCS (including, for the first time, *Renown* and *Repulse*) under Pakenham, whom Beatty was allowing to manage the entire operation – doubtless with misgivings, but a Commander-in-Chief who was a member of the War Staff did not lead such forays. Even further cover was provided by the 1st Battle Squadron.

The enemy was encountered at 0730 in poor visibility, midway between the Horns Reef and Terschelling – twenty minesweepers accompanied by ten destroyers and the four light cruisers of the 2nd Scouting Group (*Nürnberg, Frankfurt, Pillau* and *Königsberg*[3]), the entire force under Rear-Admiral Ludwig von Reuter. Under fire and clearly outnumbered, Reuter turned away under the cover of a smokescreen toward the south-east, where the battleships *Kaiser* and *Kaiserin* were positioned with, farther inshore, the battle-cruisers *Moltke* and *Hindenberg*.[4] Napier followed in pursuit without fully exploiting the high speeds of *Glorious* and *Courageous*, continuing to fire at ranges that progressively fell to 10,000 yards. Mist, and further smoke trailed by Reuter, however, made shooting extremely difficult, while Napier was aware that he was approaching an area that his charts delineated as dangerous as the result of British mines laid two years before. In fact his charts were out of date, and he might have continued in safety for a further thirty miles, but decided to rein back his two big ships and leave the chase to the light cruisers – whose charts did not show even the 1915 minefield position.

Meanwhile Pakenham, westward, had detached *Repulse* (flying the flag of Rear-Admiral R. F. Phillimore) to proceed at full speed to support Napier. *Repulse* came into contention shortly after 0900. Within a further few minutes Napier ordered his larger ships to break off the action for the reasons already given, but Phillimore in *Repulse*, with the benefit of a monthly corrected chart, pressed on in support of the 'C'-class cruisers which, already exchanging salvoes with Reuter's squadron, were now being straddled by heavy-calibre projectiles from *Kaiser* and *Kaiserin*. Commanding the British light cruisers, Rear-Admiral E. S. Alexander-Sinclair ordered his ships to fall back on *Repulse*, but not before *Calypso* (4180 tons, five 6-inch guns) had been hit by a shell that killed her captain, navigator and several others on her bridge.

*Repulse*'s guns fired in anger for the first time. One of her 15-inch projectiles found *Königsberg*, punched through all three funnels, penetrated the upper deck and burst in a bunker to start a fire. It was to be the only hit to be scored on a surface enemy by *Repulse* during her life of twenty-five years.

The German heavy ships were not to be tempted away from Heligoland, and by 1030 any further action was made impossible by thick fog. The British withdrew with a hundred killed, mostly in *Courageous*, who had suffered more damage from the enemy light cruisers' guns than she had inflicted. German casualties numbered twenty-one killed and forty wounded.

As early as 1915 the Admiralty had become aware that Germany was planning a series of battle-cruisers of about 30,000 tons, mounting eight 15-inch guns and sixteen 6-inch guns, later identified as *Mackensen, Graf Spee, Prinz Eitel Friedrich* and *Furst Bismarck*. There was nothing in the British programme to match these, and the Director of Naval Construction was instructed to prepare designs for four vessels of similar quality. As envisaged, these were to be super battle-cruisers with a displacement of 36,500 tons, eight 15-inch guns, armour similar to that of *Tiger*, and a speed of 32 knots. A design-study was approved but, initially, the Emergency War Programme was occupying all suitable building-dock capacity, and orders could not be placed before April 1916.

The four ships were to be *Anson* (Armstrong-Whitworth), *Hood* (John Brown), *Howe* (Cammell-Laird) and *Rodney* (Fairfields).

Within a few weeks, however, the loss of three battle-cruisers at Jutland, *apparently* as the result of flimsy armour, promoted a flurry of rethinking in Whitehall. In fact – in retrospect – the Jutland fatalities had less to do with the battle-cruisers' armour, however deplorable, than with a combination of indifferent magazine safeguards, ammunition-handling and cordite sensitivity. Albeit, it now seemed plain that drastic improvements in armour were necessary. If, as *Brassey* had suggested years before, battle-cruisers would inevitably find themselves trading salvoes with battleships, then they must be given battleship protection. This muddled diagnosis brought warship designers back to the old speed-versus-armour problem. Fortunately, to some extent, they were rescued by the recent adoption of small-tube boilers, of which little needs to be said except that they had drastically improved the power-to-space ratio to which designers had earlier been restricted. The innovation, proven in the 'Courageous'-class hybrids, suggested that the four projected super battle-cruisers (whatever type-name was dreamed up) would really be ultra-fast battleships.

The redrafted plans, which increased the thickness of the armoured belt from eight to twelve inches and improved the protection for magazines – including the anti-flash arrangements – resulted in a warship that would displace 45,200 tons at full load. This was two and a half times the displacement of Fisher's Invincibles, built only ten years before, on a keel three hundred feet longer and with engines of 100,000 greater horsepower, needed to achieve four knots more.

Although the additional weight of armour might have been disposed more effectively than it was, the vessels were to be well protected by the standards of the time. The 5.5-inch gun had only recently been introduced, having been installed in two cruisers being built by Armstrongs for Greece, appropriated in 1915 and subsequently renamed *Chester* and *Birkenhead*; the gun had been mounted in *Furious*. The 5.5-inch projectile, of 82 lb, was only slightly less effective than the 6-inch (100 lb) against a surface craft, but the guns were almost useless against aircraft – still regarded as a negligible threat in 1916 – and in due course those of *Hood* would become unemployable deadweight.

The hull of *Hood*, whose construction was more advanced than those of the other three, was launched on Clydebank on 22 August 1918 by Lady Hood, widow of Rear-Admiral Hood who had died in *Invincible*. By this time it had become apparent that the Germans had abandoned the building of their new battle-cruiser class to concentrate on submarines. In consequence all work on *Anson*, *Howe* and *Rodney*[5] was suspended, then cancelled, after some £860,000 had been spent on them. *Hood* might have suffered the same fate had she not been half finished. Despite the Armistice it was decided to complete her, partly to gain experience in the several novel features incorporated in her and also to lessen the blow that a sudden cessation of shipbuilding would have on the industry.

When completed, *Hood* was undeniably a warship of majestic appearance, and for the next twenty years she would have no rival in the eyes of the British public. It was difficult to understand how the same designer, E. L. Attwood, could have shaped the Navy's most stately ship and its ugliest (*Nelson* and *Rodney*) within less than a decade.

The additional armour-weight applied to *Hood* meant that she floated 3 feet 6 inches lower in the water than her original design intended and, although her handsome clipper bow and the flare of her long hull kept her fo'c'sle dry at high speed, her quarterdeck was awash in a seaway. However, she was a good sailor and a steady gun-platform. In due course, compelled to accept progressively heavier additions to her equipment in anticipation of another war, without shedding any equivalent weight, the gallant but ageing ship gradually became overladen, and her steering behaviour suffered accordingly.

Her crews wore her cap-ribbon with pride: she was always 'The Mighty 'Ood', representing all that was finest in the Fleet, and her plans had been given to the United States Navy, undoubtedly to influence the design of *Maryland, Colorado* and *West Virginia.* In *Hood*, the officers' after accommodation was considered almost luxurious by comparison with that in older capital ships, but, despite the attention given to ventilation arrangements, the lower deck quarters, forward, were surprisingly cramped, ill-lit and poorly ventilated. Still, she was the Queen of the world's greatest navy, and it would have been ungallant to draw attention to minor flaws in such a stately lady.

It is perhaps worth mentioning – but only just – that in 1912 Fisher had been contemplating the construction of *Incomparable*, a mammoth, diesel-driven, shallow-draft battle-cruiser, 1000 feet in length. Lightly hulled, but with a central citadel protected by 16 inches of armour, she would have mounted six 20-inch guns in three turrets. A coffer-dammed, honeycombed double bottom was to be filled with cork. With a speed of 32 knots plus, *Incomparable* would be capable of steaming around the world without refuelling. She was intended to last only ten years because, Fisher reasoned, all warships would have become obsolete after that time.

## Notes

1    But not quite the largest in terms of tonnage. *Renown*'s load displacement was 27,294 tons compared with *Tiger*'s 28,294, although the latter was 90 feet shorter in length. *Kongo* (Japan) displaced 27,500 tons but was 55 feet shorter.

2    These guns were later taken to Singapore. In 1946 the author stumbled on them, half buried, overgrown with grass, and with their muzzles fractured, on the island of Blakang Mati, just off Singapore, where they probably still are.

3    The second of this name. The first had been destroyed in the Rufiji river, East Africa, in July 1915.

4    The building of *Hindenberg* had been delayed because of priority given to U-boat construction. She was completed in May 1916, too late for Jutland, of 28,000 tons, mounting eight 15-inch guns and fourteen 6-inch guns.

5    All three names would be given to battleships laid down during the post-war years.

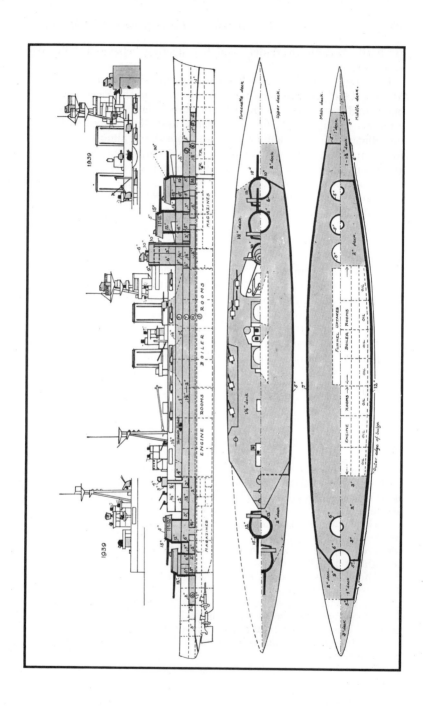

# *HOOD*, BATTLE-CRUISER

| | |
|---|---|
| *Builder* | John Brown |
| *Laid down* | 1 September 1916 |
| *Launched* | 22 August 1918 |
| *Completed* | 5 March 1920 |

*Dimensions*
Length, waterline: 810 feet. Beam 104 feet. Draught 28.5 feet. Displacement 45,200 tons. Complement 1477.

*Armament*
Eight 15-inch guns; twelve 5.5-inch guns; four 4-inch HA guns; six 21-inch torpedo-tubes (four upper deck, two submerged).

*Armoured Protection*
Hull 12-inch amidships reducing to 5-inch. Turrets, 15-inch faces, 11-inch rears, 5-inch crowns. Conning tower 11-inch. Upper decks 1–1½-inch. Main and lower decks 1–2-inch with 3-inch over magazines.

*Engines*
Brown-Curtis geared turbines of 144,000 horsepower driving four screws. Designed speed 31 knots. A mean speed of 32.07 knots was achieved in trials.

*Fuel*
Oil: 4000 tons.

*Hood* cost £6,025,000 (or about £145 per ton) with an annual upkeep of £400,000. She was the largest, fastest and arguably the finest-looking capital ship of her era, the last to have open secondary batteries and masthead control-tops.

# IV   The Ravages of Peace, the Race to Amend

## Chapter Ten

*The Armistice – growing lower-deck dissatisfaction – prize-money, pay and pensions – the assessment of the aircraft – the Washington Naval Treaty and the lean years of the twenties – the Invergordon Mutiny – prospects of another war*

CONTRARY to the usual opinion, the war did not end in November 1918 for thousands of service personnel. In addition to the British troops and flying crews that remained on Russian territory, a considerable number of warships continued to be actively deployed in the White Sea, the Baltic, the Gulf of Finland, the Black Sea and the areas around Murmansk and Archangel, all engaged in supporting the dwindling and unreliable White Russian forces which still opposed, hopelessly, the Revolution. Like all who, when the captains, the kings and the brass bands have departed, find themselves still fighting a remote war in which nobody else seems to be interested, and for a cause for which they themselves have little sympathy, the naval forces involved were becoming increasingly discontented. Conditions were harsh; in the northerly theatres the climate was bitter, provisions were monotonously poor, mail was irregular and recreational facilities almost non-existent. It was disturbing to read in weeks-old newspapers that, within the twelve months following the Armistice, 415,000 naval personnel were to be discharged into highly paid civilian life, where there were homes fit for heroes and a chicken in every pot. Those same newspapers gave few column-inches to the ice-bound ships operating from Helsingfors, Libau and Reval. In the summer of 1919 the crew of the gunboat *Cicala*, ordered up the Dvina river from Archangel, refused to comply. Then a battalion of Royal Marines mutinied in Murmansk; and finally, three months later, the aircraft-carrier *Vindictive*[1] experienced a lower-deck revolt when, having come to Copenhagen from the Gulf of Finland to embark aircraft and stores, her shore-leave was cancelled because of bad weather.

Among warships in home ports the incidence of insubordination and sabotage increased. In October 1919, in Devonport, forty men in ships under sailing orders for Russia went absent without leave to complain to their MPs in London.

Although there was undoubtedly a keen awareness of political developments in Russia, Germany and Austria-Hungary, there was never the slightest suggestion that British service personnel were thinking in terms of mutiny in the accepted sense of the word, far less of revolution. The protests were those of men, already war-weary, who found themselves distantly exiled in support of enterprises which were becoming progressively meaningless. Similar frustration would be experienced after the Second World War, when the armed forces, reduced to numbers even smaller than pre-war, were to be thinly stretched for uncomfortably long periods, to campaign in Palestine, Cyprus, Malaya and finally Korea.

During the two or three decades prior to 1914 the quality of lower-deck personnel had been steadily improving. In 1902, for instance, there were 373 courts-martial in a Navy of 104,724; in 1912 the number had fallen to 111 for a complement of 119,903. The armed services were no longer the last resort of the unemployable but were attracting men of good education, and in 1914 the general level of discipline and sobriety in the regular service was higher than at any previous period. This progression, however, was not met by any improvement in pay, conditions or promotional prospects. The chasm between lower deck and wardroom remained impossibly wide, the difference in rewards often ludicrous. Many anomalies, taken singly, were of small consequence, but in total they were overwhelmingly unfair – particularly to those long-serving and highly efficient non-commissioned officers who, on commencement of hostilities, found themselves subordinate to youthful amateurs who had undergone only a few weeks' training in a shore establishment, but who were now, of course, officers and gentlemen. As a case in point, every commander of 550 patrol launches was recruited from outside the Navy with the minimum of sea knowledge required, when there were hundreds of senior lower-deck men – warrant officers and chiefs – who might more deservedly have been given such appointments.

Lower-deck pay had always been a cause of hardship. At best it had been poor, but became markedly so during the war years when the soaring cost of living was chased by wages in the civilian sector which seemed to the fighting man to be astronomical.

The long-serving rating had always been the linchpin of the Royal

*Above left:* Sir John Fisher,
father of the modern navy,
as Vice-Admiral

*Above:* Admiral Sir David
Beatty with King George V,
June 1917

*Left:* Vice-Admiral Sir James
Somerville

*Invincible* in 1914. Later her forward funnel was raised so that her profile was not dissimilar to *Indefatigable*, below

Of impressive appearance, *Indefatigable* was too lightly armoured to survive the duel with *Von der Tann* at Jutland

*Lion*, Beatty's flagship in 1914

The construction of *Tiger* was influenced by a Japanese design study, but her fighting qualities were never exploited

*Repulse* as the Fleet first saw her in late 1916

*Hood*, the fastest and finest-looking capital ship of her era

*Furious*, as completed in 1917. Subsequent rebuilding converted her into an aircraft-carrier

*Glorious* in 1917. She, too, like *Courageous*, was converted into an aircraft-carrier in the Second World War

Admiral Sir Tom Phillips (*centre*) watches the arrival of *Prince of Wales* and *Repulse* at Singapore on 2 December 1941

*Repulse*'s ensign floats below the surface in the clear tropical sea off the east coast of Malaysia

The last of a queen. Alongside No. 3 berth at Faslane Port, *Renown* is
reduced to the level of her upper deck

Representatives of the German Naval Commander-in-Chief, Norway, surrender their fleet aboard *Renown* on 11 March 1945

Navy, and the Admiralty had stated unequivocally that 'after twenty-two years of qualifying service pensions are awarded for life', but on 3 August 1914 an Order in Council decreed that the services of time-expired men would be retained, without option, for the duration of hostilities. This was accepted as inevitable, but their pensions were to be substituted by 2*d* per day 'detained pay'. The irritation this decision generated was exacerbated by the fact that men already on pension, but recalled for service, enjoyed their full pay *plus* their pension. Nobody understood the argument, presented in Parliament, that the 'detained man' on 2*d* per day was better treated than the recalled pensioner with his pay plus pension.

Another bone of contention was the distribution of prize-money, for several centuries a financial reward to those immediately responsible for the destruction or capture of enemy ships or property. That this custom was an anachronism that favoured only those with opportunity could not be disputed, but since it was an established practice it should be justly applied. The rules governing prize-money had been amended several times since 1649, but by 1914 allowed that the crews of warships present at the taking or destruction of an enemy ship were entitled to share a sum of money calculated at the rate of £5 for each crew member of the said enemy ship at the beginning of the engagement.

This assessment was less generous than it might seem. It meant, for example, that an enemy battleship valued at, say, £2½ million would realise a prize-money figure of five or six thousand pounds – to be shared between *all* the ships present during the action in which she was destroyed.

It was not so much the modest sum involved that annoyed the lower deck; it was that sum's distribution on a basis of shares in accordance with rank.

The share system was complicated but, typically, a flag officer, if present, claimed one-thirtieth of the whole. Of the remainder, one-tenth was shared between officers commanding, or second in command, of ships (captains six shares; commanders three). After these deductions, the residue was divided between the officers and men of participating ships on a sliding scale according to rank. Commanding officers, *having already taken their share of one-tenth part*, now received eighty shares of the general distribution, a commander forty, a lieutenant-commander thirty. On the lower deck a chief petty officer had ten shares, a petty officer eight, a leading rating six, an able seaman five, an ordinary seaman three, a boy only one.

While the sailors did not dispute the officers' right to a larger reward, the system seemed unreasonably balanced in favour of the wardroom. As an example, the German cruiser *Blücher*, sunk during the Dogger Bank action in 1915, was assessed by the Prize Court as justifying a bounty amounting to £5250. Forty-seven British ships were involved in the action, so the share value was expected to be low. Even so, as Vice-Admiral commanding, Beatty received £79 4s 4d and a similar sum was shared by his three rear-admirals. Ships' captains received £15 13s 3d, commanders £7 16s 7d, lieutenant-commanders £5 4s 5d. On the lower deck each petty officer had 9s 8d and able seamen 6s 1d. Boys, at the lower end of the scale, were awarded 1s 2d.

Of naval personnel killed, 5.6 per cent had been boys of between sixteen and eighteen years – three hundred at Jutland alone. One had been posthumously awarded a Victoria Cross and more than a dozen had received Distinguished Service Medals, but the period they served before the age of eighteen (or being rated Ordinary Seamen) did not count as pension-qualifying service.

There had been trifling increases in pay and messing allowances during the war years, but these were far in arrears of cost-of-living inflation. Like those of the civilian population, rations had been progressively reduced, but in compensation civilian wages had soared. On the Navy's lower deck it had become commonplace for men to have to find twenty shillings a month – an AB's pay was 1s 10d a day – from their own pockets in order to bolster the inadequate messing allowance. In larger vessels the system of canteen messing began to be abandoned in favour of general messing, which provided all of a ship's company with the same daily fare, related to the Admiralty's victualling figure by the paymaster, and this eliminated the need for personal expenditure other than for minor acquisitions from the dry canteen. Catering was duller, but more economical than the old go-as-you-please arrangement.

These are only a few typical examples of the very many grievances during the latter part of the war and the few years following which slowly undermined the traditional tolerant loyalty of the regular Navy. It is most probable that, under peacetime circumstances, no positive co-ordinated protest would have resulted, but the war had introduced civilian trade-union elements into the service which were not slow to exploit such a situation. In July 1917, in defiance of regulations, letters from serving personnel were printed in the national press (at that time asking for pay-increases ranging from 3s 6d to 7s per week, for the easier promotion of warrant and petty officers to commissioned rank, and for pensions to be paid to all who had served twenty-one years). The Admiralty's only concession was to supplement a penny a day to 'detained pay' for every additional war-year served, i.e., 3*d* per day for the first year, 4*d* for the second, 6*d* for the third, etc.

In 1918, however, a lower-deck newspaper, *The Bluejacket* (produced by an ex-naval rating, now a civilian and thus beyond the disciplinary claws of the Admiralty) published a succinct critique of service conditions which implied that, unless the Admiralty took immediate steps toward improvement, lower-deck insurrection was inevitable. Copies of the newspaper were sent to His Majesty the King, the Prime Minister Lloyd George, all members of the Cabinet, the Board of Admiralty and selected MPs.

Indeed, acts of indiscipline leading to court-martial had increased to an unprecedented number. The Prime Minister ordered the First Lord, Sir Eric Geddes, to convene a committee of enquiry, and this was headed by Admiral Sir Martin Jerram. It was no longer possible to ignore the wide disparity between naval and civilian levels of pay. The Jerram Committee announced an immediate bonus of 1*s* 6*d* per day with an able seaman's pay increased to 4*s* and good-conduct increments trebled.

During the 1920s there were several instances of concerted insubordination, all spontaneous, none related to pay and almost invariably resulting from the lack of tact of middle-level officers, many of whom seemed unwilling to concede that human dignity was a quality to be respected. It was a bad decade for officers as a class. However, such lower-deck acts of indiscipline had never been a feature of the pre-1914 Navy. There were now new attitudes, a growing awareness that if the proper method of representing grievances proved to be a cul-de-sac, then there were other methods. It was this growing political consciousness on the one side and indifference on the other that was responsible for the progressive erosion of the sailor's regard for his officer.

Two other events of the immediate post-war years were to destroy the Navy's centuries-old position as the world's most powerful maritime service. One was the final defeat of the Admiralty's attempts to regain control of the Royal Naval Air Service, which had been transferred to the Air Ministry.[2] The other was the Washington Treaty, as a result of which Britain, the United States and Japan agreed on a ratio of 5:5:3 in capital ships. The Royal Navy was reduced to a skeleton of its former status. The fact that such a reduction was inevitable for reasons of simple economics, and did not need the Treaty for justification, failed to sweeten the sour taste of lost prestige for either British public or serviceman. True, the Navy's chief rival, the United States Navy, did not represent a war threat, but the Royal Navy had been the only British asset that was bigger and better than anything the Americans had. There seemed no reason why Japan should need a navy three-fifths the size of Britain's, but Japan was far away, and a war with the little yellow men who made cheap tin toys was inconceivable. 'A war with Japan?' scoffed Winston Churchill, Chancellor of the Exchequer. 'But why should there be a war with Japan? I do not believe there is the slightest chance of it in our lifetime.'

With the ink hardly dry on the Treaty of Versailles, the lessons of Jutland so recent and with so many large warships being consigned to the breaker's yard, it might seem remarkable that by 1921 Britain had begun the construction of four new battle-cruisers, each of 48,000 tons and mounting nine 16-inch and sixteen 6-inch guns. The United States and Japan, relatively unaffected by the war, had enjoyed a lengthy period of leisure during which to develop new warship designs whilst reaping considerable benefit from the trials and errors of the combatant navies. Soon after the Armistice the United States was ready to lay down six battleships and six battle-cruisers, all of 43,000 tons and mounting 16-inch guns, and Japan had already floated two warships of the same displacement and gun-power, was laying down four more, and was planning yet a further four mounting 18-inch guns.

Britain had nothing remotely matching such monsters, which, when completed, would relegate the Royal Navy to third place. Despite a public demand for a programme of disarmament and national economy, it was decided that to meet this threat new construction must be undertaken.

The orders for the four battle-cruisers, of the dimensions mentioned, were placed with Swan Hunter of Newcastle, Beardmore & Fairfields of Glasgow and John Brown of Clydebank. It was understood that they would carry the names *Invincible, Inflexible, Indomitable* and *Indefatigable*, would carry armoured protection similar to that of *Hood* (which was proof against all forms of attack then envisaged) and have a speed of 31–2 knots. Instead of the customary tripod mast and piecemeal bridge structure, these ships would have the compact tower citadel that later became fashionable. The nine 16-inch guns were to be mounted in triple turrets, with two turrets forward and the third amidships but with an unusually generous firing-arc. Each ship would carry a crew of 1716.

The battle-cruisers were to be followed, as soon as finances permitted, by four battleships of similar displacement but mounting nine 18-inch guns. The plans for these did not reach an advanced

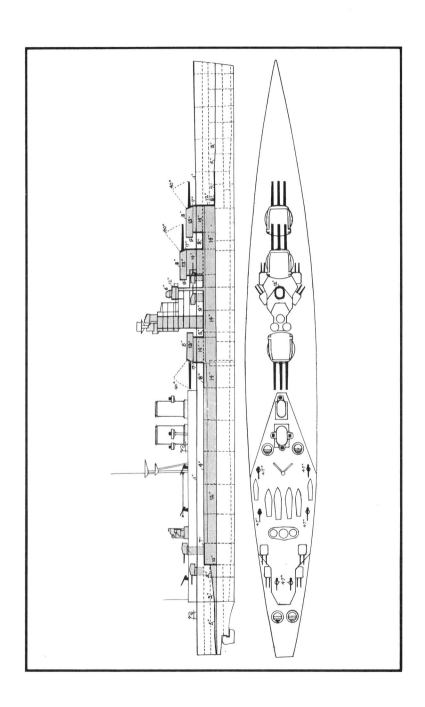

stage, but the names of these huge vessels were likely to be *St George*, *St Andrew*, *St David* and *St Patrick*.

American as well as British domestic opinion was vociferously opposed to such massive expenditure, and it was the United States Navy Department that realised that its programmed ships would now be outgunned by those of the British and Japanese. While British naval superiority was, as always, resented, it did not represent a war threat, but a naval race in the Pacific was a different matter. Moreover, this new generation of capital ships was beginning to approach dimensions too large for the Panama Canal to accommodate, while behind the scenes the American Secretary of State, Charles Evans Hughes, was concealing the unpalatable truth that in any case finances were not going to be available for all the new capital ships programmed *and* the preparation of Pacific bases to harbour them. The United States looked for a face-saving avenue of escape, and found it at the Washington Naval Conference.

The fine print of the resulting treaty does not concern us; it is sufficient to say that agreement on the possession of capital ships was reached as follows:

    1    The British and American battle-fleets should be limited to 580,450 tons and 500,650 tons respectively, Japan 301,320 tons (60 per cent), France 221,170 and Italy 182,800 tons.

    2    Capital ships should be limited in displacement to 35,000 tons with 16-inch as the maximum gun-calibre.

    3    Capital ships could be replaced by new construction twenty years after completion, and no fresh construction should be undertaken in the meantime.

    4    Reconstruction should be limited to defence against air and submarine to a limit of 3000 tons. More latitude was allowed to France and Italy.

    5    The standard displacement of a ship should be that when she was fully equipped for sea but without fuel and reserve feed-water on board.

Britain was permitted to retain 5 'Revenge' class, 5 'Queen Elizabeth' class, 4 'Iron Duke' class, 3 'King George V' class, 1 'Thunderer' as training ship, 1 'Hood', 2 'Renown' and 1 'Tiger', but was allowed to supplement these by laying down two 35,000-ton battleships in 1922. They would be *Nelson* and *Rodney*.

Doubtless as much a relief to Mr David Lloyd George as it was to Mr Warren Harding, the immediate sequel to Britain was the suspension and then the cancellation (9 February 1922) of the construction contracts covering the four 'Invincible' battle-cruisers. This was a severe blow for the shipyards concerned, which, already suffering post-war retrenchment, had anticipated employment until 1925 or 1926. The armament factories commissioned to develop and produce the new guns and turrets were almost bankrupted.

Several years before these events unfolded, however – within days of the Armistice being signed in November 1918 – dozens of great weather-worn ships were steaming southward from Scapa Flow with their long paying-off pennants snaking in the wind and their crews jubilant, to the Nore, Portsmouth and Devonport. For some, the gaunt old warriors of 1896 and 1897, the breaker's yard was very near. Others, with only four or five years of service behind them, swung slowly and forlornly at their buoys, unheeded except for the occasional visits of care and maintenance parties, waiting for bids from foreign navies. There were few, however, who wanted battle-ships when the war to end all wars had just ended.[3] One by one the proud names were struck off the Navy List as their owners were towed on their last sad journeys. In May 1921, Messrs Thomas Ward Ltd of Sheffield purchased 113 warships, including *Dread-nought*, at a flat rate of £2 10s per ton of displacement. It was the largest sale of surplus warships in history.

The 2nd Battle Cruiser Squadron, the four oldest of the Splendid Cats, was soon disbanded. In January 1919, *Inflexible* and *Indomitable* were relegated to the Nore Reserve, in which they idled until being paid off on the same day, 31 March 1920. Both were sold for scrapping in December 1922.

*New Zealand* enjoyed a brief respite, earned by her distinguished service – or perhaps by the Maori talisman she had always carried and which had brought her almost unscathed through the war. On 21 February 1919, carrying Lord and Lady Jellicoe, she left England on a world cruise during which the Admiral drew up plans for the Commonwealth's future naval strategy. *New Zealand* regained Portsmouth on 2 February 1920, to be sold for scrapping.

In 1919 the squadron's leader, *Australia*, was returned to the country that had sponsored her, now to become the flagship of the Royal Australian Navy. In due course she was listed for disposal under the terms of the Washington Treaty, and was sunk with honours off Sydney Harbour on 21 April 1924. The next of her name, a 'County'-class cruiser, was already on the drawing-board and would be laid down on Clydebank in 1925.

Meanwhile, in May 1920, the surviving battle-cruisers, now simply 'the Battle-Cruiser Squadron', had been joined by *Hood*, who hoisted the flag of Acting Vice-Admiral Sir Roger Keyes, the hero of Zeebrugge. The commissioning of the world's largest warship and her markedly improved armour and armament seemed to suggest a vote of confidence in the battle-cruiser as a class. True, *Lion* and *Princess Royal* (and the absent *New Zealand*) were transferred to the Reserve Fleet, remaining in commission, but this economy could hardly be disputed when so many fine warships were being ignominiously consigned to the scrapyard. Hopes rose, but only briefly; there was to be no escape from the Washington Treaty's condemning pen-stroke, and both *Lion* and *Princess Royal* were discarded in December 1922. Beatty's brave flagship died in a Jarrow breaker's yard in January 1924, *Princess Royal* in 1926.

From 1919, *Courageous* and *Glorious* served as floating gunnery schools, attached to Portsmouth and Devonport respectively, subsequently transferred to the Reserve Fleet until 1924 when both were converted to aircraft-carriers. Neither survived the first year of the Second World War.

That left only four Splendid Cats – *Hood, Renown, Repulse* and *Tiger.*

Specialist officers on both sides of the Atlantic were sifting through the masses of statistics that had emerged from the war, and several facts were quickly apparent. One was that the navies of 1914 had seriously underestimated the ranges at which surface actions would be fought, while the British, at least, had been over-optimistic with regard to the accuracy of their gunnery and the destructive power of their projectiles. There was no doubt that the submarine had brought Britain very near to defeat, but for several years the Royal Navy had been developing an echo-sounding detection device and keeping its cards close to its chest. If and when another war came, promised the experts, the U-boats were going to have their comeuppance.

There were many who disagreed, and there was also divided opinion on the potential of aircraft which, while their reconnaissance value was recognised, did not seem to present a threat to heavily armoured, fast capital ships. Bombing tests carried out by both the United States and Britain were inconclusive. In 1921, off the east coast of America, the German battleship *Ostfriesland* shrugged off sixteen aerial bombs before succumbing to two one-tonners, and critics pointed to the artificiality of the conditions – perfect visibility, a stationary target, no anti-aircraft fire. So the British equipped the old battleship *Agamemnon* with radio-controlled steering so that she could be manœuvred by an attendant destroyer and, in July 1924, dropped 114 bombs on her from altitudes of 12,000 down to 5000 feet. Not one hit was achieved.

In the same year the United States Navy duplicated this experiment with the condemned battleship *Washington* – and duplicated the result. Finally, on 20 January 1925 the Royal Navy used the Dreadnought *Monarch* as a target. Aircraft attacked her all morning, cruisers fired at her during the afternoon and battleships at night. At the conclusion of the shoot *Monarch* was battered but very determinedly afloat, and had to be sunk by the deliberate close-range fire of *Revenge*'s 15-inch guns, aided by searchlights.

The Admiralty's evaluation of the effectiveness of the aircraft confidently dismissed any speculation on the demise of the battleship. A bomb dropped from 12,000 feet required 28 seconds to reach the deck of a ship, during which time, at 21 knots, the ship would have travelled 1000 feet further on her course. Add to this the ship's ability to zig-zag, and the chances of hitting her with the crude bomb-sights then in use were infinitesimal. Furthermore, only bombs of 500 lb or more could seriously damage an armoured ship, and it would require twelve of such bombs to disable a modern battleship.

Trials with torpedo-carrying aircraft in 1926 proved only marginally more threatening. Against ships able to manœuvre evasively, 5 hits were achieved from 18 torpedoes fired, or 30 per cent. Against ships maintaining formation, 5 hits were made from 8 torpedoes, or 62 per cent. However, such peacetime experiments were conducted under circumstances so favourable to the attack, claimed the Admiralty (unwilling to concede anything to RAF-controlled aircraft), that the true figure would be about 11 per cent.

It was difficult for the 'salt-horse' sailor with his entrenched faith in that ultimate creation of the naval architect's genius, the battleship, to accept that aircraft were going to become progressively faster and longer-ranging, bomb-sights more sophisticated and bombs more devastating. The aircraft was not a maritime weapon in its own right but merely a useful accessory for extending the battle-fleet's range of vision, perhaps observing falls of shot if wireless became really reliable, *possibly* slowing up an enemy capital ship with torpedoes to be finished off by gunnery. Aircraft could not *sink* armoured ships. Of course, they were useful for collecting mail.

Admiral Sims, United States Navy, probably summed up the attitudes of both American and British naval hierarchies when he retorted: 'It is an astonishing thing, the conservatism of the military mind. It is absolutely historical that they never give in. You have got to shed their blood before they do it.'

The decade that followed the war saw a number of other changes for which most sailors could be grateful. Coal had almost entirely disappeared; the grimy collier had been replaced by the immaculate fleet oiler, the sweating blackened stoker by a man with clean overalls and a handful of cotton waste. The sailmaker had become a *rara avis*, and the growing importance of the non-executive officers of the engineering, electrical, medical and clerical branches had been acknowledged by allowing them the same pattern of gold stripes on their cuffs as those of seaman officers. The frock coat, full dress with cocked hat, ball dress and mess dress were no longer obligatory.

Thankfully, the rating's summer straw hat, the 'benjie', had also been declared redundant. A circular white helmet was provided for the tropics. Otherwise a committee on uniform clothing had made few changes. The sailor's appearance was still recognisably similar to that which regulations had imposed in 1864.

Personal lockers were being provided only tardily. A man's effects were still usually stowed in a kitbag supplemented by the wooden 'ditty box' and a tin cap-box. General messing had replaced canteen messing in all but the smallest vessels, with the result that breakfast became a realistic meal instead of, often, only a mug of cocoa, and, because of the greater economy of comprehensive catering, the sailor's diet, albeit somewhat predictable, was more sensibly balanced.

In the absence of coal ships were more easily kept clean, and the old mixture of brickdust and petrol for polishing brightwork had given way to Brasso; but quarterdecks were still holystoned, and men still washed their clothes in buckets with hard yellow soap. The heavy soda content of this soap and the difficulty of thoroughly rinsing it free of washed clothes, particularly underclothes, led to a high incidence of 'dhobie-itch', but there was a far more sinister threat to the health of the lower deck – tuberculosis – which was progressively to reach a level in the Royal Navy higher than that among the civilian population.

While lower-deck accommodation in many ships was cramped and ill-ventilated, even poorer conditions existed in the Navy's depot barracks, designed to house ratings drafted ashore from one ship to await assignment to another. These 'stone frigates' – *Victory* in Portsmouth, *Drake* in Devonport and *Pembroke* in Chatham – were sprawling complexities of slum buildings, condemned to demolition by successive Boards of Admiralty but always retained, never justifying the cost of renovation and so continuing to decay. Nor could compensation be found outside the barracks gate. There were shabby pubs and blowzy tarts, or bleak temperance hostels and stewed tea, and always the resentment of local townspeople. Most sailors would have agreed that there was only one thing to do when drafted into Royal Naval Barracks – volunteer for the first available ship.

Nominally a component of the Atlantic Fleet, the Battle-Cruiser Squadron of *Hood, Renown, Repulse* and *Tiger* was never, however, to serve in company and, indeed, the first three were to spend long periods of their respective commissions on goodwill cruises. Only *Tiger* remained on the Home Station. Despite her unimpressive war record she was still regarded by many as representing what a warship *ought* to look like, although her fine profile had been somewhat marred by the removal of her topmast to a position between her second and third funnels. In 1924, *Tiger* became the Fleet's seagoing gunnery training ship, attached to Whale Island until 1929, when she assumed *Hood*'s place in the Battle-Cruiser Squadron while that ship was undergoing refit. Time, however, was running out, and on 30 March 1931 she took the farewell cheers of the Atlantic Fleet, paid off in Devonport, and was sold for scrapping during the following year.

Now there were only three.

The 1920s and early 1930s were not the Royal Navy's happiest years. It was a period of parsimony and cheeseparing, the result partly of a gradually worsening economic climate and partly of several naval treaties[4] that limited warship construction anyway. Between 1918 and 1936, when the treaties were abrogated, only two British battleships were laid down, the compromise *Nelson* and *Rodney*, cynically referred to as the 'Cherry Tree'-class because they had been cut down by Washington. There were also the thirteen 'County'-class cruisers (including two for Australia), criticised as too costly when laid down but to prove superb investments in due course, and a handful of smaller cruisers; but when building restrictions were abandoned in 1936 there remained a perilously short time in which to redress the Navy's deficiencies. At the commencement of the Second World War approximately half of the Navy's ships would be legacies of the First World War.

Even so, between the wars a façade of sea-power was maintained and, despite its ageing ships, the Royal Navy was far from being merely a shop-window force. The élite Mediterranean Fleet was capable of easily destroying the Italian Navy, and was prepared to do so in 1935 when Italy invaded Abyssinia, but the League of Nations looked away; France had adopted a Maginot Line philosophy, and the United States (which had imposed the League on the world but refused to be a member) had withdrawn into isolation, declining responsibility. It was a story that had been told before but, before, Britain had grasped the nettle and to hell with the others – to the others' smug relief. This time the Royal Navy's muscle had been slashed at America's insistence and, with the territorial ambitions of Germany, Italy and Japan now becoming apparent, Britain was incapable of fighting a war on a global scale. In Whitehall the faint-hearts prevailed.

During 1920 and 1921 *Renown* had conveyed His Royal Highness the Prince of Wales on a tour of the United States and Australasia and, two years later, of India and the Far East. Both tour-parties were accompanied, in the capacity of aide-de-camp, by Lieutenant Lord Louis Mountbatten, who became engaged in New Delhi to Edwina Cynthia Ashley. In May 1923 a refit costing £979,927 increased *Renown*'s armoured belt from six to nine inches, using steel plates taken from the battleship *Almirante Cochrane*, initially intended for Chile (see page 175). Magazine protection was strengthened, and concessions to the crew included 'Petty Officer messes improved. Electric heaters, lighting improved. Reading rooms for Petty Officers and Chief Petty Officers improved by cushioned seats. Garden seats from reading rooms placed in men's smoking place and cinema house, etc.' In 1927 she again visited Australia, this time taking His Royal Highness the Duke of York, later to become King George VI.

*Renown* resumed less regal activities in home waters in 1928, but eight years later was subjected to another major refit which amounted almost to a rebuilding from the bare hull. It cost £3,088,008, or only £30,000 less than the cost of her construction, but when she steamed out of Portsmouth in June 1939 *Renown* was to all intents and purposes a new warship, well protected, re-engined and fast, achieving 29.93 knots in post-refit trials. Stripped of her obsolete triple 4-inch secondary armament, she now carried twenty 4.5-inch dual-purpose guns in ten twin mountings (to be radar-controlled after 1941) and twenty-four 2-pounder pom-poms in three eight-barrelled mountings. The elevation of the 15-inch guns had been increased to 30°.

Neither her sister *Repulse* nor *Hood* would enjoy such lavish expenditure. Following an armour-strengthening refit in 1919–20 (costing £860,684 and also utilising steel from the converted *Almirante Cochrane*), *Repulse* joined *Hood* in visiting Rio de Janeiro for the Brazilian centenary celebrations. Then both, accompanied by five cruisers, departed Portsmouth in November 1923 on 'the most successful cruise by a squadron of warships in the history of sea-power', which took them to South Africa, Zanzibar, Ceylon, Malaya, Australia and New Zealand, across the Pacific to the United States, the West Indies and Canada, and finally home again in September 1924. Although the tour was dominated by *Hood*'s presence, *Repulse* contributed substantially to an undertaking that was excellently stage-managed and outstandingly successful in strengthening friendships and reviving old alliances.

During 1925, *Repulse* took the Prince of Wales to visit South Africa and South America, but the days of easy spending were ending; the next seven years were served in home waters – the first two commanded by Captain Edward Evans (later Admiral Lord Mountevans), who had been second-in-command of Scott's last expedition to the Antarctic and whose name had later become a household word as 'Evans of the *Broke*'. In early 1927, visiting Spain, *Repulse* lost her two pilots in flying accidents between Biscay and Gibraltar.

In 1933 (three years before *Renown*) the eighteen-year-old battle-cruiser was docked in Portsmouth for her second and most extensive refit. Further armour was added to her main and lower decks and her light AA armament reinforced, but no alterations were made to 15-inch installations other than an improvement in control arrangements. An aircraft catapult was installed athwartships with hangar accommodation for up to four planes. These were to be Blackburn Shark three-seater torpedo–reconnaissance seaplanes powered by a 700 horsepower Armstrong Siddeley Tiger engine allowing a maximum speed of 152 miles per hour. They were armed with two machine-guns and could carry one 1500 lb torpedo or the same weight in bombs.

*Repulse* would be briefly docked on a number of later occasions to install further pom-poms and Oerlikon 20-millimetre cannon, degaussing gear and radar. By 1939 her displacement had been markedly increased over that when built and had reached the accepted limit of safety. It is interesting to note that, although scheduled to be fitted with seven radar equipments for different purposes, only one, for 15-inch gunnery direction, was received. The AA guns did not get their intended radar control. *Repulse* was also programmed to be docked in the United States in September 1941 to have her entire 4-inch armament modified, but before this could happen she was ordered to the Far East.

*Hood*, of course, was the ship that had captured everyone's imagination – the powerful and stately Queen of the world's battle-fleets. Throughout her life she retained her original profile, unmarred by afterthought alterations to funnels or masts. For twenty years she had no rival. 'We surrender our city to you,' said the Mayor of San Francisco. 'We capitulate.' There was an international fondness for *Hood*, conceded to no other warship before or after and only approached by RMS *Queen Mary* in the mid-thirties.

As already described, *Hood* attended the Brazilian centenary celebrations with *Repulse* in 1922, and in the following year made a second visit to Scandinavian waters, flying the flag of King Haakon of Norway as honorary Admiral. *Hood*'s world cruise, also with *Repulse*, was an outstanding triumph. She steamed 40,000 miles in ten months, during which three-quarters of a million awed people trod her decks, stared up at her massive guns and climbed her maze of ladders, doubtless comforted by the thought that this magnificent ship was 'on their side'.

Early in 1924, *Hood* was included in the Atlantic Fleet's Spring Cruise and, inevitably, was detached to Lisbon to represent the Royal Navy during the Vasco da Gama celebrations of that year. There is no evidence that other ships' crews regarded her as a *prima donna*. Indeed, *Hood*'s constant round of receptions, parades, open-ship days, the daily immaculate uniforms and the intensive attention to decks, paintwork and brass would not have made her an object of envy among her less distinguished but more leisured contemporaries. There was a limit to bull.

In 1929 she refitted, installing multiple pom-poms and, later, multiple .5-inch machine-guns, while two single 4-inch guns were replaced by twin mountings, but nothing extensive was done because it was proposed that she should undergo complete reconstruction, on the lines of *Renown*, in early 1939. This would entail the provision of new engines, the strengthening of both horizontal and vertical armour, and of underwater protection, the modification of the bridge structure, and the removal of the existing obsolete secondary armament to be replaced by eight twin 5.25-inch mountings.

As the 1930s progressed, however, the Admiralty became increasingly reluctant to withdraw the big battle-cruiser from service; once this was done she would be out of contention for two years or more. *Hood* never got her reconstruction nor even a competent refit. Wartime additions were imposed piecemeal until her deep load was increased by 2960 tons and her elegant hull floated like a log.

Both *Hood* and *Repulse* were involved in the Atlantic Fleet mutiny[5] at Invergordon in September 1931.

The red light had flickered in January 1931, when the crew of the submarine depot-ship *Lucia*, preparing for sea in Devonport, refused to muster, remaining on their messdeck after securing the hatch and, remarkably, singing hymns. Subsequently, without protest or drama, they allowed themselves to be marched under escort to Royal Naval Barracks. It is significant that the enquiry that followed conceded that *Lucia*'s discontent was largely attributable to 'want of tact and consideration on the part of the captain and executive officer and incapacity on the part of the divisional officer concerned'. The use of the word 'mutiny' was decried as unjustifiable by Commander-in-Chief Portsmouth; the *Lucia* affair had been merely a 'protest'. Such semantic varnish, however, did not save the 'protesters' from sentences of six months' hard labour, and in the House of Commons the First Lord, Mr A. V. Alexander, regretted that 'the conditions of contentment . . . and sympathy between officers and men which unquestionably exist in HM ships' had not been realised in *Lucia*. The abysmal extent to which the Admiralty was out of touch with reality was to be painfully demonstrated ten months later.

On Thursday, 3 September the National Government's Chancellor of the Exchequer, Philip Snowden, rose in the House of Commons to announce the taxation measures to be imposed on the nation as the result of a current deficiency of £75 million and an anticipated deficiency, for the following year, of £170 million. Income tax was to be increased by 6*d* in the pound, surtax by ten per cent, tobacco would yield a further £4 million, the price of petrol was to be raised by 2*d* per gallon, beer by 1*d* per pint. Other economies in national expenditure were not spelled out in detail, and the Admiralty waited until the Atlantic Fleet was at sea, exercising *en route* from the Channel ports to the north, before announcing that the Navy's pay was to be reduced in order to assist in the restoration of national prosperity.

It is not here intended to describe in detail the extent of the proposed pay-cuts but only to observe that they were brutally insensitive. For married ratings who already allotted every possible penny to their families they spelled starvation. For all, however, they represented a betrayal of assurances given by successive governments, and a memorandum from the Board of Admiralty to the Cabinet Economy Committee pointed out that 'there is no doubt that such action would be regarded by the whole Navy as a breach of faith' and 'the effect on the Navy would be deplorable'.

In fact the 'whole Navy' had a right to expect the Sea Lords to stand up and be counted, to protest on behalf of the service and, if necessary, offer their resignations (of which only the threat would have rocked the First National Government on its unsteady foundations). The Admiralty, however, did nothing. It did not even bother to warn the Navy of the proposed pay-cuts until after the Atlantic Fleet, at sea, had learned the cruel facts from BBC radio bulletins and even read of them in newspapers on anchoring off Invergordon on Friday, 11 September. During the preceding week of crisis most of the Admiralty went on leave (as did the Army Council and the Air Council), to hide their heads in the sands of Nice and Naples while the storm broke in the messdecks and barrackrooms at home.

Following meetings by libertymen in the seamen's canteen ashore during the weekend and subsequently on the fo'c'sles of the anchored vessels, on Tuesday, 15 September the overwhelming majority of the lower-deck personnel of the Atlantic Fleet refused to take their ships to sea or to contribute any activity toward raising steam or weighing anchor. In all other respects they adhered to their ships' routine, were courteous to their officers and even apologised for inconveniences. There was not one incidence of violence and, although there were reports of ratings singing 'The Red Flag', there is no evidence that this was anything more than facetious mischief which was quickly stamped on by the majority.

The ships immediately involved were the battleships *Nelson*, *Rodney* and *Valiant*, the battle-cruiser *Hood*, the cruisers *Norfolk*, *Dorsetshire* and *York*, and the cruiser-minelayer *Adventure*. Fortuitously, *Warspite* and *Malaya* were at sea for sub-calibre shooting, while *Repulse*, off Cromarty, separated from her sisters and lacking support, had secured for sea and slipped. However, all three ships were to be quickly returned to Invergordon and anchored.

There was no doubt that many officers (themselves threatened with a pay-reduction of eleven per cent) were secretly *en rapport* with the men's action, always providing it remained within controllable limits. Captain F. B. Watson, commanding *Nelson*, confessed, 'From the investigations held I cannot do otherwise than sympathize with the men's anxieties for their future and that of their wives. It is no exaggeration to say that in many cases it is not hardship they are facing but the ruin of carefully and thriftily built-up homes. These men literally budget their commitments in pence. What little margin they have disappears under the new scale.'

Despite repeated and progressively more ominous signals from Senior Officer Atlantic Fleet (Rear-Admiral Wilfred Tomkinson, in *Hood*) the Admiralty vacillated, gave orders, cancelled them, brandished the Naval Discipline Act, and finally promised investigations into the men's claims of hardship if the ships proceeded to their home ports. With some misgivings the men agreed, and by midnight on Wednesday, 16 September the Atlantic Fleet had dispersed – the first step, in the Admiralty's opinion, toward breaking the deadlock.

The next step would be the identification of the mutiny's ringleaders and the seeking of evidence necessary to charge them. When the Devonport crews went ashore there were plain-clothes officers from Naval Intelligence, MI5 and the Plymouth police in the pubs and canteens, to buy drinks, gossip and eavesdrop. What these agents thought they uncovered were plans for a resumption of the mutiny leading to a landing in force and perhaps a march on London, but these were almost certainly fabricated by a few tipsy loudmouths and were totally unrealistic. They were, however, sufficient to alarm the Admiralty into warning the King that 'mutiny was about to be resumed in a very aggravated form'. A few days later, after a massive run on gold and the value of sterling plummeting by four shillings in the pound, a harassed Cabinet agreed to adjust the services' pay-cuts to a more reasonable level.

Moreover, the First Lord (now Sir Austin Chamberlain) assured the House, there would be no scapegoats, no victimisation; 'there will be no looking back to what has happened on this occasion, but we shall go forward together in the service of the country'.

Unfortunately the Admiralty had already begun to discharge suspected ratings from ships to barracks in anticipation of expelling them from the service. That they were covered by the First Lord's amnesty was irrelevant and, indeed, on 15 October, Chamberlain himself confided to the Board that he was 'unwilling to sanction any discharges before the General Election', which was only two weeks away. With the election over, Chamberlain immediately resigned his appointment, washing his hands of the whole affair, and the Admiralty could now draw their knives. A total of 397 ratings were discharged SNLR (Services No Longer Required) on the grounds that 'there is no room in the Navy for men whose conduct, character or lack of ability renders them undesirable for retention in the service'.

The spiteful charade only deepened the damage already done – not just the abandonment of the gold standard and the fall of the pound, which were transient things of small account, but also the end of the myth of the Royal Navy, the myth of immutability that had so long been unchallenged and in which the Navy itself had believed. The lower deck would never regain complete confidence in its officers nor the Navy as a whole in the Admiralty.

In a final effort to pretend that the Invergordon mutiny had never happened, the name 'Atlantic Fleet' was abolished and replaced by 'Home Fleet'.

*

The Military Training Act, passed on 26 May 1939, required all men on reaching twenty years of age to serve for six months in the Royal Navy, the Army or Royal Air Force, followed by three and a half years in the Reserve. This was superseded on 3 September by the National Service (Armed Forces) Act, which extended liability for military service to all men between eighteen and forty-one, called up by age-groups according to occupation. Additionally, on mobilisation, some 10,000 officers and men of the RNVR were absorbed into the regular service, this time to serve in every conceivable type of vessel from battleships to landing-craft.

Had it been possible for a man discharged in 1919 to find himself again in a warship in 1939 he would have discovered that remarkably little had changed. He would have seen badges he did not recognise – those of Asdic operators and radar operators, wiremen, photographers, and several Fleet Air Arm branches – but he would have identified seamen gunners, stokers, torpedomen and signalmen, and the orders piped over the ship's amplifier would be entirely familiar.

On the messdeck he would find the same hammocks, wooden tables and stools, the same mess-traps, but the rating's personal ditty-box had been replaced by a small fibre suitcase which also made redundant the blue 'bundle handkerchief' in which sailors had carried possessions ashore. All, now, had lockers for kit stowage, and eligible men still drew a tot of rum daily.

The Navy still retained the iniquitous Kit Upkeep system by which the rating, after his first gratis issue on enlistment, was required to maintain his uniform kit and bedding at the required standard (and periodical inspections ensured that he did) by purchasing his own replacements. For this purpose his pay – fortnightly at home and monthly on a foreign station – was supplemented by a few coppers, defined as Kit Upkeep Allowance. This was not only totally inadequate but, with pay so poor and pay-days so long separated, it was also never put aside, with the result that the cash purchase from Naval Stores of a pair of shoes, a jersey or, worse, a serge suit was a crippling undertaking. Increasingly, men were finding it simpler to allot ten shillings a month to an account with one of several approved naval tailors, such as Bernard's and Fleming's, with branches in all home ports, and so be relieved of the worry of kit upkeep. Officers allotted slightly larger sums to Gieves or Moss Bros – but for the same reason.

The Royal Naval College at Osborne had been closed in 1920, after only seventeen years of existence, replaced by a new wing at Dartmouth. The latter college was, of course, quite unsuited in almost all respects for the hurried training of thousands of candidates for temporary commissions who were to deluge into the service and, in due course, outnumber regular officers by two to one. They were drilled in less distinguished, rather bleaker establishments during the war of 1939–45. Almost all of them, however, would have readily conceded that they were guided, advised and sometimes steered away from disaster by their more experienced lower-deck subordinates of the regular service. As in the earlier war, the Admiralty placed every possible obstacle in the path of lower-deck regulars who were recommended for promotion to officer status. Those few who achieved a selection interview rarely progressed beyond it. The salesmen, teachers and office executives who became sub-lieutenants RNVR for the duration of hostilities would, it was explained, soon be returning to their department stores, classrooms and office desks, but an officer raised from the regular lower deck might anticipate retaining his commission in a peacetime Navy, and that would never do.

They came from every conceivable background, the slums of Glasgow and the clubs of St James's, the industrial towns and the green shires, from public schools and state schools, to the improvised training-centres of *King Alfred* and *Royal Arthur, Collingwood, Ganges, St George, Valkyrie,* and a score of others – run-down barracks, unwanted holiday-camps or hastily raised clutters of Nissen huts on windswept peninsulas. There were training bottlenecks in some of the more technical branches, but these were overcome by the introduction of several 'sub-branches' which included coders, radio mechanics, electricians and motor mechanics, men who brought civilian skills, education and expertise into a Navy which justified many of its procedures only by the fact that they had always been done that way and nobody had considered an alternative. Thrown more closely together and for longer periods than men of the Army and RAF, the relationship between long-serving and hostilities-only ratings was nevertheless excellent; there was never an 'us-and-them' climate and, indeed, after a short time it was difficult to distinguish between the two classes.

The war of 1939–45 was to be one in which capital ships were seldom deployed in more than twos or threes; there were to be no surface actions remotely approaching the scale of Jutland, but the arena would be much vaster than in the First World War. Far more resources than had been anticipated were to be concentrated in the North Atlantic and Arctic in meeting the war needs of Russia and, while many of the smaller warships and auxiliaries involved were quite unsuited for these inclement waters, little was done to make life tolerable for their crews. Operating, as many ships were, in the bitter conditions fringing the Polar ice-cap and as far north as humanly possible, it might be thought that these men would be provided with all the protective clothing that an Arctic expedition justified. The only concession, however, was a duffel-coat for each of the crew members whose station was above decks; there was nothing for those others who, presumably, were not expected to breathe clean air for eight or nine weeks. A duffel-coat, in any case, was pitifully poor insulation against the sub-zero temperatures, winds and freezing sleet of the Barents Sea. Officers and men alike made do with football shirts and stockings, pyjamas, towels and, most of all, the balaclava helmets, gloves and scarves knitted by families and friends at home. Without this domestic supply of woollen comforts it must surely have been impossible for vessels in northern areas to remain operationally efficient for long.

Winston Churchill was returned to the Admiralty in September 1939. The suggestion, made at the time and repeated by anecdotists ever since, that the signal 'Winston is back' was warmly welcomed throughout the Navy can be regarded as war-euphoric embroidery. There could have been very few serving officers old enough to have been influenced by his performance as First Lord during 1911 to 1915, while as Chancellor of the Exchequer between 1924 and 1929 he had been no friend to the Royal Navy. To the lower deck, interested in political issues but not in politicians, he was only a vague figure; he had not held any office for ten years.

It is perhaps incredible that one of Churchill's first measures on reaching the Admiralty was to order preparations for Operation Catherine, the purpose of which was to '*force a passage into the Baltic* and maintain there a naval force'.

In his memoir of 21 October 1939 to the First Sea Lord, Sir Dudley Pound, Churchill ordered:

> . . . I want four or five ships made into tortoises that we can put where we like and go to sleep content . . . but we must make them air-proof – i.e. not afraid of a thousand pound armour-piercing bomb, if by chance it should hit from ten thousand feet. This is not so large a structural rearrangement as might appear. You have got to pull a couple of turrets out of them, saving at least two thousand tons, and this two thousand tons has to be laid out in flat armour of six or seven inches, as high as possible, having regard to stability. The blank spaces of the turrets must be filled

with AA guns. This means going down from eight guns to four. But surely four 15-inch can wipe out *Scharnhorst* or *Gneisenau*. Before the new battleship [*Bismarck*] arrives we must have *King George V* and *Prince of Wales*. Let us therefore concentrate on having five or six vessels which are not afraid of the air, and therefore can work in narrow waters, and keep the high-class stuff for the outer oceans. Pull the superimposed turrets out and plaster the decks with steel. . . . Do not let us worry about the look of the ship. . . . These four-gun ships could be worked up to a very fine battery if the gunnery experts threw themselves into it. But above all they must bristle with AA, and they must swim or float wherever they choose. . . .

# *Notes*

1    *Vindictive* had been built as the 9750-ton cruiser *Cavendish* in 1918 but completed as a light carrier. She operated twelve aircraft and also mounted four 7.5-inch guns.

2    In 1918 the RNAS, consisting of 2500 naval aircraft and 55,000 officers and men, was transferred to the newly created Royal Air Force, with the Navy permitted only to retain control of its aircraft-carriers. Thereafter the Navy's aviation needs would always be subordinate to those of the RAF, with tragic results during the Second World War when the Air Ministry gave higher priority to strategic bombing than to involvement in maritime operations.

3    Only *Canada*, completed in 1915 for Chile but appropriated, was taken by that country, after refitting, under her original name, *Almirante Latorre*. A second battleship intended for Chile, *Almirante Cochrane*, was taken over for conversion to the aircraft-carrier *Eagle*.

4    The Washington Naval Treaty, 1921; the Geneva Naval Conference, 1927; the First London Naval Treaty, 1930.

5    The deplorable circumstances surrounding the Atlantic Fleet mutiny of 1931 – a crisis sufficiently grave to force Britain off the gold standard – are historically fascinating but too complex to be covered in detail by this book. The full story has been told by David Divine in his eminently readable *Mutiny at Invergordon*.

# V Same Enemy, Different War

## Chapter Eleven

*The early rounds of the Second World War – Norway, the collapse of France and the entry of Italy – the British bombardment of Mers-el-Kebir*

NOTWITHSTANDING the heroism of RAF pilots during the Battle of Britain and the tenacity of British troops in Africa and Europe, the Second World War was won and lost in the Atlantic – not in a campaign measured in days or weeks but in a conflict which continued bitterly and without pause for five years and eight months, over 3¼ million square miles of ocean. 'The Battle of the Atlantic', Winston Churchill said, 'was the dominating factor all through the war. Never could we forget that *everything* depended ultimately on its outcome.'

For Grand Admiral Erich Raeder, commanding the German Navy, the war had begun too soon. In 1935, on renouncing the Versailles Treaty, Hitler had informed him that the Kriegsmarine would not have to fight the Royal Navy until 1944 or 1945, by which time Raeder could expect to have a fleet consisting of 13 battleships and/or battle-cruisers, 4 aircraft-carriers, 250 submarines and a sizeable force of destroyers. By 1939, however, Raeder mustered only 6 battleships with two more almost completed, 8 cruisers with one building, one aircraft-carrier building (but never completed), 56 submarines and 41 destroyers.[1] By late 1942, Hitler's disenchantment with large surface warships meant that German shipbuilding resources were to be concentrated on submarine construction, with the result that 1093 U-boats were built during the war years.

The few large ships that Raeder did have were ingeniously designed and superbly constructed. The first three – *Graf Spee, Admiral Scheer* and *Deutschland* (later renamed *Lützow*) – from which the wraps were removed during the mid-thirties, were never satisfactorily classified by other envious navies because they seemed to incorporate the best of all worlds. Within a displacement of 14,000 tons there were six 11-inch guns and a speed of 28 knots from diesel engines which not only needed no 'raising-steam' time but also afforded the ability to steam 21,000 miles (nautical) without re-fuelling. Armoured protection was to heavy-cruiser quality, made possible by an all-welding technique. There were only seven war-ships in the world capable of overhauling and outgunning them. They were Britain's three remaining battle-cruisers and, interest-ingly, the four ships of Japan's 'Kongo' class.

*Scharnhorst* and *Gneisenau*, of 38,100 tons and completed in 1938, were even faster, being designed for 32 knots – though whether this maximum was ever achieved is questionable. Thus, given sea-room, they had the speed to avoid a confrontation with any enemy mount-ing heavier weaponry than their own nine 11-inch and twelve 5.9-inch guns.

Displacing 52,600 tons at full load, mounting eight 15-inch, twelve 5.9-inch and sixteen 4.1-inch guns, *Bismarck* and *Tirpitz* were completed in 1940 and 1941 respectively. They are still regarded by many to be the finest warships ever built. The design had its weak-nesses,[2] but these ships' armament was at least the equal of anything else afloat, and their speed of 30 knots and more was close to that of the world's fastest capital ship, *Hood*; but the latter, in all respects other than speed, was never a match for *Bismarck*, and should never have been deliberately opposed to her. However, *Brassey*'s prediction of 1908 still echoed. Because a battle-cruiser looked like a battleship, sooner or later she would be expected to fight like a battleship.

Of eight cruisers, three – *Admiral Hipper, Blücher* and *Prinz Eugen* – could be said to be as good as the best in the Royal Navy, the 'Counties', of which earlier criticisms on grounds of cost were becoming noticeably muted. The three Germans' armament was marginally heavier and their nominal speed of 32 knots was about the same, but their wartime performances were to be disappointing. The earlier five vessels, *Emden, Karlsruhe, Köln, Königsberg* and *Nürn-berg*, less formidable, would make only a negligible contribution to German naval operations.

On 21 August 1939, *Graf Spee* slipped quietly out of Wilhelms-haven into the Atlantic, followed three days later by her sister *Deutschland* and the supply-vessels *Altmark* and *Westerwald*. On 1 September the old *Schleswig-Holstein* shelled Polish shore-defences near Danzig, and the Second World War had begun.

The first few months were relatively uneventful for the three British battle-cruisers. *Hood* left Portsmouth to join the Home Fleet as the flagship of Vice-Admiral Sir William Whitworth, while *Repulse* provided heavyweight protection for transatlantic convoys. In December she escorted the first Canadian convoy to the United

Kingdom. *Renown* steamed southward, with *Ark Royal*, forming Force K in the vicinity of Freetown. It was the threatened approach of this combination that undoubtedly contributed to the decision of *Graf Spee*'s Captain Langsdorf, on 17 December, that he could not prevail and should scuttle his ship off Montevideo. Meanwhile, in the North Sea, *Hood* had been bombed but had suffered no casualties or serious damage.

British and French complacency was rocked when, during the first week in April, Germany launched a seaborne invasion of Norway, pre-empting the occupation plans with which the Allies had been toying since the beginning of the year.

On the evening of 7 April, Admiral Sir Charles Forbes, Commander-in-Chief, led the Home Fleet north-eastward from Scapa Flow, aware that something was happening and suspecting a break-out by enemy heavy units to attack the Atlantic convoy-routes. Coastal Command aircraft had reported enemy warships steaming north, but it was not appreciated until later that these were the German invasion Group 1, comprising *Gneisenau*, *Scharnhorst* and ten destroyers bound for Narvik, and Group 2, comprising *Hipper* and four destroyers heading for Trondheim.

There was, however, a useful British surface force already approaching the Norwegian coast. Vice-Admiral Whitworth, now flying his flag in *Renown*, was leading four destroyers toward the Vestfjorden, the approach to Narvik, to reinforce eight other destroyers which were laying an offshore minefield. The operation, here and farther south, was intended to counter the use of Norwegian coastal waters by German ore-carrying shipping.

Weather conditions in the Norwegian Sea were foul, with gale-force winds, sleet and driving snow. One of Whitworth's screening destroyers, *Glowworm* (1345 tons), commanded by Lieutenant-Commander Gerard Roope, had been given permission to leave her station to search for a man washed overboard, but had lost contact, and during the morning of the eighth ran into two destroyers of the German Group 2. Surprise was mutual, but Roope engaged immediately and his adversaries ran. *Glowworm* followed until *Hipper* intervened with her 8-inch guns.

Hit by the first salvo and heavily outgunned, the British destroyer retreated behind her own smoke, but then, as *Hipper* closed, turned again to ram. *Glowworm* tore into the heavy cruiser's starboard bow, shearing through 120 feet of armour before rolling over and sinking. *Hipper* picked up thirty-eight survivors.

Northward, *Renown* and her remaining destroyers were still steaming into a gale and a pounding sea toward the Vestfjorden, and during the afternoon Whitworth was ordered by the Admiralty to 'concentrate on preventing any German forces proceeding to Narvik' – which was the first intimation he had of the German activity. Unfortunately the Admiralty had also ordered those destroyers in the Vestfjorden to withdraw and join *Renown*, with the result that the enemy's Group 1 passed through the area un-molested, and on the following day ten large German destroyers would land 2000 mountain troops in Narvik. However, the Group's heavy escorts, *Gneisenau* and *Scharnhorst*, were intercepted by *Renown* at dawn on 9 April.

The two battleships, commanded by Admiral Günther Lütjens, turned north-westward to draw *Renown* and her destroyers away from the Vestfjorden, where – at that time – the ten German vessels packed with seasick soldiers would have fallen easy victims to a battle-cruiser's guns. In the event Whitworth engaged the enemy he could hardly see through the swirling snow, opening fire at 0405, ranging 18,000 yards. With the three larger warships steaming at 24 knots into punishing seas and blinding snow, *Renown*'s accompany-ing destroyers could neither keep pace nor take part in the exchange.

Commanding two fast warships each of 38,000 tons, between them mounting eighteen 11-inch and twenty-four 5.9-inch guns, it is difficult to understand why Lütjens should run from one elderly battle-cruiser with six 15-inch guns and little else of consequence. To the German Navy the psychological value of a successful surface action at this time would have been immense. Although *Royal Oak* and *Courageous* had been sunk by U-boats earlier in the war, torpedo sinkings did not capture the imagination so dramatically nor seem to demonstrate the superiority of one side over the other as did a stand-up battle between capital ships. The destruction of *Renown*, also, would to some extent have compensated for *Graf Spee*'s scuttling, four months before, which nobody understood. Lütjens, however, chose to run.

At more than ten miles *Renown*'s first salvo found *Gneisenau*, disabling her main armament control. The second crippled her forward turret and the third hit farther aft but caused only negligible damage. In her first action against an enemy and in her twenty-fourth year, this was superb shooting by *Renown*. Snow and spray were obscuring her gun-sights, while *Gneisenau* and *Scharnhorst*, not so embarrassed, were able to score twice with their after guns, although without seriously hurting their pursuer. At 0500 a heavy squall hid the Germans. *Renown*, having worked up to 29 knots, glimpsed them briefly again, but the weather was closing down, and *Gneisenau* and *Scharnhorst* soon disappeared into the northerly oblivion.

Whitworth was later to transfer his flag to *Warspite* and lead a force of four 'Tribal'-class destroyers up the fjord leading to Narvik to overwhelm the German naval forces berthed there, but otherwise the story of the Norwegian campaign is one of mishandled opportunities, of plans made and unmade even after operations were set in motion, of too few and untrained land forces, inadequate RAF fighter cover and outclassed carrier-borne aircraft – and all these bunglings overlaid by unnecessary interference by a Churchill-dominated Admiralty in London which seemed completely out of touch with the realities of the situation. The few success stories of the campaign belong to the destroyers and sloops of the Royal Navy, of which ten were sunk and fourteen damaged.[3] The battle-cruisers' contribution was not significant. *Hood* conveyed 250 troops to re-inforce a British expeditionary force which was soon to be ignominiously evacuated, and *Repulse* joined forces with her sister *Renown*, later to escort *Suffolk* back to Scapa Flow after the cruiser, having shelled Sola airfield, was pounced upon by a vengeful Luftwaffe. *Suffolk*, bereft of air cover, was severely damaged but achieved haven with her quarterdeck under water.

It was the collapse of the Norwegian campaign, directed largely by Winston Churchill, that marked the end of the lacklustre premiership of Neville Chamberlain and, ironically, raised Churchill to that supreme office on 10 May. He, accepting the duty with feigned reluctance, had the grace to confess later that 'considering the part I played in these events . . . it was a marvel that I survived'.

But, of course, there was nobody else.

Five days later, at 7.30 in the morning, Winston Churchill was awakened by the ringing of his bedside telephone. The caller was Paul Reynaud, Premier of France, who choked, 'We have been defeated. We are beaten; we have lost the battle.'

The larger ships of the Royal Navy played no part in the evacuation of the British Expeditionary Force from French ports other than, by their distant presence, to deny the intervention of the German Navy. This was the hour of the little ships, the destroyers and sloops, the paddle-steamers, the fishing-smacks and pleasure-craft. The story of Dunkirk has been told repeatedly elsewhere, and has no place in these pages. Of greater, long-term relevance was the fact that the entire coastline from North Cape to the southern Biscay was in German hands, that Italy, taking advantage of France's agony, had declared war as an ally of Germany and, finally, that there was uncertainty with regard to the loyalty of the French Navy.

The advantage to Germany of harbours, U-boat bases and airfields along the entire Scandinavian and Channel coastlines was quickly apparent and would become even more regretted later; already all transatlantic convoys had to be routed by the northwestern approaches. A more immediate problem, from a naval viewpoint, was that of the French and Italian fleets.

The Royal Navy never regarded the Italians as a serious rival to the Mediterranean Fleet. Italian warships were allegedly fast, with a Latin elegance of line, but they were also 'tin cans' and their crews were ill-trained 'sunshine sailors' who might bravely swagger the streets of Naples and La Spezia but would turn a hideous green in the North Atlantic, and experience sudden colonic convulsions at hearing a gun fired anywhere. This rule-of-thumb evaluation of Mussolini's battle-fleet was not entirely justified in practice, and it is fair to say that there was considerable evidence of Italian courage and ability, particularly in smaller vessels and underwater operations. There were several occasions on which the Mediterranean Fleet burned its fingers because of an arrogant disregard for 'the Wops'' capacity.

The French Navy, however, was something different. It had earned grudging British recognition for being professionally efficient, and it was also true that during the dark days of May and June the naval service had shown no inclination to disintegrate as had the French Army.

Polish, Dutch and Norwegian warships and their crews had already thrown in their lot with the British, but these did not amount to anything like the forces commanded by Admiral Jean Darlan. Including reservists, the French Navy numbered 160,000 men, nine battleships in service and two building (one afloat and the other in the Landevanne yard from which it would never graduate) and one aircraft-carrier. Further, there was an excellent range of *contre-torpilleurs*, large, fast destroyers of up to 3000 tons and nominal speeds of 43 knots, which, with their 5.5-inch guns, were almost light cruisers, faster than anything the British had. They were ideal long-range escorts – a class of vessel in which the Royal Navy was deficient; it would be another year before Britain could provide escorts of small warships for the entire Atlantic crossing.

The inconvenience caused by a withdrawal of French ships from war operations and the German occupation of the Channel and Biscay ports was of minor consequence by comparison with the threatening situation subsequent upon the surrender of the French fleet to the enemy. The balance would be dangerously tilted. An American intelligence assessment of 13 June predicted that a

German–Italian–French naval coalition would be one-third stronger than the combined Anglo-American strength in the Atlantic, even if the Pacific Fleet were recalled from Pearl Harbor.

In response to Churchill's overtures, Darlan would only emphasise that there was no question of French warships being transferred to German control; the armistice terms stipulated that they were to be demobilised and disarmed but would otherwise remain under the jurisdiction of the new Vichy French government. Treaties signed with Nazi Germany, however, had long been regarded as meaningless, and there was little doubt in London or Washington that Germany and Italy would seize the French warships when it suited them to do so.

Fortuitously, few French warships of relevance were in metropolitan French ports when the armistice terms were promulgated on 22 June. A few were in Portsmouth and Devonport,[4] a battleship (*Lorraine*), four cruisers and three destroyers were at Alexandria with Admiral Cunningham's Eastern Mediterranean Fleet, six cruisers lay at Algiers and there were submarines in Bizerte harbour. The new battleship *Richelieu* had got away from Brest to Dakar, carrying the French Naval Academy's midshipmen, while the half-completed *Jean Bart* had scraped out of St-Nazaire to reach Casablanca in French Morocco.

The heaviest concentration, however, was at Mers-el-Kebir, the French naval base near Oran. Here, behind a mile-long stone breakwater, were moored the battleships *Dunkerque*, *Strasbourg*, *Provence* and *Bretagne*. In company were the heavy destroyers *Volta*, *Mogador*, *Tigre*, *Lynx*, *Kersaint* and *Le Terrible*, the seaplane-carrier *Commandante Teste*, and a miscellaneous collection of smaller destroyers, sloops and escort-vessels.

*Hood*, having been briefly employed in convoying New Zealand troops to the United Kingdom, was at Gibraltar, and on 28 June hoisted the flag of Vice-Admiral Sir James Somerville, appointed to command the newly formed Force H. This comprised, in addition to *Hood*, the battleships *Valiant* and *Resolution*, the aircraft-carrier *Ark Royal*, two cruisers and eleven destroyers. Three days later Somerville received orders to set into motion Operation Catapult. 'You are charged', cabled Churchill, 'with one of the most disagreeable and difficult tasks that a British Admiral has ever been faced with, but we have complete confidence in you and rely on you to carry it out relentlessly.' By Somerville's later account, he and his officers were horror-struck by the decision.

Force H was to station itself off Oran on the morning of 3 July, when Somerville would present an ultimatum to Admiral Marcel-

Bruno Gensoul, commanding the French squadron in the anchorage. Simplified, the ultimatum offered a choice of four courses of action: (1) the French warships could join the British and continue the war against Germany and Italy; or (2) proceed with reduced crews to a British port or to the (French) West Indies, where they would be demilitarised and their crews repatriated; or (3) scuttle themselves in the anchorage where they lay; or (4) be destroyed by the Royal Navy.

Admiral Gensoul would be given six hours in which to make his choice after being offered the ultimatum at 0600. (See Appendix 2.)

*Valiant* had been one of Evan-Thomas's 5th Battle Squadron at Jutland, but *Resolution* had been completed just too late to participate in that battle. Off Norway, only ten weeks before the present operation, she had been hit by one bomb of fifty aimed at her by four Heinkels, suffering two killed and twenty-seven wounded. *Hood*, too, had never been involved in a surface action, although during the Spanish Civil War she had captured the headlines by training her 15-inch guns at a Spanish cruiser, *Canarias*, that threatened interference with a blockade-running British merchant ship.

All three British capital ships were more than twenty years old.

*Bretagne* and *Provence* were of the same generation, but *Dunkerque* and *Strasbourg* were modern battleships (completed 1937 and 1938 respectively) of 27,000 tons and 29 knots, each with an all-forward main armament of eight 13-inch guns mounted in quadruple turrets. This arrangement resulted in an immense blind arc astern, and also meant that one hit could disable half the ship's heavy guns.

The destroyer *Foxhound* entered the Bay of Oran at 0600 carrying Captain C. S. Holland (commanding *Ark Royal* and sometime Naval Attaché in Paris) but remained just outside the anti-submarine nets so that, if necessary, she could withdraw without being impeded. Admiral Gensoul, for his part, refused to come out to meet Holland, and so the negotiations had to be conducted through a go-between, a Lieutenant Dufay of the French Navy, and by lamp signal – a clumsy arrangement which did nothing to ease the situation.

Gensoul transmitted the ultimatum terms to the Chief of Naval Staff in Nérac, Admiral Le Luc (Darlan was at Clermont-Ferrand). He omitted to mention the British invitation to French warships to continue fighting or at least go to a British port, probably because such a direct contravention of the armistice articles after they had so recently been ratified by the Vichy government was not to be considered. Neither, however, did Gensoul mention the option that offered his ships sanctuary in the French West Indies or the United States, and if Darlan was made aware by some other channel of the escape clause he did not relay it to the French Council of Ministers, meeting that afternoon to discuss the Oran emergency. Gensoul's signal had merely said: 'A British force comprising three battleships, an aircraft-carrier, cruisers and destroyers off Oran. Ultimatum issued: Sink your ships within six hours or we shall compel you to do so by force. My reply: French ships will meet force with force.'

The forenoon passed into afternoon with the local second-hand exchanges achieving nothing. Observing the French ships taking in awnings and apparently raising steam, Somerville, patrolling off-shore, signalled that Gensoul would not be allowed to leave harbour, repeated that the ultimatum would expire at 1400 GMT (also local time) and then ordered Swordfish from *Ark Royal* to mine the harbour entrance. The French Admiral was withdrawing into bloody-minded intractability, but the minutes were ticking by, and he needed to play for time. At 1330 he agreed to discuss terms with Holland aboard *Dunkerque*.

It was a meeting of incompatibles. While it was unthinkable that Gensoul could now scuttle his ships or tamely allow the British to sink them, Holland had no authority (nor, for that matter, had Somerville) to modify 'the irrevocable decision of the War Cabinet' that, in the event of French non-compliance, it was the 'firm intention of HM Government to destroy the ships'.

It was useless for Gensoul to plead that his acceptance of the British terms could mean that the whole of France was overrun by the Germans and Italians, and self-defeating when he quoted Darlan's orders to the effect that no French warship should be surrendered intact to an enemy, and that *adequate provisions should be made for scuttling if capture was threatened*. Ships scuttled in harbour could be raised (as many scuttled French warships subsequently were) and, if unfit for sea service, their materials re-employed or their guns mounted as shore-batteries (as, subsequently, were the 13.4-inch guns of *Provence*, at Toulon). Gensoul needed guidance from his own government, and Somerville, aware of the other's predicament and anxious to avoid bloodshed at the price of an hour's patience, extended his time-limit. But, he warned Gensoul, 'If none of the British proposals is accepted by 1730 BST repeat 1730 BST it will be necessary to sink your ships'. Any hope of compromise vanished, however, when French naval headquarters alerted all warships in the western Mediterranean by radio: 'Get under way ready for action. Report to the Admiral in *Dunkerque* at Oran.' The order, transmitted both coded and in plain language, was intercepted by Germans and British, as it was intended to be, and the Admiralty in London signalled Somerville: 'Settle the affair quickly or you will have reinforcements to deal with.'

It was a beautiful late afternoon as Captain Holland and his party descended the side-ladder of *Dunkerque* to board *Foxhound*'s motor-cutter. The shadows were beginning to lengthen, but the sea beyond the breakwater was as deeply blue as only the Mediterranean can be, flashing gold in the sun. Within the harbour the calm water peeled away from the launch's bows like torn silk, and as it passed below the quarterdeck of *Bretagne* the officer of the watch saluted Holland, who reciprocated. Bugles were sounding 'Action stations'.

Oran and its fortified harbour lay in a dun-coloured ten-mile bay with the French naval base of Mers-el-Kebir four miles to the west-ward, linked by a coastal road along which were a number of batteries. The anchorage and docks of the base were protected by torpedo-nets stretched from Point Canastel to Cap Falcon, and a mile-long stone breakwater reached into the bay from Fort Mers-el-Kebir, terminating in a lighthouse.

Gensoul's four big ships were tied inside the breakwater, with their sterns against it, at the lighthouse end. This meant that the sixteen 13-inch guns shared by *Dunkerque* and *Strasbourg* were directed shoreward. Only the ageing *Bretagne* and *Provence* could each address four 13.4-inch guns toward the sea. Such a berthing arrangement might be sensible and convenient in peacetime, but Gensoul can be criticised for disposing his tethered ships so help-lessly during wartime, particularly in the uncertain climate of July 1940. When Somerville's squadron appeared off Oran on the third the French commander could make no move to improve his deploy-ment in case the British were provoked into opening fire.

Just before 1800 the British force was ten miles to the north-north-west but steaming an easterly run at 20 knots. Two days earlier their off-duty watches had been ashore in Gibraltar, strolling the bars and well-stocked shops of Main Street and Irish Town, or swimming in Catalan Bay or from Eastern Beach – a rare pleasure, for most of these were 'cold-water ships', recently from Scapa Flow and Rosyth. Few of the crewmen in turrets, directors and engine-rooms could have said very precisely where Mers-el-Kebir was, but it was an exotic name that evoked a vision of minarets, palm-trees, bazaars and veiled women. Perhaps there would be a run ashore for the starboard watch tomorrow. . . .

At 17,000 yards the British ships opened fire.

Moored in a single group, the four French battleships were a target almost impossible to miss. The massive projectiles punched into the breakwater, and seamen and gun-crews were torn down by hurtling masonry and ragged debris. Screws churned as the big ships struggled to get under way. A 15-inch salvo from *Hood* fell, erupting, into the berth vacated seconds earlier by *Strasbourg*, astern of which *Dunkerque* and *Provence* were hauling off in an attempt to form some sort of steaming formation. *Provence* was the first to fire back at the British, her shells screaming just over the funnels of her own flagship.

*Bretagne* was hit before she could clear the breakwater. One shell wrecked her after turret and another crashed into an engine-room. The ship was in flames aft when two further projectiles found her, and then the battleship was ripped apart by a devastating explosion from which there could be no survival. Vomiting thick black smoke and hissing steam, she rolled, sinking in seconds and taking with her 977 men who, when they had climbed from their hammocks that morning, had thought their war to be over.

Gensoul's *Dunkerque* was next. Hit by three shells, a boiler-room was disabled, reducing her steam rapidly and, just after getting away one salvo – which straddled *Hood* – her fire-control circuitry was dislocated and her guns rendered useless. Nursing his remaining steam-pressure, her captain eased the ship shoreward to anchor in shallow water, out of immediate range and where Gensoul would remain only an angry spectator.

What he saw was the wide and sun-drenched Bay of Oran heavily blanketed by crawling smoke and torn by shell-splashes. There was confusion, not surprising under the circumstances of the attack, and the British had enjoyed the whole day, steaming back and forth, to calculate their ranges. The destroyer *Mogador*, from the far side of the bay, leading four of her sisters through the smoke toward the open sea, found the channel obstructed by a tug and was compelled to stop. Hit aft, her depth-charges exploded, blowing off her stern and killing thirty-seven of her crew, but she managed to claw her way toward Oran harbour, where fire-tenders met her.

Now it was *Provence*, with a turret hit, ammunition on fire and the after magazine flooded, that turned for the shallows. Commendably, she had got away three salvoes at *Hood* leading the British force which had been steaming from east to west since first firing. *Provence* beached with her bows in five fathoms, and so her undamaged forward guns could not be directed against her assailants. The 10,000-ton seaplane-carrier *Commandante Teste*, with her irrelevant 4-inch armament and complete lack of armour, got clear of the breakwater, but remained in the vicinity of the sunken *Bretagne*, taking aboard some 130 survivors.

At 14,000 yards, or about 8 miles, the British heavy squadron steamed in line ahead at 5-cable (half-mile) intervals under circumstances that could hardly have been more favourable. The sun was falling ahead, the day temperature had cooled, and the ships' speed of 20 knots – about 23 miles per hour – provoked a pleasing breeze across the bridges, flag-decks and above-deck stations, into the open sighting-ports and wind-scoops. All who could had fixed their eyes on the distant target-area, of which could just be seen the white chalk-line of the breakwater overlaid by floating smoke. It needed binoculars to see the French warships' superstructures and, beyond, the docks and derricks of Mers-el-Kebir.

Incredibly, only sixteen minutes had elapsed since the first shot of the day had been fired by *Resolution* and before Gensoul was compelled to signal a plea for a cease-fire. Somerville hoisted Flag 6 at once, and the British ships, with guns silent, steamed out of the haze of their own cordite smoke into clear air. The cease-fire was not immediately mutual. Closer inshore the destroyers were dropping depth-charge patterns to discourage several French submarines apparently attempting a torpedo attack, and then Somerville turned his squadron to the north-westerly to avoid the uncomfortably accurate fire of the coastal 6-inch gun-batteries.

It was about this time that *Strasbourg*, taking advantage of the dense crawling smoke, had escaped from the bay and, following the coast north-eastward, reached the open sea closely accompanied by *Tigre* and *Lynx*, while *Volta* and *Le Terrible* held off the British destroyers. With the channel mined by *Ark Royal*'s aircraft, Somerville was not expecting an escape, but now *Strasbourg* had somehow evaded the mines and was turning easterly with a fifteen-mile start. The Admiral swung his ships around to give chase, and ordered *Ark Royal*[5] to fly off a torpedo-carrying sortie.

The aircraft-carrier was already detached and steaming into the wind, and her Swordfish made their first run at *Strasbourg* as she cleared Point Aigulle. All torpedoes missed. A second attack was also abortive, and by now it was 2020, with *Strasbourg* forty miles from Mers-el-Kebir, twenty-five miles ahead of the pursuing *Hood*, and working up to full speed. Somerville followed until darkness fell, when he called off the operation.

Deservedly, *Strasbourg*, her accompanying destroyers and *Commandante Teste* all reached Toulon on the following day, to be joined by six cruisers from Algiers. Somerville took Force H back to Gibraltar, but on 6 July *Ark Royal* was ordered to return to Mers-el-Kebir to finish off *Dunkerque*. A dawn attack was launched in the face of intense anti-aircraft fire, yet again all torpedoes failed until a patrol-launch carrying depth-charges, alongside the anchored battleship, was hit. The resulting explosion tore a hole in *Dunkerque*'s hull, killing 150 men and putting her out of service for a year. The total Oran death-toll was now 1500.

Two days later the little aircraft-carrier *Hermes* (15 Swordfish to *Ark Royal*'s 72) showed her big sister how it should be done. Six of her aircraft carried out a single attack on the new 38,500-ton *Richelieu*, in Dakar harbour, scoring a hit aft which damaged rudders and propeller shaft, flooded three compartments, and crippled the battleship similarly for a year.

# Notes

1   The Kriegsmarine also had two 1908 pre-Dreadnoughts, *Schlesien* and *Schleswig-Holstein*, all that Germany had been allowed to retain of the Kaiser's navy. They were suitable only for coastal training, and seldom ventured out of the Baltic.

2   Contrary to modern practice, *Bismarck*'s secondary 5.9-inch guns were not dual-purpose, i.e., they were almost useless against aircraft. This deficiency necessitated the provision of a third set of 4.1-inch AA guns, an unnecessary complication. Also the German designers, usually so thorough, had exposed vital communication circuitry above armour level, to be quickly destroyed in action, while protection, although of very high quality, was somewhat irrelevantly distributed.

3   To be fair, the Norwegian adventure also decimated the Kriegsmarine, which lost the heavy cruiser *Blücher*, the smaller cruisers *Königsberg* and *Karlsruhe*, and ten destroyers, while *Deutschland* was out of commission for a year. Both *Scharnhorst* and *Gneisenau* were damaged.

4   The old battleship *Courbet*, one destroyer, three submarines, three torpedo-boats, a patrol-vessel and two submarine-chasers were at Portsmouth; one destroyer, two submarines, three submarine-chasers, six tugs, and subsequently the old battleship *Paris* were in Devonport.

5   Although *Ark Royal* was the most celebrated British aircraft-carrier of the war, the early record of her aircraft was one of almost unparalleled failure, including such slapstick incidents as two planes brought down by the blast of their own bombs and their crews taken prisoner by the U-boat they were bombing, and a fourteen-plane attack on the cruiser HMS *Sheffield*, fortunately another failure. The carrier's aircraft did, however, eventually hit *Bismarck* with two torpedoes of fifteen fired, contributing considerably to her later sinking.

# Chapter Twelve

*Communications – Force H and the Italian Navy – Denmark Strait and the loss of* Hood

THE ADMIRALTY'S communication system had been immensely improved since the days of the Grand Fleet's spark transmitters. There was now an integrated network of shore stations, rather like a vast spider's web with threads stretching thousands of miles, capable of exchanging signals with ships in any part of the world. At the centre of the web was Admiralty Wireless, situated below the Citadel – the ugly concrete blockhouse behind Whitehall which also housed Winston Churchill's war headquarters.

The terms 'wireless' and 'wireless telegraphy' were still jealously preferred to the more recent 'radio'. In general, 'W/T' was deemed to refer to Morse code communications, which represented by far the greater percentage of signals traffic and required a trained operator to transmit or read it, while 'R/T' (radio-telephony) indicated the short-range voice-exchanges of which almost anyone was capable.

In wartime ships maintained wireless silence, relaxed only in an extreme emergency. For the purpose of long-distance shore-to-ship communication the world's seas were partitioned into defined areas, each controlled by an 'area broadcast station' which continually transmitted signals intended for those ships operating in, or passing through, that area. The signals were sequentially numbered and, since the overwhelming majority were in code or cipher[1] (including the address), they all had to be read in total and logged by every operator before decoding revealed the identity of the addressee.

In theory it was possible for a signal, given priority, to be read by the captain of a ship in, say, the Arctic, only minutes after it had been written in the Admiralty, but in practice there were several delaying factors, not least of which were those of encoding before transmission and decoding on receipt. Although, in due course, there would be electrical cipher machines with typewriter key-boards, such as Typex, based on the German 'Enigma', the earlier 'One Time Pad' conversion involved a lengthy paper-and-pencil subtraction process, so that a long signal could require several hours to prepare for transmission and, when received by the ship at sea, the same time to unravel.

Thus, to reduce delay, brevity in compiling a signal became an obsession, often carried too far – and this, coupled with the Admiralty's other penchant for issuing orders to ships at sea with little or no supporting information, sometimes had serious conse-quences.

At Copenhagen, Nelson could see all his own ships and those of the enemy at the same time, assess the situation and decide to risk disobedience, confident of his own ability and that of his squadron. In a later, more complex war, a commander afloat did not enjoy Nelson's advantages. Forces far beyond his range of vision, beyond his knowledge, were of vital concern to him, and he was wholly dependent upon the intelligence conceded to him by the Admiralty. If he received orders inadequately supported by intelligence, and which also seemed to him unwise or otherwise objectionable, he had to remind himself that the Admiralty had, or *should* have, a much wider view of the over-all developing circumstances and, despite his misgivings, no commander could fight a war by obeying only those orders that happened to coincide with his own philosophy.

In August 1940, *Hood* returned to the United Kingdom, in due course to hoist the flag of Vice-Admiral Lancelot Holland, her place in Force H, at Gibraltar, being taken by *Renown*.

The threat of the Italian Navy, if regarded as something of a joke by the Mediterranean Fleet, was not to be ignored. It included some of the largest and fastest warships in the world, ideally positioned to disrupt the flow of shipping through the Mediterranean and particu-larly the reinforcement and provisioning of the British forces in Egypt, while Malta was perilously vulnerable.

The first significant clash between British and Italian heavy surface forces was delayed until late November 1940, when the Italians attempted to intercept a convoy of three merchant ships embarking 1400 troops and accompanied by the cruisers *Manchester* and *Southampton*, on passage from Gibraltar to Alexandria. The convoy was further escorted by Force H, now consisting of *Renown* (Somerville), *Ark Royal*, the cruisers *Sheffield* and *Despatch*, and nine destroyers. It was intended that, south of Sardinia, the troopships should be handed over to the battleship *Ramillies*, the cruisers *New-*

*castle, Berwick* and *Coventry*, and five destroyers of the Mediterranean Fleet, which would then shepherd them through the 'Narrows' between Sicily and Cape Bon. Somerville's Force H would return to Gibraltar while the convoy and new escort passed southward of Malta.

At 0630 on 27 November, however – before the rendezvous with *Ramillies* had been achieved – an RAF Sunderland from Malta reported sighting an Italian squadron off Cape Spartivento, the southern tip of Sardinia. This, it would be later known, consisted of the battleships *Vittorio Veneto* and *Guilio Cesare*, the 8-inch cruisers *Trieste, Trento, Bolzano, Fiume, Gorizia, Zara* and *Pola*, and sixteen destroyers.

Force H was heavily outgunned, but Somerville decided to hit first. At 1130 he turned *Renown* and his three large cruisers toward the enemy, forty miles to the north-east, and worked up to full speed.

Shortly afterwards *Ramillies* was in contact. The old battleship could not hope to keep pace with *Renown*, but Somerville was able to take *Berwick* and *Newcastle* in company. At 1230 the enemy was sighted and immediately engaged.

The Italian cruisers retreated, making smoke, and at 1300 their battleships, seen ahead, opened fire. Only *Berwick* was hit, but the British cruisers had no choice but to fall back on *Renown*. The running action that followed, with the British in pursuit of the overwhelmingly stronger Italian squadron, lasted about ninety minutes. *Ark Royal* launched eleven aircraft against the battleships but no hits were scored, and it was soon apparent that not only were the Italian ships marginally faster but also Somerville's mixed force was being drawn dangerously near to the Italian coast. His first responsibility was the safety of the convoy, and during the early afternoon he broke off the action to return to the troopships.

It was a disappointing conclusion, and the Italians broadcast the claim that Force H had run away from the Italian squadron. Churchill, who had recently criticised Admiral Cunningham (Commander-in-Chief Mediterranean) for reporting that Italian destroyers in an earlier minor action had shown considerable gallantry, was even more angered by Somerville's 'lack of offensive spirit'.

The First Lord, Mr A. V. Alexander, and the First Sea Lord, Admiral Sir Dudley Pound, taking their cue from the Prime Minister, made arrangements to have Somerville relieved of his post and replaced by Admiral Harwood, the victor of the River Plate. Churchill approved, commenting that 'should the Admiral [be found] blameworthy and unless facts emerge which are very different to those on which we have rested, I hope the relief will take place this week'.

Fortunately for Somerville a court of enquiry had already decreed that he had behaved perfectly correctly, so that his replacement now could hardly be justified on the grounds of inept leadership. Somerville survived. He was lucky; others would be less so.

The Admiralty, however, was not to concede without a Parthian shot. 'No opportunity', Somerville was admonished, 'must be allowed to pass of attaining what is in fact the ultimate object of the Royal Navy – the destruction of the enemy's forces whenever and wherever encountered.'

It is undeniable that, when doubt with regard to an officer's enterprise is expressed or implied, that doubt is regarded by the men of his command as also a reflection on their own qualities, and accordingly resented. It is similarly paradoxical that a sailor might denounce his ship as the worst in the squadron, his squadron the worst in the fleet, but an outsider who says so will get a fist in his face. The Royal Navy in general, and the Mediterranean Fleet in particular, were beginning to experience disenchantment with Winston Churchill, who seemed determined to play Prime Minister, First Lord and First Sea Lord simultaneously, and were stung by his alleged retort, in his cups, that the Navy was motivated only by rum, buggery and the lash. They, the Navy, might make that sort of jeer, but not an outsider.

For *Repulse* there was a Cinderella role in more northerly, colder seas. In late July she had searched unsuccessfully for *Gneisenau* off the Norwegian coast after the German battleship had been damaged by a torpedo from the submarine *Clyde*, but her crew had enjoyed home leave when she docked during the first three weeks in October. *Repulse* emerged in two-tone camouflage, fitted with Type 284 radar and a number of 20-millimetre Oerlikon guns. During the course of the year to follow, it was planned, the elderly battle-cruiser would be sent to the United States, to have her AA armament completely changed, superfluous torpedo-tubes removed, after armour strengthened and a slanting cowl added to her forward funnel – but none of these improvements would be achieved.

In November 1940, *Repulse* was involved in operations against German weather-ships in the Arctic and, during the same month, covered a raid on the Norwegian island of Jan Meyen, when an enemy scientific expedition was captured and the wireless station destroyed.

None of these activities, however, made news; they were overshadowed by more dramatic events elsewhere. Half of the Italian battle-fleet had been disabled at Taranto, and the auxiliary cruiser *Jervis Bay* had achieved immortality by engaging *Admiral Scheer* while her convoy scattered. Nearer home the Blitzkrieg continued in unprecedented ferocity; 500 bombers razed the centre of Coventry, and Birmingham and Southampton suffered badly. Worst of all, large areas of London were destroyed and St Paul's Cathedral only just saved. For the first time merchant seamen and civilian losses were heavier than those of the fighting services.

*Hood*'s crew, returning from the Mediterranean in the summer of 1940, would not have regarded the desolate wastes of Scapa Flow as a profitable exchange. The Orkneys were allegedly a part of the United Kingdom but, for all that it mattered, they might as well be on the moon. The men of Beatty's Invincibles, a quarter of a century before, had felt the same way.

Then, in September, *Hood* was ordered to Rosyth, 150 miles nearer to the English Channel across which a German invasion was still feared. *Hood*'s men were delighted – and even more so in January 1941 when the old ship was warped into dry dock for a two-month refit.

It was at this time that her 5.5-inch guns were removed, being considered, rightly, of little relevance, and she was equipped with both navigational and gunnery radar. Also fitted were five UP batteries.

UP (Uprotated Projectile) batteries were twenty-barrel rocket-launchers, carried as defence against low-level air-attack and weighing between six and seven tons. The projectiles fired were PAC (Parachute and Cable) rockets of 170 millimetres (6.7 inches) diameter and weighing 35 lb. They had a ceiling of 2000–2500 feet and were intended to release bombs (or 'aerial mines') attached to wires and suspended by parachute in the anticipated path of enemy aircraft.

The weapon had been developed by Professor Frederick Lindemann (later Lord Cherwell), Churchill's principal adviser on scientific and technical matters, who, in the 1930s, had argued against the promotion of radar in favour of infra-red detection, and had always been convinced that his rocket-propelled aerial mines could be more effective than AA guns.

The trouble with the UP was that it was a persistent and expensive failure. The Navy did not like it, nor did they like the exposed crates of explosive warheads on decks and turrets. The men preferred their familiar 4-inch HA, their Oerlikons and pom-poms.

However, Lindemann's UP could not be refused. *Hood* had one battery fitted to the roof of 'B' turret, forward, one each side of the forward funnel, and one each side of the boat-deck.

*Repulse* had spent the second Christmas of the war covering mine-laying operations off the south-east coast of Iceland, and in January 1941 joined the unsuccessful hunt for *Scharnhorst* and *Gneisenau* – now dubbed 'Salmon and Gluckstein' – which had broken out into the Atlantic via the Denmark Strait and would between them sink 22 ships totalling 115,000 tons before regaining Brest two months later.

On 18 May, *Repulse* lay in the Clyde, awaiting the assembly of convoy WS8B, destined for Malta and the Middle East. It was about time, her company rejoiced, that they were given a chance to get their knees brown – although, knowing their luck, they would probably be required to hand over the convoy to *Renown* at Gibraltar, after barely a sniff of the Mediterranean, and then return to the gales and sleet of the North Atlantic.

*Renown* had fared rather better than her sisters. At dawn on 9 February, still flying Vice-Admiral Somerville's flag, she led *Malaya*, *Ark Royal*, *Sheffield* and ten destroyers on an audacious foray into the Gulf of Genoa to subject the shipbuilding yards and installations of Genoa, Leghorn and La Spezia to a destructive sea and air bombardment. More than 300 tons of shells flung at Genoa started large fires in the Ansaldo electric works at Cornigliano Ligure and the central power station, and severely damaged oil-tanks, the marshalling-yard, dry docks, the inner harbour and moored merchant ships. The Italians were taken completely by surprise, and the raiders suffered no casualties.

On 18 May, *Renown* lay anchored at Gibraltar with her fellows of Force H – *Ark Royal*, *Sheffield* and the destroyers – awaiting the sailing orders that would take them out to rendezvous with *Repulse* and WS8B.

*Hood* was in Scapa Flow, in company with the flagship of the Home Fleet, *King George V*, the new battleship *Prince of Wales*, and the equally new aircraft-carrier *Victorious*, which, loaded with 48 crated Hurricane aircraft assigned to Malta, was under orders to join convoy WS8B, and *Repulse*, in the Clyde estuary.

Scapa Flow had been stripped of its defences after the First World War and no attempt was made to re-equip the location until 1940. It was still the most miserable anchorage in home waters, and any sailor of 1916 landed by his ship's drifter at Flotta's landing-stage in 1941 would have immediately recognised the huddle of ugly buildings to which the narrow puddled road led him. He would have seen the same empty expanses of rain-lashed heather with a scattering of bedraggled sheep, the same sagging goal-posts standing in lakes of water. A Salvation Army canteen still served the same tea, beans on toast and bread-and-jam – although the Nissen-built cinema now boasted a small organ that led half-hearted community singing prior to each film-showing. Flotta's major attraction and almost its sole redeeming feature was the Fleet Canteen.

It was a building of aircraft-hangar proportions – necessary to accommodate the thousands who poured ashore with no other objective – bleakly furnished, and with twenty barmen behind a long counter swimming with spilt beer, filling glasses without pause, exchanged for tickets purchased in strips from cash-windows. The air was thick with tobacco smoke. Hundreds drank to get drunk, sang, blasphemed, looked for quarrels with men of other ships, and the patrols waited with swinging batons. It was a place where old animosities surfaced, real or imaginary, and it was wise to remain in the proximity of others from the same ship, particularly if one's ship was a battleship or battle-cruiser which left the enclosed anchorage of Scapa Flow only rarely for a brief screening operation, manoeuvres or gunnery practice, and then always carefully escorted by a brood of destroyers. Otherwise, for months, they swung idly at their cables. It was a painfully monotonous existence, but to the crews of those other ships that spent the same months continuously at sea – like the 'County'-class cruisers patrolling the white-shot wastes north of the Arctic Circle – it was a secure lotus-eating existence behind anti-submarine nets and shore-batteries. Even Scapa Flow was a haven of peace and comfort compared with the sleet-drenched Denmark Strait or the icy hell of Bear Island, and when the opportunity arose the men of the 'Counties' said so, loudly.

And during the evening of Sunday, 18 May the German battleship *Bismarck* and the heavy cruiser *Prinz Eugen* steamed out of the Gulf of Danzig, hoping to slip unreported through the Kattegat to begin a voyage of destruction that had been code-named *Rheinübung*. Aboard *Bismarck* was Admiral Günther Lütjens with orders to proceed to the Arctic, oil from one of five tankers already on passage to remote rendezvous positions, and then turn southward at high speed through the Iceland–Faeroes gap into the Atlantic.

In the event Lütjens would choose the longer route southward via the Denmark Strait, which he had negotiated before and considered more secure. Also he did not pass through the Kattegat unseen, for soon after dawn on the twentieth the squadron was sighted by the cruiser *Gotland* of the Royal Swedish Navy, which transmitted a report to the Ministry of Marine in Stockholm. More unfortunately, the two German warships and their escorts were later seen by a member of the Norwegian resistance from the shore near Kristiansand.

Captain Henry Denham, RN, British Naval Attaché in Stockholm, had already passed an O-U (Most Immediate) despatch to the Admiralty in London: 'Kattegat today 20th May at 1500 two large warships escorted by three destroyers five escort vessels ten or twelve aircraft passed Marstrand course north west = 2058/20.'

The other message, tapped out from an illicit radio transmitter on the Norwegian coast, confirmed the Admiralty's fears. *Bismarck* and *Prinz Eugen* were at sea – but where were they going? The ocean was vast and the Royal Navy's patrolling cruisers were ridiculously thinly spread, while, so far as the bigger warships were concerned, it was unlikely that any could be successfully matched with *Bismarck*. Despite the pride and the propaganda, those sufficiently armed were too slow, and those sufficiently fast were too flimsy.

*Raise steam with despatch.*

The signal had been flashed across the darkness of Scapa Flow by *King George V*, the flagship of Admiral Sir John Tovey, Commander-in-Chief Home Fleet, shortly after 2300 on Wednesday, 21 May, to *Hood* and *Prince of Wales*, and by telephone and light to the flotilla in Gutta Sound – *Achates, Antelope, Anthony, Echo, Electra* and *Icarus*.

Ships were expected to raise steam for 20 knots in four hours; they were required to raise steam *with despatch* in two. It was a black night, mild but with no stars, as the destroyers dropped their slip-ropes. As the little ships passed through the Switha gate into the Pentland Firth, dawn visibility hazed and it began to drizzle. *Hood*, flying the flag of Vice-Admiral Lancelot Holland, and followed by *Prince of Wales*, slipped from the Flow at 0052.

*D'ye hear there? Secure for sea. Close all scuttles and watertight doors. Special sea dutymen close up. Ship will assume second state of readiness. . . .*

There had been a hum of speculation during the entire previous evening. Now, as *Hood* and *Prince of Wales* slid southward through the Hoxa gate into the black Firth, increased speed and then turned westward to rendezvous with the waiting destroyers, few men slept. Second state of readiness meant watch and watch about, only one step removed from action stations, to which every man would be summoned by a marine bugler's 'General Quarters'. Doors were already being closed and their clips hammered home. Damage-control parties checked their hoses, hydrants and baulking-timber, and communication circuits were being tested. In engine-rooms which were labyrinths of steel ladders and walkways under organ-lofts of tangled pipes clad in white asbestos jackets, artificers watched the brass-rimmed pressure-gauges; the ships were working up to 27 knots, and the deck-plates were shuddering underfoot. The familiar, slightly sweet smell of warm oil was beginning to permeate the messdecks, and the ventilation system hummed quietly.

At 0815, shortly after the Forenoon watchkeepers had closed up, all aboard *Hood* paused in their activities to listen to the slow voice over the amplifying circuit that reached to every corner of the ship.

'This is Captain Kerr speaking. Intelligence has been received that *Bismarck* and *Prinz Eugen* have passed through the Skagerrak and were last reported as having reached a fjord near the Norwegian port of Bergen, where they are probably refuelling. There is every likelihood that they intend to break out into the Atlantic where, as you will understand, they can cause immense damage to even our most strongly escorted convoys, of which there are eleven at sea – including one vital troop convoy on passage to the Middle East. *Bismarck* and *Prinz Eugen* must be stopped.

'We cannot predict which route the enemy will choose. The cruisers *Norfolk* and *Suffolk* are covering the Denmark Strait, *Manchester* and *Birmingham* the Iceland–Faeroes gap.' The voice paused. 'It's C-in-C's guess they'll go for the Denmark Strait, but none of our cruisers can trade punches with *Bismarck*. We, therefore – *Hood* and *Prince of Wales* – have been ordered to support *Norfolk* and *Suffolk*.'

There was a longer pause, then: 'The Admiral has asked me to assure you of his complete confidence in the ships and men under his command. Be of good heart. We have in company a flotilla of seasoned destroyers in addition to the Navy's newest battleship, while other powerful forces are being widely deployed. If every man does his duty, we shall prevail.'

The men of *Hood* would not have chosen *Prince of Wales* as their consort. Despite being commissioned only four months earlier, she was already earning a reputation for being unlucky – a 'Jonah'. Within minutes of leaving her Liverpool fitting-out berth she had been run aground on a sandbank. Pulled off, she steamed for Rosyth with two of her four screws lashed to her upper deck; there had been no time to fit them. In Rosyth a pom-pom crew had fired two rounds in error and injured a dockyard worker. Three fires, albeit small, had erupted in the shell-room of 'B' turret, and two ratings had been injured by bad falls. Her captain, John Leach, not wishing to be excluded from Tovey's deployment, had assured the Commander-in-Chief that his ship had completed her working-up programme and was an efficient fighting unit. This was most unlikely and, indeed, even as she steamed northward with *Hood* civilian armourers of Vickers-Armstrong were still working on her defective 14-inch turrets. However, during the evening of the twenty-second Leach cleared lower deck and, from the roof of 'Y' turret, spoke to his men as Holland's flag captain had to the men of *Hood*.

Vice-Admiral Lancelot Holland had hoisted his flag in *Hood* only ten days earlier. Aged fifty-four, he was a slight white-haired man of restrained temperament but undoubted determination; aboard *Manchester* he had led Somerville's cruiser force during the action off Sardinia and had not hesitated to attack two battleships. Today, however, neither of his big ships was in good fighting condition and both were good for only about 28 knots. Even so, like another battle-cruiser commander, twenty-five years before, if Holland met *Bismarck* he would fight.

Meanwhile, in Scapa Flow, Admiral Tovey was waiting for further news of the enemy's movements, holding back what few resources he still had. They comprised his own flagship *King George V*, four cruisers and the carrier *Victorious*, which, because she was already loaded with crated aircraft for the Mediterranean, had accommodation for only nine Swordfish and six Fulmars. Flown on two days before from RNAS Hatston, in the Orkneys, few of the pilots had any operational experience and most had just landed on a carrier for the first time. At 2000 hours Tovey learned that the Bergen fjords were empty; *Bismarck* and *Prinz Eugen* were loose, somewhere in the Atlantic.

Nothing, now, would be gained by sitting in Scapa Flow. In addition to *Victorious*, the cruisers *Kenya*, *Hermione*, *Galatea*, *Aurora* and the destroyers *Punjabi*, *Inglefield*, *Intrepid*, *Active*, *Lance* and *Windsor* were ordered to prepare to slip and proceed to sea with *King George V* at 2245.

*Repulse* had just shepherded the ships of WS8B out of the Clyde, only hours from steaming southward to Gibraltar, sunshine, oranges and flamenco dancing, when new orders were piped and the messdecks howled. The battle-cruiser was to leave the convoy and rendezvous with *King George V* north of the Hebrides during the next morning.

At 1815 on the evening of 23 May the cruiser *Suffolk*, on White Patrol in the Denmark Strait, established a radar contact. A few minutes later, seven miles distant on the starboard quarter, *Bismarck* and *Prinz Eugen* emerged from a bank of mist, and *Suffolk* swung away to port, her main wireless transmitter hammering at full power.

'—O – 1822z/23 = 1BS1CR – 02024007. . . .'

'Immediate. One battleship one cruiser in sight bearing 020 degrees course 240 distance 7 miles. . . .'

Unfortunately no H/F shore station, and neither Holland in *Hood*, now three hundred miles away, nor Tovey in *King George V*, six hundred miles to the south-east, heard *Suffolk*'s enemy-report because the cruiser's aerials were clogged with ice, but her sister *Norfolk*, with Rear-Admiral Frederick Wake-Walker aboard and only fifteen miles distant, did hear it. Cleared for action, *Norfolk* came pounding out of the fog to sight the enemy only six miles away and with the gap closing rapidly. *Bismarck* altered course to open her firing-arcs and fired five salvoes. *Norfolk*, outmatched, plunged back into the fog, and it was her sighting-report that was picked up by Admirals Tovey and Holland, by the Admiralty to be rebroadcast immediately to all British men-o'-war, and so unavoidably by *Bismarck*.

Now began a classic 'shadow-and-report' operation by the two cruisers, intended to vector the approaching British heavy ships on to the enemy – as indeed it did. The concussion from *Bismarck*'s guns had disabled her own forward radar mattress on the fore-top range-finder, so she could not probe ahead. Lütjens therefore ordered *Prinz Eugen* to overtake *Bismarck* and assume the leading station. It was a manœuvre that would have a crucial effect on later events.

*Norfolk*'s relatively primitive Type 79Y radar could *only* see directly ahead and, since she was positioned on the enemy's port quarter, Wake-Walker had to rely on *Suffolk*, fitted with a more sophisticated, all-round Type 272 equipment, to maintain contact with an enemy who was going to twist and turn at 30 knots in trying to shake off the shadowers. *Suffolk*'s radar had a range of 13 miles – rather less than the range of *Bismarck*'s 15-inch guns.

Lütjens was annoyed at having been located by British surface forces so early in his operation, but not deeply concerned. Amid the fog and frequent snow-flurries, or in the dark of night, he could use his 30 knots to lose the tracking cruisers. Sadly for Lütjens, *Norfolk* and *Suffolk* were two knots better, and they were not going to be lost; each time the Germans twisted so also did the British, increasing speed, reducing speed. There were six hours to dawn.

*Bismarck*'s southward course, despite the British ships deployed, was bringing her nearer every hour to vulnerable convoy-routes. The Admiralty's Service 5 wireless link with Gibraltar carried an Operational Priority order, and within an hour *Renown*, *Ark Royal*, *Sheffield* and the destroyers of Force H were easing past the break-water to head west, then north-west, into the black Atlantic.

*

The British cruisers remained at action stations. Below, the lighting in the deserted messdecks and communicating passageways was reduced to the occasional red 'police lights' on bulkheads at knee-level and shaded downward. The chapel and the officers' bathroom flat were rigged for casualty reception, with tables covered with brown rubber sheets, anaesthetics machines, cylinders, trolleys of coldly gleaming instruments and mounds of dressings. Elsewhere, damage-control parties waited, talking in low voices, their hoses unrolled and snaking along the shadowed main deck. From widely separated stations above and below, and by laborious routes, men found their way to the galley to collect pails of cocoa, thick sand-wiches of corned beef and, if the Chief Cook was conscientious, soup maintained over a slow heat at all hours.

*Suffolk*'s bridge had been glass-enclosed and heated during her last refit, but *Norfolk*'s bridge was open to the weather, and with the ship pounding through the sea at 35 miles an hour the Arctic wind cut through the heaviest of clothing like a knife. The cold climbed sleeves, numbed faces and chilled the lungs; men stood with shoulders hunched, eyes stinging. If they had to speak, their voices were rusty croaks. Hell, they would have agreed, wasn't hot; it was icily cold, and situated just off the coast of Greenland.

A hundred miles to the south-east the situation aboard *Hood* and *Prince of Wales* was very similar. All irrelevant locations were shuttered and silent – the bakery, the dry canteen, the pay, regulat-ing and victualling offices, the bookstall, the 'goffer bar', which sold aerated soft drinks during the dog watches. All were in darkness. Neither ship was using radar for fear of the transmissions being detected by the enemy (although, in fact, the German ships were not equipped with the necessary FuMB radar detectors). There was strict wireless silence, but transmitters were tuned to ship–shore frequencies and all W/T positions manned – main office, auxiliary office, third office and bridge wireless office, with telegraphists, duplicated, reading the area broadcasts BN and HD on 107 and 78 k/cs, Fleet Wave and the mercantile distress bands. In anticipation, coders wrote out the coded groups that meant 'I have struck a mine', or 'I have been torpedoed', or 'My position at — was —'. If it happened, there might be only seconds in which to hammer out those few Morse symbols before power failed; there might be no time at all.

On the flag-deck muffled signalmen checked again the letters, changed every four hours, which might or might not be flashed in challenge at an unidentified contact, checked again their Aldis lamps and the pneumatic blower from the Signals Distribution

Office below, blew on cold fingers and hungered for tobacco. A steward brought a pail of hot coffee to the bridge, balancing with cups on a circlet of wire, from the wardroom pantry. It was not fully dark, and would not be until about two in the morning, but dark enough for the binnacle and chart-table to need a glimmer of illumination. Admiral, flag captain, navigator and officer of the watch stood with feet apart, seeing ahead, through the curious dusk light, the slate-coloured sea thrust aside and splintering white as *Hood* smashed through it at 27 knots.

The British ships had gone to action stations at 0015, and the stream of situation-reports from *Norfolk* and *Suffolk*, clinging to the Germans' flanks, indicated that the two battle-groups, now only 120 miles apart and closing each at something like 55 miles per hour, would collide in about two hours. That meant an action in darkness.

Between the wars, as the result of a mediocre performance in the first, the Royal Navy had trained unsparingly in the techniques of night fighting and had achieved an extremely high level of expertise. On this occasion, however, Holland had *Prince of Wales* in company, of doubtful efficiency and with technicians still working on her guns. He did not relish a night action, and would prefer either to bring the confrontation forward, i.e., before darkness closed down, or delay it until dawn. It was at about this time, however, that *Suffolk* reported: 'Enemy hidden in snowstorm.'

Only a few minutes earlier Holland had altered from a westerly intercepting course to roughly north-north-west, reducing his speed to 25 knots. Had *Suffolk* only temporarily lost sight of *Bismarck* in a flurry of snow or, more seriously, lost radar contact?

In the event of the latter, Lütjens (whose B-Dienst officers were decoding the British signals within minutes) would almost certainly attempt to shake off his pursuers completely by swinging away from his original course. He could not turn westward because *Bismarck* and *Prinz Eugen* were hard against the Greenland pack-ice, but now that he was emerging from the confinement of the Denmark Strait[2] he could wheel south-easterly. Once having slipped past Holland's squadron into the open Atlantic he would have all points of the compass from which to choose. He would be running free.

It is possible only to speculate at Holland's reasoning because neither he nor anyone in his confidence survived the day. He ordered his ships to turn due north, to hoist battle-ensigns and to expect action at any time after 0140. That, at least, was perfectly logical under the circumstances. At 0028, however, *Suffolk* confirmed that she had indeed lost radar contact and, as a result, Holland informed his command that if they had not met the enemy by 0210 he would turn *Hood* and *Prince of Wales* southward. Thus, at worst, he would be going in the same general direction as *Bismarck* until contact was re-established, which was better than missing Lütjens in the darkness with, disastrously, Holland continuing northward at high speed as the enemy sped in the opposite direction.

Sixty miles of further steaming achieved nothing. There were no reports from *Norfolk* and *Suffolk*, and the short night was ending. At 0203 Holland hauled around to the south-south-west, on 200° (which was the last-known course of the enemy). At the same time he ordered Commander Cecil May, in *Electra*, to continue with all destroyers in company on their northerly course, spread out at fifteen-mile intervals. Within a few minutes the two capital ships had settled on their new course, unescorted, and the flotilla was opening formation as it vanished northward.

Holland has been criticised for splitting his force in trying to anticipate alternatives. In retrospect it can be seen that he should have kept the destroyers with him; they and the German ships, on an almost reciprocal course, passed each other – although only ten miles apart during reduced visibility. Holland's own turnabout, with *Hood* and *Prince of Wales*, was of little relevance, for at 0247 *Suffolk* reported that she had again made radar contact with *Bismarck*, which, steering 220° (against Hood's 200°), was only 35 miles to the north-west.

Holland increased speed to 28 knots and altered course slightly so that he converged on *Bismarck*'s. By 0430 visibility was twelve miles and improving, so *Prince of Wales* was ordered to launch her Walrus aircraft, but had to confess that this was impossible as the plane's fuel was contaminated with sea-water. The battleship was still cursed by ill luck.

'Enemy in sight, green one-one-oh!'

It could only be the enemy on that north-westerly bearing, and it was 0535. The director-control tower was already turning, followed by the guns.

'Two ships bearing two-nine-oh, course two-two-five, speed twenty-nine knots. It *must* be them, sir.' All glasses were levelled to starboard, searching. It *must* be. Distant and blurred, yet there was no mistaking the low sinister silhouettes that raced on an almost parallel course and slightly astern. These were *Bismarck* and *Prinz Eugen*, the hunters at bay.

Vice-Admiral Holland turned from the bridge-screen. 'Alter course, please, forty degrees to starboard in succession. And Chief Yeoman – take a signal for W/T. "Enemy in sight. Am engaging."'

Then hoist Flag Five.' The cutting northerly wind was almost abeam, the sea slate-grey, the long rollers crested with white. From the mainmast the huge ensign streamed, half hidden by the tumult of dense smoke from the funnels. 'Preserve us from the dangers of the sea and from the violence of the enemy,' the chaplain had earlier spoken from the address system, 'that we may return in safety to enjoy the blessings of the land with the fruit of our labours.' It was too late for prayers now. The Chief Yeoman's voice carried from the flag-deck. 'Blue Four – *hoist!*' – then: 'Bend on Flag Five.'

Holland walked to the bridge-wing to raise his glasses at *Prince of Wales*, five cables astern, and saw her answering pennant climb to her yardarm. There was something comfortingly solid in the diffused bluff profile that dogged *Hood* through the white spindrift flung off the whipped sea. Captain Kerr was watching the enemy and the range-dial as the great ship turned her bows almost directly toward the enemy.

It was Holland's intention to concentrate the fire of his two ships on *Bismarck* while leaving *Prinz Eugen* to *Norfolk* and *Suffolk*, but he had not wirelessed any orders to the British cruisers. Holland also assumed that the leading German warship was *Bismarck* – an excusable error at long distance because the two German vessels, although of different size, were of almost identical outline. He flashed to *Prince of Wales*: 'Stand by to open fire. Target left-hand ship.'

In attempting to close the range at high speed, *Hood* was being placed at a serious tactical disadvantage, in effect deliberately allowing her own T to be crossed, albeit for only minutes – exactly as Beatty had done in the opening exchanges at Jutland. With the Germans fine on the starboard bow only the battle-cruiser's four forward 15-inch guns could bear. Of *Prince of Wales*'s six forward guns in two turrets one was inoperative and, indeed, she would quickly be reduced to three-gun salvoes. *Bismarck* and *Prinz Eugen*, during these crucial minutes, were free to engage with all sixteen of their heavy guns.

*Hood*'s bows knifed through the sea, lifting a great bow-wave that streamed along her flanks to join the white froth of her wake. On the bridge nobody spoke unless he had to, and then in clipped syllables. A voice from the DCT was intoning the range as it narrowed ominously, and the massive gun-barrels sniffed at the air.

'Twenty-eight thousand . . . twenty-seven five hundred. . . .'

'On the ready to fire,' confirmed the DCT. The gun-ready lamps were glowing red.

'Permission to open fire, sir?' Captain Kerr enquired, as politely as if asking a lady for the pleasure of this dance.

Admiral Holland considered. 'Thank you. Yes. Open fire.'

Kerr nodded toward the Chief Yeoman, then lifted the DCT handset. 'Open fire.'

The Chief Yeoman whirled. 'Flag Five. *Hoist!*'

In the DCT the Gunnery Officer spoke into his microphone. 'Shoot!'

The fire-gong said, 'Ting-ting.'

The range was 26,500 yards, the time 0553.

There was a shuddering roar as 'A' and 'B' turrets fired. Four 15-inch projectiles each weighing 1920 pounds were in flight at more than twice the speed of sound. The great barrels lurched backward in recoil, shrouded in thick caustic cordite smoke, then slid forward again slowly.

It was *Prince of Wales*'s gunnery officer who, realising that *Hood* was firing at *Prinz Eugen*, directed his own ship's guns at *Bismarck*. No countermanding order was issued by Holland, who merely ordered a two-point turn to starboard to open *Prince of Wales*'s firing-arcs.

'When the *Hood* opened fire,' said Ordinary Signalman Albert Briggs, on the flagship's compass-platform, 'the *Prinz Eugen* definitely turned away, and the *Bismarck* was thought to turn away. This I gathered from a conversation between the Admiral and the Captain. We altered course 30 degrees together and closed to twelve miles range. We hit *Bismarck* with our second salvo right amidships and the *Bismarck* did not open fire until we had fired about four or five salvoes. And then she hit us, according to the Squadron Gunnery Officer, "on the starboard side of the boat deck aft" causing a fire in the 4-inch ready-use lockers.'

In such a tense situation young Briggs can be forgiven for mistaking what could only have been the distant flare of *Bismarck*'s first salvo for a hit, for it is certain that *Hood* did not engage the German battleship, which was found by only three projectiles during the entire course of the action. *Prince of Wales* was overestimating the range by about a thousand yards because (almost predictably) none of her radar sets was functioning, but her sixth salvo straddled *Bismarck*.

The operator on *Hood*'s Type 279 radar could see the salvoes detaching themselves from the enemy ships and speeding across the trace toward their target – *Hood*.

'Salvo coming . . . coming towards . . . coming towards . . . going right . . . going right. . . .'

*Prinz Eugen*, with her more rapid rate of fire, scored a hit within the first minute. An 8-inch shell struck *Hood* just aft of the after

funnel, where a number of motor-boats were decked which may
have had small but significant quantities of petrol in their tanks.
Here, too, were ready-use ammunition lockers for the nearby 4-inch
AA guns and, even more lethal, 9½ tons of useless UP rockets, also
stowed in exposed, light steel lockers. The fire that inevitably resulted
blazed high, enveloping the entire midships area in blinding smoke.

AB Robert Tilburn, of one of the forward 4-inch guns' crews, had
been sheltering under the bridge:

'A fire started and it was a very fierce blaze, a pinkish colour. . . .
There were fairly small explosions, rather like a big Chinese cracker.
I heard the explosions but could not see any results of them. The
order to put the fire out was given and then countermanded because
of exploding ammunition. After the fire had been going for a good
while and about six salvoes had been fired altogether, when we
started going round to port, we were hit somewhere and the ship
shook all over and a lot of debris and bodies started falling all over
the decks.'

The fire represented no immediate danger to *Hood*; it was merely
an annoying distraction. Holland, however, could not continue on a
course that reduced his gun-power by half. He urgently needed to
bring *Hood*'s four after guns and the four of *Prince of Wales* into
contention. At 0559 he ordered a turn of 20° to port. The range had
now fallen to 19,000 yards.

Coloured bunting was wrenched from a flag-locker. 'Two Blue –
*Hoist!*' The Chief Yeoman had his telescope riveted on *Prince of
Wales*, then – '*Down!*'

As both ships began to turn, *Bismarck* fired her fifth salvo, and in
*Hood* the radar operator watched the venomous little flecks closing.

'Salvo coming . . . coming towards . . . coming towards . . . coming
towards—'

Understandably, not all eye-witness accounts coincide exactly.
Different eyes saw different things. From *Prince of Wales* the disaster
was reported as 'a muffled roar, not a bang or an explosion. There
was no flame, just a huge release of boiling smoke. The ship had
been moving at around twenty-eight knots, but she stopped as if
somebody had put his foot on a car-brake. And she lifted. She lifted
right out of the water along her entire length, and bits of her, like
15-inch gun turrets, were thrown hundreds of feet into the sky. Then
her back broke and she sank. Just like that. I couldn't believe it, nor
could anybody else who saw it.'

Yet observers in both *Norfolk* and *Prinz Eugen* described a huge
column of flame, four times the height of the mainmast, which

'nearly touched the sky'. Lieutenant Esmond Knight, RNVR, also in *Prince of Wales*, saw a 'long, pale red tongue', and *Suffolk*'s Lieutenant-Commander Havers a 'stick of red rhubarb' – but all these may well have been seeing the fire on *Hood*'s boat-deck. AB Usher (*Prince of Wales*) said that 'all amidships seemed to lift up into the air. After that the ship was surrounded by yellow smoke. . . . All along the upper deck it seemed to be bubbling up as if boiling. This was the fo'c'sle only, the deck of which seemed to be bubbling like a fried egg. . . . The next thing I saw was the quarterdeck coming up into the air and I saw the screws. . . .'

A number of observers were categorically and independently of the opinion that the explosion made no noise, but, on *Hood*'s bridge, Briggs declares that

there was a terrific explosion, but the officer of the watch said to the Admiral that the compass platform had gone and the Admiral said move to after control. During that she had listed six to seven degrees to starboard and shortly after the Admiral spoke she listed right over to port. She had gone about twenty-five degrees to port and the crew were trying to get away (by the crew I mean the men on the bridge) but the Admiral did not make any attempt to get away. I got out of the starboard door and there was the navigator just in front of me and the Squadron Gunnery Officer just in front of him. I had just got out of the door and the water by that time had got level with the compass platform. I do not remember anything more then until I found myself on the surface. The bows of the *Hood* were vertical in the water about fifty yards away and I was looking at the bottom of the ship.

Briggs was one of only three survivors. Another was Midshipman Dundas, in the DCT, washed out of its window after being 'flung about a bit'. The third was AB Tilburn, who threw himself from the holocaust of the boat-deck into the sea, then surfaced and narrowly missed being run down by *Prince of Wales* as she ploughed through the smoke and debris with guns thundering. All three, separately, hauled themselves on to Carley floats and were picked up by *Electra* soon after 0800.

'But there *must* be more of them,' gritted Lieutenant Frank McLeod, the engineer officer, as the destroyer steamed at slow speed among the pitiful flotsam. 'There *can't* be only *three* of them. Where the hell are all the others?'

Only three from a ship's company of 1419?

*

There will always exist a slight element of doubt with regard to the precise series of events leading to the loss of *Hood*. The Admiralty convened two boards of enquiry, the first provisional report being issued on 2 June 1941 and the second, more searching, on 12 September. Evidence was given by 177 witnesses drawn from *Norfolk*, *Suffolk*, *Prince of Wales* and *Hood* herself.

It was concluded that the fire on the boat-deck, involving 4-inch and UP rocket ammunition, made no significant contribution to the disaster, nor was it possible for an explosive flash in a gun-turret to penetrate to a magazine, as had occurred in *Indefatigable*, *Queen Mary* and *Invincible* in 1916. The post-Jutland design of *Hood*'s turrets had incorporated the fullest safeguards against such a consequence.

The probability is that either one or two of *Bismarck*'s fifth salvo, presumably of four shells, penetrated *Hood*'s after 4-inch magazine, situated below the turrets and shelter-deck, which in turn detonated the 15-inch magazine immediately aft. The projectile(s) may either have entered beneath the narrow armoured belt or, more likely, have pierced the horizontal armour around the turrets. This consisted of the two-inch upper deck, three-inch main deck and two-inch lower deck, i.e., a total of seven inches, which would be vulnerable to high-velocity armour-piercing shells descending (from 19,000 yards) at a steep angle.

The Admiralty learned of the loss of *Hood* from Wake-Walker's signal: '*Hood* blown up' – which could hardly have been briefer or more dramatic. The news was broadcast by the BBC at 9 a.m. and in later news bulletins during Saturday, 24 May, inflicting a shock on the nation almost as traumatic as those of Dunkirk and the later fall of Singapore. To millions the name *Hood* was synonymous with unchallengeable British sea-power; the world would never be the same again, and the loss of three cruisers and six destroyers in the battle of Crete – then in progress – would cause hardly a ripple of concern.

Oddly (assuming the Germans to be monitoring BBC broadcasts) the report of *Bismarck*'s success did not reach the Propaganda Ministry in Berlin until the afternoon, but it was then fully exploited, supported by Wagnerian music, in enhancing the splendid communiqués from Greece and Crete and to offset the embarrassment of Rudolf Hess's desertion two weeks earlier.

With *Hood* destroyed, both German ships turned their guns on *Prince of Wales*, and within the next twelve minutes the British battleship, still struggling to keep her turrets firing, was hit by four shells from *Bismarck* and three from *Prinz Eugen* that wrecked her compass-platform (killing or wounding every man on it except Captain Leach), the forward 5.5-inch director, the radar office and the aircraft-crane. A 15-inch projectile penetrated the side below the armoured belt, passed through several bulkheads and came to rest, unexploded, alongside the room housing the diesel dynamo. Two 8-inch shells penetrated below the waterline aft, admitting 500 tons of water, while yet another smashed into a shell-handling room without exploding.

In this now unequal exchange *Prinz Eugen*[3] remained unscathed except for superficial damage from the blast of her own guns. *Bismarck*, however, sustained three 14-inch hits from *Prince of Wales*. One only wrecked a motor-boat and the aircraft catapult, the second pierced the ship's side to destroy a dynamo-room and No. 2 boiler-room, but the third, most seriously, struck *Bismarck*'s port bow above the waterline but below the bow-wave, which meant that the damage could not be welded without stopping the ship. The feed-line from the forward oil-bunker was severed, spilling valuable oil fuel and letting in brine. The immediate effect was to reduce *Bismarck*'s speed to about 28 knots, which was no great penalty, but an unchecked loss of a thousand tons of fuel meant that the German ship must seek a haven as quickly as possible; her Atlantic foray was no longer possible.

Leach broke off the action behind smoke to place *Prince of Wales* under the command of CS1, Rear-Admiral Wake-Walker in *Norfolk*, which, with *Suffolk*, had been unable to overtake the action in time to make any contribution. As the wounded battleship turned away her after quadruple turret jammed, leaving each gun with only two rounds until the defect could be cleared. There was little more that could go wrong for *Prince of Wales*, and her frustrated crewmen could anticipate another storm of ribaldry when they next reached the Fleet Canteen in Scapa Flow.

In the massive hunt for *Bismarck* that was now to be set in motion the last remaining battle-cruisers, *Repulse* and *Renown* – although their crews were desperate to come to grips with the enemy – would play only a minor role. Both were even older than *Hood*, and Tovey had no desire to throw them into the battle unless he had to. He had *Repulse* in company with *King George V* and the 2nd Cruiser Squadron, 300 miles from *Bismarck* but closing fast, while *Renown*, leading Force H, was still pounding northward from Gibraltar. *Rodney* and four destroyers, then about 550 miles south-east of the enemy, were ordered to close; *Ramillies* was ordered to abandon her Halifax-bound convoy and *Revenge* to leave Halifax. The cruisers *London* and *Edinburgh* were drawn from their patrol-area north-east of the Azores, and *Dorsetshire*'s Captain Benjamin Martin, unbidden, handed over his convoy, 700 miles to the southward, to the armed merchant cruiser *Bulolo*, and steamed his ship at 26 knots to get into the action.

In terms of desperate suspense and see-sawing fortunes the next three days have no equal in the history of the Royal Navy. During the afternoon of the twenty-fourth Lütjens parted company with *Prinz Eugen*, ordering the cruiser to undertake an independent commerce-raiding operation while *Bismarck*, losing fuel, made for Brest. The shadowing British let the cruiser go; they were determined to remain with *Bismarck*. Then, during the night that followed, eight Swordfish of No. 825 (FAA) Squadron, flown from *Victorious* by pilots on passage to Malta, made a torpedo attack on *Bismarck*, achieving one hit but inflicting only negligible damage. All the Swordfish regained *Victorious*, but two escorting Fulmars had to ditch. Aboard *Bismarck*, Lütjens broadcast to his crew that the ship had shot down five of twenty-seven attacking aircraft, of which only one had regained its carrier. Meanwhile, the RAF's Coastal Command had positively identified *Prinz Eugen* as *Admiral Scheer*.

During the Morning watch of the twenty-fifth *Bismarck*'s commander caught *Suffolk*'s weary radar operators off guard; the German battleship disappeared as if she had never existed, and Captain Ellis ruefully flashed Wake-Walker: 'Have lost contact with enemy.'

Against the forces that the Admiralty were deploying – six battleships, two battle-cruisers, two aircraft-carriers, eleven cruisers, twenty-one destroyers and six submarines – it might seem impossible that *Bismarck* could long remain undetected, but more than thirty hours of frantic air–sea searching would elapse before the fugitive would be sighted again. Meanwhile, several of the British warships involved, steaming continuously at high speed, were running seriously short of fuel oil. *Repulse* had been burning almost sixty tons an hour since leaving the Clyde and, during the forenoon of the twenty-fifth, Tovey ordered her to turn away to Newfoundland to refuel, searching as she went. *Repulse*'s place astern of Tovey's *King George V* was taken by *Prince of Wales*, no longer needing the cover of *Norfolk* and *Suffolk*.

Lütjens, indeed, might have got clear but for the fact that he still believed himself to be followed by Wake-Walker's ships. This would not have been too serious if he did not also suffer from the inherent German carelessness with the use of wireless – or, more accurately, a disregard for British expertise in radio direction-finding. Lütjens transmitted a long wireless signal to Adolf Hitler describing his action with *Hood*, his damage, the excellence of British radar and the shortcomings of his own. Long before the thirty-minute signal had ended British D/F stations had pounced, and bearings were being reported to the Admiralty.

This should have spelled the end for *Bismarck*, but luck had not entirely deserted Lütjens. The Admiralty chose to send Tovey the enemy's bearing rather than his position, a deficiency that was compounded in the flagship by erroneous plotting which suggested that *Bismarck* was attempting to return to Germany via the Iceland–Faeroes gap, which had always been a possibility. The Commander-in-Chief broadcast this interpretation on Fleet Wave to all ships, with the result that almost the entire weight of the sea-search was turned to the north-east. It was not until the afternoon of 25 May that it was realised that Lütjens was indeed making for France and, at 1810, Tovey again altered course for the Bay of Biscay. *Bismarck*, however, had now stolen a lead of 150 miles and was only hours from U-boat and Luftwaffe cover.

It was Catalina Z of 209 Squadron[4] Coastal Command that made the final, vital sighting at 1030 on Monday, 26 May and, as shell splinters punched through the fuselage, the condemning Morse signal was transmitted: 'one battleship bearing 240–5 miles – course 150. My position 49.33N 27.47W.'

The report placed *Bismarck* 690 miles due west of Brest, which meant that she could call on massive Luftwaffe cover by the evening of the next day. The nearest British capital ship was *Renown*, a hundred miles to the eastward with *Ark Royal* and *Sheffield*, directly between *Bismarck* and Brest. Tovey's *King George V* was 135 miles away to the north, *Rodney* 125 miles to the north-east.

## Notes

1 Correctly, a code converts plain language into meaningless groups of letters, a cipher into groups of figures, but both terms are often loosely given to either form of symbology.

2 The Greenland ice-edge on one side and the British minefield (known to the Germans) laid off Iceland limited the navigable channel between to about forty miles.

3 Later a large splinter from a 15-inch shell (which could only have come from *Hood*) was found resting at the base of *Prinz Eugen*'s funnel.

4 The Catalina was piloted (but not captained) by Ensign Leonard Smith of the United States Navy, one of sixteen American pilots in Britain as 'special observers'. As a neutral, he should never have been flying on an operational commitment.

# Chapter Thirteen

*The hunt for* Bismarck

*Renown*, however, was twenty-five years old, with only six heavy guns, and at this moment was hammering northward through heavy seas into the teeth of a savage north-westerly gale to meet a ship that outclassed her in every statistic except speed – and there was a doubt about that. The previous day Vice-Admiral Somerville had ordered the Force H destroyers, low on fuel, back to Gibraltar, and now only *Ark Royal* and *Sheffield* were in company. He had flown his flag in *Hood* until August of the previous year, and with regard to Holland, his successor in that ship and an old comrade-in-arms, he might have mused, 'There, but for the grace of God. . . .'

Only three days before, in the warm sunshine of the Mediterranean, Force H had flown off forty-eight Hurricanes from *Ark Royal* and *Furious* to Malta. Today, Monday, 26 May, Somerville had not only *Bismarck* to consider but also the possibility of *Scharnhorst* and *Gneisenau* putting to sea from Brest in support of Lütjens. He had ordered Captain Loben Maund, commanding *Ark Royal*, to fly off a search-detail toward Brest at first light, but during the night the weather had worsened, compelling the carrier to reduce progressively to seventeen knots. She had steamed a hundred thousand miles since her last engine-refit, the centre of her three shafts had ruptured its stern gland twice in recent weeks, and these were just the conditions to provoke a third such disaster.

Commander (Air) Traill had sent the flying-programme to the Operations Room late during the previous night, and at 0630 – half an hour before planned take-off – the pilots and observers, with eyes still swollen with sleep, were subjected to a final briefing. By now, however, the wind-speed over the flight-deck was exceeding fifty miles per hour and the ship was rising and falling fifty-five feet in a sea that repeatedly exploded over the bows, but the Admiralty and Somerville needed to know that no enemy sortie was being made from the direction of Brest. At 0645 the pilots were piped to man the aircraft rocking on the flight-deck, and five minutes later the order was given to 'man the chocks, stand clear of propellers, stand by to start up!' *Ark Royal* turned into the wind, the latticed wireless-masts fell slowly, and then the radial Pegasus engines coughed, roared into life. From the greying bleak void to eastward a signal-lamp blinked. It was *Renown*, only a silhouette at which the sea clawed, ahead of her *Sheffield* plunging her bows deep. The aircraft-carrier's deck trembled, handlers were scattering and the tannoy was spitting orders again. From his perch in the island Traill lowered the green flag that the wind almost tore from his grasp, and the leading Swordfish trundled forward into drenching spray. Another was only seconds behind.

If there was only one aircraft capable of getting airborne from a deck with a thirty-degree roll it was a Fairey Swordfish. This obsolete biplane, constructed of steel tubing and fabric, with fixed landing-gear, open cockpits, and a maximum speed of only 139 miles per hour, possessed outstanding handling characteristics for carrier employment. The 'Stringbag's' load was one 18-inch torpedo 'for letting in water' or the equivalent weight in bombs 'for letting in air', and small strike-forces of Swordfish had performed brilliantly at Taranto and in the engagement off Cape Matapan, with negligible losses.

This morning's first aircraft climbed jerkily away, and a telegraphist in the bridge wireless office listened through the crackle of H/F for their observers to tell off with their call-signs. Ten more Swordfish were being brought up the hangar-wells on bell-clanging lifts, and the oilskinned handlers, mechanics and electricians jostled around them, leaning into the wind on unsteady feet as the deck rolled. The reduced speed imposed by the previous night's bad weather, however, had meant lost mileage; *Ark Royal* was not where she had anticipated being at dawn, and there was no sign of conditions improving. The air-search for *Bismarck* was delayed until 0900.

Of the ten Swordfish that lurched off *Ark Royal's* flight-deck two hours later, two located *Bismarck*. Somerville, eastward and out of sight of *Ark Royal*, turned Force H accordingly, steering for a position from which he could launch a torpedo strike. *Renown* was still between *Bismarck* and sanctuary, and if the old battle-cruiser had to engage, alone, then Somerville intended to do so from astern, so that Lütjens would have to turn to reciprocate, conceding the weather-gauge and, at the same time, interrupting his retreat. At 1315 he detached *Sheffield*, ordering her to push ahead, make contact and shadow. *Bismarck* was only forty miles away.

Somerville wirelessed a situation report to the Admiralty and *King George V*, repeating the signal, for information, to *Ark Royal*. The Admiralty, alarmed, ordered that *Renown* must not engage unless *King George V* and *Rodney* (which had now joined Tovey) were involved. Meanwhile *Ark Royal*, to whom Somerville's situation-report was not specifically addressed, did not decipher the signal until *after* fourteen torpedo-carrying Swordfish had taken off, at 1450, to attack *Bismarck*. The crews knew nothing of the presence of *Sheffield* in their operational area; the first warship they sighted would be *Bismarck*.

The second crewman of each aircraft, even if his pilot might quip that he was 'just along for the ride', was at the same time an observer, navigator and signalman. Today, several had been burdened with yet another responsibility; their Swordfish had been fitted with ASV (Anti-Surface-Vessel) radar. Within only forty minutes of taking off, and twenty miles from *Bismarck*'s estimated position, the radar warned of a vessel just ahead. It had to be *Bismarck*. The strike aircraft dropped through the cloud; they saw what they wanted to see, and jockeyed into an attack position.

*Sheffield* twisted desperately at high speed to avoid eleven torpedoes launched at her – three pilots recognised their error at the last moment – and the British cruiser's survival was little less than a miracle. The magnetic firing pistols of two torpedoes exploded on striking the water, three more in *Sheffield*'s tumbling wake. The remaining six missiles streaked harmlessly past the ship as she combed their tracks, and then the Swordfish climbed away, heading back toward *Ark Royal*. As the sailors below stared up at the retreating planes an Aldis lamp flickered back at them. 'Sorry for the kipper!'

With *Repulse* and then *Prince of Wales* out of the chase for lack of fuel, *King George V* – reduced to *Rodney*'s 22 knots – was also running low, and *Bismarck* was still ninety miles ahead. If the enemy's speed could not be reduced by midnight, Tovey told the Admiralty, then *King George V* would have to break off the pursuit, and *Rodney* could continue only until the following morning. Everything depended on *Ark Royal*'s aircraft.

And *Ark Royal*'s shamefaced airmen had landed on at 1720. Somerville, in *Renown*, decided that at such a moment nothing would be gained by reporting the attack on *Sheffield*. He wirelessed Tovey, simply, 'Estimate no hits,' and a little later was able to add, 'Second strike force will leave *Ark Royal* about 1830.'

The second strike would almost certainly represent the last opportunity for preventing *Bismarck* coming within range of the Luftwaffe and perhaps a U-boat screen. This time the torpedoes slung from the fifteen aircraft on *Ark Royal*'s deck were armed with contact firing pistols instead of the earlier, apparently defective, Duplex detonators. Refuelling and rearming was no simple business when flight-deck and hangar-deck were heaving and twisting like some crazy fairground amusement, and it was 1900 before the last engine-cowling had been replaced, the last fuel-line thrown off, and the ship could turn off course and into the wind. Pilots and observers had been rebriefed; this time they would contact and identify *Sheffield* before they attacked *Bismarck*.

Taking off into a north-westerly gale at 1910, the Swordfish located *Sheffield* half an hour later, only to lose her almost immediately in the atrocious weather. They found her again at 2035, and now the cruiser could signal, 'The enemy is twelve miles dead ahead.'

Lütjens had sighted *Sheffield* and knew that *Renown* and *Ark Royal*, the other components of Force H, must also be closing on him. He was not entirely surprised, therefore, nor seriously alarmed, when, at 2047, the slow torpedo-biplanes began to tumble out of the low thick cloud. *Bismarck*'s 12½-inch 'Wotan' armoured belt had little to fear from 18-inch torpedoes. He was almost right. Of the thirteen torpedoes launched in the face of a drenching AA fire, eleven missed. One struck the battleship squarely amidships on the port side but did no observable damage, but the third, approaching from starboard as the ship was swinging evasively to port, exploded under her starboard quarter, wrecking her steering and jamming the rudders 15° to port. *Bismarck* began to turn in a wide circle and, no matter how her three screws were used to counter the discrepancy, she insisted on returning her bows into the wind and steering an erratic north-easterly course – which was only slightly to be preferred to steering a continuous circle.

In the confused circumstances of the attack, the strike force's senior pilot, Lieutenant-Commander Tim Coode, had seen no detonations and, as he turned away for home, wirelessed, 'Estimate no hits.' Somerville in *Renown* relayed this to Tovey in *King George V*, and now, it seemed, all hope of stopping *Bismarck* had gone for ever. When *Sheffield* signalled that, incredibly, the enemy was suddenly steering north-north-west, there was disbelief. Two aircraft confirmed it, then *Sheffield* again. On the bridges of a dozen pursuing ships tired men looked at each other and grinned. They'd got her.

But not quite yet. *Bismarck* was a scorpion that was not to be rashly handled. She had already warned off *Sheffield* with several salvoes, and the British cruiser wisely kept her distance, but more shadowers were joining the hunt. At 2152, as daylight was fading, the 'Tribal'-class destroyers *Cossack*, *Maori*, *Zulu* and *Sikh*, and the Polish destroyer *Piorun*[1] made contact. They would cling relentlessly to *Bismarck*'s flanks for the entire night, tormenting her with long-range torpedo attacks as her damage-control personnel fought desperately but unsuccessfully to free the jammed rudder. By dawn it was clear that the damage could not be repaired, and the enemy was gathering. Lütjens bolstered his crew's spirits by announcing that seven of *Ark Royal*'s Swordfish had been shot down, one destroyer sunk and two severely damaged, that three tugs and an oiler were racing to the ship's assistance, and eighty German aircraft would be overhead by first light. In fact no aircraft had been shot down, no destroyers hit, and the battleship was beyond the reach of any help. Lütjens was whistling in the dark.

At 0500 *Bismarck* attempted to fly off her Arado aircraft to France with the ship's log and a reel of film covering the sinking of *Hood*, but now the damage to the catapult from one of *Prince of Wales*'s shells was discovered. The aircraft was jettisoned. On each horizon the fiendish destroyers still steamed, and at 0753 they were joined by a ship that Lütjens had cursed before – *Norfolk* – which had steamed hard for thirty-six hours to be in at the kill. *King George V* and *Rodney* were sixteen miles to the south-east.

During the previous evening, when Tovey had reported to the Admiralty his dwindling fuel-supply, Somerville had immediately offered to add *Renown* to the Commander-in-Chief's force, but Tovey had preferred that the battle-cruiser remain with *Ark Royal*. At dawn on the twenty-seventh Somerville was still anxious to do more than merely hang on the fringe of the action, and asked *Ark Royal* when another strike force could be ready to fly off. Captain Maund, still smarting from the *Sheffield* embarrassment and aware of the increasing number of ships in the vicinity and the poor squally visibility, replied: 'Not until such time as aircraft can differentiate between friend and foe.'

In London the Admiralty's Operations Centre had been crowded all night. The Prime Minister, the First Sea Lord, Sir Dudley Pound, and the Vice-Chief of the Naval Staff, Rear-Admiral Sir Tom Phillips, had been watching the distant situation with interest and no small degree of anxiety. Any operational signal originating in the Admiralty was assumed to carry the authority of Sir Dudley Pound, but the directive that was transmitted to the Commander-in-

Chief afloat during the early forenoon of the twenty-seventh was, by admission, drafted by Winston Churchill. 'We cannot visualise the situation from your signals. *Bismarck* must be sunk at all costs and if to do this it is necessary for *King George V* to remain on the scene she must do so even if it subsequently means towing *King George V.* $= 1137B/27$'.[2]

This was not only arguably the most naïve signal ever to have emanated from the Admiralty, it was also one of the most presumptuous. Only four days earlier, when *Hood* had been steaming to engage *Bismarck*, Admiral Tovey had been briefly tempted to suggest to Holland that *Prince of Wales*, better armoured, should take the leading station in order to draw the enemy's fire away from the battle-cruiser, but quickly decided it would be wrong to dictate tactics to an experienced commander. To allow a battleship to be halted in a battle-area through lack of fuel would have been criminal, and the possible consequences of towing her were mind-boggling. The signal, read with amusement by some and indignation by others, was accorded the only treatment it deserved; it was ignored.

Lütjens had exchanged heroic signals with Adolf Hitler, unaware that the German Admiralty had already requested the Spanish naval authorities to despatch ships to the rescue of *Bismarck*'s survivors, and that the cruiser *Canarias* – the ship at which *Hood* had trained her guns in 1936 – would be ordered to sea from Ferrol with two destroyers. Shortly after 0830 *Bismarck* could see her executioners approaching: *King George V* and *Rodney* to westerly, *Norfolk* to northward, and to the southward, after 600 miles of hard pounding, *Dorsetshire*.

At 0847 *Rodney* opened fire at 16,000 yards and, before the 16-inch salvo erupted in the sea fifty-five seconds later, the guns of *King George V* and *Norfolk* followed suit.

*Bismarck* replied within two minutes, and her first few salvoes fell very close to *Rodney*, but the odds against her were hopelessly overwhelming. Once the British had found the range, at distances reducing to a point-blank three and a half miles, their massive projectiles were smashing into the German battleship with horrendous effect. Both of her forward 15-inch turrets were disabled by one of *Rodney*'s salvoes, and by 1000 hours all her heavy guns were silent, her mast blown away and the shambles of her upper deck littered with dead and wounded. The crews of her secondary turrets began to leave their guns to abandon ship.

'We had the impression', Ordinary Seaman Manthey recalled later, 'that we were being fired upon from all sides. As the hits increased the anti-aircraft crews went under cover. First I was with a group of twenty men in the after gunnery position. After a few hits nearby we fled behind turrets "C" and "D" on the upper deck.' A few moments later Manthey and several others were flung over the side by the splash of a near-miss and scrambled aboard a rubber dinghy in the wake of the shattered burning *Bismarck* among dozens of other struggling men. He would be one of only three to be picked up by a German submarine after nine hours in the sea.

To the chagrin of her company, *Renown* had been ordered to remain with *Ark Royal* and *Sheffield* twenty miles to the southward, out of sight, but thirty minutes of distant thunder was too much for Somerville. He ordered another torpedo attack, and at 0930 twelve Swordfish lifted off from *Ark Royal*. When they reached the battle-area, however, *Bismarck* was still being shelled by *Rodney, King George V, Norfolk* and *Dorsetshire*, with six or seven destroyers prowling in the hope of making some contribution. The aircraft did not interfere, but turned back to their carrier.

*Bismarck* refused to be sunk by gunfire. 'Any ship with torpedoes', Tovey signalled to all ships in company, 'to close *Bismarck* and torpedo her.' As *Dorsetshire*, the only vessel with torpedoes remaining, closed to within three thousand yards of *Bismarck*, the German battleship's turbine-engineer-officer was ordered to detonate explosive charges that would destroy the sea-valves. At 1036 *Dorsetshire* fired two torpedoes into the starboard side of *Bismarck*'s hull, then a third into the port side. The massive wreck rolled to port, sinking by the stern, turned her keel to the sky and disappeared completely.

Of *Bismarck*'s complement of 2084, *Dorsetshire* and *Maori* picked up 102 survivors before the threat of U-boat and Luftwaffe attacks compelled the British to abandon all further rescue-attempts. Of the hundreds left in the sea, three were found by *U74*, as mentioned, and two were hauled aboard the German weather-ship *Sachsenwald* on the following day. The remaining 1977 perished.

Members of the House of Commons cheered jubilantly when Winston Churchill interrupted proceedings to announce that *Hood* had been avenged. The NAAFI bars in Devonport, Portsmouth, Chatham and Rosyth were crowded with happily blaspheming sailors, and in every mess and wardroom through the Navy midday glasses were raised in celebration.

A ramrod gunnery officer strode into the mess-hall of HMS *St George*, the Boys' Training Establishment. A bosun's pipe shrilled, and the officer shouted, 'For what we are about to receive, thank God!' Then – '*Silence!*' Twelve hundred boys froze. The officer thrust out an angry chin. 'We have sunk the *Bismarck!*' Seconds later the mess-hall exploded into roaring cheers. They shouted themselves hoarse, climbed on tables, and even the instructors grinned. They had sunk *Bismarck*, and *Hood* was avenged.

Force H regained Gibraltar, to be fêted. *Rodney*, *Norfolk* and *Maori* came into the Clyde, and so, briefly, did *Victorious*, before resuming her passage to the Mediterranean. *Dorsetshire* docked in Newcastle, and *King George V* anchored in Loch Ewe for much-needed fuel. The vast Fleet Canteen in Scapa Flow was almost deserted, but within the next few days the Fleet's drifters would be landing swarming hundreds of libertymen ashore – although nearly fifteen hundred of those who had sailed from the anchorage six days earlier would never return to it.

In his report to the Admiralty during the forenoon of 27 May, Tovey said that he would 'like to pay the highest tribute for the most gallant fight put up [by *Bismarck*] against impossible odds'. The Admiralty snapped back very quickly: 'For political reasons it is essential that nothing of the nature of the sentiments expressed in your 1119 should be given publicity, however much we admire a gallant fight.'

In Britain the loss of *Hood* was little less than a national disaster. Almost unnoticed was the fact that during the few days of the *Bismarck* chase the Royal Navy had also lost the cruisers *Gloucester* and *Fiji* and the destroyers *Greyhound*, *Juno*, *Hereward*, *Imperial*, *Kashmir* and *Kelly* (the latter commanded by Captain Lord Louis Mountbatten), with 2000 men, off Crete.

In Germany the brief exultation at the destruction of *Hood* was silenced by the news of *Bismarck*'s sinking. A queen exchanged for a queen was no gain, and, materially, the Germany Navy could afford its loss less comfortably than the British. Nor was there consolation for the thousands of bereaved in the knowledge that *Bismarck*'s sister *Tirpitz* was carrying out her sea and battle trials in the Baltic.

The Germans insisted (and still insist) that *Bismarck*'s own crew was responsible for her sinking only after all her ammunition had been expended, and that *whilst sinking* she was struck by *Dorsetshire*'s torpedoes. They are possibly right, but the point is academic – as also is the unanswered question of *Hood*'s destruction; whether by the penetration of a magazine or the explosion of deck torpedoes. The end was the same.

*Prinz Eugen*, having parted company with *Bismarck* on 25 May, was still at large. Churchill was anxious that the enemy cruiser should somehow be involved in a confrontation with an American warship, and confided to the First Sea Lord: 'It would be far better,

for instance, that [*Prinz Eugen*] should be located by a United States
ship, as this may tempt her to fire upon that ship, thus providing the
incident for which the United States government would be so thank-
ful.'

*Prinz Eugen*, however, did not oblige. She oiled from the *Esso
Hamburg* on 28 May and reached the sanctuary of Brest four days
later. She would survive the war to be destroyed in American atom
bomb experiments at Bikini Atoll in July 1946.

As in the Falklands battle twenty-seven years before, it was probably the cruisers that emerged from the *Bismarck* action with the
greatest credit. The shadow-and-report role played by the hardly
youthful *Norfolk* and *Suffolk* (both were built in the 1920s) might be
thought beyond criticism. Gliding like phantoms through the Arctic
mists in the wake of the enemy for hour after weary hour, the
slightest miscalculation could have been disastrous. The cruisers
lacked the majestic power of the battleships or the dash of a destroyer, 'Yet . . . the gallant Counties,' wrote an officer in *Electra*,
racing northward with *Hood*, 'side-stepped smartly from their baited
quarry's fire, hugging his flanks and never losing sight of him – were
pinpointing the location of the enemy on this wide expanse of ocean
as if the speeding ships were as stationary as church steeples set
down on an ordnance map.'

During the thirty-two hours that contact with *Bismarck* was lost.
*Suffolk* was compelled to abandon the operation through lack of fuel
and seek replenishment in Scapa Flow, and *Norfolk*, too, was running dangerously low. Rear-Admiral Wake-Walker began making
for Iceland, changed his mind, and turned again in search of
*Bismarck*, steaming *Norfolk* a total of 2000 miles to rendezvous with
her again.

When *Hood* was sunk, the unfit *Prince of Wales* automatically became subordinate to *Norfolk* and took station astern of her. Although
aware that *King George V* and *Repulse* were closing, the Admiralty
impatiently signalled Wake-Walker to enquire what his intentions
were with regard to *Prince of Wales* re-engaging. It was a question
that not only implied that Wake-Walker lacked offensive spirit but
might also have stung him into another action against his better
judgement. Fortunately Wake-Walker was not to be provoked.

Some weeks later Sir Dudley Pound, supported by his deputy,
Rear-Admiral Sir Tom Phillips, proposed that Wake-Walker and
Captain John Leach (*Prince of Wales*) should be court-martialled for
not re-engaging *Bismarck* after *Hood*'s sinking. However, Tovey –
who had totally approved of Wake-Walker's behaviour – informed

Pound that if this intention was proceeded with he would haul down his Commander-in-Chief's flag and appear at the trial on behalf of the accused. On 25 September, Winston Churchill wrote 'Leave it' across the relevant Admiralty memo, after which, recalled Tovey, 'I heard no more about it'.

Both *Norfolk* and *Suffolk* survived the war, to be subsequently scrapped. *Dorsetshire* was sunk in the Indian Ocean, with her sister *Cornwall*, by Japanese dive-bombers in April 1942.

## *Notes*

1    *Piorun* was originally the British *Nerissa*, manned by the Polish Navy from 1940 to 1946, then renamed *Noble* for a further ten years of service in the Royal Navy.

2    The suffix letter 'B' after the time of origin indicates that the Admiralty's 'local' clocks were two hours ahead of GMT, i.e., on Double British Summer Time. The ships at sea would be adhering to GMT (suffix 'Z').

# VI  Same War, Different Enemy

## Chapter Fourteen

*The Eastern Fleet and the threat to Singapore – the sortie of Force Z*

JOHN F. KENNEDY, son of the Irish-American Ambassador in the United Kingdom, had visited Germany and subsequently provided his father, Joseph Kennedy – already an anglophobe – with an enthusiastic description of the Nazi military and industrial potential. The Ambassador had early reported to President Roosevelt: 'I have yet to talk to any military or naval expert of any nationality this week who thinks that . . . England has a Chinaman's chance . . .', and continued to communicate pessimistic assessments, while a number of other prominent Americans, including Henry Ford, who had already announced that history was bunk, and Charles Lindbergh, friend of Goering and an admirer of the Luftwaffe, declared that Britain would go the same way as all the other countries that had opposed Hitler.

After a year of war Britain was bloodied but still on her feet. There were still bastions of isolationism in the United States; with regard to Roosevelt's decision to transfer fifty old destroyers to the Royal Navy in exchange for bases in the West Indies, the *St Louis Post Despatch* retorted: 'Of all sucker real estate deals in history this is the worst, and the President of the United States is the sucker.' In the main, however, public opinion was swinging heavily in favour of the British cause. 'Between us and Hitler stands the British Fleet!' claimed the Committee to Defend America by Aiding the Allies, pointing out that the United States deployed only one-sixth of its navy on the eastern seaboard, and it was the British and Canadians who were fighting 'to stop the international gangsters from reaching the loot across the Atlantic'. If most Americans were more worried about *what would happen to the United States* if Britain failed than with the fate of the British, the end result was the same.

The neutrality of the Republic of Ireland (Eire) was beginning to strain the patience of Winston Churchill. The Irish premier, Eamon

de Valera, had refused to restore base facilities at Berehaven and
Lough Swilly (surrendered to Ireland in 1938), which would have
increased the range of Atlantic convoy escorts by 200 miles. The
Irish Government also refused to allow British air–sea rescue-
vessels to venture within territorial limits, while its own rescue
services were quite inadequate for the location and recovery of
survivors who had crashed or drifted into coastal waters. That many
British sailors died while transporting oil, wheat and other cargoes
upon which Ireland was dependent did not shake de Valera's
determination to remain uncommitted and allow the Republic to be
a haven for enemy agents and observers who could cross and recross
the border at will. When (to British satisfaction) a German aircraft
dropped its bombs on Dublin in error, killing twenty-eight people,
the Irish claimed that British Intelligence had deliberately 'bent' the
Germans' navigational radio beam signals. More than once
Churchill toyed with the possibility of sending troops into the
Republic, but was dissuaded by his Chiefs of Staff. There were far
more urgent problems, and one of them was the growing militancy
of Japan.

By mid-1941 those men who had entered the Navy on mobilisation
or in the early days of the war were competent seamen and leading
hands; two years of war service were worth ten of peacetime ritual.
From whatever background they had come, they had all learned one
thing – that nobody outside the service knew *anything* about it. The
films they had seen and the books they had read about the Royal
Navy had all painted a totally different picture from the real one,
because authors, scriptwriters and film advisers had invariably been
drawn from too remote a social stratum. Nobody thought of inviting
a three-badge gunlayer or a killick torpedoman to advise on messdeck protocol, dress and behaviour, the sailor's humour, the closely
bonded comradeship that prevailed across the white-scrubbed
tables of the lower, forward decks. Films like Noël Coward's *In Which
We Serve* would dismiss ratings as poorly spoken Cockneys with
terraced homes in Clapham North or inarticulate Glaswegians with
aspirations that did not reach beyond a sailors' doss-house or an
intimate hour with Slack Alice – but always showing a dog-like
devotion to their captain and ready, at his word, to give three rous-
ing cheers when clinging to a raft as the brave old ship plunged. Nor,
as the film directors insisted, did ratings wear their caps at the
mess-table, their boots in their hammocks or, indeed, sling their
hammocks during daytime. Naval ratings were simply ordinary men
with ordinary decencies and the same emotions as all ordinary

men – fear, love, hate, homesickness, moments of happiness and moments of despair – who had adapted to an extraordinary environment. Probably the commonest attitude on the lower deck was one of resignation; they talked of 'after the war', not knowing how far distant the end was or how it would come, but only that the most valuable years of their lives were being poured away in a war engineered by a completely different species, compared with which they – the ordinary men – were hopelessly insignificant.

With *Bismarck* sunk and the new 'King George V' battleships coming into commission, the Admiralty could afford to take a look at the Far Eastern situation with a view to discouraging Japanese expansionist ambitions. While the Navy was still short of long-range escorts and anti-submarine vessels, there was now a superfluity of old battleships, and it was decided that, beginning in mid-1942, an Eastern Fleet would be built up, consisting of the four surviving 'R'-class battleships, *Revenge, Resolution, Ramillies* and *Royal Sovereign*,[1] the battle-cruiser *Renown*, and the slightly younger but slow *Rodney* and *Nelson*. To these would be added one aircraft-carrier, ten cruisers and twenty-four destroyers.

In August 1941, however, during the Anglo-American Atlantic Conference, Churchill was informed by Roosevelt that American economic pressures on Japan were about to be intensified and that a war in the Far East was a possibility. Churchill ordered the Admiralty immediately to reinforce the Far Eastern station with a squadron 'including capital ships'.

The Admiralty did not wish to release one of their latest battleships from European waters. There was still *Tirpitz* (working up in the Baltic) which, with any combination of *Scharnhorst, Gneisenau, Admiral Scheer, Lützow* and *Prinz Eugen*, was a force to reckon with. Still, it was quite plain to Churchill and others that the 'R'-class battleships earmarked for the Far East were too slow and outdated to serve any useful purpose against a hostile Japanese fleet. Churchill wanted a 'King George V' battleship to supplement either *Repulse* or *Renown*, with an aircraft-carrier. A modern capital ship, he argued, would have a similar influence on the Japanese as the *Tirpitz* had on the British – a 'paralysing effect upon Japanese naval action'.

It was all too apparent that the Admiralty's interpretation of the requirements was different from Churchill's. The Admiralty was visualising a defensive force to secure Singapore and Malaya, but Churchill, who was by no means convinced that Japan was intent on war with the United States, Britain and possibly Russia, or, if she was, that she would attack Singapore, wanted a powerful but fast and compact *offensive* force – rather, an improved Force H. Much later, in retrospect, he would claim that once the force had reached Singapore and made its arrival known to the Japanese it should 'then disappear into the immense archipelago'; the last thing intended was that the ships should intercept a Japanese invasion force.

In any case, there was not much time. The three ships chosen to formulate Force G, for the Far East, were *Prince of Wales*, *Repulse* and the aircraft-carrier *Indomitable*. To placate Admiralty misgivings, Churchill intimated that he might like to see these three joined by *Nelson* when repairs to the latter had been completed in April 1942.

*Prince of Wales*, less efficient than *King George V* but preferred to the newly commissioned *Duke of York*, had taken Churchill to Newfoundland, where the Atlantic Charter was agreed, and had then served briefly in the Mediterranean, where, in a convoy action, she had shot down two Italian aircraft and one of *Ark Royal*'s before returning to the United Kingdom and Scapa Flow in October.

The choice of *Repulse* was decided largely by the fact that she was already at Cape Town, having escorted Convoy WS11 that far on the long route to Suez. It was the first time that the battle-cruiser had experienced warm sunshine on her old armour since 1938; it was mildly reassuring to know that *Renown* had returned to the United Kingdom and the cold drizzling rain of Scapa Flow.

*Indomitable* was a new aircraft-carrier of 24,680 tons, carrying 48 aircraft (Albacores, Fulmars and Hurricanes) and with a speed of 31.5 knots. She had, however, been in commission only since 1 October, a mere nineteen days before the Admiralty added her name to those of *Prince of Wales* and *Repulse*, and she had been sent to the West Indies to work up. To what extent *Indomitable* and her three squadrons might have changed the history of the Far East will never be known, for on 3 November the carrier damaged her hull on an uncharted reef when about to enter Kingston and was ordered to Norfolk, Virginia, for repair. She was at sea again in twelve days to fly on her aircraft and then hasten for the Cape and Singapore, but she would never overtake *Prince of Wales* and *Repulse*.

What sort of Britain were the ships leaving behind them during those closing weeks of 1941?

It was a shabby grey country of queues, shelters, static water-tanks and barrage balloons, night shifts and the blackout. BBC programmes included 'ITMA', 'The Brains Trust' and Vera Lynn singing 'We'll Meet Again', while CBS commentator Ed Murrow spoke nightly across the Atlantic so that Americans could savour the realities of war by proxy. Air raids were not as frequent or as severe as they had been a year earlier, and civilian wages were rising faster than prices; but sugar, butter, bacon and ham were rationed and most other foodstuffs tightly controlled. Meat was rationed by price – 2s 2d per person per week – eggs were limited to one per person per fortnight, and the cheese ration fluctuated wildly. The worst was very shortly to come; the tea allowance was about to be reduced to two ounces per person weekly.

There was remarkably little black-market activity. Parks, public gardens and golf courses had been ploughed up, and housewives were being exhorted to experiment with new foods and recipes – boiled cabbage-tops, swede-tops and radish-tops, the green fronds of young bracken (which allegedly tasted like asparagus), mock bacon made from lettuce and dripping, and eggless, sugarless cakes, potato flour, potato pastry, potato soup, potato balls, potato sauté, potato croquettes, potato pudding, potato turnover. . . .

The colony to which the ships were steaming was so different from war-worn Britain that it might have been on a different planet. The European community of Singapore, during the last days of 1941, was among the most spoiled and certainly the most complacent in the world. Its contempt for the native Malays, Chinese and Tamils was equalled only by a disdain toward the British servicemen whose presence had to be tolerated but did not call for fraternisation. At the Raffles, the Adelphi and the Seaview hotels in Singapore, the Eastern & Oriental in Penang, the civil officials and police officers, planters, engineers and mining superintendents took tiffin or ordered chota pegs, swam in their exclusive pools, played tennis on the courts of their private clubs, confident in the knowledge that Singapore was a fortress defended by the soldiers and sailors who, however, *were* rather you-know. The men of the local squadron of old light cruisers, *Danae*, *Dragon* and *Durban*, and the Gordon High-landers, were more cordially provided for by the Union Jack Club, or the city's amusement parks – New World, Happy World and Beauty World – where they could dance with Eurasian girls of startling beauty but debatable morals for 30 cents, drink cold 'Tiger' beer, watch wrestling or boxing, or 'Please lay down and have yourself A Massage here so that you will be able to recover from your fatigue which you have received from the battle field. We always have very beautiful massage girls to welcome you Soldiers and Sailors and Seamen. Sanitary Conditions Heating System is Perfect! From A.M. 10 to P.M. 9.'

*Prince of Wales* and *Repulse*, the former accompanied by the destroyers *Electra* and *Express*, had joined forces in Ceylon before moving on to

Singapore. Sailors tend to be superstitious, and *Repulse*'s would have been made a little uneasy by the knowledge that one of their escorting destroyers had accompanied *Hood* on her last sortie; they were also resentful at finding their own ship subordinate to *Prince of Wales*, flying the flag of Admiral Sir Tom Phillips. Although both were 'Guzz' ships, i.e., manned by Devonport personnel, the battleship's reputation as a 'Jonah' had preceded her. Moreover, *Repulse*, the older ship, had a crew of which seventy per cent were regular servicemen, competent and highly disciplined, and aware that they were, while the unsettled morale in *Prince of Wales* – a ship that had been hustled from one enterprise to another before achieving below-decks coherence – was no secret.

'This ought to serve as a deterrent on Japan,' Churchill had cabled Roosevelt on 7 November. 'There is nothing like having something that can catch and kill anything.' He also telegraphed General Smuts, South Africa's Prime Minister, that Phillips was on the way to the Far East, and that 'he is a great friend of mine and one of our ablest officers . . . he knows the whole story back and forth . . .'.

This was one of the most fanciful claims of the war. Sir Tom Spencer Vaughan Phillips, KCB, aged fifty-three, had been behind a Whitehall desk since 1939 and he had last experienced action in 1917. A very small man – he needed to stand on a box when on the compass-platform and was nicknamed 'Tom Thumb' – he was notorious for his angry impatience and, more seriously, his strong conviction that aircraft were no match for properly handled warships, arguing that only greater resolution on the part of ships' commanding officers was needed to defeat the dive-bomber. He had always refused to listen to anyone who tried to persuade him that fighter protection was necessary for all ships operating within reach of enemy bombers.

Phillips was not popular among his contemporaries. 'I shudder to think', Somerville wrote to Admiral Cunningham (Commander-in-Chief Mediterranean), 'of the Pocket Napoleon and his party. All the trials to learn and no solid sea experience to fall back on. They ought to have someone who knows the stuff and can train that party properly on the way out.'

On leaving the Admiralty, where he had been Vice-Chief of Naval Staff, to take up his new appointment, Phillips had been promoted from Rear-Admiral to the temporary rank of Admiral – a double step. When he reached Singapore (having flown from Ceylon to arrive before his ships) he took over the role of Commander-in-Chief Eastern Fleet from Rear-Admiral Sir Geoffrey Layton,[2] who was not only Phillips' substantive senior but had been Commander-in-Chief China Fleet since mid-1940 and was far more familiar with the problems and circumstances of the station. Layton did not complain, then or later, when the Admiralty ordered that he should reassume command of a débâcle, with far fewer resources than Phillips had been given.

And Phillips' resources were lean enough. As he stood on the jetty of Singapore's naval base on 2 December he could see *Prince of Wales* alongside and *Repulse* moored in the Johore Strait. With them were the destroyers *Electra, Express, Jupiter* and *Encounter* – the last two having been released by the Mediterranean Fleet to accompany the force and both with chronic engine deficiencies. In addition to the three old 'D'-class light cruisers already mentioned there was the local destroyer force of *Tenedos, Stronghold* and the Australian *Vampire*, all of First World War vintage. In dock, undergoing refit, was the 8000-ton cruiser *Mauritius*, while *Exeter*, of 8390 tons, was several days away in the Bay of Bengal. In Hong Kong, if it mattered, were the old destroyers *Scout, Thanet* and *Thracian*, and the gunboat *Cicala*, built in 1915.

Six hundred cars had met the warships at Cape Town to carry off the shore-going sailors, and hospitality had been overwhelming. In Singapore the new arrivals were quickly to learn that even officers were regarded as poor whites, and other ranks as only marginally more socially acceptable than natives. In the naval base on the north-east of the island the Admiralty civilians had their own clubs, shops, churches and amusements, their houses with servants. The men from the ships, when released from duty, could go to the NAAFI canteen in the base (HMS *Sultan*[3]) or catch a rickety bus to travel the fifteen miles of Bukit Tima Road to Singapore City, southward, where there were excellent Chinese-owned bars and restaurants, Greta Garbo in *Mata Hari* at the Alhambra, Tyrone Power in *Blood and Sand* at the plush air-conditioned Cathay. The Malays and Chinese were friendly, at least while the British were still masters, but the gunnery officer of *Electra*, taking tea with a colleague at the Raffles, tells of a depreciating female voice from a neighbouring table: 'Yes, they may very well be officers, my dear, but if so they must be terribly, terribly junior officers – and temporary, too, of course.' Still, there were so many compensations for the men from Scapa Flow. The sun was warm and the island richly green, with monkeys and squirrels among the palms and groves of rubber-trees, red roads and fine white houses, and pineapples, lichis, mangoes and mangosteens. 'This must be a wonderful change for you,' patronised a resident. 'A regular holiday.' It was, so far.

At military level, however, both British and Americans were aware of ominous Japanese movements, and Service 6, the wireless link between Singapore and Whitehall, was heavy with priority traffic. On Monday, 1 December the forces in Malaya were ordered to assume a state of emergency, and two days later Phillips was advised by the Admiralty to get his ships out of the base, where they could be trapped by aircraft or submarines. The British were haunted by the possibility of a war with the Japanese without the United States being involved. A few weeks earlier Churchill had promised that if Japan attacked America a declaration of war would follow from Britain 'within the hour', but Roosevelt could make no reciprocal pledge. Phillips now asked the Admiralty to send him the four 'R'-class battleships with, in addition, *Warspite*. Of these, *Revenge* was in Colombo, but two or three months would elapse before all the others could be mustered in Singapore and, although Phillips did not know it, the Japanese were only four days away.

On 4 December, Phillips flew to Manila to consult with Admiral Thomas Hart, commanding the United States Asiatic Fleet, and General Douglas MacArthur. Hart was persuaded to allow four of his own First World War four-stack destroyers to accompany Phillips' force on a reconnaissance in strength toward the Gulf of Siam. At 1800 hours on the sixth Hart and Phillips were still discussing the situation when an aide brought in a despatch transmitted from Singapore. A patrolling aircraft had sighted a Japanese convoy of twenty-five transports escorted by thirteen warships south of Saigon and steering 240°.

'Did you say you were flying back to Singapore tomorrow morning, Admiral?' Hart asked Phillips. 'If you want to be there when the war starts, I suggest you take off right now.'

Phillips moved quickly. During his absence from Singapore, *Repulse*, with *Vampire* and *Tenedos*, had steamed for Darwin, partly to get the battle-cruiser out of harbour but also in the hope that the Australians would add HMAS *Hobart*, a 7105-ton 'Leander'-class cruiser, to the force. Now, however, the three British ships were ordered back to Singapore at top speed. Hong Kong, with a garrison of only 11,319, had always been regarded as indefensible, and now Phillips told the colony's destroyer force to abandon the station and join him.[4] The four promised American destroyers, *Whipple, John D. Edwards, Edsall* and *Alden*, were instructed to prepare for passage from Balikpapen to Singapore within twenty-four hours, and *Exeter*, convoying in the Bay of Bengal, turned for the base, working up to 28 knots.

By midnight on 7 December the entire Malayan Command was

alerted; British, Indian and Australian troops were standing to arms, searchlights probed Singapore's night sky, and the codeword for invasion was 'Raffles'.

The first Japanese landed at Kota Bharu, in the remote north-eastern state of Kelantan at 0045 local time on Monday, 8 December, about seventy minutes before the attack on Pearl Harbor (where, because of the intervening International Dateline, the time was still 0800 on Sunday, 7 December).[5] All land and air forces in Malaya were commanded by Air Chief Marshal Sir Robert Brooke-Popham, aged sixty-three. He had 86,895 British and Commonwealth troops (but no tanks because the jungle was allegedly impenetrable) and 158 operational aircraft – a mixed bag of elderly types of which the best were Blenheim medium bombers and American-built Brewster Buffalo fighters, though neither type was likely to be a match for the Mitsubishi squadrons soon to be flown from Indo-China. Lieutenant-General Tomoyuki Yamashita led 26,000 men accompanied by a few tanks who, however (according to the *Malaya Tribune*'s military correspondent), were 'caught in a trap of their own making, and neither by land nor sea nor in the air do they have even a glimmer of a chance of victory . . . against the preponderance of forces which encircle them . . .'.

The Admiralty had taken care not to have its Eastern Fleet under the supervision of an Air Marshal who had retired in 1937 to become Governor of Kenya, and had been recalled to the RAF only in November 1940. Vice-Admiral Layton, and now Phillips, were their own masters, but, by the same token, the Navy would have to request any air support from an RAF which had always taken pleasure in thumbing its nose at the senior service. When that pleasure could be justified by a very real shortage of aircraft, the Navy's chances of achieving operational co-operation were not good.

At 0400 on the morning of the eighth Japanese planes made a brief bombing attack on Singapore, killing sixty-three. With breakfast came the news of Pearl Harbor.

Churchill telephoned Roosevelt from Chequers. 'Mr President, what's all this about Japan?'

'It's quite true,' Roosevelt confirmed. 'They have attacked us at Pearl Harbor. We are all in the same boat.'

Churchill was secretly elated. At last the United States, the sleeping giant, had been provoked, and Britain was no longer alone. There was still a long hard road, but it had only one possible end. 'So,' he mused, 'we won the war after all.'

*

By noon it was apparent that the enemy was landing at Kota Bharu, near the mouth of the Kelantan river and slightly farther north at Singora in Siam, and, if the activities were going to be disrupted, now was the time to do it. However, when Phillips reviewed the forces immediately available for a sortie he discovered that he had only *Prince of Wales* and *Repulse*, the old light cruiser *Durban*, and the destroyers *Electra, Express, Vampire* and *Tenedos*. The Admiral had three choices of action: he could remain in Singapore until his resources improved but risk being the victim of another Pearl Harbor attack; he could retire to a safer area – Ceylon or Australia; or he could go out and fight with what he had. To Phillips there was no alternative. It was, he told the officers gathered in his day-cabin, like 'taking the Home Fleet into the Skagerrak without air cover. Nevertheless, I feel we have to do something. So, gentlemen, we sail at fifteen hundred.' The Air Officer Commanding, Air Vice-Marshal C. W. Pulford, had already agreed that the RAF would do its best to provide cover during the following day, but his airfields in north Malaya were already being evacuated and it was doubtful if any planes could be made available on 10 December. Layton, the outgoing Commander-in-Chief, strongly disapproved of a five- or six-day operation without air support, but had no authority to inter-vene and had planned to leave Singapore in the *Dominion Monarch* on the following day.

*Durban*, Phillips decided, would remain in Singapore, and, indeed, the destroyers would return before action was joined by the capital ships because of their vulnerability to air attack and also their limited fuel-capacity. Any Japanese aircraft encountered, he calcu-lated, would not be carrying torpedoes, or bombs sufficiently heavy to embarrass *Prince of Wales* and *Repulse*. Even so, despite Phillips' poor opinion of aircraft, he was uneasy. 'I'm not sure', he told Captain Bell, his senior aide, 'that Pulford realises the importance I attach to fighter cover over Singora on the tenth. I'm going to write him a letter stressing the point, and asking him to let me know for certain what he can do.'

The letter was taken ashore minutes before the ships slipped, to be delivered by hand. As the warships emerged from the Johore Strait into the open sea Pulford's answer was passed by Kranji Naval W/T Station.

'Regret fighter protection impossible.'

'Well,' Phillips shrugged, 'we must get on without it.'

The squadron, now designated Force Z, turned north-eastward at 17½ knots. Below decks only a privileged handful knew where they were going; the most favoured designation was the Philippines to join forces with the United States Asiatic Fleet, which consisted of one heavy cruiser, one light cruiser, thirteen destroyers (including the four on passage to Singapore) and twenty-nine submarines. *Prince of Wales* and *Repulse*, the British sailors agreed, would add a little class to that shabby bunch of amateurs.

With Force Z steaming through a quiet tropical night. *Repulse* four cables astern of *Prince of Wales* and the destroyer-screen deployed, there is time to examine Phillips' situation. His intention was to attack first the Japanese shipping off Kota Bharu and then proceed a further 140 miles up the coast to Singora. He had asked Pulford for air reconnaissance a hundred miles northward of Force Z at daylight on the ninth (the following day), a reconnaissance off Singora at first light on the tenth, and fighter protection off Singora during daylight of the tenth. With regard to fighter protection, Pulford had already answered with an emphatic refusal, but some eight hours after the ships had sailed the Naval HQ in Singapore wirelessed a situation-report which confirmed that *one* Catalina would reconnoitre as requested on the ninth and it was *hoped* that a dawn reconnaissance could be flown over Singora on the tenth. Once again it was emphasised that no fighter aircraft would be available, but General MacArthur in Manila had been requested to attack the Japanese airfields in Indo-China with long-range bombers as soon as possible.

Phillips maintained radio silence. His ships were reading the continuous area broadcast transmitted by Stonecutters Wireless Station (GZO) in Hong Kong, but were free to communicate directly on H/F with either Hong Kong or Kranji Wireless Station (GYL) in Singapore. Signals from Singapore for Phillips had first to be relayed to Hong Kong for broadcast transmission, but this entailed a delay of only minutes.

At this stage of the operation Phillips' prospects of success, although risky, remained reasonable *while he remained undetected by the enemy*, particularly if the Americans were about to launch heavy bombers against the Japanese air-bases. He was convinced (wrongly) that enemy torpedo-aircraft could not fly the 400 miles from Saigon to the target-area and he had little to fear from light bombs. What he did not know was that on the previous day all but three of MacArthur's thirty-five B-17 Flying Fortresses had been destroyed on the ground at Clark Field.

But neither did Phillips know that the RAF, too, were hedging their bets. They had been stung by criticisms on other occasions – in Norway, at Dunkirk, over the Atlantic and off Crete – for allegedly failing to support the Navy when it mattered, and they could see a situation developing in which those criticisms might be repeated.

Pulford had warned Phillips, but on Sembawang airfield eleven Brewster Buffalos of No. 453 (Australian) Squadron had been ordered to be held in readiness to take off in the event of an attack on the British warships – *if* they were within range and *if* sufficient warning was received.

Finally, there was a joker in the pack of which nobody was aware, yet. Malayan airfields were being bombed and machine-gunned, and there was a sickening repetition of British planes being caught on the ground. Personnel were firing buildings and equipment and departing hurriedly, whereupon the Army decided that if the RAF were not concerned about the airfields, then neither were they. The joker was an officer of the RAF, a native of the Irish Republic, who, pursuing his country's feud with the British, was caught signalling the Japanese.[6]

The dawn of 9 December was grey, wet and overcast. The ships went to dawn action stations at 0600 and stood down at 0730. By noon they would have covered almost half the distance to their first target-area. There was a moment of excitement when *Vampire* reported sighting an unidentified aircraft which had subsequently disappeared, but it was decided that, if the aircraft had been an enemy, it had not seen the warships. They steamed on.

Nobody knew that at 1345 the Japanese submarine *I-65*, the most easterly of the 30th Submarine Flotilla, sighted *Prince of Wales* and *Repulse* but, because of the distance involved, not the destroyers. Radio conditions were bad, and it was not until 1500 that the submarine's enemy-report reached Rear-Admiral Sadaichi Matsunaga, commanding the 22nd Air Flotilla in Saigon. The Japanese were surprised and alarmed. Only that morning two high-flying Japanese aircraft had reported that the two British capital ships were still moored in Singapore's naval base, yet now they were suddenly approaching the sensitive landing-areas on the east coast. There was worse to come. The submarine *I-65* had lost contact with the enemy, so briefly seen.

The alarm was sounded to all Japanese ships and ship-borne aircraft. Find the British.

Force Z was still steaming 345° at 18 knots. There had been no interception of enemy transmissions because none of the ships was carrying 'Y' wireless operators, trained to read the very peculiar Japanese Morse code, and it is doubtful if any such men were in the Singapore area. However, everything seemed to be going well.

In *Repulse* the quartermaster's voice over the address system had announced that the ship would remain at first state of readiness following tomorrow's dawn action stations, and anti-flash gear would be worn. Supper was better than usual: soup, cold beef, ham, meat pie and fresh pineapples, coffee for the wardroom and tar-strong tea for the messdecks. 'Them Jap ships with the pagodas,' opined a three-badge AB who had served in the China Fleet in 1926, 'if they fires a broadside they turns over. And them Japs is slant-eyed monkeys, mate. I was thinking of bringing one 'ome for my missis, on a string.'

As the officers of the day made their rounds of the messdecks at 2100 the slant-eyed monkeys were firmly established in northern Malaya and were closing around Hong Kong, although in Penang, Kuala Lumpur and Singapore the clubs and bars, out of bounds to servicemen, were still thronged with European residents drinking gin slings, brandies-and-dry, whisky sours and horse's necks. They were still planning to attend the Penang races, spend Christmas at Cameron Highlands or dance to Dan Hopkins and his band at the Raffles, the Reller band at the Adelphi, or have dinner by moonlight among the palms and orchids of the Cathay's roof-garden. 'Boy! Chota peg, chop chop!'

During the afternoon, and ending only when dusk forbade further communication by light, Phillips ordered an 'all-round' nine-part policy-signal to be flashed to ships in company, and the signalmen on other flag-decks pencilled sheet after sheet of signal-pad, cursing a flag officer who suffered from verbal diarrhoea.

In earlier communications with the Admiralty, Phillips had referred to 'a line of battle' and to his desire to carry out the 'Fleet training of battleships', which might be considered quaintly outmoded concepts in the third year of the war; and now, in this contiguous series of signals (see Appendix 2), he mentions 'aerodromes' when most servicemen talked of airfields or air-bases. The first two paragraphs merely repeat 'sitrep' information which all ships would already have received on the area broadcast, while Phillips' advice to Captain John Leach (*Prince of Wales*) and Captain William Tennant (*Repulse*) that they should not offer themselves as end-on targets, and on the availability of fuses, may have stung those experienced officers.

The reference to 'clothing such as overalls or suits which keep arms and legs covered against risk of burns from flash' is perhaps a reminder that, although the anti-flash gear with which all personnel were provided protected the head and neck, hands and forearms, it was possible that men might be tempted to go to action stations in tropical shorts or even without shirts. One can think of all sorts of things to remind men about, in anticipation of action, but, even if

this warning merits inclusion above all others, the signal is rep-
etitious and overlong; it might with advantage have been limited to
half this length. (See Appendix 3.)

The British were hoping to be soon hidden by darkness, but
shortly before sunset *Prince of Wales*'s Type 272 radar found aircraft
to the eastward and she hoisted Flag A. The contact soon materialised into three Japanese floatplanes which, however, remained well
out of range, low on the horizon, before turning away. It was a
sobering moment – the first real evidence of an enemy presence.
Phillips held his course, and soon after sunset ordered *Tenedos* to
return to Singapore while the old destroyer's remaining fuel allowed
her to do so safely. Force Z began working up to 26 knots, turning to
north-west.

There was no doubt that now, in so far as secrecy was concerned,
Force Z's operation was compromised and, if there was a right time
for abandonment, it was now – but that, of course, is a retrospective
observation and there were several factors of which Phillips remained ignorant. One was that the invasion location toward which
he was speeding had been abandoned by the transports; they were
on their way back to Indo-China. Another was that Force Z was on
a collision course with a powerful enemy force of cruisers and
destroyers, while fifty land-based aircraft, in three-plane flights,
were searching the darkness for the British ships earlier reported.
The Japanese were worried. They still had irons in the fire, and
Force Z could impose a costly disruption of a hairline timetable.

The First watch, the final period of 9 December, was less than an
hour old when several things happened in rapid succession. *Electra*
reported a flare, estimated five miles ahead. At that moment neither
Phillips' Force Z nor Vice-Admiral Ozawa's cruiser force, which
also saw it, knew that it had been dropped by a Japanese aircraft
which, by incredible luck, had sighted the white wakes of the British
capital ships in the black void below. It was a million-to-one sighting, but it changed everything.

Admiral Ozawa, in the cruiser *Chokai*, wheeled his force around to
northward, reporting to Saigon that there were three attacking
planes above him, protesting, 'It is *Chokai* under the flare!' Ozawa
might have been even more disturbed had he known that he was
well within the range of *Prince of Wales*'s surface surveillance radar,
but the British obviously failed to detect anything unusual.

Phillips ordered an emergency turn to port (almost due west) to
avoid the flare. Then, before he could resume the original course
expected by all five ships, he was handed a signal from Naval HQ
Singapore.

'Most Immediate. One battleship one M-class cruiser eleven destroyers and a number of transports reported close to coast between Kota Bharu and Perhentian Island by air reconnaissance afternoon.'

Perhentian Island was just south of Kota Baru, but an amplifying signal minutes later revealed that the sighting-report was eleven hours old, so that any landing operation had probably already been carried out and, since the Japanese were apparently aware of the proximity of Force Z, the invasion transports would have scattered or be well on their way back to Indo-China. In that case there was no longer a surface force justifying the attention of Phillips' big guns, but come the dawn he could find himself, without air cover, in an area swarming with enemy aircraft and almost certainly submarines, for no real purpose. The Japanese would go to suicidal lengths to prevent this prize slipping out of their hands.

The decision reached by Phillips must have been one of the most courageous of his life. He had never made a secret of his conviction that warships, commanded resolutely, were more than a match for aircraft, and he knew what happened to admirals who showed 'a lack of offensive spirit'. There is little doubt that Phillips would have relished a stand-up fight with the battle-cruisers *Kongo* and *Haruna*, suspected to be somewhere to the north-eastward; but the odds were now far too high against achieving anything worthwhile and withdrawing safely. He had to eat his words, and even now it might be too late.

At 2025 Force Z turned back toward Singapore, and thirty minutes later a masked lamp from *Prince of Wales* was blinking apologetically.

'I have most regretfully cancelled the operation because having been located by aircraft surprise was lost and our target would almost certain to be gone by the morning and the enemy fully prepared for us.'

In *Repulse* Captain Tennant gave the news to his wardroom, concluding, 'I know you all share with us the disappointment in not engaging the enemy at this time, but I am sure you will agree with the Commander-in-Chief's judgment.' According to Cecil Brown, an American correspondent of CBS accommodated in *Renown*, 'the officers groaned in disappointment and bitterness', while on the messdecks 'men were sitting around long tables, some with tears in their eyes'. One can accept a few groans from anyone who, for hours, has steeled himself in anticipation of battle only to be dumped into a slough of anticlimax, but tears on the messdeck are totally unbelievable. There were doubtless a few obscenities, with the luckless OD of the mess being ordered away to make tea or fetch kye (cocoa), but speculation would revolve around whether the ship would regain Singapore tomorrow in time for shore leave, which was the off-duty watch, and who had twenty dollars to lend because that was the price of a slant-eyed little darling in Lavender Street.

Twenty years later an eminent American author could still write: 'The three planes which had just forced Phillips to turn back were not Japanese, but Allied. They either did not see the British Fleet or neglected to report it.' Of such dross are history books written.

The day following the attack on Pearl Harbor, President Roosevelt announced to Congress that a state of war existed between the United States and the Empire of Japan. He did not mention Germany, but waited a further three days for Hitler to declare war on the United States of America. They must have been the longest three days in Winston Churchill's life.

## Notes

1    *Royal Oak* had been torpedoed in Scapa Flow in 1939.

2    Layton had been ordered to haul down his flag on 10 December, then return to the United Kindom. The take-over, however, was brought forward by Phillips when the Japanese began their attacks on 7 December.

3    The name *Sultan* was subsequently transferred to the naval quarters on the little island of Blakang Mati, off Keppel Harbour, Singapore, and the base became HMS *Terror*.

4    *Thanet* and *Scout* got clear, the first to be sunk within the next few weeks but the other to survive the war. *Thracian, Cicala* (which had mutinied in Archangel in 1919) and the 2nd MTB Flotilla remained in Hong Kong and fought it out to the bitter end. The sunken *Thracian* was salvaged by the Japanese to become the *IJN Patrol Boat No. 101*, recovered in 1945 and scrapped in 1946.

5    It was also Sunday mid-morning in Washington and still Sunday evening (about 1715 GMT) in the United Kingdom.

6    Details of the betrayal were kept secret, and will presumably remain so until the relevant files are opened for public inspection in 1998.

# Chapter Fifteen

*The loss of* Repulse *and* Prince of Wales

PHILLIPS had not broken W/T silence to inform Naval HQ that he was returning to harbour, and his Chief of Staff in Singapore, Rear-Admiral Arthur Palliser, was keeping his seaborne superior provided with situation-reports on the assumption that Phillips was continuing in the direction of Kota Baru (now in enemy hands) and Singora. At 2352 he scrawled 'Immediate' over a single sentence, knowing that for the second time that night the whole situation was in the melting-pot.

'Enemy reported landing Kuantan latitude 03.50N.'

If true, it meant that the Japanese were ashore only 200 miles north of Singapore and that same distance *behind* the British forces defending northern Malaya, astride important road-communications, in a position to cut the peninsula in half, and in possession of Kuantan airfield (which the RAF had abandoned during the ninth). The consequences could be disastrous.

In fact not a single Japanese soldier was anywhere near Kuantan. Nervous Indian troops had sighted several distant small craft, opened fire, and reported the approach of a Japanese landing force. The report reached Singapore and was relayed to Phillips. When dawn revealed the Kuantan shoreline to be peacefully deserted, it was too late.

Phillips, of course, had no choice but to deviate shoreward on his southward route. He was correct in assuming that Naval HQ had alerted him to the alleged Kuantan landing *because* they knew he would decide to intervene. Besides, the Japanese would be taken unawares; their last sighting-report (so far as Phillips could guess) placed Force Z far to the northward and steaming toward Kota Baru and Singora. He did not break W/T silence to tell Palliser in Singapore of his intentions. There was no reason why he should. Palliser was pointing a finger at Kuantan, and a wirelessed confirmation would do nothing except lose Force Z the advantage of surprise. It was a pity because, it will be remembered, the Brewster Buffalo fighters of 453 Squadron were waiting at Sembawang, held in reserve by an RAF that waited for a cry for help from Phillips. Even had Phillips known (and he *might* have known) that aircraft had been specifically detailed to play nursemaid to him, he would have been reluctant to ask for them before he was in serious trouble. He would be hoping that Palliser would make an offhand suggestion to the RAF that the fighters might fly a patrol over Kuantan, within range, next morning.

Phillips' wireless silence meant that Naval HQ could only *assume* that Force Z was heading for Kuantan, and so waited for more positive information before asking for air cover, while the RAF, completely ignorant of Force Z's movements, did nothing.

All Phillips' caution counted for nothing, however. Only minutes *before* Force Z altered course for Kuantan the Japanese submarine *I-58* sighted the British ships, fired all her torpedoes – which all missed – and transmitted a positional report, indicating that the enemy was steering 180°, due south, at 22 knots. This was absolutely correct. The submarine's next report, warning of Phillips' alteration of course, south-westward toward Kuantan, never reached Saigon, but the damage had been done. Force Z, lost for hours, had been found again – no longer steering northward but speeding southward for Singapore. Clearly, the British would never be caught by surface forces, but in Saigon were ninety-four aircraft with the speed and range to overhaul the enemy squadron before it reached sanctuary.

None of the ships knew anything of *I-58*. Their crews were at second state of readiness, a tiring watch-and-watch-about discipline, and they went to dawn action stations at 0500, which meant only an hour's sleep for the Middle watchkeepers. Dawn rose over a calm sea, empty except for an inoffensive-looking tug, which could hardly have come from Indo-China, towing several barges eastward. An hour later an aircraft could be seen, low to northward, but it could not be identified before disappearing. One watch went to breakfast – to boiled haddock in *Repulse*, bacon and tinned tomatoes in *Prince of Wales*, bread, margarine, strong tea heavily laced with Nestlés milk. At 0700 the flagship's Walrus amphibian was ordered to prepare for catapulting. Everyone now was anxious to abandon the operation, to return to Singapore, to provision and refuel, take stock of the ships refurbishing, to liaison with American and Dutch naval forces – and attend to ordinary tasks like dhobying, messdeck-cleaning, letter-writing. The usual spectators gathered to watch the aircraft climb away on its reconnaissance of Kuantan, beyond the horizon ahead.

Within forty-five minutes the Walrus was circling *Prince of Wales* again. Its crew had seen no enemy ships in the little harbour of Kuantan or in the estuary. The beaches seemed deserted, the roads quiet. In short, there was no Japanese landing.

It might be thought that Phillips could now cut his losses and make for home and safety, but by 0800 Force Z was off Kuantan, steaming parallel to the shore, while *Express* was detached to take a closer look at the harbour and confirm the aircraft's report that there was no hostile activity in the vicinity. The other ships watched the destroyer disappear into the estuary.

All was peaceful. 'The estuary glittered in the rays of the sun,' wrote *Electra*'s gunnery officer, 'the mist rose like steam from the warming shore. The rollers moaned softly over the roots of leaning trees, dark green against the silver of the sand. In the mess of Kuantan airfield, only thirty miles away, they would be thinking, we said, of breakfast. . . .'

When *Express* came into view again her lamp was flashing.

'All as quiet as a wet Sunday afternoon.'

Phillips was showing no sense of urgency, and perhaps he felt justified. Even if Force Z had been sighted by a few enemy patrol-aircraft, the British were five hundred miles from Saigon, from where, presumably, any competent attack would have to be mounted, and the inferior Japanese planes flown by short-sighted Japanese pilots could never carry torpedoes that far. There was, of course, the possibility of submarines in the area, and Phillips accepted a suggestion that one of *Repulse*'s Walrus aircraft should fly an anti-submarine patrol. The stubby little biplane puttered happily among the patches of cotton-wool cloud, as obsolete as anything the enemy was alleged to possess.

It was Tennant, of *Repulse*, who proposed that the tug and barges sighted earlier should be relocated and investigated more closely, but it was surely not that officer's intention that the whole of Force Z should be employed in a task for which a destroyer could have been detached. Albeit, Phillips turned all five ships almost due east, holding this course for thirty precious minutes until, just after 1000 hours, telegraphists below decks were reading signals from *Tenedos* reporting that she was being attacked by enemy aircraft – *and she was 140 miles nearer to Singapore than Force Z.*

The news was almost unbelievable, but when a single aircraft was seen approaching from the south-east at 1015 it was too high to be identified; it could well be an RAF plane from Kuantan, only a few minutes' flying-time away. Nobody knew that Kuantan airfield had already been abandoned. Phillips turned Force Z also to the south-eastward, not because of the aircraft but to look more closely at an old freighter, the SS *Haldis, en route* from Hong Kong to Singapore. It was only at 1040, when radar detected an aircraft formation closing from southward, that the red and yellow Flag A climbed to *Prince of Wales*'s yardarm and anti-aircraft readiness was ordered. It was all rather unreal. The day was beautiful, the sky clear, the sea blue and dazzling gold. Most men were thinking about their rum or calculating whether or not the ships would reach Singapore in time for watchkeepers' shore-leave. It was doubtful, unless the Admiral took his finger out. There was an awakened appetite among the men so recently from the bleakness of the United Kingdom, not just for alcohol and sexual adventures but also for plates filled with large beefsteaks or pork cutlets, eggs and chipped potatoes drenched with tomato sauce, for neon lights and shops spilling with silks and brocades, carved ivories and teaks, clockwork toys and tea-sets, the Tiger Balm Gardens, Whiteway Laidlaws and Robinson's emporiums, the Cold Storage, Kelly & Walsh, the British Pharmacy. Of course, there *was* beer – ice-cold at thirty cents a bottle on a puddled table in the Naval Base canteen or thirty-five cents in a Chinese bar with free potato crisps, salted peanuts, toothpicks and obsequious civility, not to mention the other. . . .

The aircraft had been on the radar screens of *Prince of Wales* and *Repulse* for some twelve minutes before the first wave of enemy bombers was sighted, to southward and high – eight snub-nosed single-wing aircraft, painted yellow that gleamed in the sun. The British could not have named them because outdated recognition-charts did not feature the Mitsubishi 'Nells', each carrying two 550 lb bombs, but among those men who had experienced air-attacks before there was little concern. Even the Germans, the best in the business, had not been very successful in high-level bombing of ships manoeuvring at speed; no capital ship, Allied or enemy, had been sunk *at sea* by aircraft.

'Barrage – commence, commence, commence. . . .'

*Prince of Wales*'s starboard HA 5.25-inch turrets opened fire, ranging 12,000 yards, *Repulse*'s older, manually operated 4-inch guns at 11,000. Immediately, however, Phillips betrayed his lack of ship-handling experience by ordering an evasive Blue Three alteration of course, turning all ships 30° to port *together*, which meant that the starboard guns were losing sight of their targets. The port batteries got a few rounds away, but then Phillips compounded his error by an attempt to rectify it; he ordered a Five Blue – reversing the turn – and the ships began swinging back to starboard, with the inevitable consequences. The gun-crews blasphemed. If Tom Thumb would only make up his bleedin' mind, they might soddin' hit something other than their own bleedin' flag-deck.

The cumbersome manœuvring by flags of an entire squadron was no way to avoid aircraft or allow guns to fire effectively, and Phillips had learned his first lesson. He ordered all ships to disregard the flagship's movements; each would manœuvre independently.

The enemy ignored *Prince of Wales* and the destroyers. Around *Repulse* the sea was torn by white eruptions. An observer in *Electra* records that the battle-cruiser 'disappeared completely in a forest of cascading bomb-bursts' – which must have shaken a few complacent convictions with regard to Japanese fighting efficiency – but when she emerged from the welter of spray she seemed unhurt except for a feather of smoke rising from her starboard side. One bomb had struck, to penetrate the hangar and upper deck, bursting against the main deck, killing one man and injuring several, mostly stokers scalded by steam from pipes fractured by blast in the boiler-room below. The remaining Walrus aircraft had been toppled from its trolley and, leaking petrol, was quickly jettisoned. Meanwhile the enemy aircraft, having each dropped one bomb, had droned away northward followed by the fire of every gun that could bear, seemingly unscathed. In fact five of the eight had been hit, two sufficiently seriously for them to abandon the attack immediately.

The action had lasted twenty minutes and *Repulse* was only scratched. There was cause for satisfaction. Phillips ordered twenty-five knots, but still refrained from using W/T to ask for assistance, and now there could be no credible explanation for the omission. There was no longer anything to be gained by silence and it could hardly be concluded that the one attack would be the last.

It was not. Shortly after 1130 two groups of aircraft, of nine and eight respectively, were detected to the south-easterly, and any hope that they might be British disappeared as they began to lose height and jockey into an attack-pattern. On *Prince of Wales*'s bridge the torpedo officer, Lieutenant-Commander Harland, lowered his glasses. 'I think, sir,' he suggested, 'they're going to make a torpedo attack.' In his high chair Phillips shook his head, unruffled. 'No, they're not. There are no torpedo aircraft around.'

If there is ever a dictionary of famous last words, these of Phillips must be included. Nine torpedo-bombers were flying directly toward the flagship.

The squadron's navigators, bent over voice-pipes, waited to choose the moment for turning, and the AA barrage began – first the heavier-calibre guns, then pom-poms, Bofors, Oerlikons, .5-inch machine-guns and even Lewis guns. The enemy flew low into a hurricane of fire, some of the pilots approaching to within 700 yards before launching their torpedoes, and yet they seemed divinely protected. The aircraft were much faster than any torpedo-carriers the British had experienced and, when they had released their missiles, they did not climb away above the ships, offering their bellies, but continued on course to machine-gun the decks. Whether fanaticism or courage, it was rewarded. Only one aircraft was destroyed by *Prince of Wales*'s AA armament, considered among the most sophisticated afloat. None was shot down by *Repulse*'s old guns as the enemy contemptuously raced down both her sides, firing at point-blank range. *Repulse*, however, at thirty knots and twisting like a destroyer, had escaped harm so far. *Prince of Wales* had been seriously hurt.

Had Phillips survived, he could not have claimed in justification – as could the United States Navy after the attack on Pearl Harbor – that he had been caught unaware, at anchor and not even at war. The British ships were ready, waiting and fully armed for the enemy. Phillips, and only Phillips, was responsible for the ships being where they were, and he seems to have been almost alone in totally dismissing at least the *possibility* of torpedoes being used against him. One can hardly criticise him for taking his force to sea in the first instance – indeed, it is difficult to think what else he could have done in the circumstances – but immediately it became apparent that the operation was achieving nothing he should have steamed Force Z southward at utmost speed.

To be fair, Phillips had suffered some unbelievably bad luck. Had he *Indomitable* in company, as the Admiralty had planned, there might have been a very different sequence of events, but it is not easy to understand why the Admiralty had not ordered *Hermes*, in Simonstown when *Prince of Wales* called there on her outward passage, to accompany Phillips as a stop-gap measure. Although carrying only fifteen machines, the little carrier could have proved vitally useful. It must have been supposed that the damaged *Indomitable* had ample time to join Force Z before anything uncomfortable happened in the Far East.

Early in the action it was painfully evident that the guns of Force Z were having little or no effect on the attacking aircraft; the highly regarded 5.25-inch turrets of *Prince of Wales* were particularly disappointing. There is little doubt that these guns (or perhaps more accurately their fire-control systems) were still not combat efficient. *Repulse*'s old 4-inch weapons were simply inadequate, and both ships' pom-pom guns suffered repeated stoppages as the result of defective ammunition – some as often as eight or twelve times during a single attack. None of these deficiencies, however, contributed significantly to the loss of *Prince of Wales* and *Repulse*. William Sims, United States Navy, had already said everything as long ago as 1925, when he commented: 'It is an astonishing thing, the conservatism of the military mind . . . they never give in. You have got to shed their blood before they do it.' Despite more than two years of war and the bitter lessons of Norway, Dunkirk and Crete, warships without fighter cover were still being expected to function in waters known to be dominated by the enemy's air forces.

However, Phillips can be forgiven for shrugging aside the possibility of his ships being hit by bombs of modest weight dropped from high level. His cardinal errors were, first, his unshakeable belief that he would not meet torpedoes and, second, not ordering an enemy-report to be transmitted when first attacked at about 1100. However thinly stretched the RAF might have been, they would surely have felt compelled to make a special effort to prevent the loss of the two capital ships and, indeed, we know that eleven Brewster Buffalos were waiting at Sembawang within about an hour's flying-time of Phillips' position. This means that, if alerted, those fighters, albeit few, under-powered and under-gunned, could have been over Force Z in time to counter the twenty-six Mitsubishi 'Bettys' approaching for the final ruinous assault.

Afterwards, the RAF's liaison officer suggested that, had Phillips agreed, there *could* have been a CAP (Combat Air Patrol) of six aircraft flying over Force Z at all times during daylight providing the squadron did not proceed farther than a hundred miles north of Kota Baru or more than sixty miles from shore, but this would have placed uncomfortable restrictions on Phillips' movements and, in any case, it is not clear if he was offered such a facility before departing Singapore.

The heaviest responsibility for the Force Z calamity, which was only a small part of the over-all Far Eastern débâcle, must be borne by the RAF. No, not by RAF Malaya, nor Air Vice-Marshal Pulford, nor even Air Chief Marshal Brooke-Popham, but by an Air Ministry which had assumed the principal responsibility for the defence of Singapore and Malaya and had done almost nothing to meet that responsibility. An obsession with the heavy bombing of Germany, approved and even encouraged by Churchill, resulted in not a single modern aircraft being allocated to the Far East. Only a few squadrons of Spitfires or Hurricanes, Halifaxes or Stirlings, might have pulverised Japanese operations almost before they had begun. It is infuriating to discover that, when Malaya's airfields were being abandoned to the Japanese advance, the RAF was able to produce – like a conjuror from a hat – fifty Hurricanes, with pilots, and embark them in *Indomitable* at Port Sudan. As the men of *Prince of Wales* and *Repulse* would snarl at the Brewster Buffalos later that fateful day, it was too bleedin' late, mate. Phillips was undeniably an obstinate old shellback and he made several tactical miscalculations based on outdated experience. He was probably unqualified for the task he had been given – but he also deserved better support than he got.

Many other factors can be paraded as contributing to the loss of an empire, but they amount to excuses rather than reasons. In the event Force Z's losses, in terms of lives, were to be measured in hundreds; ashore, the British lost 138,708 military and civilian personnel, including more than 130,000 prisoners.

At 1210, *Prince of Wales* hoisted two vertical black balls.[1] She had been struck by a torpedo in the Achilles' heel of all armoured ships, the stern extremity, and the damage resulting was out of all proportion to that expected from one missile. A massive hole had been torn in the hull but, much more seriously, the 240-foot shaft of the port outer propeller had been distorted and, still churning viciously, had fractured bulkheads, riveting and fuel-piping along its entire length before it could be stopped. Within minutes flooding had disabled several engine-, boiler- and machine-rooms. Diesel and turbo dynamos failed, depriving salvage-pumps of electrical power. Lighting, communications and ventilation failed, the steering-motors were dead and four of the eight AA turrets were inoperative. *Prince of Wales*, for the moment, was crippled, with a 10° list, wallowing at 15 knots and with her quarterdeck only two feet above sea-level.

Manœuvring independently and three miles distant, Tennant, in *Repulse*, had been astonished to learn from his own W/T office that the Admiral had still not transmitted an enemy-report. His flag-deck flashed PT53 (Prince of Wales's pennant number), enquiring what damage had been sustained and if her wireless was out of action, but the flagship made no response.[2] 'We have dodged 19 torpedoes so far, thanks to Providence,' Tennant added, and confirmed that the earlier bomb-damage to *Repulse* was under control; she could still make 25 knots. Phillips did not answer, so at 1158 Tennant originated the signal which should have been sent an hour before.

'Enemy aircraft bombing. My position 134NYTW22X09.'

The signal, in simple direct-conversion Fleet Code, was broadcast to GBXZ, the call-sign for 'All British Men of War' – perhaps a little odd since the only possible provider of assistance was Singapore, but the point is of little relevance since Kranji Naval W/T Station, near Yew Tee village in the north-west quarter of Singapore island, read the transmission at 1204, decoding it and rerouting it within minutes to RAF HQ. The eleven Brewster Buffalos took off from Sembawang airfield at 1231.

They would never reach Force Z in time. Even as the aircraft climbed over the Johore Strait, turning north-east with an hour's flight ahead of them, twenty-six more Mitsubishi 'Bettys' in two groups were sweeping in fast and low toward *Prince of Wales* and *Repulse* – 'grey shadows almost wave-hopping,' said a man in *Electra*. 'The Japs seemed to come at us from twenty different directions, and we couldn't be everywhere at once.' But the enemy had no time for destroyers. They had taken off from Tu Duam, north of Saigon (one of several military airfields conceded to the Japanese by the Vichy French government), at 0645 that morning, and had already turned back to their base with fuel running low, abandoning the search, when *Repulse*'s Walrus was sighted through the cloud. Then they had seen *Electra*, *Express* and *Vampire* – and then the valuable quarry they had sought for six hours. *Prince of Wales* was almost helpless, with several of her turrets inoperative and others, because of the ship's list, unable to depress sufficiently to meet the aircraft's low approach. Of six torpedoes launched by the first wave, four struck, and in five minutes the battleship was reduced to 8 knots, almost all electrical power gone, thousands of tons of water pouring into her and her great hull settling ominously lower.

Yet it was *Repulse*, until this stage of the attack a fully efficient fighting unit and with her engine-room personnel working her up to nearly 28 knots, who was the first to succumb. Tennant had manœuvred the battle-cruiser brilliantly, and now, caught in a pincer movement involving eight torpedoes approaching from starboard and three from port, it was miraculous that he should avoid all but one of them. That one torpedo struck amidships, its detonation being largely absorbed by the bulge. *Repulse* shivered, then ploughed on, but her luck was running out. Two 'Bettys', insolently leap-frogging the ship's bows, were turned into spinning fireballs by a forward pom-pom; a third plane screamed clear. The gun-crews cheered, but all three aircraft had got their torpedoes away and all three smashed home. One disabled the battle-cruiser's steering – and, so like another brave warship of another navy in another sea,

*Repulse* could now steam only in a wide circle. And, like Lütjens before him, Tennant knew his ship was finished. A fourth torpedo, seemingly coming from nowhere, hammered into her starboard side as she listed to port. 'Clear lower deck,' Tennant ordered. 'Muster all possible men to starboard.'

*Repulse* died with the dignity of her years and lineage – quickly and without fuss. Nor did her crew disgrace her. Despite a list of almost 30° there is no record of a single man leaving his station until told to do so, and nobody went over the side until Tennant, leaning over the side of the bridge, gave the order to abandon ship. Mercifully, the loudspeaker system was still functioning. 'God go with you,' he said, but God would, or could, do nothing for the hundreds of officers, men and boys trapped in dozens of compartments below.

At 1232, *Repulse* rolled, momentarily to lay on her side as if seeking to repay her crew's loyalty with a few more minutes of grace, but then turned her keel to the sky. Even now she hesitated. Men swam frantically to escape the final plunge that might drag them down. *Repulse*'s screws rose, then surrendered, and the sea pounced. Only eleven minutes had elapsed since the first torpedo had struck the ship.

Watching *Repulse*'s dying movements, Phillips had at last broken W/T silence. 'Emergency. Have been struck by a torpedo on port side NYTW022R06 – four torpedoes. Send destroyers = 1220GH/10 +'

Read and then decoded by Kranji W/T Station, it was being studied by Naval HQ by 1240. Apart from the signal's ambiguity, which was hardly important, it is incredible that the Admiral should ask for destroyers rather than fighter aircraft. The three destroyers he had left in Singapore, *Jupiter*, *Encounter* and *Stronghold*, even if they were battleworthy, were an impossible distance away and, in any case, could have contributed nothing to Phillips' salvation, while *Tenedos* was racing for home to land a rating wounded by bomb splinters.

The enemy struck their final, and in the event unnecessary, blow at 1244, when a flight of eight bombers attacked from 10,000 feet. Only one 1100 lb bomb hit, penetrating the catapult-area and exploding against the 5-inch main deck amidships. *Prince of Wales*, however, was already sinking – though neither Phillips nor Captain Leach seemed to think so, because at 1252 Phillips initiated another signal asking for 'all available tugs' to be sent to position 003.40N, 104.30E. Two further, similar requests were transmitted by the stricken flagship within the next half-hour, two by *Electra*. The destroyers, at least, did not doubt that the battleship was finished and, unbidden, began to close to take off survivors. Determinedly, Leach had come down to the upper deck, asking for volunteers to remain on board to work the ship back to harbour – and he got them – but within minutes even he was forced to concede defeat. *Prince of Wales* was settling. 'Abandon ship,' he nodded.

Phillips, having ordered his staff away, remained on the bridge until the last moment, when the ship began her last roll to port, and then he and his secretary, Captain Simon Beardsworth, walked down the ship's side together, into the sea. The corpses of both Phillips and Leach were later both seen floating; neither was recovered.

The Brewster Buffalo fighters arrived just in time to see the last of *Prince of Wales*. In the water hundreds of struggling men, oil-filthy, scalded and choking, raised fists to the sky and screeched obscenities. Aboard the destroyers the gun-crews had to be restrained from opening fire.

'I flew low over them,' the senior pilot would later report. 'I witnessed a show of that indomitable spirit for which the Royal Navy is so famous . . . as I flew around, every man waved and put his thumb up . . . waving, cheering and joking as if they were holidaymakers at Brighton. . . . I take off my hat to them, for in them I saw the spirit which wins wars. . . .'

The RAF fighters remained over the area for an hour, then returned to Singapore, leaving the three destroyers to the long and shuddering task of picking up survivors. Between them they took aboard 2801, which meant that 513 had died with *Repulse*, 327 with *Prince of Wales*. Among the lost were thirty boy seamen, a boy bugler of the Royal Marines and two sixteen-year-old NAAFI canteen assistants.

The cost to the Japanese Naval Air Service was three aircraft destroyed and twenty-eight damaged (of which one crashed on landing) with eighteen crewmen killed.

Tokyo Radio was the first to broadcast the news, even as the last survivors were being dragged from the sea. Winston Churchill informed a subdued House of Commons at 1130 (London time) and the BBC's midday news bulletin told the nation before *Electra*, *Express* and *Vampire* reached Singapore with the survivors. The senior officer afloat was Commander Cecil May, of *Electra*, who had rescued the sole three survivors from *Hood* six months before.

In the Irish Republic, where cinema audiences applauded newsreels that featured a British reverse, or booed every success, the jeers were cautious now that they could be interpreted as being also levelled at the United States. In Berlin, too, the news, coupled with that of Pearl Harbor, was received with mixed feelings, for Germany was tied to Japan by treaty. However, Hitler told the Japanese Ambassador: 'You gave the right declaration of war. This method is the only proper one. One should strike as hard as possible and not waste time declaring war.' To General Jodl, his closest adviser, he confided, 'Victory can no longer be achieved.'

There was an unsavoury postscript that has to be recorded. Of the two thousand survivors of *Repulse* and *Prince of Wales*, about 900 were returned to the United Kingdom, but the remainder were drafted to the warships remaining in Singapore,[3] to crew ferry-craft evacuating Europeans on the west coast, or to form two combatant companies which were absorbed into the Argyll and Sutherland Highlanders. Some forty of these survivors were killed during the subsequent fighting in Malaya, including a fifteen-year-old boy seaman. With so many others less deserving being allowed to depart for home, it was perhaps not surprising that the morale of the re-employed survivors was at a low ebb, and there were incidents of insubordination. Vice-Admiral Layton, reinstated as Commander-in-Chief, retorted, 'This is not at all inspiring. Officers and men do not seem to realise that war is not always a very pleasant game. . . . I wish to hear no more sentimental rubbish about survivors not being fit for the next job that comes along. They should be only too ready to get their own back.'

Before Singapore fell, however, Layton and his staff took passage to Ceylon, leaving the naval base in the charge of Rear-Admiral E. Spooner (who had commanded *Repulse* prior to Captain Leach). 'I have gone to collect the Eastern Fleet,' Layton reassured the naval forces left behind. 'Keep your heads high and your hearts firm until I return.' Spooner and his RAF counterpart, Air Vice-Marshal Pulford, died of starvation. Some perished in small craft attempting to escape the final reckoning, but still more passed into the hell of Japanese captivity.

It was singularly tragic that both *Prince of Wales* and *Repulse* were manned by the Royal Navy's Devonport Division. The two great ships lay in a clear tropical sea, eight miles apart, *Prince of Wales* 155 feet below the surface, *Repulse* only 105. Today, Britain regards them as Crown property, the war-graves of 840 men which shall never be disturbed. Several requests by the Japanese to salvage the vessels have been firmly refused.

The position has been surveyed several times; in clear conditions the ships can be seen as huge shadows, a haven for shoals of angelfish, barracuda and jewfish. In 1966 divers of the Royal Navy and Royal Australian Navy descended to both wrecks, and from the propeller shaft of *Repulse* they fastened a six-foot white ensign that floated proudly in the crystal sea. One of the divers was forty-three-year-old Petty Officer Norman Edwards, of Somerset, a survivor from *Repulse*.

'I volunteered to dive,' he said. 'The sight of that flag flying in the water as though it was in the wind brought a lump to my throat. Memories of the ship and the men I had known aboard her came flooding back. *Repulse* was lying on the bottom like a huge cathedral.'

The divers were forbidden to enter the hulls of either ship but, when the thirteen-day operation was completed, Lieutenant-Commander David Lermitte made a final descent to photograph the ensign. He subsequently presented the prints to Mrs Frederick C. Darwell, the daughter of Commander H. B. C. Gill, DSC, *Repulse*'s surviving navigating officer.

## Notes

1   The definition of two black balls, by day, is 'Ship not under command', but more sensibly 'not under *control*', because of lack of steering or propulsion.

2   *Prince of Wales* was quite capable of signalling by wireless or light until a few minutes before she sank.

3   Including the cruiser *Exeter*, which was to be sunk in the Java Sea some weeks later, as were the destroyers *Electra*, *Encounter* and *Jupiter* and the Australian cruiser *Perth*.

# VII   The Cat That Survived but Not to Live

## Chapter Sixteen

Renown, *the last battle-cruiser – operations in the North Atlantic – the rebirth of the Far Eastern Fleet and sorties against the Japanese – the reduction of Sabang*

AND NOW there was only one.

During the first seven months of 1941, *Renown*, the senior partner of Force H, had been involved in no fewer than twelve operations applied to the provisioning of Malta and to convoying troops and supplies to Egypt. At another time they would have made shouting headlines, but, with the passage of so many dramatic events – particularly the German assault on Russia in June, the invasion of Yugoslavia and the fighting in Greece, Crete, Syria, Somaliland and Abyssinia – there were few column-inches or broadcasting-minutes to spare for repetitive accounts of convoying and screening missions, however perilous. Ships at sea, whether in the Arctic, Atlantic or Mediterranean, did not win anything tangible which could be marked on maps by flags or pencilled lines. To people at home an account of one convoy-battle read pretty much the same as any other. Food-coupons equalled rations, and it was difficult for any housewife in Pontypool or Kilmarnock or Stow-on-the-Wold to calculate the real cost of her family's sugar, tea, meat and bread. The reckoning was far distant, the rations always seemed inadequate.

*Renown* had left Gibraltar in early August 1941, and on the fourteenth docked in Rosyth for a brief refit. The period she had spent in the Mediterranean in Somerville's force had been one of notable success against a much stronger enemy. Somerville, because of his outspoken views on some of the more capricious stratagems suggested by Churchill, was not the Prime Minister's favourite admiral. One such scheme was that for the capture of the Italian island of Pantellaria, another for the seizure of the neutral (Portuguese) Cape Verde Islands and the Azores. Both adventures would have involved Force H, which Churchill considered was merely 'lying under the Spanish howitzers at Gibraltar'. If taken, Pantellaria – which had been of only small inconvenience to the British – would have proved disproportionately expensive to garrison and supply when Malta was already stretching the Fleet's resources to the limit. The occupation of the Portuguese islands would undoubtedly have had damaging international repercussions. In the event, fortunately, both proposals were so strongly opposed by the Chiefs of Staff that they were abandoned. Equally fortunately, the fire-eating sixty-nine-year-old Admiral Sir Roger Keyes, Director of Combined Operations, was relieved on 19 October by Captain Lord Louis Mountbatten, who was given the rank of Commodore 1st Class and subsequently Acting Vice-Admiral.

The battle-cruiser joined the Home Fleet in Scapa Flow on 22 November, a cold drizzling day on which her sister *Repulse* lay in sun-drenched Trincomalee harbour awaiting the arrival of *Prince of Wales* from Cape Town and, in Hitokappu Bay in the Kuriles, the Japanese task force assembled for the attack on Pearl Harbor was awaiting final sailing orders from Tokyo. During the forenoon of 10 December, as *Renown*'s quartermaster piped 'Up Spirits' and then 'Hands to the Mess for Rum', her company learned that this was, indeed, the last of the battle-cruisers. The knowledge inspired no ribaldry, no chaff.

During the first few months of 1942 *Renown* would experience again the bitter conditions of northern waters; long-forgotten duffel-coats, long underwear, gloves and woollen helmets were dragged from the depths of lockers, consignments of 'comforts' from the WVS were distributed, and cocoa was in demand. *Tirpitz, Admiral Scheer, Prinz Eugen* and the destroyers *Hermann Schoemann, Friedrich Ihn* and *Z-25* were in Trondheim, ideally poised for attacks on convoys making for North Cape, and on 6 March *Tirpitz*, accompanied by the three destroyers, steamed out of Trondheimsfjord to intercept convoy PQ12.[1]

In anticipation, Admiral Sir John Tovey, Commander-in-Chief Home Fleet, was already only a hundred miles from PQ12 with *King George V, Duke of York, Renown, Victorious* and a destroyer-screen, and now, warned by an enemy-report from the patrolling submarine *Seawolf*, he turned to place his ships between *Tirpitz* and the convoy. If he could destroy *Tirpitz*, he would eliminate the one enemy warship that tied down so many British heavy ships to the North Atlantic and so release them for the Indian Ocean.

It was a tantalising possibility but, as so often before, the vicious Arctic weather foiled the plans of both Tovey and Admiral Otto

Ciliax in *Tirpitz*. On 7 March rough seas, snow and severe icing prevented both forces from flying off reconnaissance aircraft. Could *Victorious* have done so, *Tirpitz* almost certainly would have been located. At noon that day PQ12 and the home-bound convoy QP8 met and passed through each other in a snowstorm that fortuitously also blinded the German destroyers which had been detached on a search-sweep. Only one straggler from QP8, a Russian freighter, was sighted and torpedoed.

For all that day and most of the next *Tirpitz* searched for the convoy which was not where it was expected to be because, as a result of the superb interception, decipherment and analysis of German wireless traffic by the Admiralty's Operational Intelligence Centre, it had been rerouted. Tovey, gambling that the Germans, characteristically, would run for sanctuary as soon as their operation began to turn sour, turned back toward Iceland with his destroyers running low on fuel. It was not until the evening of 8 March that it became apparent that *Tirpitz* was persevering with her search, and Tovey turned, once again, to intercept. Time and distance, however, were both against him.

At dawn on the ninth the two forces were 115 miles apart, and *Victorious* launched six search Albacores, one of which sighted *Tirpitz* and *Friedrich Ihn* at 0800. As twelve more torpedo-carrying Albacores took off from the flight-deck of *Victorious*, Tovey flashed the carrier.

'A wonderful chance which may achieve most valuable results. God be with you.'

It was not supposed that a handful of aircraft would succeed in sinking the German battleship, but if they could slow her there could be another *Bismarck* finale. The crews of both forces were at action stations, the Germans in their purpose-made fleece-lined leather clothing, the British in their football stockings and mittens, scarves and balaclavas knitted by sweethearts and mums and those many other unknown ladies who had never known to what ship or man the products of their weeks of dedicated needle-clicking had reached.

The torpedo attack at 0925, unfortunately, was a failure, its lack of co-ordination and poor timing exacerbated by the fact that *Tirpitz* was steaming 30 knots into a 35-knot wind. All torpedoes missed, and two aircraft were shot down. *Tirpitz* and her destroyers ran for Vestfjord, and by 1700 hours all were anchored in Bogen Bay, near Narvik.

*Renown* was employed once more with the covering force for convoys PQ13 and QP9, when the former was attacked by Luftwaffe bombers and destroyers 85 miles off North Cape, losing six ships. Russian convoys were now suffering twenty-per-cent losses, heavier than those on the Gibraltar–Malta run, and there were few regrets expressed on *Renown*'s messdecks when it was learned that the ship had been reassigned to the Mediterranean. Duffel coats and 'long johns' went back into lockers, white caps were pipe-clayed.

Reaching the familiar harbour of Gibraltar, *Renown* found *Rodney* already berthed, with the small aircraft-carrier *Eagle* and the submarine depot-ship *Maidstone*. The situation in the Mediterranean was at its most critical stage. Malta was experiencing almost daily air-attacks and had been reduced to only six aircraft, and it was estimated that the Germans and Italians had strewn 30,000 mines between Sicily and the coast of Africa. Ships at Gibraltar had to be constantly on the alert for Italian frogmen, carrying limpet mines, swimming from Algeciras and other bases with the tacit approval of the Spanish authorities.

On 20 April, *Renown* escorted USS *Wasp* when, on that day, the carrier flew off 47 Spitfires for the RAF in Malta. Tragically, 30 of the 46 that landed were destroyed on the ground before they could be refuelled. On 9 May the operation was repeated, with *Eagle* reinforcing *Wasp*, and 17 aircraft touched down safely, most of the remainder having been lost by inexperienced pilots unable to conserve their fuel over the long flying-distance. Malta, with food, ammunition, petroleum and aircraft almost consumed, was on the brink of collapse, and the award of a George Cross to the people of the island by King George was badly timed. During June, mercifully, the Axis attacks were not sustained. More ships got through and 59 Spitfires arrived from carriers on the third and the ninth. The crisis had been survived.

Regaining Gibraltar, *Renown*'s company was astonished to be informed that they were to accompany *Wasp* to Scapa Flow, departing on the fifteenth. It defied comprehension, but they hastened ashore to buy nylons, cosmetics and bags of oranges, then returned their whites to their lockers and unrolled duffel-coats and football stockings. Someone, said the inevitable three-badger, ought to make up what they call their bleedin' minds.

*Wasp* was ordered to the Pacific, where she would be torpedoed and sunk four months later, but the Stars and Stripes was flying from several ships in Scapa Flow, including the battleship *Washington* and the cruisers *Wichita* and *Tuscaloosa*. Otherwise Scapa was still the same old Scapa with the same noisy beer-canteen, the shunting NAAFI lighters alongside, side parties and painting parties, the ferry from Thurso off-loading tired draftees, kitbags and hammocks on to *Iron Duke*, the anchored transit-ship. At least it was springtime, the evenings progressively lengthening until twilight met the following dawn. Hundreds of Italian prisoners, taken in north Africa, were beginning to lay a causeway, the Churchill Barriers, to link four islands with Mainland and so close the entrance that *U-47* had penetrated to sink *Royal Oak*.

The Home Fleet deployment leading up to the massacre of convoy PQ17 off North Cape in early July did not involve *Renown*, although it is fair to add that her participation would not have influenced the outcome in any way. After the next convoy, PQ18, which sailed from the west coast of Scotland on 6 September (to lose 13 of 40 ships) all further convoys to Russia by the northern route were suspended by the Admiralty until the darkness of the Arctic winter could be exploited, and also in order that shipping could be accumulated for the Allied invasion of north Africa – Operation Torch.

It was hardly possible to hide the passage of more than a hundred transports and two hundred warships, and little attempt was made to do so. *Renown* had reached Gibraltar at the end of October, once again to supplement Force H which, since leaner times, had become a sizeable force consisting of *Duke of York*, flying the flag of Vice-Admiral Sir Neville Syfret, *Rodney*, the carriers *Victorious*, *Formidable* and *Furious*, three cruisers and seventeen destroyers. There was a degree of apprehension because it seemed probable that the French forces in north Africa would fight, but Admiral Darlan initially misjudged the Allied armada's destination, and no French naval units sallied from Toulon, which was being watched by five submarines. (There is some evidence that both Darlan and Pétain were hoping for an invasion of southern France, always providing that French honour could be seen to be served.) The fiercest French resistance was met by the American landings at Casablanca. Force H suffered the loss of the destroyer *Martin* by torpedoing, but during the heavy-calibre bombardment of the Oran area the crews were more discomfited by the heat and lack of ventilation below decks than by any action on the part of the Vichy French or Italian naval forces.

The year 1943 was the one in which *Renown*'s company would claim that everybody wanted the battle-cruiser's services; others would riposte that nobody did. The ship was returned to the United Kingdom in February, reaching the Clyde on the fourth and, three days later, being docked in Rosyth for a four-month refit. Then, again, she found herself in Scapa Flow. There was a growing confidence, now, that the Allies were going to win this war. The only questions were how soon and by precisely what means. Bitterness between the Admiralty and the Air Ministry over the deployment of aircraft intensified. The Navy urgently needed long-range cover for its convoys and for anti-submarine patrolling, particularly in the Bay of Biscay, which could only be provided by land-based squadrons; while the RAF insisted that maximum resources should be applied to the bombing offensive against German industry. 'The naval employment of aircraft', argued Air Marshal Harris, Commander-in-Chief Bomber Command, 'consists of picking at the fringes of enemy power . . . of looking for needles in a haystack.' Churchill agreed; thousands of naval and mercantile seamen disagreed, obscenely.

Now, as in the earlier war, there was a rising swell of discontent among all British servicemen with regard to pay, particularly that of junior officers and other ranks. From the viewpoint of the naval rating, the relatively inflated pay of his American counterpart was accepted with envious reluctance. All Americans were millionaires. There was keener resentment, however, toward the considerably higher rates of pay allowed by the British Government to French, Polish, Dutch, Norwegian and Belgian personnel, many of whom did not seem to exert themselves very strenuously in exchange.

Even more provoking was the widening disparity between service and civilian pay-levels, painfully apparent to the sailor when his ship docked for refit or repair of battle-damage. Even unskilled dockyard labourers were being paid five or six times as much as a highly skilled chief or petty officer, and were not slow to demand more. Nor was the civilians' work-rate impressive or their honesty above question. In early 1943, when the cruiser *Norfolk* docked in Portsmouth (she was a 'Westoe', or Devonport, ship) local voices were raised in protest. Such a ship, it was claimed, would only invite enemy air-attacks on the docks; she should be taken somewhere else – anywhere else, but not Portsmouth. Aboard, civilian dockyard workers found obscure corners in which to play cards, scrounged tea and cigarettes from the crew, and stole anything that could be crammed into pockets or tool-boxes – tobacco, clothing, shoes, personal items and even rations from mess lockers. There were limits to patriotism.

In late August, *Renown* steamed for Halifax, Nova Scotia, to embark Winston Churchill following the Quebec Conference, and executed the return passage to Scotland at 23½ knots through considerable fog. Churchill, anxious to achieve a degree of involvement in the Pacific theatre, had offered to loan *Illustrious* and *Victorious* to the Americans, but the anglophobe Admiral Ernest King, USN, was unwilling to have British ships in company with his own – as he was equally opposed to having American ships under British command ('I fought under the goddam British in the First World War, and if I can help it, no ship of mine will fight under them again!'). Churchill, however, was determined that the Royal Navy should do something in the Far East and, enthused by the leapfrogging operation that had lifted invasion forces from north Africa into Sicily and then Italy, was contemplating an amphibious landing in the Andaman Islands and then Sumatra. It would, he suggested, require a force of five capital ships, one fleet and five light carriers, six cruisers, 'one or two destroyer flotillas', and at least six submarines. When, in due course, Mountbatten estimated that the project would also require 50,000 troops, Churchill was scathingly incredulous. The Admiralty agreed, in view of the Italian Fleet's surrender, that a naval force of less ambitious dimensions than that envisaged by the Prime Minister could be made ready during the following year.

Racing back from Halifax, the men of *Renown* were unaware that she would be following in the wake of her late sister, *Repulse*.

She was first, however, to be chosen again to convey the Prime Minister and the First Sea Lord to the Cairo Conference, leaving Plymouth on 12 November and reaching Alexandria on the twentieth. This was at a time when the ill-provided British attempt to reoccupy some of the Aegean Islands, which the Americans had firmly refused to support, had collapsed with nothing to show but six destroyers sunk and four damaged, two submarines sunk and four cruisers damaged. *Renown* returned to the United Kingdom via Oran and Algiers, arriving in Rosyth on 2 December. By now, during several brief docking-periods, the midships catapult had been removed, its place being employed for boat stowage, the close-range AA armament had been reinforced by 20-millimetre Oerlikons, and four of the eight above-water torpedo-tubes dispensed with. Since her 1943 refit the ship had been progressively burdened with an additional 425 tons, and now her draught of 32 feet was considered to be the absolute safe limit.

By the end of 1943, Sir Andrew Cunningham had succeeded Sir Dudley Pound as First Sea Lord. Admiral Eric Raeder had resigned his command of the German Navy and would be succeeded by Admiral Karl Doenitz. Mussolini had been deposed and, if the Allies' progress was still cautious, the entire balance of the war in Europe had shifted in their favour. There were still stinging losses at sea, both naval and mercantile; many of the fine ships that had operated in company with *Renown* had been lost, including the carriers *Ark Royal*, *Eagle* and USS *Wasp*, the cruisers *Southampton*, *Manchester* and *Coventry*.

Hoisting the flag of Vice-Admiral Sir Arthur Power, Second-in-Command Eastern Fleet, *Renown* departed Rosyth for Scapa Flow on 27 December 1943, joining *Queen Elizabeth* and *Valiant*. All three ships, now the 1st Battle Squadron, sailed from the Orkneys on the thirtieth, to be further supplemented by the aircraft-carrier *Illustrious* (Rear-Admiral Clement Moody) and *Unicorn*. All were ordered to reinforce the Eastern Fleet[2] based on Trincomalee. It would be the first time that *Renown* had travelled east of Suez since 1922, the first time ever for the two old battleships.

The squadron reached Colombo on 27 January 1944 without incident. There was an old friend waiting for them – Admiral Sir James Somerville, Commander-in-Chief East Indies since March 1942. His fleet had already included *Ramillies*, the escort carrier *Battler*, the cruisers *Suffolk*, *Ceylon*, *Danae*, *Emerald*, *Hawkins*, *Frobisher*, *Newcastle* and *Kenya*, and eleven destroyers. Admiral Lord Mountbatten had been appointed Supreme Commander South East Asia Command in October 1943.

Colombo was a city-port of contrasts, of dazzling white breakers exploding over the long mole, a vast harbour dotted with ships, palm-trees and bright flowers, aloof Europeans in immaculate whites, air-conditioned hotels with liveried servants, native rickshaws and bullock tongas, skeletal sore-corroded dogs, poverty and squalor, staff officers in limousines, ramshackle buses painted silver, red and blue, women in saris, pleading vendors of fruit, betel nut and sticky sweetmeats, beggars, soldiers in starched khaki drill. The ships' officers made for the Galle Face Hotel, the Colombo Club, the Grand Oriental or the British India to relax in cane chairs with iced drinks, ratings for the YMCA and the temptations of Pettah. The war, here, seemed very far away.

It was, however, going to get nearer, because in February 1944 the Japanese moved the greater part of their battle-fleet to Singapore. To meet the possibility of renewed enemy raids into the Indian Ocean, Somerville staged the intercepting operation Diplomat in March and a seaborne air strike against Sabang (Operation Cockpit) on 19 April. The following month *Renown* steamed 4000 miles to Exmouth Gulf in Western Australia in support of a heavier air-attack on the port and oil refineries of Surabaya in Java (Operation Transom), and Winston Churchill, who only a few months earlier had fiercely criticised the Eastern Fleet (and, by implication, Somerville) for its 'idleness', now declared that the Admiral was 'keen and sprightly in the last degree . . . the right man in the right job'. For Operation Pedal on 21

June, against Port Blair in the Andamans, *Renown* accompanied *Illustrious*, which flew off 15 Barracudas and 8 Corsairs. Surprise was achieved but results were poor, and two aircraft were lost. This sort of operation was thin fare for the big British ships. They had twenty-two 15-inch guns between them, and to these could now be added the eight of the French battleship *Richelieu*, refitted in the United States and anxious to sharpen the morale of the rehabilitated Marine Nationale. The speed of Somerville's squadron was limited to that of *Queen Elizabeth* and *Valiant*, but the old ships carried a punch. One 15-inch shell was considerably heavier than the total bomb-load of a Barracuda, and a bombardment by battleships more satisfying than a hit-and-run raid by carrier-borne aircraft.

The target was to be Sabang again, the enemy base off the northernmost tip of Sumatra, dominating access to the Malacca Strait and the route along which the Japanese supplies to Burma travelled. The 1st Battle Squadron left Trincomalee on 22 July, with Somerville flying his flag in *Queen Elizabeth* and leading *Renown*, *Valiant* and *Richelieu*, the heavy cruiser *Cumberland*, the Dutch light cruiser *Tromp* and a screen of destroyers. Two days' steaming across the Bay of Bengal brought them off Sabang, and the ships went to action stations before dawn.

Some of the men on deck said they could smell a tropical off-shore fragrance. If they could, the pleasure was short-lived. For most there was a sadistic cold pleasure in the knowledge that the huge shells hissing into the gun-breeches would, in a few minutes, be smashing into the still-sleeping Japanese, tearing to red ruin the sub-humans that had raped nurses in Hong Kong, bayoneted prisoners in Malaya and employed Europeans and Americans as slaves until they died of malnutrition, exposure or disease. 'Crimson' was a well-chosen code-name for this operation. It was going to be a beautiful day. Flag Five climbed to *Queen Elizabeth*'s yardarm and thirty 15-inch guns erupted, recoiled, erupted again, and again, until paint-blisters like tennis-balls swelled and burst on the hot gun-barrels.

Two years earlier the Dutch Rear-Admiral Karel Doorman, in the cruiser *De Ruyter*, had led a hastily gathered British–American–Australian–Dutch force of warships out of Surabaya to meet the Japanese and, since the ships had had neither an operational plan nor a common code of tactical signals, Doorman had simply ordered, 'Follow me, the enemy is 90 miles away'. Now, at dawn on 25 July 1944, the sweating sailors in *Tromp* blasphemed gleefully as their ship led the destroyers inshore, all guns firing at anchored shipping and shore installations at point-blank range. It was a beautiful day as *Tromp* and her following flotilla pounded through the outer bay at 33 knots, releasing eight torpedoes into the inner harbour as they passed its entrance. All done, Somerville's force withdrew, leaving climbing columns of smoke from oil-tanks and burning ships that obliterated from view the receding slate-coloured coastline.

Trincomalee was regained in high spirits on 27 July, but this first real strike by the Navy against the Japanese would pass almost unnoticed. In Normandy the Allies had taken Caen and St-Lô, the Russians had advanced into Poland, V1 flying bombs were landing in southern England, and the Americans had wiped out 30,000 Japs on Saipan. The bombardment of Sabang seemed rather small beer.

The repair facilities in Trincomalee, less than adequate for a battle-squadron, had been supplemented by a floating dry dock that had been built in the United Kingdom, taken to India in three sections to be assembled in Bombay, and then towed to the Ceylon base. It was planned that *Renown* should be the first large ship to be taken into the dock but, in the event, it was *Valiant* that was accorded that privilege. The battleship was successfully negotiated into the massive caisson and then raised, but at dusk her searchlight was flashing 'SOS. Dock collapsing.' Assembled by semi-skilled dock labour, the dock had failed under its burden and its sections had begun to separate with all pumps and electrical circuitry in-operative. *Valiant* almost toppled, but was eased out of her predica-ment, seriously damaged. Emergency repairs were carried out and she was despatched to the United Kingdom, only to run aground at the southern end of the Suez Canal. Getting clear after six hours, she then proceeded via Cape Town, arriving home in January 1945. Her repairs continued until the end of the war.

It would be wrong to suggest that *Renown*'s company did not feel themselves unjustly treated by fate. The ship in the dry dock should have been *Renown*; to be incapacitated without a shot fired and returned to the United Kingdom was a circumstance that sailors only dreamed of.

In August the battle-cruiser supported a strike against the island of Car Nicobar. For some time, now, there had been friction between Admiral Somerville, Commander-in-Chief Eastern Fleet, and Lord Mountbatten, Supreme Commander South East Asia, largely the result of the latter's accelerated advancement over older and more experienced flag officers, not helped by the fact that Somerville's area of responsibility extended far outside Mountbatten's command. The Admiralty's directions on who commanded what were loosely framed and interpreted differently by both men. However, the details of this distasteful quarrel between two fine commanders have no place here. On 23 August 1944, Somerville was relieved by Admiral Sir Bruce Fraser.[3]

Meanwhile the assembly of a British Pacific Fleet (four battleships, six fleet carriers, four light fleet carriers, sixteen cruisers, forty destroyers and ninety escort-vessels) was being completed. Based on Sydney, it would be a considerably more impressive force than the Far East Fleet, and the impracticability of both Indian Ocean and Pacific being controlled by one commander was soon apparent. Fraser became Commander-in-Chief British Pacific Fleet. The Eastern Fleet was given to Sir Arthur Power, already with his flag in *Renown*.

The Royal Navy and the United States Navy had long hammered out their differences of procedure and terminology. There was a common phonetic alphabet for radio-telephony exchanges, and signals now had a date–time group instead of a time of origin – although the British never could stomach 'left rudder' and 'right rudder' instead of port and starboard, nor 'go topsides' instead of climbing on deck. The masses of printed operational instructions issued by the Americans prior to the simplest adventure would continue to baffle the British, who had always managed very well with an informal pre-departure briefing and a typed sheet of dispositions, communications responsibilities and the challenge codes. In mid-October 1944, *Renown*, with three destroyers, was Task Group 63.1. *Cumberland*, *London* and *Suffolk*, with a destroyer screen, formed Task Group 63.2, and *Indomitable*, *Victorious* and the light cruiser *Phoebe* were the Carrier Task Group 63.3.

Between 17 and 19 October, Task Force 63 carried out Operation Millet, involving further bombardments of Japanese installations in the Nicobars. On the return passage to Trincomalee an attack by ten enemy torpedo-bombers was broken up by the British carriers' Fulmars, which destroyed seven for the loss of three. Then, to everyone's surprise, a small Japanese freighter steamed naïvely through the middle of the Task Force, to survive for only seconds. It was the last time that *Renown* was to use her 15-inch guns. The following week she struck her flag and proceeded to Durban for a three-month refit.

At the beginning of 1945, *Renown* was one of only two heavy ships attached to the East Indies Station, the other being *Queen Elizabeth*, and it was intended that one of these should be relieved by *Richelieu*, briefly at Gibraltar, during March. Power wanted to retain *Renown*, to give him two heavy ships with a high speed capability; *Richelieu*'s 30 knots would be irrelevant with *Queen Elizabeth* in company. Provisional arrangements were made to dock *Renown* again in June for the installation of long-range gunnery radar and the improvement of close-range AA armament, but none of these plans would materialise. *Renown* was going home for the last time.

## Notes

1   The serial number of each Russian convoy was suffixed 'PQ' for the outward voyage and 'QP' when returning.

2   Not to be confused with the British Pacific Fleet, later operating under United States Navy command.

3   Somerville had, in any case, been on the East Indies Station for 2½ years. Churchill did not approve of his recall but accepted that the clash of personalities at high level could not be allowed to continue. Somerville went on to lead the British Naval Mission in Washington. See Stephen Roskill, *Churchill and the Admirals*.

# Chapter Seventeen

*Victory in Europe – a surrender delegation – the meeting of a king and a president – reduction to a training role and condemnation to a breaker's yard*

WITH THE U-boat bases in France captured and the Baltic becoming progressively untenable for German naval forces as a result of the Russian advance from the east, an increasing number of enemy warships were seeking bases in Norway. The possibility of Hitler establishing a 'Bavarian redoubt' was receding, but the German Navy showed no signs of cracking. 'There may be a fair proportion of fanatical Nazis among the officers,' Admiralty Intelligence assessed, 'and it is probable that some may prefer to sacrifice themselves in a desperate attack rather than survive to suffer the defeat that is now generally accepted.' In short, there could be a last-ditch fight to the death similar to that planned in 1918. *Tirpitz* had been capsized by bombing during the previous November, and *Scharnhorst* sunk by *Duke of York* in December 1943, but there still remained a useful surface force which could prove an embarrassment if it embarked on a 'death ride' adventure.

With all four 'King George V'-class battleships now assigned to the British Pacific Fleet, the twenty-nine-year-old *Renown* was the only remaining ship capable of *overhauling and outgunning anything afloat* in home waters.

Before departing Colombo on 30 March there had to be endured the painful process of selecting 500 of her company to be left behind, replaced by a similar number from other ships who had served several years on the station. Lord Mountbatten bade farewell, and then, to show that there was life in the old lady yet, *Renown* achieved the 7642 miles to the United Kingdom in 306 steaming-hours – an average of 24.9738 knots.

Ironically, as the battle-cruiser pushed her bows out of Gibraltar on the last stage of her homeward journey, *Admiral Scheer, Hipper* and

*Emden* were being crippled by RAF bombing in Kiel, and the day after *Renown* docked in Rosyth on 15 April *Lützow* was similarly disabled near Swinemunde.

The ship was still anchored off South Queensferry on VE Day. It had been expected that she would hoist the flag of Commander-in-Chief Home Fleet, but everything now was uncertain. On 11 May, *Renown* was designated the venue for a confrontation between British naval authorities and a delegation of nine German officers from Norway who had brought their charts of minefields, buoys and swept channels in Norwegian waters. The German party, led by Captains Krueger and Loewisch, was received by Vice-Admiral the Hon. E. R. Drummond, CB, MVO, Captain R. St V. Sherbrooke, VC, DSO, and five other captains including two of the Royal Norwegian Navy. The Germans, representing the Naval Commander-in-Chief, Norway, had flown by Junkers 52 transport aircraft from Stavanger. They were escorted by marines aboard *Renown*, and their first greeting was a reprimand for arriving twenty-four hours after the time laid down in the terms of surrender. Krueger explained that there had been difficulty in assembling his delegation within the limited time available and, additionally, the weather had been unsuitable for flying. He and his party were able to satisfy the British that the charts they brought accurately recorded all minefields, and that all German forces in Norway were aware of the surrender terms and would co-operate fully.

'Anyone want to buy a second-hand battle-cruiser?' someone asked. After the jubilation of VE Day, the bonfires and singing crowds, there was a strange silence. Ships were returning to harbours and estuaries from the Arctic, the Western Approaches, the far Atlantic – tired weather-beaten ships that dropped their anchors or tied alongside jetties, and waited. Germany was defeated, but the war was not finished yet. There was still Japan to settle with, and there were few illusions about the difficulties involved. The Japanese could still muster 2½ million troops, and the losses suffered by the Americans in the bloody battle for Okinawa suggested that the final subjection of Japan could cost a million Allied lives. Nobody yet had heard of an atom bomb.

*Renown* left Rosyth on 12 May for Portsmouth. She was going to refit, it was understood; that could only mean further active service, and the only theatre that needed 15-inch guns was the Far East. The supposition was reinforced when the ship's six forward 4.5-inch below-deck mountings were lifted out for conversion to remote power control. No warship's armament was improved unless there was a likelihood of it being used. Then, on 23 July, *Renown* left Portsmouth for Devonport, and on her arrival her company was ordered to paint ship. It all figured. Nobody painted a battle-cruiser unless it was going somewhere.

*Renown*, however, was not. Her new paint had scarcely dried on 2 August when President Truman landed at nearby Yeovilton Naval Air Station, interrupting his journey home from the Potsdam Conference for a meeting with King George. Travelling by train from London overnight, the King boarded *Renown* at 1020, and two hours later the battle-cruiser's launch carried the President from the United States cruiser *Augusta*, lying in harbour with *Philadelphia*. He was piped aboard, and the Stars and Stripes was hoisted in company with the royal standard.

This was to be the graceful old lady's last flourish before the limelight died. She had been reduced to two-fifths complement, and on 26 November 1945 she moved up the Hamoaze to moor just below Brunel's great bridge at Saltash, with *Resolution* and *Revenge* forming a training establishment for stokers – all three, ignominiously, sharing the name *Imperiuse*.

The final chapter, dreaded but inevitable, had been reached. The veteran battleship *Warspite* had been struck in March 1946 and, in a last act of defiance, she had parted her towline when on passage to the ship-breaker's on 23 April 1947 and gone ashore in Prussia Cove, Cornwall. She was being slowly dismantled where she lay. By the end of 1947 the Admiralty had decided that five more capital ships must go, and they would be *Nelson*, *Rodney*, *Renown*, *Queen Elizabeth* and *Valiant*, accompanied by the cruisers *Berwick*, *Suffolk*, *Orion*, *Ajax*, *Leander*, *Arethusa* and *Scylla*.

There could be no reasoned argument. The Royal Navy's postwar requirements were amply met by the four 'King George V' battleships and the recently completed *Vanguard* – and with the mass exodus of National Service personnel the Navy's bigger problem was not a lack of warships but the shortage of sailors to man them. In reply to pleas that the older ships might be retained it was estimated that, to restore them to only a modest standard of operational viability, *Nelson* and *Rodney* would require refits lasting two years and each costing £2 million, *Renown* and *Queen Elizabeth* needed refits of eighteen months, each costing £1 million, and *Valiant* would cost £750,000. Moreover, of the ships listed for disposal, none was really suitable for modernisation and only *Renown* had the speed to operate in company with a carrier task force.

On 19 March the Admiralty announced that *Renown* had been

sold to Metal Industries Ltd and would be dismantled for scrap in Faslane, off the Clyde.

The paying-off ceremony was carried out during the evening of 1 June, with the ship's company mustered on the quarterdeck. At 1830 Royal Marine buglers sounded Sunset, the Last Post and Reveille, the ensign was lowered for the last time, and the sailors were marched away to Royal Naval Barracks. *Renown* had served her flag for 31 years and 9 months.

A few weeks later the tugs *Englishman, Manxman* and *Seaman* towed the old battle-cruiser on her last passage to Faslane. Her arrival in the Clyde estuary excited little interest, but so many scarred old ships had ended their lives here that perhaps one more was hardly worth comment. Still, she found herself in good company, for in the loch, in various stages of dismantling, were *Renown*'s old comrades *Malaya, Resolution* and *Iron Duke*. Between them, could they have spoken, these four could have told stories to clog the throat of any sailor.

From the maintenance and repair ship *Mull of Galloway*, Chief Petty Officer T. J. McCafferty saw *Renown*'s berthing. He had served in her between 1943 and 1946.

'Then one day I saw a number of tugs towing up another . . . and I recognised HMS *Renown*. I remember saying, "Oh, no – not her." But she ended up in the floating dock. And so day by day I watched her becoming smaller and smaller . . . deck by deck was removed until all that was left was the huge keel. That also disappeared in a matter of weeks, and then *Renown* was no more.'

# Postscript

THE WHITE ENSIGN of the Royal Navy was lowered for the last time in Scapa Flow on 29 March 1957. A stranger is surprised at the immensity of this grey expanse of water, but it is forlornly empty now. From the cliffs of the guardian South Isles he will see no lines of battleships, no darting pinnaces nor panting drifters filled with singing libertymen. Only the gulls remain, wheeling and crying, a few cormorants, and still the unkempt sheep that have grazed here for centuries. Even the fishing-boats have disappeared, and the native population dwindles as more young people seek employment elsewhere. In late summer migrating lapwings gather in their lamenting thousands among the old cairns and barrows where wild fuschia and lupins grow, and always the wind blows, ruffling the heather and stippling the surface of the great Flow.

Of course there are ships here, but they cannot be seen. *Royal Oak* lies deep in the north-east quarter of the anchorage, the grave of 833 men who drowned on 14 October 1939, and there still remain the hulks of three battleships and four light cruisers of the Kaiser's High Seas Fleet, scuttled on 21 June 1919 and too deep to be salvaged. Visitors come occasionally, British and German, grey-haired men who halt their cars on the narrow Orphir Road and stand in silence on the cliffs, shrugged into their coats and silent as they gaze down at the vast abandoned harbour. What do they see, these ageing men? Do they still hear the distant shrill of bosuns' pipes, the far music of a quarterdeck bugle? Do they recall the good times, the camaraderie and the songs, or do they remember only the months of heaving green seas, bitter cold, stinging rain and debilitating fatigue? It is impossible to guess, but their eyes are sad as they turn away, and they grow fewer each passing year.

# Appendixes

# Appendix One

*Service histories*

## INVINCIBLE

Completion delayed by faults in electrical turret machinery. Commissioned 20 March 1909. 1st Cruiser Squadron, Home Fleet. March–May 1911 refit and modifications. Rejoined 1st BCS. 17 March, in collision with submarine *C34* in Stokes Bay but no damage. August 1913 to Mediterranean Fleet until December 1913, then returned to Home Fleet. On mobilisation stationed first Queenstown then Humber. 28 August 1914 Heligoland Bight. Grand Fleet and 2nd BCS. 4 November flagship Admiral Sturdee, departed Cromarty for Devonport, restored then proceeded South America 11 November. Engaged von Spee's squadron 8 December in company with *Inflexible*, sinking *Scharnhorst* and *Gneisenau* off Falklands. Sustained 22 hits, none serious, one casualty. Rejoined Grand Fleet March 1915 as flagship of 2nd BCS. May 1915 flagship of Rear-Admiral the Hon. Horace Hood, 3rd BCS. 31 May 1915 engaged Battle of Jutland. At 1834 after several hits from *Lützow*, *Derfflinger* and *König*, was struck in 'Q' turret amidships and blew up, sinking in two halves. 1021 crew lost, 2 officers and 3 ratings saved.

## INFLEXIBLE

Commissioned Chatham 20 October 1908. Attached to Nore Division of Home Fleet until April 1909, then transferred to 1st Cruiser Squadron. September–October 1909 attended Hudson–Fulton celebrations in New York as flagship of Admiral of the Fleet Sir Edward Seymour. 26 May 1911 in collision with battleship *Bellerophon* off Portland, damaging bows. November 1912 flagship Mediterranean Fleet. During 3–10 August 1914 engaged in unsuccessful pursuit of *Goeben* and *Breslau*. 19 August returned to Humber, and during 1–10 October to Shetland patrol to escort Canadian convoy. 4 November joined *Invincible* on passage to South America and engaged *Scharnhorst* and *Gneisenau*, both enemy ships being sunk off the Falklands on 8 December. No damage suffered by *Inflexible*. Returned United Kingdom 19 December, refitting Gibraltar *en route*. 24 January 1915 relieved *Indefatigable* as flagship Admiral Carden, Commander-in-Chief Mediterranean. Took part in Dardanelles operation including attack on the

Narrows 18 March. Suffered heavy damage and 29 killed. Towed to Gibraltar for repairs. Rejoined Grand Fleet 19 June 1915. With 3rd BCS at Jutland 31 May 1916. No casualties. Reduced to Nore Reserve January 1919 and paid off 31 March 1920. Considered for purchase by Chile but sold for scrapping in December 1922.

## INDOMITABLE
Commissioned 25 June 1908. Conveyed HRH George, Prince of Wales to Quebec Tercentenary celebrations. Attached Nore Division Home Fleet until April 1909, when assigned 1st Cruiser Squadron. Refit November 1911. February 1912 to 2nd Cruiser Squadron (flagship). December 1912 attached temporarily to 1st Cruiser Squadron as private ship. January 1913 to 1st BCS and in August transferred to Mediterranean Fleet. 3–10 August 1914 engaged in search for *Goeben* and *Breslau*, then blockade of the Dardanelles. 3 November 1914 long-range bombardment of Sedd-el-Bahr. Returned United Kingdom December to refit. Rejoined Battle Cruiser Force. 24 January 1915 Dogger Bank action, towed home *Lion* at 7 knots. 31 May 1916 at Jutland with 3rd BCS; no damage or casualties. Remained 2nd BCS from June 1916 to January 1919. Reduced to Nore Reserve (flagship) February to July 1919. Paid off 31 March 1920, sold December 1922 and scrapped in 1923.

## INDEFATIGABLE
Commissioned 24 February 1911 and assigned 1st Cruiser Squadron, which in January 1913 became 1st BCS. Transferred to 2nd BCS Mediterranean Fleet December 1913. Shared search for *Goeben* and *Breslau* 3–10 August, then Dardanelles blockade. Bombarded Cape Helles 3 November. Flagship of Admiral Carden until relieved by *Inflexible* January 1915. Refitted Malta. Returned to United Kingdom, 2nd BCS, February 1915. At Jutland 31 May 1916 engaged in duel with *Von der Tann* and struck by salvo of three shells which generated magazine explosion. Sank with loss of 1017 crew. Two survivors.

## AUSTRALIA
Built for the Royal Australian Navy, completed June 1913, proceeded to Australian waters. Flagship RAN 1913–14. August 1914 convoy escort duties south-west Pacific (now flagship North American and West Indies Station). 9–15 September operations against German New Guinea. December 1914 ordered to United Kingdom, and on passage sank German SS *Eleonore Woermann* near Falklands on 6 January 1915. Arrived Portsmouth 28 January 1915 to be assigned flagship 2nd BCS (Rear-Admiral Pakenham). 22 April 1916 in collision with *New Zealand* in fog, heavily damaged and docked in Rosyth until 5 June. Rejoined 2nd BCS. 19 August 1916 deployed against German fleet operations in North Sea. 12 December 1917 in collision with *Repulse* and under repair until January 1918. Released from Grand Fleet and departed for Australia 23 April 1919. Flagship RAN until

12 December 1921 when taken out of service in accordance with Washington Treaty. 12 April 1924 sunk with honours off Sydney Harbour.

## NEW ZEALAND

Completed November 1912, paid for by New Zealand and presented to the Royal Navy. 7 February 1913 proceeded on world cruise, visiting the Dominions and several colonies, rejoining the Battle Cruiser Force December 1913 for a visit to Russian Baltic ports. Assigned 1st BCS then 2nd BCS. Participated in Heligoland Bight action 28 August 1914 and Dogger Bank 24 January 1915. During the latter succeeded to command when *Lion* was damaged. In collision with *Australia* 22 April 1916 and docked until late May. At Jutland 31 May 1916 received one hit on 'X' turret; no casualties. 1st BCS June 1916. Replaced by *Renown* in September and returned to 2nd BCS for remainder of war. 17 November 1917 in action in vicinity of Heligoland Bight. February 1919 conveyed Admiral Jellicoe on world cruise, covering 33,000 miles, when he drew up plans for future Commonwealth naval forces. Listed for disposal under Washington Treaty and sold for scrapping December 1922.

## LION

Commissioned 4 June 1912. 1st Cruiser Squadron, then 1st BCS. Flagship of Battle Cruiser Force (Rear-Admiral Beatty) 1915–18. At Dogger Bank action 24 January 1915 received 12 hits and was towed home by *Indomitable*. Four months' repair at Elswick, when director-control was installed. At Jutland 31 May 1916 sustained further heavy damage with 100 killed and 50 wounded. Ready for service again from 19 July. 17 November 1917 in action off Heligoland Bight. 1919–22 flagship 1st BCS. Discarded under Washington Treaty, sold January 1924 and scrapped in Jarrow.

## QUEEN MARY

After 2½ years' construction, delayed by industrial action in Palmers yard, Newcastle, commissioned January 1913. Assigned 1st BCS. Heligoland Bight 28 August 1914. Refitting during Dogger Bank action. At Jutland 31 May, engaging simultaneously *Seydlitz* and *Derfflinger*, was struck by plunging salvo which generated magazine explosion. She sank with the loss of 1266 men. There were eight survivors.

## PRINCESS ROYAL

Commissioned 14 November 1912. Joined 1st Cruiser Squadron January 1913, then 1st BCS. Heligoland Bight 28 August 1914, no casualties. October to December 1914 escorting convoys from Canada to United Kingdom. Dogger Bank action 24 January 1915. At Jutland 31 May 1916 suffered severe damage and casualties and survived the day only with difficulty, but was ready for action again from 15 July. In action off Heligoland 17 November 1917. Discarded under Washington Treaty December 1922 and sold for scrap in January 1926.

## TIGER

Joined Grand Fleet at Scapa Flow 6 November 1914 after less than a month's work-up. Assigned 1st Battle Squadron, then 1st BCS. At Dogger Bank 24 January 1915 was hit several times, sustaining 10 killed and 11 wounded. Further damaged at Jutland 31 May 1916 by 21 hits, killing 24 and wounding 37, but was ready for service again by 2 July. On 19 August 1916 deployed against German operations in North Sea and in action off Heligoland Bight 17 November 1918. Atlantic Fleet (BCS) 1919–22, then sea-going gunnery training ship 1924–9. Relieved *Hood* as flagship BCS 1929–31. Taken out of service 30 March 1931 under life-duration clause of Washington Treaty. Sold to breakers March 1932.

## RENOWN

Joined Grand Fleet (1st BCS) September 1916 to 1919. Tour of United States and Australasia with Prince of Wales 1920–1, India and Japan 1921–2. Major refit 1923–6, then BCS, Atlantic Fleet. Conveyed Duke of York to Australia 1927. BCS 1928–36. Refitted 1936–9. In action with *Scharnhorst* and *Gneisenau* off Norway 9 April 1940. Force H, Gibraltar, August 1940. Running action in company with cruisers against Italian force on 27 November 1940. Bombardment of Genoa 9 February 1941. Returned United Kingdom August 1941 as VA Home Fleet. In April 1942 Commodore-in-Command Force 'W' escorting USS *Wasp* when ferrying aircraft to Malta, then returned Home Fleet. Again with Force H to cover north African landings October 1942. Based Gibraltar until February 1943. Refit Rosyth. August 1943 took Prime Minister from Halifax, Nova Scotia, to United Kingdom and in November embarked Prime Minister and First Sea Lord for Alexandria. Returned United Kingdom. 27 December 1943 flagship Vice-Admiral Sir Arthur Power 2 i/c Eastern Fleet. February–April 1944 working up at Trincomalee. April 1944 screened air attack on Sabang. May 1944 air strike against Surabaya and in June against Port Blair, Andamans. 22 July bombardment of Sabang. August bombardment of Car Nicobar. Refit in Durban. Returned United Kingdom 30 March 1945. Reduced complement and then assigned to training role at Devonport. Towed to Faslane for scrapping July 1948.

## REPULSE

Joined Grand Fleet (1st BCS) September 1916 to 1919. In action 17 November 1917 off Heligoland Bight. Refitting 1919–22, then BCS Atlantic Fleet. Joined *Hood* in visit to Rio de Janeiro 1922 and following year engaged in world cruise. Returned United Kingdom September 1924. During 1925 conveyed Prince of Wales to South Africa and South America. Remained United Kingdom 1926–32. Refitting until 1936. Mediterranean Fleet 1936–8. December 1939 escorting trooping convoys, Atlantic. In April 1940 operating off Norway. November 1940 deployed against German weather-ships off Jan Meyen Island. December 1940 covered minelaying operations south-east of Iceland. In Cape Town October 1941 transferred to East Indies Station in company with *Prince of Wales*. 8 December 1941 departed

Singapore (with *Prince of Wales* and four destroyers) to intercept Japanese invasion force off Kota Baru. Two days later attacked by torpedo-planes and high-level bombers. Sunk with loss of 513 crew.

## ✢ FURIOUS

Laid down in June 1915 as a light battle-cruiser but before completion (July 1917) was converted to aircraft-handling. On 19 July 1918 operated against German airship-base at Tondern. During 1922–5 further modifications turned the ship into an orthodox aircraft-carrier, and as such served until May 1945. Scrapped in Dalmuir and Troon in 1948.

## COURAGEOUS

Joined Grand Fleet January 1917, first with 3rd Light Cruiser Squadron then 1st Cruiser Squadron. In action with German light forces 27 November 1917, suffering damage and casualties. From 1919 gunnery training ship at Portsmouth, then flagship of Reserve. Converted to aircraft-carrier between 1924 and 1928 in Devonport. 17 September 1939 sunk by *U29* off west coast of Ireland with loss of 514 crew.

## GLORIOUS

Joined Grand Fleet January 1917, first as flagship of 3rd Light Cruiser Squadron then 1st Cruiser Squadron. In action with German light forces 27 November 1917. From 1919 gunnery training ship at Devonport, then flagship of Reserve. Began conversion to aircraft-carrier February 1924 in Rosyth and towed to Devonport for completion January 1930 (because the Rosyth dockyard was closed). 8 June 1940 sunk by *Scharnhorst* and *Gneisenau* off Narvik.

## HOOD

Commissioned May 1920 as flagship BCS. With *Repulse* attended Centenary Celebrations Rio de Janeiro 1922. World cruise with *Repulse* and 1st Light Cruiser Squadron 1923, steaming 40,000 miles. Atlantic Fleet 1924. Vasco da Gama celebrations Lisbon, and routine cruises Home and Mediterranean. Refitting 1929–31. Recommissioned flagship Atlantic Fleet. Collided with *Renown* 23 January 1935, repaired at Portsmouth. From April 1936 patrolling northern Spanish waters during Civil War. Autumn cruise of Mediterranean ports. February–August 1939 refitting in Portsmouth, then Home Fleet. October bombed in North Sea but no casualties. March to May 1940 refitting in Devonport. June 1940 convoying Australian and New Zealand troops to United Kingdom from Cape Finisterre, involving *Queen Mary*, *Empress of Britain*, *Mauretania*, *Aquitania*, *Andes* and *Empress of Canada*. Force H, Gibraltar, June 1940. Frequently bombed by Italian aircraft. Bombardment of French warships in Mers-el-Kebir, 3 July 1940. Returned United Kingdom August. Refitting Rosyth January to March 1941. Departed Scapa Flow with *Prince of Wales* 19 May to intercept *Bismarck* and *Prinz Eugen*. Sunk 24 May with loss of 1416 crew. Only three survivors.

# Appendix Two

THE ADMIRALTY's signal regarding the ultimatum to Admiral Gensoul was timed 0435 of 29 June 1940, marked Most Secret, addressed to Flag Officer Force H, repeated to Commander-in-Chief Mediterranean. Its text was as follows:

His Majesty's Government have decided that the course to be adopted is as follows.

(A) French Fleet at Oran and Mers-el-Kebir is to be given four alternatives:

1. To sail their ships to British harbours and continue to fight with us.

2. To sail their ships with reduced crews to a British port from which the crews could be repatriated whenever desired.

In the case of the alternatives (1) or (2) being adopted, the ships would be restored to France at the conclusion of the war or full compensation would be paid if they are damaged meanwhile.

If the French Admiralty accepts alternative (2), but insists that ships should not be used by us during the war you may say we accept this condition for as long as Germany and Italy observe the armistice terms, but we particularly do not wish to raise the point ourselves.

3. To sail their ships with reduced crews to some French port in the West Indies such as Martinique.

After arriving at this port they would either be demilitarised to our satisfaction, or, if so desired, be entrusted to United States jurisdiction for the duration of the war. The crews would be repatriated.

4. To sink their ships.

(B) Should the French Admiral refuse to accept all of the above alternatives and should he suggest that he should demilitarise his ships to our satisfaction at their present berths, you are authorised to accept this further alternative provided that you are satisfied that the measures taken for demilitarisation can be carried out under your supervision within six hours and would prevent the ships being brought into service for at least one year, even at a fully equipped dockyard port.

(C) If none of the above alternatives is accepted by the French, you are to endeavour to destroy ships in Mers-el-Kebir, but particularly *Dunkerque* and *Strasbourg*, using all means at your disposal. Ships at Oran should also be destroyed if this will not entail any considerable loss of civilian life.

The signal added that French ships should be dealt with in harbour, not at sea, and because the defences at Algiers would make it impossible to avoid the destruction of the town a separate operation against that place was not justified.

The instructions contained in the signal were final.

# Appendix Three

THE SIGNALS passed by Admiral Tom Phillips to the ships of Force Z on 9 December 1941 were recorded as follows:

*To Force Z from Commander-in-Chief Eastern Fleet*

1. Besides a minor landing at Kota Baru which has not been followed up, landings have been made between Patani and Singora and a major landing 90 miles north of Singora.

2. Little is known of enemy forces in the vicinity. It is believed that *Kongo* is the only capital ship likely to be met, three 'Atago'-type, one 'Kako'-type, and two 'Zintu'-type cruisers have been reported. A number of destroyers possibly of fleet type are likely to be met.

3. My object is to surprise and sink transports and enemy warships before air attack can develop. Object chosen will depend on air reconnaissance, intend to arrive objective after sunrise tomorrow 10th. If an opportunity to bring *Kongo* to action occurs this is to take precedence over all other action.

4. Subject to CO's freedom of manœuvre in an emergency, Force Z will remain in close order and will be manœuvred as a unit until action is joined. When the signal 'act independently' is made or at discretion of CO *Repulse* will assume freedom of manœuvre remaining in tactical support but engaging from a wide enough angle to facilitate fall of shot.

5. Intend to operate at 25 knots unless a chase develops and subsequently to retire at maximum speed endurance will allow.

6. Capital ships should attempt to close below 20,000 yards until fire is effective but should avoid offering an end-on target. Ships must be prepared to change from delay to non-delay fuses according to target.

7. *Prince of Wales* and *Repulse* are each to have one aircraft fuelled and ready to fly off if required. If flown off, aircraft must return to land base. Kota Baru aerodrome is understood to be out of action.

8. *Tenedos* will be detached before dark to return independently to Singapore.

9. Remaining destroyers may be despatched during the night 9/10 should enemy information require a high speed of advance. In such case these destroyers are to retire towards Anamba Islands at 10 knots until a rendezvous is ordered by W/T.

*To 'Prince of Wales', 'Repulse', from Commander-in-Chief Eastern Fleet*
Inform ships companies as follows begins
The enemy has made several landings on the north coast of Malaya and
has made local progress. Our army is not large and is hard pressed in
places. Our air force has had to destroy and abandon one or more aerodromes. Meanwhile fat transports lie off the coast. This is our opportunity before the enemy can establish himself. We have made a wide
circuit to avoid air reconnaissance and hope to surprise the enemy shortly
after sunrise tomorrow Wednesday. We may have the luck to try our
metal against the old Japanese battle-cruiser *Kongo* or against Japanese
cruisers and destroyers which are reported in the Gulf of Siam. We are
sure to get some useful practice with the HA armament. Whatever we
meet I want to finish quickly and so get well clear to the eastward before
the Japanese can mass too formidable a scale of attack against us. So
shoot to sink. Ends.

*To 'Prince of Wales', 'Repulse', from Commander-in-Chief Eastern Fleet*
From dawn action stations and through daylight tomorrow Wednesday
all ranks and ratings are to wear clothing such as overalls or suits which
keep arms and legs covered against risk of burns from flash.

*To Force Z from Commander-in-Chief Far Eastern Fleet*
Course will be altered to 320 degs at 1800 by signal. Course is to be
altered to 280 degs at 1930 and speed increased to 24 knots without
signal. At 2200 destroyers are to part company without signal and proceed to southeastward subsequently adjusting course and speed so as to
r/v at point Charlie at 1600/10 unless otherwise ordered.

*To 'Prince of Wales', 'Repulse', from Commander-in-Chief Eastern Fleet*
Unless further information is received intend to make Singora at 0745
and subsequently work to eastward along coast. I have kept to eastward
so as to try and remain unlocated today which is the most important
thing of all.

# Select Bibliography

**Official Records**
ADM 199/1187–8; ADM 116/4352; ADM 199/1149; ADM 199/357; ADM 1/18189; ADM 116/5669.

**Archives**
The Fleet Air Arm Officers' Association
The Imperial War Museum
The Naval Historical Branch of the Ministry of Defence
The Public Record Office
The Royal Naval Museum, Portsmouth

**Books**
Allison, R. S., *The Surgeon Probationers* (Blackstaff Press, 1979).
Apps, Michael, *Send Her Victorious* (William Kimber, 1971).
Bacon, Admiral Sir R. H., *The Jutland Scandal* (Hutchinson, 1925).
Barnett, Correlli, *The Swordbearers: Studies in Supreme Command in the First World War* (Eyre & Spottiswoode, 1951).
Beesly, Patrick, *Very Special Intelligence* (Hamish Hamilton, 1977).
Bennett, G., *The Battle of Jutland* (Batsford, 1964).
—, *Coronel and the Falklands* (Batsford, 1962).
Berthold, Will, *Sink the 'Bismarck'* (Longman, 1958).
Braddon, Russell, *The Naked Island* (Laurie, 1952).
Breyer, Siegfried, *Schlachtschiffe und Schlachkreuzer 1905–1970* (Munich: J. F. Lehmanns Verlag, 1970).
Browne, Courtney, *Tojo: The Last Banzai* (Angus & Robertson, 1967).
Butler, J. R. M., *Grand Strategy*, vol. II (HMSO, 1957).
Cain, T. J., *HMS Electra* (Frederick Muller, 1959).
Calvocoressi, P., and Wint, G., *Total War* (Allen Lane, 1972).
Carew, Tim, *The Fall of Hong Kong* (Anthony Blond, 1960).
Chatfield, Lord, *It Might Happen Again* (Heinemann, 1947).
—, *The Navy and Defence* (Heinemann, 1942).
Churchill, Winston S., *The Second World War* (Cassell, 1949–51).
—, *The World Crisis* (Thornton Butterworth, 1927).
Costello, J., and Hughes, T., *The Battle of the Atlantic* (Collins, 1977).
Cunningham, Sir Andrew, *A Sailor's Odyssey* (Hutchinson, 1951).

Dewar, Vice-Admiral K. G. B., *The Navy from Within* (Gollancz, 1939).
Divine, David, *Mutiny at Invergordon* (Macdonald, 1970).
Dorling, T., *Endless Story* (Hodder & Stoughton, 1931).
Falk, Stanley, *Seventy Days to Singapore* (Robert Hale, 1975).
Fawcett, H. W., and Hooper, G. W. W., *The Fight at Jutland* (Hutchinson, 1920).
Frost, H. H., *The Battle of Jutland* (Washington, DC: United States Navy Institute, 1936).
Harper, Captain J. E. T., *Reproduction of the Record of the Battle of Jutland* (HMSO, 1927).
Harvey, W. B., *Downstairs in the Navy* (Brown, Son & Ferguson, 1979).
Hoehling, A. A., *The Great War at Sea* (Arthur Barker, 1965).
Hough, Richard, *The Pursuit of Admiral von Spee* (Allen & Unwin, 1969).
Ireland, Bernard, *Warships* (Hamlyn, 1978).
James, W., *Admiral Sir William Fisher* (Macmillan, 1943).
*Jane's Fighting Ships* (Sampson, Low, Marston, 1914, 1939).
Kemp, P. H., *Victory at Sea, 1939–1945* (Frederick Muller, 1957).
Kennedy, Ludovic, *Menace: The Life and Death of the 'Tirpitz'* (Sidgwick & Jackson, 1979).
—, *Pursuit: The Sinking of the 'Bismarck'* (Collins, 1974).
Lenton, H. T., and Colledge, J. J., *Warships of World War II* (Ian Allan, 1970).
Lohmann, Walter, and Hildebrande, Hans, *Die Deutsche Kriegsmarine 1939–1945* (Verlag Hans-Hanning Podzun, 1956).
Lyon, Hugh, *Warships* (Salamander, 1978).
McGowan, A., *Sailor* (Macdonald & Jane's, 1977).
Manning, T. D., *The British Destroyer* (Putnam, 1961).
Marder, A. J., *Fear God and Dread Nought* (Cape, 1952, 1956, 1959).
—, *From the Dreadnought to Scapa Flow* (Oxford University Press, 1961).
—, *Portrait of an Admiral* (Cape, 1952).
Mars, A., *British Submarines at War, 1939–1945* (William Kimber, 1971).
Masters, John, *Fourteen Eighteen* (Michael Joseph, 1965).
Middlebrook, M., and Mahoney, P., *Battleship* (Allen Lane, 1977).
Mordal, Jacques, *25 Siècles de Guerre sur Mer* (Editions Robert Lafont, 1959).
Mountevans, Admiral Lord, *Adventurous Life* (Hutchinson, 1946).
Northcott, Maurice, *'Renown' and 'Repulse'* (Ensign, 1978).
*Ocean*, HMS, Welfare Committee, *Ocean Saga* (Privately printed, 1953).
Oram, H. K., *Ready for Sea* (Seeley Service, 1974).
Padfield, Peter, *The Battleship Era* (Rupert Hart-Davis, 1972).
Parkes, Oscar, *British Battleships* (Seeley Service, 1974).
Pears, Randolph, *British Battleships, 1892–1957* (Putnam, 1957).
Price, Alfred, *Instruments of Darkness* (Macdonald & Jane's, 1977).
Raven, Allen, and Roberts, John, *County Class Cruisers* (RSV Publishing Inc., 1978).
Roskill, Captain Stephen, *Churchill and the Admirals* (Collins, 1977).
—, *Naval Policy between the Wars* (Collins, 1969).
—, *The War at Sea, 1939–1945* (HMSO, 1954).

Schmalenback, P., *Die Geschichte der Deutsche Marineartillerie* (Koehlers, 1970).

Schofield, B. B., *Loss of the 'Bismarck'* (Ian Allan, 1972).

Smith, Peter C., *Hit First, Hit Hard* (William Kimber, 1979).

Snyder, Gerald S., *The 'Royal Oak' Disaster* (William Kimber, 1976).

Sperry Gyroscope Company, *Sixty Years On* (1973).

Toland, J., *But Not in Shame* (Anthony Gibbs & Phillips, 1962).

Tuchman, Barbara W., *The Guns of August* (Constable, 1962).

Vader, John, *The Fleet without a Friend* (New English Library, 1971).

Westwood, John, *Fighting Ships of World War II* (Sidgwick & Jackson, 1975).

Whitehouse, Arch, *The Zeppelin Fighters* (Robert Hale, 1968).

Wilson, H. W., and Hammerton, J. A., *The Great War*, vols I–XIII (Amalgamated Press, 1914–18).

## Newspapers and Magazines

*The Daily Express*
*Hansard*
*The Nautical Magazine*
*Navy News*
*The Navy Pictorial* (West of England Newspapers)
*Picture Post*
*Purnell's History of the First World War*
*The Scottish Field*
*The Straits Times* (Singapore)
*The Sunday Times*

# Index